P9-CMY-976

MEDIA MYTHMAKERS

MEDIA MYTHMAKERS

how journalists, activists, and advertisers mislead us

BENJAMIN RADFORD

59 John Glenn Drive
Amherst, New York 14228-2197

Published 2003 by Prometheus Books

Inquiries should be addressed to
Prometheus Books, 59 John Glenn Drive, Amherst, New York 14228–2197
VOICE: 716–691–0133, ext. 207; FAX: 716–564–2711
WWW.PROMETHEUSBOOKS.COM

07 06 05 04 03 5 4 3 2 1

Library of Congress Cataloging-in-Publication Data

Radford, Benjamin, 1970–.
Media mythmakers : how journalists, activists, and advertisers mislead us / by Benjamin Radford.
p. cm.
ISBN 1–59102–072–7 (cloth : alk. paper)
1. Mass media—Objectivity. 2. Mass media—Psychological aspects. I. Title.

P96.O24R33 2003
302.23—dc21

2003005667

Printed in Canada on acid-free paper

For my parents, Jeff and Martha, with love and thanks.

CONTENTS

PART 3: PROFITING FROM FEAR AND MYTH

PART 4: THE WAGES OF FEAR: THE CONSEQUENCES OF A PUBLIC BLINDED BY MYTHS

ACKNOWLEDGMENTS

Though writing is largely a solo effort, few books are truly written alone, and help comes from many quarters. Time spent poring through files, hunched over copy machines, and staring blankly at computer screens is time taken from friends, family, and loved ones. For support, inspiration, and encouragement, I wish to thank Marcus Aurelius, Chris Ayles, Robert Bartholomew, Barry Glassner, Paul Kurtz, Patty Melquist, and all my other colleagues and friends who provided feedback and criticism. Thanks also to my editor, Meg French, whose red pen only improved my writing.

INTRODUCTION

There is only one quality worse than hardness of heart and that is softness of head.

—Theodore Roosevelt

The world is shaped by myths. Our understanding of ourselves and our culture is based largely upon what we are told by the media. Yet much of the media's content includes unexamined assumptions and myths. These myths are stories, themes, and ideas that embody an aspect of culture. Politicians, advertisers, activists, journalists, and others create myths to manipulate how we think, what we value, and what we fear.

Frequently these myths are also myths in the sense that they are fictions: They are erroneous half- or nontruths provided by others to alter our picture of the world around us. Our culture puts stock in the myth of child abduction by strangers, when in fact such abductions are very rare. We accept the myth that simply throwing money at a social problem will fix it. We allow myths to frighten us, then we spend money and pass laws to protect us from our phantom fears.

The media create myths all the time. Magazines claiming to have their fingers on America's collective pulse jockey to be the first to name the latest trend, identify the next big star, and sell their prepackaged zeitgeist report to hip-hungry consumers.

Our myths change over time, but the efforts to commercialize and label them remain the same. In the past twenty years, for example, America has seen its heroes cycle among a handful of archetypes: saviors (firemen and police, for example), warriors (sports and military figures), creators (businessmen, artists, and actors), and victims or martyrs.

When strong currents of our victim-centric culture came to the fore, we saw a new set of heroes arise. Those with dread diseases and some measure of fame who spoke of their struggles became heroes. Thus actors such as Christopher Reeve and Michael J. Fox were transformed from modestly successful but unremarkable B-list actors to courageous heroes telling their inspiring stories.

For a while, many of America's heroes were aggressive and wealthy businessmen. The luster of those heroes gradually tarnished as one after another got indicted in fraud, junk bond, and corporate scandals that left millions of investors billions of dollars poorer.

The September 11, 2001, attacks breathed new life into our hero myths. Many of our old ideas of heroes seemed to pale in comparison to the brave firefighters and policemen who risked their lives in the attacks—as well as those on a doomed plane who sacrificed themselves to save others.

The cycle will continue, and eventually other hero myths will emerge. What they all have in common, though, is that they are largely driven by the media. They are media myths not in the sense that they are necessarily falsehoods, but in the sense that they are part of a story, a narrative created in the symbiotic relationship between the popular media and the public.

Deborah Tannen, in her book *The Argument Culture*, says that "culture, in a sense, is an environment of narratives that we hear repeatedly until they seem to make self-evident sense in explaining human behavior."[1] Many of these narratives take the form of myths, and before we act on those myths we should examine them closely.

When advertisers promise that we will be smarter, richer, or more popular if we use certain products, we are being told a myth. This myth manipulates our fears and illusions to get us to spend our money. When the news media report on current events, they frequently cast them in time-honored themes and motifs dating back to Shakespeare and earlier. The media build up heroes, such as Princess Diana and John F. Kennedy Jr., and then follow their tragic deaths. Often the news media create myths and give us merely the illusions of news and content. Advocates and politicians offer up their own myths—some true, others false, but most exaggerated—to manipulate public opinion and policy. They give us illusions of problems to fix—and sometimes the illusion that they're fixing them.

Without realizing it, we frequently act out the prescripted roles given us: buying products, giving money, and even crying on cue. But while we're all busy with our comfortable lies, pretending that advertising copy means something and that network news is actually unbiased and informative, real problems are ignored and fester. Common sense proves not so common in the face of manipulated emotion, fear, and panic. Our children are *not* being protected and social problems are *not* being seriously addressed, due largely to the illusions we are fed.

Carl Jensen, professor emeritus of communications studies at Sonoma State University in California, points out that the news media frequently fail in their role as providers of useful information:

> Few would deny that the United States has problems, serious problems, that need to be confronted and resolved if we are to succeed and survive in the future. . . . And yet, how many of our citizens are fully informed about, or even aware of, those issues? There has been a breakdown in America's early warning system. Only occasionally, when the problem gets totally out of control . . . , are the media inspired to provide the information the public needs to know. Even then, the media tend to provide too little too late.[2]

Sometimes the incidents that spark moral and social outrage—and calls for change—are based upon misunderstandings, lies, or hoaxes.

In 1987 a young black girl in New York named Tawana Brawley claimed that she had been kidnapped by a group of white men who repeatedly raped her, smeared her with feces, and scrawled racist names on her chest. Racial tensions erupted, fueled by activists such as Al Sharpton; Bill Cosby and Mike Tyson offered money for information on her attackers, and the nation was outraged and saddened by the vicious and racist assault. After extensive investigations, Brawley's story fell apart and the attack was discovered to be a hoax.[3] While the Brawley case was still unfolding, another case two years later, also in New York, fanned racial flames and unfairly blamed blacks.

In the spring of 1989, a female jogger was attacked in Central Park. The woman was repeatedly raped, beaten until nearly dead, and left until passersby found her. The victim was in a coma for nearly two weeks and suffered permanent damage. The woman couldn't remember anything about that night and was unable to identify her attackers. Prosecutors, though, quickly affixed blame: five young black and Hispanic teenagers "wilding" in the park. Though there was no forensic or eyewitness evidence linking the youths to the crime, the police got convictions.

And so that case stood for nearly fifteen years, as a high-profile reminder of the danger of young, violent black men on rampage. Then, in 2002, a jailed and convicted rapist named Matias Reyes confessed to the crime. He acted alone, he said, and DNA evidence linked him to the crime scene. The five young men originally convicted had since served their time in prison, the longest serving thirteen years. Despite the evidence of their innocence, the men had to register as sex offenders under Megan's Law for the rest of their lives. "Because the suspects were black and Latino, this became an international case. It didn't matter who was convicted," said lawyer Roger Wareham.[4] Their records were eventually cleared.

We as a culture must be careful where we place our faith and beliefs. Beliefs that are fed or created with lies and hyperbole are in danger of collapsing beneath us. We risk wasting valuable time and resources, and in some cases our very lives, when we blindly follow those who manipulate us. The rush to judge, whether in giving donations, enacting laws, or identifying role models, is dangerous. Cynicism may not be good for America, but skepticism would go a long way toward inoculating us against predatory appeals.

As the effects of corporate media ownership squeeze out truly independent voices, hard news gets diluted and manipulated by private interests with financial motives. This increase in corporate ownership has fueled a disturbing shift in priorities: Instead of the news media being valued for their important social and democratic functions, news reporting is frequently seen by those who finance it as simply another type of programming. A recent example was the apparent willingness of the broadcast network ABC to replace its venerable hard-news program *Nightline* with a talk show. (*Nightline* stayed on the air.)

Corporate ownership of the news media is also fraught with conflicts of interest and a strong propensity to deemphasize coverage of certain topics. Whether subtle or overt, those in the newsrooms are keenly aware of which topics may affect and upset their owners. Later, we'll look at several cases in which corporate directives and lawyers, instead of news editors, have determined the content and angle of the news.

In this book I discuss how the media help shape our concerns and priorities—and how easily those concerns and priorities can be manipulated for personal gains and agendas. In part 1, I discuss advertising and the illusion of meaning. Advertisers use fear and emotion to sell their products, while placing meaningless phrases and "puffery" on their labels. It's no secret that advertising can be shady and deceptive, but the lines between advertising, news, and entertainment have become even more blurred in recent years. We expect truth and accuracy from the news media, and when the lines blur, they do so in favor of lending veracity and importance to advertisement. When news and advertising become indistinguishable, the public loses out.

In part 2, I examine the biases and manipulations of the news media. Though the news media usually try to make sure their reporting is not obviously politically biased, there are other, less recognized biases that plague this powerful business, ranging from how journalists choose what news to emphasize to the subjects they interview. They often emphasize bad news, minor fears and risks, and their biased reporting gives the public a skewed view of reality. This illusion of content and information is dangerous because people *think* they are being informed when they are not.

Other times, the media provide the illusion that viewers and readers are participating in causes and influencing the world around them. The public is presented with emotional, simplistic solutions to complex problems. In response, the public sends in their opinions, their money, or both, under the illusion that they are making a difference.

The news media use tragedy as license to abandon responsible journalism and wallow in sensationalism and hyperbole. Writing emotion into a story is easy; it's getting the facts right that takes effort. Many reporters "juice up" their articles with loaded words; others have simply found the facts too cumbersome and instead spin wholly fictional "articles."

Part 3 discusses how people and the press line up to profit from emotions and tragedies. The news media are among the worst; *Time* magazine, for example, exploited the tragedy at Columbine High School not once but several times in its quest to sell more magazines, under the guise of "helping the community."

I examine how advocates and lobbyists use emotional manipulation to create crises and manufacture martyrs in their efforts to promote their agendas. From AIDS testing to hate-crime legislation to Christian martyrs, people lobby for their causes—at times stretching the truth while they tug on heartstrings. Competing causes fight for limited public money, and frequently resort to emotional, alarmist, and inaccurate claims to gain support and funding. Many hold rallies and memorials to "raise awareness," substituting good feelings for action, creating the illusion of influence when in fact little is done.

In part 4 I discuss the damage caused by the media's myths. In some cases there is little consequence if people are misled; not every deception has important repercussions. But many myths have dramatic consequences on our lives, health, liberty, and security. I examine many such cases, including the hysteria following the Columbine High School shooting; medical scares surrounding breast implants, birth control, and autism; false accusations of satanic ritual child abuse; and the loss of trust and money to hoaxers and liars.

In the last section, I suggest some positive recent trends toward more responsible journalism, how the news media can do better, and the role of emotion in manipulation—and how to overcome it.

In this book I take the news media to task for many faults, ranging from sensationalism to bias. But it is also true that *media* is a plural noun, and in this regard it is a broad brush indeed—perhaps unfairly so, lumping megamonopolies such as Viacom in with small hometown newspapers, nestling ABC News next to *Mother Jones*. Of course, there are many socially responsible journalists and editors in all news fields. Bias and sensationalism are not bound by political ideologies.

Huge multinational corporations try to influence public opinion, but so do small bands of grassroots activists. The difference is that the corporations can afford slick ad campaigns from Madison Avenue, while the activists may be armed with little more than flyers and determination. Both sides are trying to sell you something, and a healthy dose of skepticism is needed as an antidote to the lies and exaggerations on both sides.

All things being equal, the informed consumer should make more of an attempt to get the activist's point of view, if for no other reason than in the interest of balance. It's easy to find out what R.J. Reynolds or General Electric wants you to know about them; it's somewhat harder to find out what their critics want you to know. I have attempted to draw examples from across the political and journalistic spectrums, though surely my own biases will surface now and then. I am not above them, though I have done my best to minimize them here.

Wherever possible, I give specific examples of the abuses I mention. The problems are not limited or peculiar to the individuals and organizations I cite, of course. I come from a long line of journalists, have been in the business for over a decade, and I am proud to carry on this work. At times—and at its best—journalism is a noble pursuit of the truth, without, as they say, fear or favor. Other times, perhaps much of the time, it's simply fallible people doing the best they can under deadline. Many in the news media work hard and get it right; this book is not about them.

It's time to call an end to this game of "Let's Pretend," in which advertisers and the news media pretend to give us useful information and the news media warn us of pretend problems so that publicity-seeking politicians can pretend to solve them with real-world legislation involving real-world consequences. On and on this game goes, while real problems get little attention because few with vested interests want to point out that the emperor has no clothes.

Cynthia Crossen summed it up well in her book *Tainted Truth*: "The tacit acceptance of untruth in daily life eats away at belief in right and wrong. If nothing is true, how can one solution be better than another?"[5]

NOTES

1. Deborah Tannen, *The Argument Culture: Moving from Debate to Dialogue* (New York: Random House, 1998), p. 13.

2. Carl Jensen, "What Happened to Good Old-fashioned Muckraking?" in *Into the Buzzsaw: Leading Journalists Expose the Myth of a Free Press*, ed. Kristina Borjesson (Amherst, N.Y.: Prometheus Books, 2002), p. 334.

3. Robert D. McFadden, *Outrage: The Story Behind the Tawana Brawley Hoax* (New York: Bantam Doubleday Dell, 1990).

4. Araminta Wordsworth, "DNA May Clear Five Jailed for Central Park Rape," *National Post*, September 7, 2002.

5. Cynthia Crossen, *Tainted Truth: The Manipulation of Fact in America* (New York: Simon & Schuster, 1994), p. 238.

Part 1

ADVERTISING AND THE ILLUSION OF MEANING

1

ADVERTISING AND THE ILLUSION OF MEANING

Americans are flooded with words. We are targeted wherever we turn by people trying to sell us products, persuade us to vote a certain way, or convince us to support their cause. Much of this persuasion—advertising, really—consists of meaningless words and phrases. Meaningless words are not simply a nuisance; they are a form of mental and visual clutter. Our children spend years in school learning how to read so they can understand the meaning of words and sentences, yet as they grow up, they encounter more and more words and phrases that *have* no meaning.

Perhaps nowhere is the illusion of meaning more clearly seen than in advertising. Red and yellow shock waves emerge from labels in 2-D, telling the consumer that the products are New, Improved, or, paradoxically, New *and* Improved. (Of course, a product cannot be both new *and* improved: If the product is new, it didn't exist before and therefore can't have been improved; an improved product existed before and therefore isn't new.)

That consumerist America is targeted by advertising is nothing new; as long as capitalism thrives, there will be choice, and where there is choice the providers of goods and services do not want consumers to choose too freely. Choice, the mantra goes, is important. But what is important is *informed* choice, not blind choice. Some products, ideas, and solutions are better than others. But when those promoting them give no substantive content on which the consumer can judge, the idea of informed choice becomes irrelevant. Informed choice is hard to come by when many product labels are meaningless, misleading, or both. As philosopher Sissela Bok wrote, "To be given false information about important choices in [our] lives is to be rendered powerless."[1]

Take, for example, a bottle of the dishwashing liquid Ajax. The label says, "Guaranteed Clean! Great Value! Tough on Grease!" I'm pretty clear on what the latter two phrases mean, but what in the world does "Guaranteed Clean" mean? Is the Colgate-Palmolive Company, the maker of Ajax, guaranteeing that my dishes will be clean if I use their product? What if I don't use enough of it? What if I'm not a very thorough washer? How can a company *guarantee* that my dishes will be clean? When I called the company to inquire, Terry, the customer service representative, couldn't find the label information on his computer. When I assured him that's what it said, he agreed and said, "We're here to help. We have a money-back guarantee regardless of the situation." He asked if I was unhappy with the product, and I said no, I just didn't understand what the label meant. He politely repeated that he would be happy to refund my money. He seemed a little hesitant to imply that his employer was directly guaranteeing that my dishes would be clean under any circumstances. Finally I gathered that "Guaranteed Clean" doesn't really imply any actual guarantee of dish or utensil cleanliness, but simply to an overall money-back guarantee.

A talk radio station in Buffalo, New York, advertises that it provides "breaking news first . . . guaranteed!" I looked up the word *guarantee* in my dictionary, and found "an assurance of the quality of a product offered, often with the promise of reimbursement." I wrote to the station to ask what, exactly, the guarantee meant. If the station isn't first with breaking news, is there some recourse or refund offered to listeners? Or was the guarantee just meaningless verbiage? Despite several queries, no one from the station would respond.

Breyer's Homemade Strawberries and Cream Ice Cream is another example. How can an ice cream made in a factory possibly be called "homemade?" Does Breyer's think consumers will be surprised when they see it in the store and exclaim, "Wow! That's the exact same ice cream I made at home!"? It seemed like a clear-cut oxymoron to me, so I wrote the company a polite letter asking if they were using some special meaning of the word "homemade." A representative, displaying little of the good humor one might expect from a Good Humor spokesman, wrote, "I believe it means it [*sic*] formulated to taste like homemade ice cream. Thank you." That's all well and good, but that's not what the label says.

Apparently "homemade" has joined the legion of weasel words such as "natural" that mean little. Even the high-priced and much-touted "organic" label doesn't necessarily mean that the product was grown without insecticide. In fact, according to the 1996 International Certification Standards published by the Organic Crop Improvement Association, the use of crop treatments such as *Bacillus thuringiensis*, copper sulfate, strychnine (a rat poison), and pyrethrum (a pesticide) are allowable on "organic" foods.

Another favorite advertising technique is telling the consumer not that something good *is* in a product, but that something bad is *not*. That's the rationale behind phrases like "sugar free" and "caffeine free." (In case you're wondering, advertisers don't use phrases like "no sugar" because product label designers don't want to use negative words like "no," even when making a positive claim. The assumption—right or wrong—is that consumers are childlike in that they don't like to be told "no.")

Even the question of what a product actually *is* can get tricky. Here's a quick quiz: What are the following products: Pringles __________, red Twizzlers __________, and Country Time __________. If you responded "Pringles potato chips," "Twizzlers licorice," and "Country Time lemonade," then you're not reading labels. Pringles are potato *crisps*, not chips (they aren't actually chips of potato, but simply mashed and formed potato pulp); cherry Twizzlers are simply called "twists" (a ridiculously broad term), as they have no actual licorice in them; and Country Time is a "lemonade *flavor* drink," no more lemonade than Country Time cherry flavor drink is made from real cherries.

Most consumers simply fill in what they *think* the product is. Advertisers are required by law to be truthful about their products, and when consumers make wrong (but positive) assumptions, companies are happy to perpetuate those misunderstandings.

One of my all-time favorite meaningless words is "goodness." Many products, including Grape-Nuts and Roman Meal bread, have at one time or another claimed to have "goodness" in them. Oddly, "goodness" doesn't appear on the ingredient labels. Perhaps the companies are trying to suggest that their competition's products have "evilness" in them, or at least are lacking the U.S. Recommended Dietary Allowance of vitamin G, "goodness."

Speaking of dubious vitamins, Robert Park notes an example in his book *Voodoo Science*:

> There was a full-page ad in *USA Today* recently for "Vitamin O." Beneath a photograph of an attractive group of vigorous, smiling people, the ad said "Vitamin O" was helping thousands of people to live healthier lives. . . . Indeed, the ad included a number of testimonials, which said things like, "After taking 'Vitamin O' for several months, I find I have more energy and stamina and have become immune to colds and flu." . . . "Vitamin O" was to be taken orally as a supplement. The recommended dose was fifteen to twenty drops two or three times a day. . . . A two ounce vial, which sold for twenty dollars plus shipping charges, should last a month. . . . So what is "Vitamin O"? The ad says exactly what it is: "stabilized oxygen molecules in a solution of distilled water and sodium chloride." In other words, it's salt water.[2]

Labels for juice drinks promise they're "100% Juice"—but are they?

Though meaningless words and phrases are common in advertising, they often pop up in news as well. Since 1976 Detroit's Lake Superior State University has compiled an annual list of misused, overused, and generally useless words and phrases. For the year 2000, compilers cited "at risk," "for the children," and "wake-up call" among the offensive and worthless political terms to be eliminated. Not coincidentally, these are the same hackneyed phrases that make up much of the news media's staple dialogue.[3]

Another meaningless advertising gem is "So Good It Has Been Awarded a Patent!" But of course a patent is no guarantee of quality or utility: Virtually any item or process can be patented, regardless of quality. Even some items that *cannot* work have been "awarded" patents (such as perpetual motion and free-energy machines).

The label of the vegetable drink V8, made by the Campbell Soup Company, states proudly not once but twice that it is "100% Vegetable Juice." Yet a glance at the ingredient list reveals that the company has ingeniously managed to define such diverse ingredients as salt, citric acid, vitamin C, and flavoring as "juice." "If," I asked Maria, the pleasant customer service representative at Campbell Soup, "100 percent of your product is juice, then how is there space for what seem to be nonjuice ingredients?" At first she didn't understand what I was talking about, so I repeated the question. After a few seconds, she said, "It's not vegetable juice *only*." "But if V8 is 100 percent juice," I countered, "that doesn't leave any percent for the non-juice, does it?" We both noted that at the bottom the label said, in small print, "From concentrate with added ingredients," though that didn't help much.

Maria then tried to change the subject: "Were you unhappy with the product, sir?" I assured her that I liked V8 and didn't want a refund, just an explanation of a phrase that the company placed twice on its label. The best she could come up with was, "100 percent of the first ingredients *up to salt* is juice." "So the juice part is all juice?" I asked, trying to keep a straight face. "That's right," she replied. When I asked her why they put the label "100 percent juice" on a product that (to anyone except Campbell Soup consumer service representatives) is clearly not 100 percent juice, her answer was, "I guess they didn't think that anyone would call and ask." (I later received a note from Campbell Soup thanking me "for making a difference," along with a coupon for more V8.)

In January 2000 the aspirin maker Bayer settled after the Federal Trade Commission (FTC) charged that a series of Bayer ads made unsubstantiated claims. The commercials strongly implied that regular aspirin use could help the general population prevent heart attacks and strokes. This isn't true, according to Dr. Rodman Starke of the American Heart Association. In fact, there is little evidence that aspirin prevents a heart attack in someone who doesn't already have vascular disease. Bayer paid $1 million for a consumer education campaign to clear up misleading information about who can truly benefit from taking aspirin daily.[4]

Crystal Geyser, the bottler of alpine spring water, has a curious bit of information on its labels. The water, which comes from "Tennessee's Cherokee National Forrest [*sic*]," apparently goes bad and expires after about two years. A bottle I bought in March 2000 listed an expiration date of December 2001. I had never heard of water going bad, and couldn't imagine what sort of perishable ingredients might be in this "pure" spring water, so I called the company. After some questioning, the spokeswoman admitted that water "doesn't really go bad," but rushed to add that nonetheless, Crystal Geyser likes to make sure that the product is rotated to assure the "freshest" water possible for the consumer.

The ad copy on the back of the bottle says that "Pure rain and snow fall upon the peaks of the Blue Ridge Mountains. . . . The geological layers of these historic mountains naturally filter this pristine water. Years later some of this water emerges at our protected spring source in the nearby foothills." So by the company's own admission, the water has been sitting around for "years." Yet, suddenly, inexplicably, as soon as it's bottled and shipped, the water is once again "fresh" and subject to a perishable goods date. It then joins expiration-dated carbonated beverages and beer, including Budweiser and Michelob's oddly anthropomorphized "Born On" dates.

I also contacted the bottler of Dannon Natural Spring Water to ask about its expiration date. I was told that it "doesn't really go bad," and that in New Jersey a state law requires the expiry date because the product is bottled and therefore considered a food product. I was told that the expiration dates are there "to ensure your safety."

It's good of the companies to be reassuring about the safety of their bottled water, because a 2000 study found that regular tap water was often safer than bottled water. Dr. James Lalumandier of the School of Dentistry at Case Western Reserve University tested bacterial counts and fluoride levels of samples of bottled water and regular tap water. He found that although most of the bottled water had lower bacterial counts, the fifteen samples of bottled water that were not as pure had anywhere from ten to one thousand times the bacteria levels of water from Cleveland water plants. Lalumandier also expressed concern that the lack of fluoride in bottled water would lead to increases in dental caries in the population.[5]

A package of Rold Gold Original Snack Mix touts that the contents are "Lighthearted and Crunchy!" Now, I know what crunchy is, and the adjective's use to describe the snack mix therein seemed appropriate. But "lighthearted"? According to one source, the *Macmillan Contemporary Dictionary*, "lighthearted" means "free from care or anxiety; cheerful; gay." I opened the package carefully, so as not to disturb any cheerful or gay pretzels cavorting around. I called Frito-Lay, Inc. to inquire as to how a one-ounce bag of crackers, bread bits, and pretzels could be considered "lighthearted." The customer service representative I spoke with explained that the word is just meant to remind consumers of happy thoughts. "They [Frito-Lay] know that pretzels don't have feelings," he assured me.

Companies are not used to being called on the spot to explain their meaningless packaging blurbs. They act surprised that anyone would take what they say literally or hold them to the words on their labels.

Most candy bars—especially at Halloween—now come in a "fun size" package. They're smaller than the standard version of the candy, and typically contain just one bar or piece. Notice how the candy isn't "small" but "fun size," as if *less* of something is somehow *more* fun. If anything, I would assume that kids would want more candy, not less, and would therefore have more fun with a regular or king-sized candy bar. But the interesting thing here is the evasive terminology.

Are "small" and "fun size" interchangeable? Imagine being promised a "fun size" raise at work, or choosing between a "fun size," medium, or large shirt. "Fun size," alas, seems to have meaning only in the minds of marketers and ad agencies, not in the real world.

Who is in charge of making sure that advertisers are truthful in their claims? Though there are a handful of consumer watchdog organizations, ultimately this Herculean task falls to the Federal Trade Commission (FTC).

As Cynthia Crossen explains in *Tainted Truth*, the FTC is limited in

A sample of meaningless, vague, and contradictory advertising slogans.

what it can do. "[T]he FTC can tackle only a handful of the most egregious claims, usually national in scope. 'Do you have the world's largest Ford dealer in your area?' asked a spokesman for the FTC. 'Well, I've got the world's largest Ford dealer down here too. It's not worth it for the commission to challenge a claim like that. It's just not going to stop.'"[6] The beleaguered and underfunded organization dramatically watered down its definition of deceptive advertising in 1983; the standard became ads which "were likely to mislead," instead of simply having the "capacity" to mislead.

LEGALESE, PUFFERY, AND THE LOSS OF MEANING

Then there are the near-meaningless phrases and warnings on products that are taken seriously only by lawyers and anal-retentive types. Typical commercial glass coffeepots fall into this category. Written on the side of most pots is a list of a half dozen or so warnings intended "to avoid breakage or injury." A common item on the list states, "Discard if cracked, scratched, or heated empty." This warning is there to protect the manufacturer from lawsuits brought by people who might use a cracked coffeepot and spill boiling coffee on themselves or others.

But seriously, folks: in the office where I work, if we threw out a coffee pot every time some idiot emptied it and put it back on the burner or a pot got scratched, we'd go through a dozen a week. Our litigious society has slapped thousands of (to most people, irrelevant) warnings and directions on a wide spectrum of products, from coffee cups gently warning that the contents might be hot to tubes of toothpaste that helpfully suggest we squeeze from the end. I collect boomerangs, and I own a boomerang that says, "Not suitable for children under 36 months due to small size of components." Well, there's only one component, and that's a sixteen-inch, L-shaped piece of rounded plastic. The legalese facet of this warning comes right after it, in endearingly fractured English: "You are advised to this information."

A group called the Michigan Lawsuit Abuse Watch holds an annual Wacky Warning Label Contest. In 1999 the winner was a notice on an iron: "Never iron clothes while they are being worn." Runners-up included a thirteen-inch wheelbarrow tire that warned, "Not for highway use" and a bathroom heater that cautioned, "This product is not to be used in bathrooms."[7]

A package of Sunbird Hot & Sour Soup Mix notes on the back, "For hotter flavor, add hot sauce." Good thing it's mentioned bright red lettering; it wouldn't have occurred to me that adding hot sauce would make the soup hotter. From a Cumberland Ridge Confections Peanut Roll candy wrapper: "Allergen information: Manufactured in a facility that processes peanuts." One might think that someone allergic to peanuts wouldn't buy and eat a candy that has "peanut" in its name and is clearly coated in peanuts.

Some warnings are simply inscrutable. Several books published by Godsfield Press include warnings on the copyright page that state, "Every effort has been made to ensure that all the information in this book is accurate. However, due to differing conditions, tools, and individual skills, the publisher cannot be responsible for any injuries, losses, and other damages which may result from the use of information in this book." That's an exhaustive standard disclaimer, so one might assume the information in the book is potentially dangerous. A title on explosives, perhaps? Or home medical remedies? No, this indemnification appears in, among others, *Taoist Wisdom* and *Zen Made Easy*, both by Timothy Freke.

What sort of "injuries, losses, or damages" could possibly come from a book of Zen quotations? Is there an epidemic of Taoist deaths due to excess wisdom that has somehow escaped media attention? Is the voyage to self-discovery and enlightenment fraught with mortal bodily dangers?

Another irritating, meaningless phrase that plagued the world recently was, "The Official (insert product here) of the Millennium." If it's a joke, it's a tired one, and if it actually means something, what the hell is it? Of course, usually a sponsorship means that a company has given money to be the "Official" sponsor of an event. Soon, companies realized that, with careful selection, they could be the "Official Sponsor" of anything. The A&E Channel thus became the "Official Channel of Every Millennium," Miller was the "Official Beer of the Millennium," while Coors was the "Official Beer of Y2K." Even Viagra, tongue in cheek, was touted as "An 'Official Sponsor' of Valentine's Day." While some may find this cute or amusing, such claims have no meaning.

The companies insist, in Orwellian doublespeak, that "Guaranteed" doesn't really mean guaranteed, "100% Juice" means "mostly juice," and "Homemade" really means exactly the opposite. Some labels are obviously literally untrue: "Ice Cold" beer isn't ice cold, of course; who wants to gnaw on frozen beer? But shouldn't "100% Juice" be literally true? One product, Juicy Juice, has made its name (and found its market niche) based on the fact that its claim to be 100 percent juice is actually true. Shouldn't "100% Juice" mean the same thing, at least between juice products? And what does it say about the state of affairs when the selling point of the product is essentially, "Buy our product because we're not misleading you when we say it's 100 percent juice?"

(As it turns out, even Juicy Juice isn't 100 percent juice. Along with juice, the product has natural flavoring and ascorbic acid. Though most

Pfizer
WISHING YOU A HAPPY VALENTINE'S DAY
VIAGRA®
(sildenafil citrate) tablets
An "official sponsor" of Valentine's Day
www.viagra.com
HC639A99C
© 2000, Pfizer Inc

Viagra touts itself as an "official sponsor" of Valentine's Day.

people probably would have little objection to those added ingredients, the fact remains that the product is simply not 100 percent juice, as it is labeled and promoted.)

Aside from the problem of meaningless and misleading labels, what happens when people with severe allergies or strict diets need accurate information about what's in and on the products they buy? A person with a milk allergy who buys a product touted as "nondairy" that nonetheless contains dairy products could be at serious medical risk. In the case of V8, each serving has 620 mg of sodium, more than a quarter of the Recommended Daily Value. Consumers on a low-salt diet (such as those with high blood pressure) might want to know that the "100% Juice" product has much more salt than would be found naturally in a drink that is truly 100 percent juice, with no added ingredients. Problems with food products containing ingredients not listed at all on the label led to notices on many baked goods notifying consumers that the item "may contain traces of peanut" or was "manufactured in a plant that that handles nuts."

Perhaps some readers feel I'm being obstinate. But if these phrases don't mean anything, why are they on packages? Do companies assume that the public is stupid, or just that we don't care? I posit it is a mixture of both. Imagine what life would be like if real people talked to us in such meaningless babble:

> Client (walking into a bank): Hi, I'd like to set up an account.
>
> Banker: Great. We have a new fund you might like, the all-natural plan.
>
> Client: What does that mean?
>
> Banker: It means it's all natural.
>
> Client: Oh . . . okay. Are my funds insured?
>
> Banker: Absolutely. One hundred percent.
>
> Client (after reading contract): But this says it's only insured to $90,000.
>
> Banker: Well, the part that's insured is insured 100 percent.
>
> Client: But you said it's all insured.
>
> Banker: That's right!
>
> Client: That doesn't make sense. Is it insured or isn't it?
>
> Banker: It's fully, 100 percent insured. Except the part that's not.
>
> Client: Hold on. Is the contract right or are you right?
>
> Banker: We're both right.
>
> (Client walks out)
>
> Banker (calling out): Would you like to hear about our guaranteed goodness plan?

If we wouldn't accept such imbecility in real life, why do we accept it on the products we buy and in the advertisements we watch?

Yet the consumer "tunes out" the meaningless junk at his or her peril:

Important information may be buried amid the crap, ranging from legally binding fine print and caveats to crucial warnings about drug interactions. Hidden and misleading information buried in the sea of fine print on the backs of credit card and telephone bills, for example, have led to complaints of fraud and misrepresentation.

Similar complaints have been filed against Publisher's Clearinghouse and American Family Publishers. Hundreds of people have claimed that the companies' advertisements, designed to look like official notifications, misled them into thinking they won money or needed to buy magazine subscriptions to win. Several states' attorneys general have stepped in and filed lawsuits of their own—and won.

In June 2001 a New Jersey man won a million dollars from H&R Block—but refused to claim his prize, believing it was a scam. The man was selected out of 17 million people to win the grand prize. Said company spokeswoman Janine Smiley, "We're a little bit amazed that there is such growing skepticism."[8] And in January 2000 several Milwaukee, Wisconsin, taxpayers threw away their tax rebate checks from the State Department of Revenue because the checks were packaged in envelopes that looked like a coupon, campaign mailing, or advertisement.[9]

"Puffery" is a term from advertising law that basically means a claim by an advertiser that doesn't mean anything to consumers and (presumably) can't be actually substantiated. If a pharmaceutical company claims that more hospitals use its product, that is a verifiable assertion; either it's true or it isn't. (By the way, the reason more hospitals use that brand of pain reliever often has nothing to do with its effectiveness; it simply costs the hospital less and is therefore used more.)

By contrast, the claim that the A&E Channel is the Official Channel of Every Millennium clearly means little in concrete terms. But, writes Leslie Savan, "Hyperbole can communicate all sorts of information—much of it may not be 'objective,' but it can still be highly persuasive. One customer is now opposing an advertiser's puffery defense in an Ohio court. E*Trade had advertised its online brokerage as 'reliable, convenient, fast and efficient' and its technology as 'state of the art,' saying trades could be 'executed and electronically confirmed within seconds.' But a client, Truc Hoang of Westlake, Ohio, says that service outages stopped her from completing trades and cost her $40,000. She filed a class action lawsuit against E*Trade. . . . E*Trade filed for dismissal, citing other cases in which ad claims were considered 'mere puffery.'"[10]

Another type of misleading occurs when print ads for a film feature glowing blurbs from reviewers across the country. These folks are known in the trade as "quote whores," those who don't mind misleading readers as they gush lovingly about the worst dreck ever put on film.

As an example, recent critical failures and box office duds such as *The*

Legend of Bagger Vance and *Pay It Forward* garnered abysmal reviews among most of the best-known (and most-credible) film reviewers. Yet in full-page ads in the November 3, 2000, *New York Times*, both films managed to cull enough quotes from various reviewers to fill their ads with glowing praise. Also in that edition, a review of *Charlie's Angels* by A. O. Scott questioned the filmmaker's competence, said the copious fight scenes were "carelessly edited and ploddingly staged," and called the whole film "trash." Yet don't fear, angels: a double-page, full-color ad for the film on the previous two pages included eight blurbs telling moviegoers what a gem the film was.

Certainly, reviewers may have legitimately different takes on films—and that's their defense, that it's ultimately subjective opinion—and arts reviewers should be applauded for bucking the popular opinion and telling it as they see it. But when the same critics shill over and over for movies that are simply bad, or seem incapable of writing a negative review, it becomes clear what their agenda is. As *Washington Post* critic Desson Howe points out, "This country is overpopulated with helium-filled movie critics who like anything."[11] *Newsweek*'s John Horn explains: "Reading the glowing newspaper-ad recommendations for even the lamest movie, you might wonder if those quoted critics are real. . . . Many are habitués of the junket circuit, an all-expenses-paid gravy train where the studios give journalists free rooms and meals at posh hotels and the reporters return the favor with puffy celebrity profiles and enthusiastic review blurbs."[12] The studios walk on thin ice, however: At least ten class-action lawsuits have been filed by moviegoers who were duped into paying to see bad films by biased reviewers.

In one notable case, the film reviewer himself was a fiction. Sony Pictures created a fictional film reviewer named David Manning to promote their films. Gushing about the film *A Knight's Tale*, Manning wrote that the male lead was "this year's hottest new star," and that *The Animal* (a dog of a film by most measures) was "another winner!" The film studio's deception came to light when *Newsweek* reporter John Horn challenged Sony about Manning's authenticity. Sony admitted using "incredibly bad judgment" and promised an investigation.[13] In March 2002 Sony Pictures agreed to pay $325,000 to the state of Connecticut for using the fake reviews.[14]

In the fallout from the Manning affair, other studios—including 20th Century Fox, Universal Pictures, and Artisan Entertainment—admitted using employees or actors in television commercials posing as moviegoers.[15]

There is a cumulative effect of all these lies, half-lies, and meaningless words: a completely justifiable abrasion of trust in what we are being told. Politicians lie to us, the government lies to us, advertisers try to deceive us, and on top of it all, we're bombarded by words that don't mean anything. Even photographic evidence, once considered difficult to fake, can easily be manipulated with modern technology. Using old film footage, long-dead celebrities can be brought back from the grave to promote new products. Doctored photos of famous nude celebrities can be found all over the Web. Nothing is beyond suspicion.[16]

EMOTION AND THE CORPORATE IMAGE

An examination of a recent advertising campaign by Philip Morris Companies, Inc. shows how the tobacco company uses emotional appeals to salvage its corporate image. The campaign, which reportedly costs $150 million per year, is intended to repair the company's image following the disclosures that Philip Morris (along with all the other tobacco companies) knew about the health risks of their products for decades and lied to the public about it, earning billions in the process.

Double-page print ads in national magazines feature sympathetic photographs of people on the left page and their (presumably genuine) quotes and personal stories on the right. Each ad tackles a social problem and uses an individual person or case to illustrate that problem and how Philip Morris has helped them out. For example, an ad that ran in the May 2000 issue of *Atlantic Monthly* showed an old man with a cane, along with the quote: "Dignity . . . is life without hunger." It goes on to say, "Lewis Niblack didn't want to be a burden. As one of a growing number of homebound seniors, his daily struggle to get nutritious food limited his cherished sense of dependence. Thanks to . . . *The Philip Morris Fight Against Hunger*, Lewis and thousands of hungry seniors across the country are no longer kept on waiting lists by their neighborhood meals-on-wheels programs. Now that the wait for food is over, Lewis has regained his self-sufficiency. And with it, his sense of dignity."

Another ad that ran the same month in *Brill's Content* focused on domestic violence. It begins, "With their [Philip Morris's] help, I survived domestic violence. Now I can dream again." Below, the text begins, "When Sarahrose Snyder took refuge at Hope House, a domestic violence shelter, she found the support she needed to change her life. . . . Sarahrose regained her dignity and discovered a new future. . . . Through initiatives such as *Doors of Hope*, the people of Philip Morris have been helping communities in need for more than forty years."

In a 1998 ad whose slogan was "Sharing the commitment. Building the solution," Philip Morris showed us Warren Brice, a volunteer at a Houston food bank. "I help hungry people get fresh and wholesome food," Brice is quoted as saying, "and that just feels good." Again, the ads goes on to tell of the tobacco company's good deeds in glowing detail.

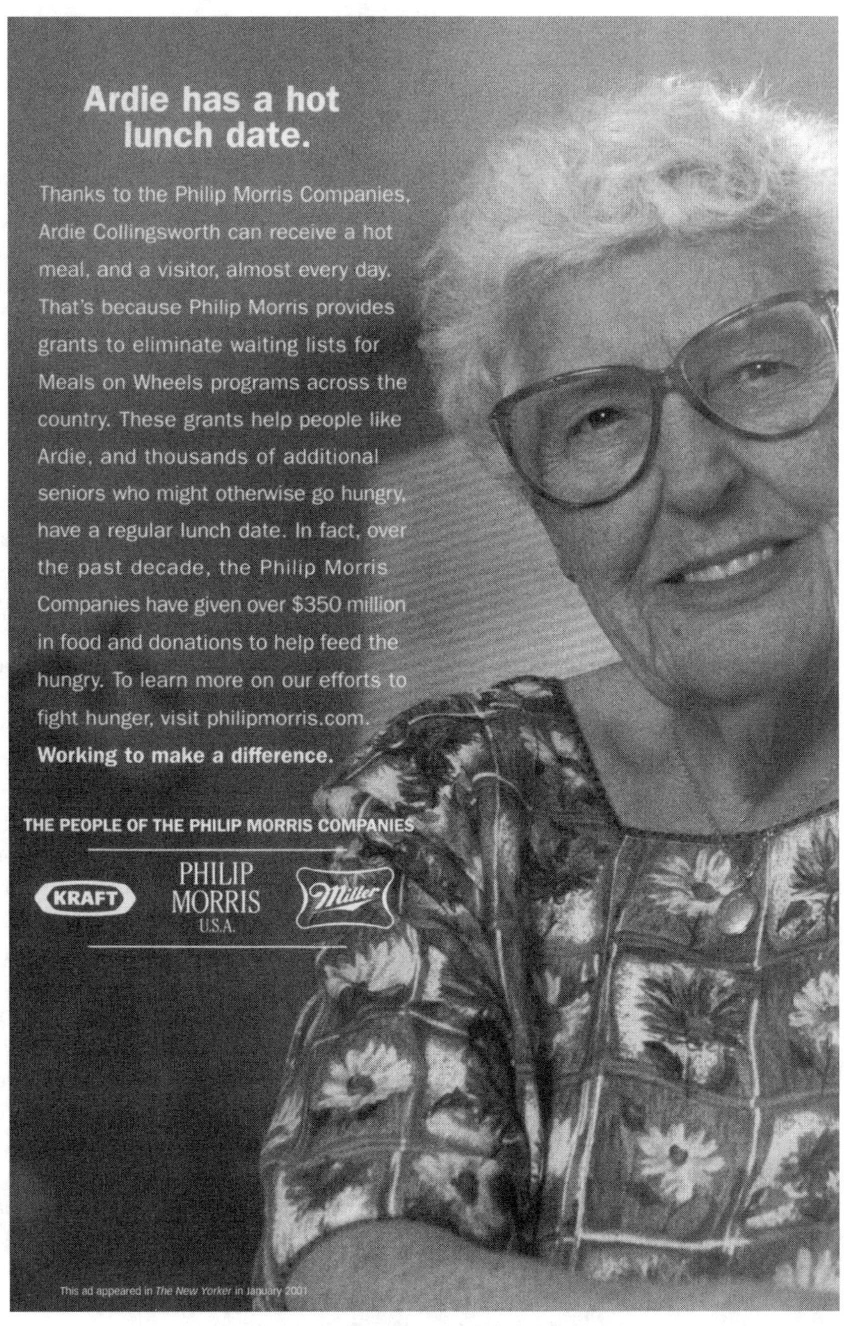

An advertisement for the tobacco company Philip Morris uses emotional appeals to counter bad publicity.

These ads, and many others in the series, tell us that the people of Philip Morris are feeding our hungry elderly, giving them back their dignity, and protecting women and children from abuse. They like to use the phrase "the people of Philip Morris" to subtly try to counter the public image of a faceless corporation.

The ads are clever: They show Philip Morris as not just doing charity efforts, but restoring seniors' "dignity" and helping a former battered spouse to "dream again." This sort of emotionalism is hard to combat: Who doesn't want the elderly to have dignity or a battered woman to have dreams? Of course, the ads don't mention the seniors who have lost their dignity and independence confined to an oxygen tank or hospital bed from emphysema due to a lifetime of smoking cigarettes.

Studies show that alcohol plays a significant role in contributing to domestic violence and spousal abuse. Says Dr. Brian Quigley, research associate at the Research Institute on Addictions in Buffalo, New York, "Alcohol use is not simply a reaction to the violence, it is predictive of later violence. It seemingly plays a role in the development of violence." Who do we find in the Philip Morris "family" of companies working so hard to combat domestic violence? Miller brewing company, the second largest brewer in America.[17]

Many large companies are responsible corporate citizens that don't toot their own horns—and haven't deceived the American public for decades about the safety of their products. Philip Morris's repeated and public self-congratulations for its humanitarian efforts is a display of astounding hypocrisy. It is an attempt at emotional manipulation and misdirection.

Certainly, companies that support community programs should be acknowledged. But, as *Time* columnist Roger Rosenblatt has noted, "Here is where the problem of these efforts at redemption lies. Yes, they are worthy. Without Philip Morris, many of the best arts programs would be hanging by a thread. But there is also a shell game in progress. Every one of these good works is meant to draw one's eyes away from main purposes. One is tempted to say, 'Duh,' but Philip Morris would not need to worry about selling cigarettes to minors if it did not sell cigarettes at all." And, if the ad campaign is successful—and $150 million a year buys a lot of success—the public will eventually come to associate Philip Morris with the polar opposite of what it really does for a living.[18] ABC newsmagazine *20/20* correspondent John Stossell profiled the Philip Morris ad campaign in his February 9, 2001, "Give Me a Break!" segment. He noted that although the company had spent $150 million the previous year on advertising its good deeds, it actually spent $35 million less—$115 million—on its charitable work. In terms of money spent, announcing its good deeds is clearly more important than performing them in the first place.

It's also unclear just how much of the image makeover is heartfelt, and how much is marketing strategy. In June 2000 Philip Morris CEO Michael Szymanczyk testified before a Florida jury, trying to dissuade it from granting a multibillion-dollar punitive damages request on behalf of three hundred thousand to five hundred thousand sick Florida smokers. Szymanczyk told jurors that, as the top decision maker in the company, he intended to make changes because the company was facing "substantial litigation."

Plaintiff's attorney Stanley Rosenblatt argued that Szymanczyk shouldn't be allowed to give the jury "a public relations spiel about how they do business today." Circuit Judge Robert Kaye noted that Szymanczyk had been employed by Philip Morris for a decade, saying, "I'm certain he knew and understood what was going on in the company, way back in 1990. To come in and say that now that I'm CEO in 1997, 'I just realized what we were doing wrong,' I think, well, it stretches one's credulity."[19]

NOTES

1. Cynthia Crossen, *Tainted Truth: The Manipulation of Fact in America* (New York: Simon & Schuster, 1994), p. 73.
2. Robert Park, *Voodoo Science: The Road from Foolishness to Fraud* (New York: Oxford University Press, 2002), p. 46.
3. Alexandra Moses, "'Millennium' on Banished Words List," Associated Press [online], http://wire.ap.org [January 1, 2000].
4. Lauran Neergaard, "It's Not for Everyone: Bayer Pays for Making Unsubstantiated Claims about Aspirin," ABC News [online], abcnews.go.com/sections/living/DailyNews/aspirin000111.html [January 11, 2000].
5. The study was published in the *Archives of Family Medicine* in 2000; story available at fluoride.oralheath.org/papers/2000/reutershealthtapwatersafety031400.htm.
6. Crossen, *Tainted Truth*, p. 93.
7. Available at www.power-of-attorneys.com/wacky_warning_labels.asp.
8. "Reluctant Winner," ABC News [online], abcnews.go.com/sections/us/DailyNews/reluctant_winner010630.html [June 30, 2001].
9. "Rebate Checks Resemble Junk Mail," Associated Press [online], www.getacoupon.com/pages/coupon_news.html [January 7, 2000].
10. Leslie Savan, "Truth in Advertising?" *Brill's Content* (March 2000): 114.
11. Nancy Chandross, "Fooled Ya!" ABC News [online], abcnews.go.com [June 26, 2001].
12. John Horn, "The Reviewer Who Wasn't There; Sony Resorts to Some Questionable Marketing Practices to Promote New Movies," *Newsweek* Web Exclusive, June 2, 2001.
13. Ibid.
14. Pat Eaton-Robb, "Sony Settles Phony Film Review Suit," Associated Press [online], http://wire.ap.org [March 12, 2002].

15. "Sony Promises Not to Use Fake Movie Reviews," Associated Press [online], www.cnn.com/2001/LAW/08/14/fake.review [August 14, 2001].

16. William J. Mitchell, "When Is Seeing Believing?" *Scientific American* (February 1994): 69.

17. "Alcohol Consumption and Marriage: A Good Mix?" Research Institute on Addictions [online], www.ria.org/news/2001-06-05.html [July 14, 2000].

18. Roger Rosenblatt, "Redemption: It's Good for Business," *Time*, May 22, 2000, p. 160.

19. Rachel La Corte, "Philip Morris CEO Testifies," Associated Press [online], www.no-smoking.org/june00/06-13-00-1.html [June 12, 2000].

2

ADVERTISING, NEWS, AND ENTERTAINMENT

Emotion and fear are used by the media and drug companies to sell their respective products. Consumers react as expected, reaching for their wallets and generating money for those tugging on heartstrings.

Ads for Michelin tires feature adorable babies sitting happily inside a stack of tires. A voice-over intones a quasi-extortionistic, "Because so much is riding on your tires." The message? If you don't want your beautiful baby killed or horribly maimed in an auto accident, buy our tires. In reality, the simple use of seat belts is much more critical in assuring kids' safety than which brand of tires are on the vehicle. Recent studies have shown that fewer than one in five children are properly buckled in; buying a set of "safer" tires is much easier than making the efforts to consistently restrain children. By purchasing Michelin tires, parents can give themselves the illusion that they're protecting their children. I deal more with the illusions of influence in part 2.

When Scope mouthwash is touted as "Make-out Insurance" in Procter & Gamble's ads, and Close-Up toothpaste's jingle is "Want Love? Get Close-up," the implication is clear. A contented audience happy with who and how they are is an advertiser's nightmare: They don't want you to be happy without their products, and if they can't convince you to buy, they'll create the illusion that you *need* what they have. This mentality was satirized in the 1980s TV show *Max Headroom*, which featured a multinational conglomerate named ZikZak: Its slogan was, "We make everything you need and you need everything we make."

Advertisers want consumers whose self-worth is tied to what kind of car they drive, what kind of shampoo they use, and how big their diamond engagement ring should be. In a particularly audacious move, ads by the South African diamond monopoly DeBeers went so far as to suggest how much a man should spend on diamonds: two months' salary. (Presumably the diamond given should be accompanied by a receipt and detailed pay stubs proving that the giver loves her because he has tithed DeBeers its 16 percent.)

Notice that few ads offer real information. The bulk of advertising trades on changing not minds but hearts, and playing on such fear and insecurity is both powerful and manipulative. "Am I saving all I can on long-distance?" the American consumer is requested to ask himself. "Do I love my kids enough to buy them real Jell-O instead of the store brand? Do I have acid reflux syndrome? Should I ask my doctor about the latest drug? How can I slim my thighs enough to ride a roller coaster with Fabio?"

To some degree, this need-oriented approach is at once both personal and universal: If we're lonely, we can fix it by buying the right mouthwash; if we're having "intimacy" problems, we can pop some Viagra; if we have that "not-so-fresh" feeling, we can discuss it with our mother during a walk along a sunny beach. As always, the message is that money (properly distributed) will solve the problem—any problem. The view that you can solve problems yourself—or that there's nothing wrong with you to begin with—is seldom heard.

THE BLURRING LINES BETWEEN ENTERTAINMENT, ADVERTISING, AND NEWS

The marriage of entertainment and advertising is a natural one. People enjoy entertainment, and people are consumers, therefore advertisers want their names and logos in front of entertainment audiences. The "sponsored by" tag on TV shows and sports events is certainly nothing new: Early game shows were prominently sponsored, such as *Twenty-One,* "brought to you by Geritol" as the program announcer intoned at the beginning of the show.

Though the partnership is by no means a new one, the venues for advertising seem to have proliferated in the past decade. TV, radio, billboards, magazines, and the Internet are obvious places for advertising, but so are more mundane places such as the handles on gas pumps and small placards on shopping carts. Anywhere consumers spend time, even briefly, is seen as an opportunity for ads. Not so long ago, a person going to a theater to see a film might sit through two or three short previews, then enjoy the feature. These days it's not unusual to sit through ten to fifteen minutes of advertisements before the film you paid your money to see comes on. And the ads not only sell Coke and popcorn, but everything from cars to dental services.

A cursory look at the naming of sports venues further illustrates the overt commercialization and blending of entertainment and advertising: Riverfront Stadium in Cincinnati became Cinergy Field; San Francisco's Candlestick Park became 3Com Park, and Superbowl XXXII was played at Qualcomm Stadium, formerly Jack Murphy Stadium, in San Diego. Race cars are emblazoned with patchwork ads, tennis players shill for Nike or Reebok as they play. You might think that pro beach volleyball players, wearing little anyway, would have no space to advertise. No matter: players don temporary tattoos for their sponsors.

THE LINE BETWEEN NEWS AND ADVERTISING

Television and print news media have largely been careful about keeping advertising and news coverage separate, while the merger craze of the past decade has created many news outlets that, though ostensibly independent, are actually owned by a handful of huge conglomerates. Corporate ownership of news organizations is a troubling trend, largely because of the influences that may be brought to bear on coverage of topics sensitive to the parent corporations.

The proliferation of television newsmagazines (for example, *60 Minutes* clones and their spin-offs) has led each network to have its own stable of prime-time news shows to plug. Not content with the standard routes of advertising, a few years ago the networks turned to having the nightly news anchors themselves encourage viewers to tune in. It's usually encapsulated in a brief "program note," as in, "Here's a preview of *48 Hours* (or *Dateline* or *20/20*) later tonight." But make no mistake, it's an advertisement. Though perhaps innocuous, the door has been opened for other reporters or anchors to promote other programs, or possibly other products.

Press releases have been around in some form for centuries. When a company or special interest group wants to put out its biased point of view to the public, the press release is principal among its tools. Some public relations firms put out press releases that, at first glance, look exactly like legitimate news stories. The copy reads like a news story, complete with city of origin, date, quotes, and at times even a "reporter's" name.

America Online, the top Internet service provider in the United States, does nothing to help its subscribers tell the advertising from the news. The press releases are presented along with the real news, in the same format and viewfield. Many firms who do this work use deceptive names, such as U.S. Newswire and PRNewswire. Yet they are not newswires at all, but shills for anyone paying their bills.

Compare this approach with the initiative taken by the Web search engine Google. Those trying to find information amid the millions of Web pages use search engines to sort out what they're looking for. Many search engine companies allow companies to pay to have their advertisements pop up in search results. So, for example, if a person is looking to find information on how to repair a classic car, ads for cars might appear along with the Web pages of information the user requested.

But Google decided to take a stand. In a statement titled, "Why We Sell Advertising, Not Search Results," the company states that "like a news organization, we believe we have an obligation to present information as objectively as possible. That's why we don't bias our search results based on what people are willing to pay. . . . Every ad on Google is clearly marked as a 'Sponsored Link' and is set apart from the actual search results. . . . Some online services don't believe the distinction between search results and advertising is all that important. We do."[1]

The Infomercial Boom

It wasn't until the 1980s that the idea of "infomercials"—those late-night and weekend thirty-minute advertisements hawking everything from car waxes to fitness machines to food processors—came up. The infomercial is a curious blend of entertainment, advertising, and news formats.

The idea was to frame an advertisement (which most people would typically regard as a necessary nuisance) as a seemingly informative, educational program. Although by now most infomercials are recognizable as such, many early ones clearly copied the newsdesk format, complete with a news "anchor," "special reports," and interview subjects, all as faux as any cubic zirconian "diamond" on the Home Shopping Network. The idea, of course, is to capitalize on the authority of the news format, to make people think (perhaps subconsciously) that what they are being told has equal weight, value, and truth as a news broadcast.

"For the business community and for politicians," writes David Shenk, author of *Data Smog*, "the prospect of bypassing journalists holds the allure of circumventing public skepticism, intellectual curiosity, and rational analysis. It is the promise of being able to make an elaborate sales pitch completely uncontested. Conservative Republicans, for example, have already established two cable television networks, GOP-TV and National Empowerment Television (NET), funded by the conservative Free Congress Foundation. NET broadcasts programs produced by the National Rifle Association and the American Life League, an anti-abortion group. 'Though these programs can look like Discovery Channel documentaries,' reports the *Columbia Journalism Review*, 'they are in fact unrestrained, unfiltered, political infomercials.'"[2]

Much as print publishers try to warn readers of which material is advertising, television stations still air the common bumper blurbs saying, "The following is a paid advertisement . . . and not endorsed by this television station." Television stations know that viewers might (or are likely to) mistake ads for news. The fact that the news media go to such lengths shows that at least some people have difficulty telling the difference between the two.

Infomercial hosts are typically dredged from a sorry field of minor and/or washed-up celebrities, most of whom would otherwise never have been seen again unless *The Love Boat* returns or *Hollywood Squares* lowers its standards. I imagine there's nothing like the resounding depression of hearing "I'll take Charles Nelson Reilly for the block" day after day to send quasi celebrities clamoring for infomercial gigs.

Knowledge of the product or expertise in the field (e.g., cars or food) is usually unnecessary. Occasionally, a former athlete will pitch a health product (George Foreman's grill comes to mind), but more often the hosts and hostesses need only be gushing, vacant, and gullible, the kind who can keep a straight face while asking, "Gee, Ron, how *can* I have whiter teeth in four easy steps?" or "Wow! It's a floor polish *and* a dessert topping!"

The entertainment portion of the show usually involves manic and flamboyant guests or hosts along with flash and spectacle: We get to see a geriatric geezer drink his freshly made vegetable juice cocktail and then make like an ox and tug a truck onstage; another sets fire to a car hood to show off a car wax; a third pours sand into a mounted, running car engine. The studio audience *oohs* and *aahs*, and now that everyone's attention is caught, the show goes on. (And yes, those "studio audiences" are frequently full of paid actors, not just random homemakers and businesspeople pulled off the street.)

In one infomercial for the Minute-Brite Tooth Whitening System, host Erik Estrada can be seen talking with an authoritative-looking man in a lab coat. As they discuss revolutionary breakthroughs in tooth whitening, a small disclaimer appears briefly at the bottom of the screen: "Individual in white coat is not a medical or a scientific expert. White coat is for dramatic effect only."

Occasionally, ads in newspapers and magazines are formatted to look exactly like a news article, complete with byline, city of origin, and headline. To keep readers from mistaking the ads for news, the publications frequently add a small notice that says "advertisement" above the "article." The advertiser's intended effect is clear: to capitalize on the legitimacy and respected status of the news story.

Or take, for example, a publication titled *Journal of Longevity: Medical Research Reviews in Preventive Medicine Fields*. A magazine with glossy covers, it features articles with titles such as "Male Sex Hormone Offers Three Keys to Longevity" and "Overcoming the Life-Threatening Risks of Cholesterol Drugs," by people with M.D.s after their names. The journal even has a Letters to the Editor section and a table of contents. But all is not kosher in this scholarly medical journal.

The first hint that something is amiss can be found in the business reply envelope stapled in the middle. The return address doesn't list a reputable medical organization, but instead Gero Vita Laboratories in Toronto. The articles use lots of impressive medical terms and jargon but, oddly, have no references. And in each "research review" of the latest medical literature, we find that the authors invariably recommend that the malady under discussion (high blood pressure, weight loss, varicose veins, etc.) can be alleviated or cured by a product from Gero Vita Laboratories. The last sentence in each "article" leads readers to the convenient ordering form the inside back cover.

The *Journal of Longevity* made national news in September 2001, when the Senate Special Committee on Aging held hearings into unscrupulous retailers who bilk Americans out of billions of dollars each year selling worthless dietary supplements. The supplements, marketed to the elderly, were touted as cures for everything from memory loss to arthritis to impotence. Many of the ingredients are worthless, but some can actually harm those who take them. The *Journal of Longevity* is published by Almon Glenn Braswell, who owns a dozen supplement companies said to be worth more than $200 million. In Senate testimony, former employees of Braswell accused him of knowingly promoting false claims about his products. Braswell was asked directly by the chairman of the Special Aging Committee, "Do you really use any of these products yourself?" Braswell managed a wry smile and asserted his Fifth Amendment right against self-incrimination.[3] In 1983 Braswell was convicted on charges of mail fraud, perjury, and tax evasion, and at the time of the hearings he was under investigation on suspicion of money laundering and tax evasion.

Even legitimate medical journals can be suspect. One of the nation's most prestigious medical journals, the *New England Journal of Medicine*, drew criticism in 1999 for not disclosing that some of its authors had close financial ties to drug companies whose products they were writing about. In one case, an article by Dr. Vera Price praised the antibaldness medications Rogaine and Propecia without disclosing that she was a paid consultant to the companies that produce the drugs. Though Price had disclosed this information to the journal, editor-in-chief Dr. Marcia Angell omitted the information from the article, claiming that the affiliations were not "relevant."[4]

In 2001 the potentially corrupting influence pharmaceutical companies can have over doctors and medical researchers caused enough unease that a group of prestigious scientific and medical journal editors created new guidelines to deal with the problem.

The *Journal of Longevity*, an advertisement in journal format.

Editors of the *New England Journal of Medicine*, the *Lancet*, and the *Journal of the American Medical Association*, among others, published a joint editorial on September 10, 2001. The editorial said that the journals would reject studies funded by drug companies regarding one of their drugs if, among other criteria, the researcher has not controlled the decision of whether or not to publish and has not had access to all the data.

As journalist Jeff Carpenter explains, "In the past, most clinical trials were done in the academic setting in order to test a new hypothesis. But now more and more trials are performed in order to gain approval of a new device or drug. Consequently, pharmaceutical companies have taken a larger role in conducting these trials. . . . In order to control costs, the pharmaceutical industry has shifted the majority of its funding to private nonacademic research groups, or contract research organizations." The concern is that nonacademic researchers, being more dependent on funding, may be more likely than an academic organization to serve as an advocate of the company funding their research.[5]

In 2002 the federal government warned drug companies against offering financial incentives to doctors, pharmacists, or other health care professionals to prescribe or recommend certain drugs. The new standards were issued by the inspector general of the Department of Health and Human Services. Pharmaceutical companies that continue to offer physicians payments or other "tangible benefits" (such as free weekend vacations, dinners, and event tickets) could be charged under federal fraud and kickback statutes.

PUSHING THE BOOKS

In the past few years, television journalists have branched out into writing books. CBS News anchor Dan Rather wrote several books, including *People of the Century* and *Deadlines and Datelines*. NBC News anchor Tom Brokaw penned *The Greatest Generation*, while *ABC Nightly News* anchor Peter Jennings wrote *The Century* (which was later turned into a series). ABC's Ted Koppel scribed *Off Camera: Private Thoughts Made Public*, and *Today* coanchor Katie Couric wrote a children's book titled *The Brand New Kid*. Even perennially perky Al Roker cranked out a book on parenting called *Don't Make Me Stop This Car!*

Tara Weiss of the *Hartford Courant* looked into the practice of journalists promoting their own books and found it to be widespread. She found that journalists from all three major networks have promoted their own books on their own airwaves. Asks Weiss, "How can viewers really know if it's a quality book or if their colleagues are just helping each other out?" Anchors-turned-authors found it very easy to get interviewed and promoted on the same network's other news shows, and the interviewers tended to be very complimentary. How Couric promoted her book is instructive: She shamelessly used her connections as coanchor of *Today* to push her book. Couric even sat for an interview about her book with Matt Lauer, her *Today* coanchor.

Weiss again: "Couric's book made *Today* several times of late. One of the most blatant displays came in a conversation with Willard Scott. Couric told Scott that while she knows *Today* tries to stay away from blatant commercialism, she just had to get the cameraman to show the two women standing outside the studio holding her book!"[6]

When ABC News veteran David Brinkley took a job promoting the agricultural giant Archer Daniels Midland (ADM) in 1998, some in the news media expressed dismay at Brinkley's easy crossover from respected journalist to corporate shill. ADM was the most visible sponsor of Brinkley's long-running television show *This Week*. In one commercial, Brinkley said, "I will still speak straight and true. I'll never change that. But now I will bring you information about food, the environment, agriculture; issues of importance to the American people and the world." Archer Daniels Midland, by the way, was forced to pay a fine of $100 million for antitrust violations. The business giant was fined for price-fixing and participating in international cartels in food and feed additives. ADM's vice chairman, Michael Andreas, and another ADM executive also faced charges of conspiring to fix the price of lysine, a feed additive.[7]

We expect advertisers to shout at us to buy their products, we expect them to inflate their claims with hyperbole. But when the news media do the same thing, there is something unseemly about it, because the veneer between advertising and news is shown to be thin. Instead of a calm, authoritative news anchor telling us what stories are coming up, we get a dose of pitchman, trying to find the right mix of words and images to lure, threaten, or cajole us into watching. This is due in large part to increased competition among television newsmagazines. And, as with any product or service, more competition means more selling and more advertising. News departments that once focused on content quality now must spend time and resources promoting themselves in a crowded marketplace.

The News Format

The power of the news format hasn't been lost on advertisers. Over the past few years Tylenol has run a series of ads that strongly resemble a public service piece. The ads in this campaign, Tylenol House Call, begin with what is ostensibly an informative segment on colds, flu, or other such maladies. A typical ending line is, "Doctors recommend lots of fluids, rest, and, for the temporary relief of your symptoms, Tylenol." The commercials give little hint of their purpose at the beginning, and look to the casual viewer like public service announcements.

Columnist Richard Reeves notes, "One of the great recent breakthroughs in the clouding of the American mind is the realization that if something looks like news, people perceive it as news. Now anchorpersons, interviews with 'consultants,' . . . and all the techniques of network news are used to lend credibility to made-up tabloid television reports and publicity on the news and entertainment of the day."[8]

In one sense, entertainment and news have always commingled; news directors typically want more than just "hard" news stories. Audiences also want human interest stories, or "soft" news, and those almost by definition are geared more toward entertainment than news. An example would be a piece on the long lines of people at a local store waiting for the latest Harry Potter book. It's mildly interesting (especially to Harry Potter fans) and good advertising for the book and store featured, but isn't particularly important.

Sports as a form of entertainment is rarely covered in national nightly news shows unless it involves larger issues, a hook that makes it newsworthy for reasons that go beyond the normal seasonal wins and losses. That's why, for example, Mark McGwire, Sammy Sosa, and Tiger Woods all made national news. In the same vein, although "entertainment news" is presumably a legitimate category of news coverage, it is only occasionally seen on the nightly news.

This void is filled by programs such as *Entertainment Tonight*, *Access Hollywood*, *Inside Edition*, and their ilk. You can tune in to these shows to hear the latest on Hollywood romances, Barbra Streisand's garage sale, and other such important information. Every night *Entertainment Tonight* lauds itself in its tag line as the "most-watched entertainment news program in the world." Though by now few people would mistake the eerily cheery Mary Hart for a real news anchor, the show borrows heavily from the network news format, and phrases such as "the latest news" and "coverage" are common.

As *Entertainment Weekly* writer Ken Tucker noted, "*Entertainment Tonight* [*ET*] was never the *New York Times* of celebrity journalism, but at least it reported stories that informed its audience about what their favorite celebrities were doing. Now, however, *ET* too often reports on what they're *not* doing. The July 10 [2000] broadcast, for example, was a paragon of non-news: A breathlessly hyped story about Britney Spears' engagement to *NSYNC's Justin Timberlake? *ET* quotes a Britney spokesperson as saying it's 'completely untrue.' Who's going to play Harry Potter in the upcoming movie? 'The decision could be announced later this week.' 'Rachel Hunter sets the record straight,' we're told, 'about reports she had cancer.' After a commercial, Hunter says she doesn't have it. Again and again, spectres of scoops and scandals are espied, only to be denied. What's the point?"[9] Alas, this analysis applies much more broadly to television than Tucker may realize.

Along with fluff fare like exclusive tours of Burt Reynolds's bathrooms and Jay Leno's motorcycles, the program frequently has "sneak peeks" and "first looks" at upcoming films, projects, and the like. Interviews with stars and directors, "preview" film footage (usually just the trailer), and behind-the-scenes information are treated as (and called) news, though a moment's thought will clarify their purpose: advertising. Just as film trailers are a blend of entertainment and advertising (though blatantly advertising), the purpose of such segments is to get the audience to see the film or buy the CD.

Often, celebrities grant access and interviews only to reporters and publications that will treat them favorably. As Adam Sternbergh of the *National Post* noted, "This arrangement—stars and their handlers bartering exclusive access in exchange for favorable press coverage—had traditionally served both parties very well. Only one partner in the transaction gets shortchanged: the reader."[10]

What's wrong with watching a star being interviewed about her new film? Nothing at all, except that the viewers are told they're getting entertainment "news" when in fact they get mostly ads. Viewers who would indignantly object to watching a four-minute commercial on television will happily watch it on *Entertainment Tonight*, as long as it's called "entertainment news."

Many companies tread on thin legal and ethical ground by designing their advertising to look like official government notices. Take, for example, an organization named the United States Trademark Protection Agency. They send businesses a document with a banner reading, "Urgent notice of EETM service registration," and quotes the United States Trade Marks Act: "No Trademark shall be refused registration unless it so resembles a mark registered as to be likely to cause confusion." It is accompanied by what appears to be a government form, giving the impression that the trademark registration is a government requirement.

Sounds very official, doesn't it? Well, the whole thing is just an advertising pitch. For a mere $375 per trademark (and a company may have more than one), the "agency" will, for one year, look through the U.S. Patent Office's weekly listing and alert the subscriber if anyone else registers a trademark similar to his so he can contest it. The previous sentence is the boiled down-version of the pitch; the verbose and confusing ad copy runs 246 words in six paragraphs of government-style stilted prose. It is filled with official-sounding phrases: "This process is an annual subscription, commencing upon receipt of your response, under which you will receive notification . . ." and "To enable the monitoring of your mark(s) . . . please complete the sections to the right and return to the United States Trademark Protection Agency."

Apparently aware of the misleading nature of its ad (and hoping to head off any sweepstakes-type litigation) the "agency" includes four lines of very fine print down at the bottom. It reads: "Electronic Trademark Monitoring provided by the United States Trademark Protection Agency is an elective service and is neither a legal requirement nor a mandatory registration. [The agency] is a trading name and style of a private corporation providing trademark monitoring services." The disclaimer copy is exactly one centimeter high; all the other copy on the page makes it look like a government agency requesting payment for an existing trademark.

Another trick companies use to get consumers to read their advertisements is to send mail with misleading or ambiguous return addresses. For example, in 2001 I got a letter in the mail that said "Time sensitive notification. Open at once." I checked the return address: "World Financial Center" in New York. Yet a quick glance at the cancellation meter clearly indicated that it was sent bulk mail. How important could this "notification" be if it was sent for seventeen cents using bulk mail? The "important notification" inside was just a subscription solicitation from the *Wall Street Journal*. It's curious that the *Journal*, which prides itself on having intelligent readers, uses dubious marketing practices that presumably intelligent readers would see right through. Of course the *Journal* knows that, had it put who *actually* sent the junk mail on the return address, I probably would have tossed it right away.

EETM104A 00/01 - SUPPLEMENTARY

USTPA **UNITED STATES TRADEMARK PROTECTION AGENCY**

P.O. Box 94368 • Seattle, Washington • 98134-6668 • 1-800-783-0122

TRADEMARK: REGISTRATION #: REGISTRATION DATE:

SKEPTICAL INQUIRER
CSICOP

URGENT NOTICE OF EETM SERVICE REGISTRATION

ATTN: TRADEMARK OWNER
CSICOP, INC.
Amherst NY 14228

ATTENTION:
Trademark Owner

REGARDING:
Elective Electronic Trademark Monitoring (EETM)

PLEASE NOTE: Section 2 of the United States Trade Marks Act:
No Trademark shall be refused registration unless it so resembles a mark registered as to be likely to cause confusion.

This has resulted in the United States Patent and Trademark Office (the "USPTO") allowing Trademarks that might be considered conflicting.

Be advised, protecting a Trademark from registration of confusing or conflicting marks is ultimately NOT the responsibility of the normal Trademark registration process, but of the Trademark Owner.

The USPTO publishes a *Weekly Trademarks Gazette* listing all names and designs which have been approved by USPTO examiners to receive the status of Trademark. Approximately 220,000 Trademark applications are *published* each year. This process is intended to give the general public the opportunity to oppose any Trademark that may infringe upon their rights, prior to its registration. Confusing or conflicting marks that are registered may require legal representation to reverse.

Opposition to a name or design which has been published must be received by the USPTO within 30 days of the publication or the confusing or conflicting name or design receives the status of registered trademark.

Trademark monitoring is the ongoing electronic review of all Trademark applications received by the USPTO. This process is an annual subscription, commencing upon receipt of your response, under which you will receive notification of the publication of confusing or conflicting marks before they become registered trademarks.

The responsibility to detect other Trademark applications which could be prejudicial to your rights rests with the Trademark Owner. Elective electronic monitoring gives the Trademark Owner information which is important to maintain its Trademark rights.

To enable monitoring of your mark(s) (listed above) please complete the required sections to the right and return to the United States Trademark Protection Agency in the envelope provided.

CONTACT NAME

TITLE

ADDRESS

CITY

STATE

ZIP

PHONE

FAX

PLEASE INDICATE METHOD OF PAYMENT BELOW:

AMERICAN EXPRESS NUMBER

VISA NUMBER

MASTERCARD NUMBER

EXPIRY DATE /

SIGNATURE

CHECK PAYABLE TO:
UNITED STATES TRADEMARK PROTECTION AGENCY (USTPA)

FEE AT $375.00 PER TRADEMARK	$ 750.00 US

Electronic Trademark Monitoring provided by the United States Trademark Protection Agency is an elective service and is neither a legal requirement nor a mandatory registration. The United States Trademark Protection Agency is a trading name and style of a private corporation providing trademark monitoring services. Information received by the USTPA for Trademark Monitoring is for internal use only. It is not distributed nor disseminated under any circumstances.

State taxes included where applicable.

VISA MasterCard

PAYMENT MUST ACCOMPANY COMPLETED FORM
(RETAIN COPY MARKED "TRADEMARK OWNER" FOR YOUR RECORDS)

An official U.S. government form? No—an advertisement for the private company United States Trademark Protection Agency.

An even more insulting letter came from the auto insurance company AIG. The envelope said, "Immediate Action Advised" and "Confidential Disclosure." The return address said the letter came from an "Interstate Advisory Center" in Delaware. Again, the bulk mail postmark betrayed

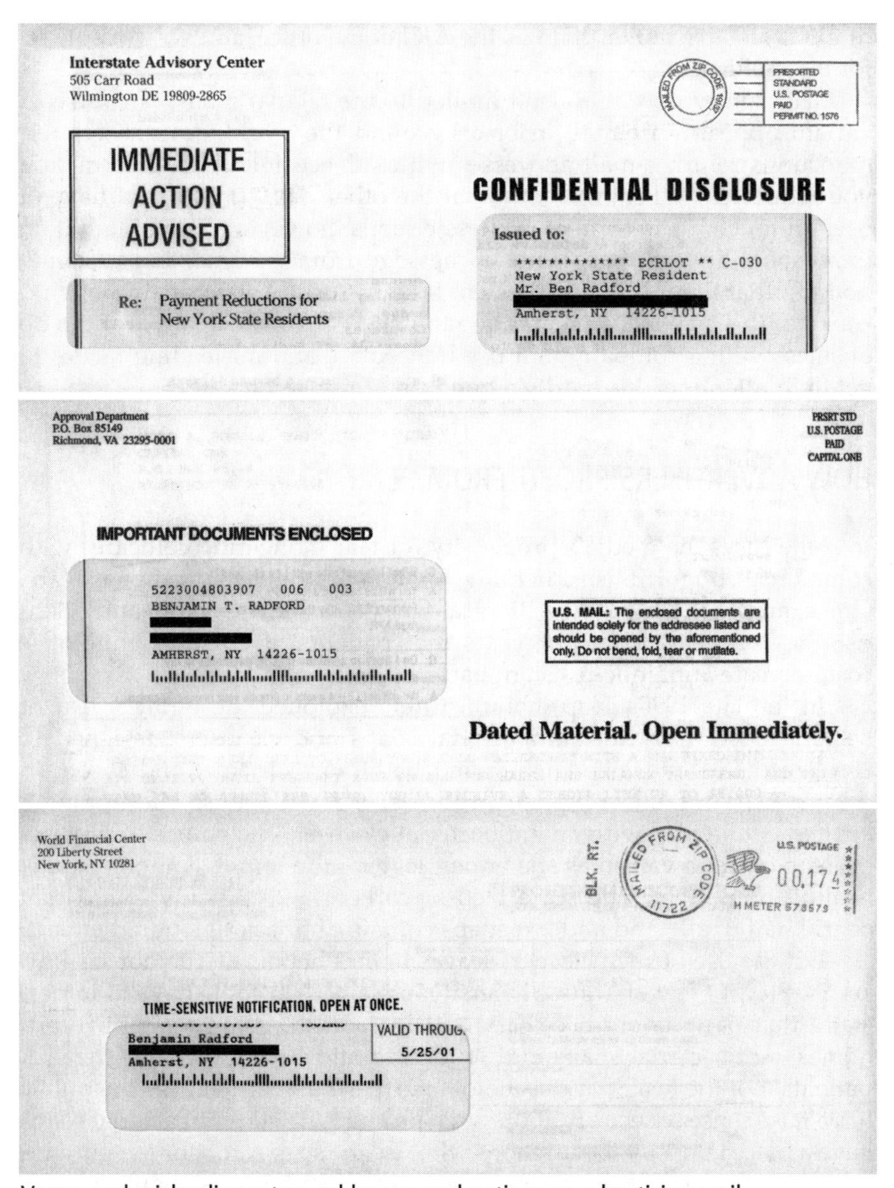

Vague and misleading return addresses and notices on advertising mail.

---

the ruse: Inside was nothing more than a mass-mailed ad wanting my auto insurance business. Just to be certain I wasn't mistaken, I called the 800 number provided and asked about the organization on the return address. The operator admitted that the "Interstate Advisory Center" didn't really exist other than as the AIG home office, and was "just used for the mailings."

This sort of deception isn't limited to the regular mails, of course. A variant appears in e-mail in boxes around the world. Advertisers use innocuous return e-mail addresses with subject lines like "Information you requested," "I enjoyed our chat the other day," or "Sorry I haven't been in touch." The content of these e-mails, however, is nothing but an impersonal advertisement, not a message from a friend and certainly nothing that the receiver requested. It seems odd that companies would consider this an effective marketing tool. Do consumers really want to do business with a company that used deceptive and misleading tactics to get their attention? It's hardly a good first impression.

HOW ADVERTISERS PROFIT FROM FEAR

In some cases the media's propensity for fear mongering coincides with commercial opportunism, helping foment the public's irrational fears. One example is the public's illogical fear of bacteria. Doctors and scientists have been worried for years that patients' overuse of antibiotics would create antibiotic-resistant bacteria.

In the late 1990s soap manufacturers exploited the public's fear of bacteria by introducing antibacterial soaps and cleansers designed to sterilize plates, utensils, kitchen and bathroom surfaces, and so on. In commercials for one of these products, a joyful housewife sprays a kitchen countertop with an antibacterial cleanser. The names of disease-causing bacteria vanish as she wipes, leaving the impression of a sterile, healthy household. The scare tactics worked: a 2000 study found that nearly half of all hand and bar soaps contain antibacterial ingredients.

But the use of such cleaners leaves homes neither sterile nor healthy. As Dr. Stuart Levy of Tufts University explained, "People have to understand that bacteria are necessary and we are not going to sterilize our homes. Antibacterial soaps and lotions should be reserved for the sick patients, not the healthy household." Furthermore, he believes the public has a false sense of security about such products. While antibacterial soaps have a place in hospitals, surgeons who use the soap scrub for ten minutes under hot water. The average washing time in a home is about five seconds, Levy said. A quick swipe on a kitchen counter will not kill most bacteria. In 1998 Levy found that *E. coli* bacteria can develop a resistance to one of the common antibacterial ingredients in store-bought soaps.[11]

It is also possible that the overuse of such cleansers may help create a new drug-resistant form of tuberculosis. The problem is so serious that in June 2000, the American Medical Association's (AMA) House of Delegates asked government regulators to expedite their review of antibacterial products and determine if they might aggravate the health threat from drug-resistant bacteria. Although the group did not explicitly call for the public to stop using the products, it did express doubts about their usefulness. Said Myron Genel, chairman of the AMA's Council on Scientific Affairs, "There's no evidence that they do any good and there's reason to suspect that they could contribute to a problem."[12] In the case of antibacterial soaps, the results may be catastrophic: More and more people are dying of infectious diseases because they are infected with strains that have become resistant to antibiotics.

Not surprisingly, the trade group representing antibacterial product manufacturers immediately responded that the public should not be deterred from using antibacterial products, and that the AMA's action was based on "untested scientific theory." It is ironic that an industry that has tried so hard to scare consumers into buying its products ("protect your family from *E. coli*!") is so concerned about having consumers scared away by science.

Some research indicates that children exposed to germs may in fact grow up to be healthier adults than those raised in more sterile environments. A study conducted at the University of Arizona College of Medicine found that children who attended day care in their first six months or had two or more older siblings were about half as likely to have asthma at age thirteen as children who had one or no older siblings and did not attend day care at that age. Protection from asthma came from frequent exposure to other youngsters if that exposure occurred during the first six months, an important time for the developing immune system. Two studies in Germany found similar results. This finding about asthma is important, as it is the most common chronic childhood disease.[13]

In any event, using antibacterial soaps is not as important as simply washing your hands. Regular soaps wash away about 99 percent of the unwanted bacteria, according to Dr. James Todd, a professor of pediatrics and microbiology at the University of Colorado Health Sciences Center. And anyway, he says, "The antibacterial substance may take many minutes to hours to work. You can't kill bacteria instantaneously with the stuff you can put in soap. The only thing that can kill bacteria instantly is fire."[14]

Who benefits from fanning the public's fears, both real and unfounded? Lots of people. Drug companies alone spent nearly $4 billion on advertising in 1998, trying to make viewers feel that something was wrong with them that medications could fix. Fear opens wallets and purses, and the more advertisers can convince people that something's wrong with them, or that they or their loved ones are in danger, the more money they make.

Profiting from Flu Fears

The winter of 1999 was, by many media accounts, the worst flu season in years. The epidemic made national news, and television was saturated with ads for flu remedies. Of particular interest were two new medicines designed to reduce the duration and severity of flu symptoms, Tamiflu and Relenza. Both medicines were brought to market with much fanfare and advertising.

Correctly diagnosing the flu (as opposed to a simple cold) suddenly became very important. ABC News reporter Shawna Vogel explained why:

> A few months ago, it wasn't all that important whether doctors made an accurate diagnosis. But now there are two new antiviral drugs, Relenza and Tamiflu, that are effective against both influenza A and B. . . . "Drug companies are pushing hard and dumping tons of money into ads,' [physician Kimberle] Chapin says. "[*Seinfeld*'s] Newman is the flu showing up in your living room. People see this and say, 'I've got the flu, I want that Relenza stuff.'" Out of 168 flu tests requested by doctors at [Chapin's] hospital, only 39 percent turned out to be the flu.[15]

The intent and effect of the ad blitz was to create demand for the drugs, whether the patients needed them or not. Consumers feeling a little ill, having seen alarmist news reports followed by ads promising flu relief, rushed out to buy the medicines. Since both Tamiflu and Relenza should be started within the first two days after flulike symptoms appear, the rush to medicate was made all the more urgent. It is likely that many people who took the medicines never had the flu at all—yet the pharmaceutical companies made their profits either way.

As it turned out, much of the hype over the flu season—translated into demand for drugs—was manufactured by drug companies trying to convince consumers to buy their products. Once the hype, sensationalism, and hysteria died down, the Centers for Disease Control and Prevention reported that although the flu levels were high, they were no worse than in the previous five years. Not only that, but the strain of influenza was the same as the previous year's, and the widely available vaccine was still effective at preventing it. The much-hyped "epidemic" vanished.[16]

Roche Laboratories and Glaxo Wellcome, already among the richest drug manufacturers in the world, benefited greatly from the coverage. The news media, intentionally or otherwise, could not have done a better job of raising alarm and sending patients racing to their doctors to get prescriptions. Although the drug manufacturers would defend their advertising as simply an effort to help raise consumers' awareness about a dan-

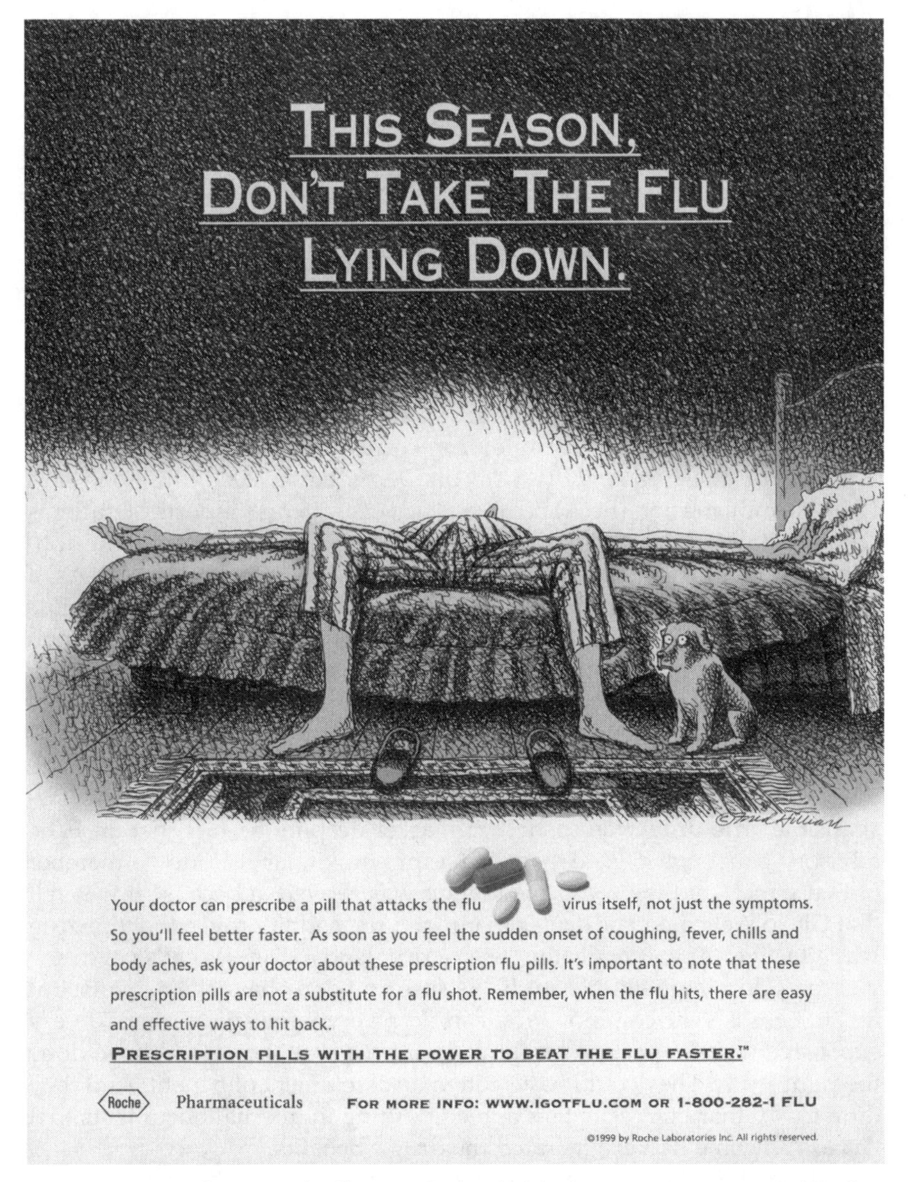

THIS SEASON, DON'T TAKE THE FLU LYING DOWN.
Your doctor can prescribe a pill that attacks the flu virus itself, not just the symptoms. So you'll feel better faster. As soon as you feel the sudden onset of coughing, fever, chills and body aches, ask your doctor about these prescription flu pills. It's important to note that these prescription pills are not a substitute for a flu shot. Remember, when the flu hits, there are easy and effective ways to hit back.
PRESCRIPTION PILLS WITH THE POWER TO BEAT THE FLU FASTER.™
Roche Pharmaceuticals
FOR MORE INFO: WWW.IGOTFLU.COM OR 1-800-282-1 FLU
©1999 by Roche Laboratories Inc. All rights reserved.

Heavy advertising for flu remedies and alarmist news coverage combined to fuel a baseless flu scare that reaped huge profits for drug companies.

gerous disease, it is a fair question to ask whether their advertising was intended to merely inform consumers or to use fear to sell their products.

Eventually the Centers for Disease Control (CDC) grew concerned that doctors (many responding to their patients' requests) actually endangered patients by relying too heavily on the drugs. America Online didn't help matters much when it featured two directly contradictory stories on the flu drugs in the "Today in Health" section on January 13, 1999: "Two New Ways to Fight Flu: You may have seen ads already for two new drugs available by prescription this year to fight the flu. . . ." Directly beneath this "story" (actually a de facto advertisement for the flu drugs), was the following: "FDA Warns of Overuse of New Flu Drugs: The government warned that doctors appeared to be relying too heavily on two new influenza drugs and said some patients might have died because they did not get the more aggressive treatment they needed."

The media's aggressive promotion of the flu medicines came back to haunt them the next year, when one of the drugs, Relenza, was linked to the deaths of eighteen people. As correspondent Sharyl Attkisson reported on the *CBS Nightly News* on December 4, 2000, the Food and Drug Administration (FDA) received "adverse events" reports of patients who had taken Relenza and died (only in corporate or government doublespeak are the deaths of human beings termed "adverse events"). As of late 2000, more than a million people had tried the drug, and complaints about dangerous side effects have gradually piled up. The most common complaint was of respiratory problems, which were also noted in seventy serious or life-threatening cases associated with Relenza.

Questions have been raised about not only the safety of the drug, but also its effectiveness. It's one thing for a *useful* drug to have dangerous side effects, but for a drug with limited effectiveness to also be dangerous is irresponsible. The drug was rushed to market despite the fact that an FDA advisory panel voted 13-to-4 against approving it. Janet Wittes, a member of that panel, said the recommendation was arrived at because it was felt that Glaxo Wellcome, the drug's manufacturer, hadn't proven that the drug was effective: "If you're dealing with a drug and a disease that's very rare, you can't do a large sample study because you don't have the patients. But for flu? Flu is very common. You can do a very large study in not a very expensive way. So part of the thinking for me was they could have done the right study. They could have gotten an assessment of benefit. And they didn't."[17] Other FDA scientists agreed, writing in internal documents that Glaxo Wellcome had exaggerated the drug's benefits.

Meanwhile, the company responded that all drugs have side effects (true enough) and insisted that the drug is safe and effective. In fact, Glaxo Wellcome said it is hoping to get the drug prescribed for *preventive* use in groups (such as students in school and nursing homes) where one person has the flu and there is fear that it might spread. Think about this: the company wants to prescribe its drug—one that has been associated with reports of respiratory problems and death—*for perfectly healthy people.*

Perhaps if Glaxo Wellcome, Roche Laboratories, and the news media hadn't pushed the drugs so hard on the public in the first place in pursuit of profits, lives would have been saved.

A 2001 study found that almost two-thirds of those who take prescription allergy medications such as Claritin, Allegra, and Zyrtec don't need them. Dr. Sheryl Szeinbach of the Ohio State University studied 265 patients taking the medications. She found that the vast majority did not suffer from allergies at all but were instead suffering from a reaction to something else in the environment, such as chlorine. The costly anti-allergy medications were useless against these irritants. It was clear that many doctors had misdiagnosed the source of the symptoms, and many patients demanded the allergy medications in response to heavy advertising. Szeinbach presented the findings of the study at the American College of Osteopathic Family Physicians' annual meeting on March 28, 2001, in Philadelphia.[18]

Attention-Deficit/Hyperactivity Disorder: A Created Crisis?

Attention-deficit/hyperactivity disorder (ADHD) is a disease affecting between 4 and 12 percent of school-age children, mostly boys. The symptoms include short attention span, impulsive behavior, and inability (or unwillingness) to sit still. As *Frontline*'s Martin Smith noted, "On average, two to three kids in every classroom are on some kind of behavior-modifying drugs and the numbers are increasing. It is largely an American trend; school-age children in the U.S. consume at least four times more psychoactive medicine than the rest of the world combined."[19]

By far the most common drug used to treat ADHD is Ritalin (the brand name for the stimulant methylphenidate), manufactured by the pharmaceutical company Novartis. In 2000, lawyer Richard Scruggs filed two lawsuits accusing the American Psychiatric Association (APA) of encouraging overdiagnosis of the disease to benefit Ciba-Geigy Corporation and Novartis. Scruggs claims that 4 million children are being medicated unnecessarily, possibly endangering their health.

According to Scruggs, the companies worked with the APA to include the diagnosis of attention-deficit and hyperactivity disorders in the *Diagnostic and Statistical Manual of Mental Disorders* in 1980, thereby effectively creating (or, at the very least, inflating) both the disease (ADHD) and the treatment (Ritalin). The influence began, Scruggs alleges, in the 1950s, when the makers of Ritalin encouraged the APA to include the diagnosis of attention deficit disorder (ADD). That diagnosis was later expanded to the current ADHD, and along with that expansion came a larger number of children to be classified with the disease.

In a Reuters interview, Scruggs summed up the allegations:

> The main complaint is that they have inappropriately expanded the definition of ADHD to include "normal" children so that they can promote and sell more drugs and treat more people. These suits represent the latest class-action battleground in the U.S., but since it involves kids, this is that much more important. . . . Right now, virtually every child would fit the diagnostic criteria for Ritalin. They are exploiting the fears of parents for the welfare of children to gain inappropriately, and I think that is very reprehensible and it can have a widespread effect on the health of American kids.[20]

The APA and the drug companies contend the assertions are meritless and that they will prevail in court. And they may, but troubling questions about ADHD and Ritalin remain.

One critic of Ritalin overprescription, John Leo, notes that American children consume 90 percent of the world's Ritalin. Why, he asks, is it that 5 to 10 percent of American children have the disease, yet in England only 0.03 percent have it? And why does the incidence vary not only between countries but also between school districts? "In one school district in Virginia, for example, 20% of the children are diagnosed with ADHD. Is this due to an overabundance of ADHD genes in Virginia, or overzealous school psychiatrists?" writes Leo.

Leo believes that Ritalin is being used to drug unruly children, and that it is used as an easy substitute for good parenting and schools. Leo quotes medical expert Dr. Dean Edell, who says that "we just can't drug all the kids who won't fit into the mold. Our culture needs people who think and act differently and there is nothing more frightening to me than looking into a classroom in America where every little kid is the same, all paying attention, all doing their homework and marching to the same drummer."

Leo makes several points about ADHD and Ritalin:

- The symptoms of ADHD may simply be in the upper range of "normal." "Every human trait falls into a range of values. Some people are tall, some are short, some are dark skinned, some are light skinned, some are outgoing, and some are shy. With height, for example, if we measure the general population we see a bell-shaped curve with the very tall and very short at either end of the spectrum. Regardless of a person's height, or what factors cause a person to be tall or short, we do not label the people in the upper 10% as diseased. . . . The ADHD experts have convinced the American public that the description of a personality trait is actually a disease. This is perhaps the biggest flaw and mistake of the ADHD proponents. They do not understand normal human variation."
- Basic assumptions underlying the use of Ritalin are flawed: "[T]he

major scientific evidence for ADHD is that hyperactive children can be helped, at least in the short run, by taking Ritalin, a drug that increases a neurotransmitter called dopamine. So, the argument goes, if we know that Ritalin both increases dopamine levels and subdues hyperactive children, then the original hyperactivity must have been due to a dearth of dopamine. This line of reasoning is flawed. We do not use a parallel argument to explain the effects of other drugs such as aspirin. Aspirin relieves headaches but that doesn't mean that a shortage of aspirin caused the headache." This methodology is further flawed because for ADHD no biological test exists to detect a shortage of dopamine, and because some one-third of ADHD children do not in fact benefit from Ritalin.

- ADHD is always diagnosed not in a laboratory but in a school, usually during a subjective evaluation. At a 1998 National Institute of Mental Health consensus conference, the final report noted that "we don't have an independent valid test for ADHD; further research is necessary to firmly establish ADHD as a brain disorder; existing studies come to conflicting conclusions as to whether the use of psychostimulants increases or decreases the risk of abuse; and finally after years of clinical research and experience with ADHD, our knowledge about the cause or causes of ADHD remain largely speculative."

Like Scruggs, Leo also questions the link between Ritalin manufacturers and those demanding the drug: "CHADD (Children and Adults with Attention Deficit Disorders) is a national organization that promotes the concept that ADHD is a neurobiological disorder, and it has received close to a million dollars from the drug companies that manufacture Ritalin." Clearly Novartis has a financial interest in making the public believe that the problem is biological and their drug can fix it.[21]

Another company that tried to make money off of the ADD scare was Natural Organics, Inc., which marketed a dietary supplement named Pedi-Active A.D.D. The company, doing business as Nature's Plus, claimed that the supplement would mitigate or effectively treat ADHD or its symptoms. This claim was challenged by the Federal Trade Commission (FTC), and in August 2000 the FTC issued a complaint against the company, saying that Nature's Plus had no reasonable evidence or basis to support its claims. Without admitting that it had violated any laws, Natural Organics settled the FTC charges and agreed, among other things, not to claim that Pedi-Active A.D.D. would improve children's performance and not to use the term "A.D.D." in its advertising.[22]

We have advertising that looks like news, advertising that looks like entertainment, entertainment that looks like news, and other permutations, all washing over each other in different strengths and combinations. This is a problem because each medium has different values of accuracy and importance. News should, ideally, be both accurate and important. Entertainment may be just as accurate but is likely to be less important. And the bias inherent in advertising makes the accuracy low (or at least quite suspect); the importance is likely nil. (Advertisers might balk at that, claiming that, to a person with a medical condition, news of their offers of prescription medication may be very important. But compared to such real news as flooding, warfare, and crisis, the importance of an inducement to buy a product must be considered low indeed.)

This premium on entertainment also leads to programming being judged largely on its entertainment value. Not all news needs to be "hard" news, but by the same token not all programming should be judged by whether or not it is entertaining.

When valuable, important information looks the same as (and may be mixed with) worthless information, the audience loses the ability to distinguish between the two. Like gold coins mixed with gold foil chocolates, it's hard to tell which are valuable, which are tasty but worthless, and which are hollow.

NOTES

1. "Why We Sell Advertising, Not Search Results," About Google [online], www.google.com/honestresults.html.
2. David Shenk, *Data Smog* (New York: HarperCollins, 1997), p. 164.
3. Tony Pugh, "Supplements Stuff of Fraud, Senators Told," *Philadelphia Inquirer*, September 11, 2001, p. C01.
4. Scott Gottlieb, "Medical Societies Accused of Being Beholden to the Drugs Industry," WHALE [online], www.whale.to/vlconf2.html [November 20, 1999].
5. Jeff Carpenter, "Banding Together: Medical Journal Editors Strike Cautionary Tone," ABC News [online], abcnews.go.com/sections/living/DailyNews/medicaljournals010910.html [September 10, 2001].
6. Tara Weiss, "Selling or Shilling?" *Buffalo News*, October 28, 2000, p. E1.
7. Douglas Barricklow, "Blind-sided by Brinkley," *Coffee Shop Times* [online], www.coffeeshoptimes.com/brinkley.html [January 12, 1998].
8. Richard Reeves, "Jaded America Indifferent to Truth," *Albuquerque Journal*, May 15, 1996.
9. Ken Tucker, "Biz Buzz Kills," *Entertainment Weekly*, July 26, 2000, p. 163.
10. Adam Sternbergh, "'Check Out My Blue Aura!' Britney's Meltdown," *Saturday Post*, September 7, 2002, p. SP1.
11. "Clean Freaks?" ABC News [online], abcnews.go.com/sections/living/DailyNews/sops000907.html [September 7, 2000].

12. "Antibacterial Soap 'May Not Work,'" BBC News [online], news.bbc.co.uk/2/hi/health/791934.stm [June 16, 2000].

13. Linda A. Johnson, "Germ Exposure May Be Good for Kids," Associated Press [online], dailynews.yahoo.com/h/ap/20000824hl/childhood_asthma_2.html [August 24, 2000].

14. Maggie Fox, "Common Disinfectant Could Breed Superbugs," Reuters [online], www.lindachae.com/articles_of_interest.htm [June 1, 2000]; "Doctor's Group Questions Anti-bacterial Soaps," Reuters [online], www.anapsid.org/drkoop.html [June 14, 2000]; Julie Stafford, "Waging War on Germs," *Albuquerque Journal*, May 12, 1997, p. C1.

15. Shawna Vogel, "Is It Flu or Is It Hype?" ABC News [online], abcnews.go.com/sections/living/DailyNews/is_it_flu000111.html [January 11, 2000].

16. "Final Figures Show Annual Flu Fears Overplayed," Canoe Health [online], www.canoe.ca/Health0003/09_flu.html [March 10, 2000]; Christine Gorman, "Don't Be Flued," *Time*, January 24, 2000.

17. Sharyl Attkisson, "Doubts Surface on New Flu Drug," *CBS Evening News with Dan Rather*, December 4, 2000.

18. Robert Bazell, "Allergies Often Misdiagnosed: Study," NBC News [online], www.msnbc.com/news/579946.asp#BODY [May 29, 2001].

19. Martin Smith, "Medicating Kids," *Frontline*, PBS, April 10, 2001.

20. Amy Westfeldt, "Lawsuits Accuse Ritalin Makers, APA," Associated Press [online], www.resultsproject.net/APA_editorial.html [September 15, 2000]; Edward Tobin, "Tobacco Foe Takes Aim at Ritalin," Reuters [online], www.resultsproject.net/Reuters_editorial.html [September 14, 2000].

21. Jonathan Leo, "Attention Deficit Disorder: Good Science or Good Marketing?" *Skeptic* 8, no. 1 (2000): 64.

22. "Natural Organics Settles FTC Charges That They Made Unsubstantiated ADHD Treatment Claims," press release, Federal Trade Commission, July 31, 2001. The full text is available online at www.ftc.gov/opa/2001/07/natorgan.htm.

Part 2

THE MEDIA PERSPECTIVE

3

THE NEWS BIAS

distorting reality and feeding fears

> *We [at* 60 Minutes*] haven't done an ambush interview in a long time. Perhaps at the beginning we made our reputation with it. But then people came along and began to ape it, and it turned into a caricature of itself. We asked ourselves, "What are we after: light or heat?"*
>
> —Mike Wallace, *Playboy* interview, December 1996

"Light or heat" is an apt paradigm for the differing emphases of the news media. While light is what's needed to illuminate and bring context and informative content to issues, all too frequently it's heat—sensationalism and hype—that the public gets.

There are many claims and counterclaims of bias in the news media. Perhaps the most common form of bias is political. In his book *Bias: A CBS Insider Exposes How the Media Distort the News*, Bernard Goldberg mostly focuses on liberal biases.[1] There are, however, less-examined biases that transcend politics. The biases that are inherent in the modern news-gathering process—including sensationalism, predefining news events, and selective news coverage—I have collectively called the *news bias*. The news bias distorts reporting and changes how we understand and react to the world around us.

The news media also create myths that come to shape our world. At times they take a grain of truth and weave an elaborate story out of it. One example is the much-hyped "soccer moms," touted by endless media pundits and pollsters as a powerful, previously unrecognized key demographic whose votes might decide the 1996 presidential election. Columnist John Leo writes that "the newsroom ought to be embarrassed about inventing the 'soccer moms' phenomenon. These married, college-educated suburban moms with school-age children didn't turn out to be this year's juggernaut after all, but only 4 percent to 5 percent of the electorate."[2]

Mike Pride, editor of the *Concord* (N.H.) *Monitor*, discussed the propensity for journalists to predefine news events and write them according to common myths. He cites journalism scholar Roy Peter Clark's admonition to journalists to "beware of stories that fit familiar patterns" (such as the little old lady who beats City Hall—or the stock market; see p. 264). His point, according to Pride, "was that journalists sometimes go on automatic pilot when they report such events, relying on preconceptions and writing stories that omit or discount facts that don't fit the mold."[3]

The media profit from fear mongering through sensationalized headlines. Nothing gets viewers to tune in to a news program like fear: fear of war, fear of disease, fear of death, fear of harm coming to loved ones. This can easily be seen in teasers for news, with implicit threats like "Violence in the schools: Is your child safe? A special report every parent must see. Tonight at eleven." Thus many parents, possibly already feeling guilty about not spending enough time with their kids (and busy putting food on the table, paying bills, and dealing with other daily pressures) have news anchors asking them if they love their children enough to tune in to find out how to protect them. Of course, the logic in this emotional blackmail is flawed: Parents can love and protect their children without watching the program, and "every parent must see" is clearly more meaningless hyperbole.

Though the television news media have blossomed into dozens of channels over the past decade, much of my discussion addresses the "big four" networks. Television news is the most credible, dominant source of mass information in America, with 35 million nightly viewers. Because it has such a pervasive influence, a basic understanding of the nature of news is important. News events don't just come to be shown on television on their own; there are many steps involving judgment, selection, and interpretation between the actual, objective event and the version of it that the audience views or reads.

German cultural theoretician Rudolf Arnheim predicted in the 1930s that people would come to confuse the world perceived by their senses and the world interpreted by thought, and would come to believe that seeing an event is understanding it. As Ryszard Kapuscinski wrote in *Le Monde Diplomatique*:

> The confusion between seeing and knowing, and seeing and understanding, is used by television to manipulate people. In a dictatorship, censorship is used; in a democracy, manipulation. The target of these assaults is always the same: the ordinary citizen. When the media talk about themselves, they conceal the basic problem behind the form: They

> substitute technology for philosophy. They discuss how to cut, how to edit, how to print. They talk about problems of layout, or databases, or the capacity of hard disks. They do not concern themselves with the problem of the content that they are about to cut, edit, and print.[4]

Here I discuss content, for it is just that content (or lack thereof) that is the problem. Audiences watch news programs and pretend that they understand—and that they are given enough information *to* understand—what really happened. But reality can't be packaged into one-minute sound bites, and this is especially true for complex, important stories with many nuances. A rare exception to the short-segment news format, *Newshour with Jim Lehrer* on PBS, usually does a good job of sacrificing lots of little stories for deeper coverage of bigger ones.

"NEWS IS WHAT NEWS PEOPLE SAY IT IS": THE NEWS PERSPECTIVE

As David Altheide notes in *Creating Reality: How TV News Distorts Events*, his book on network news, "[P]eople tend to equate media presentations with significance; if something is [on] the news, then it *must* be important." But this view is mistaken; not everything you see on the news is newsworthy, and not everything newsworthy is on the news. Altheide again: "The taken-for-granted—and often explicated—pronouncement that the world has been adequately combed for the strongest news fiber to weave a significant account of the day is another central feature of the news perspective: News is what news people say it is."[5]

Implicit in Walter Cronkite's signature sign-off, "And that's the way it is . . . ," is the message that the news media are simply reporting the world's state of affairs. But, as Altheide points out, "In order to make events news, news reporting decontextualizes and thereby changes them. . . . [N]ews messages may do more than inform viewers about events; they may also change the meaning and significance of events."[6] How a particular story is reported, and how the facts are filtered by the journalist, can greatly influence the audience. Time and space constraints strip away valuable information needed to really understand a news event.

The question of what is newsworthy falls mainly to news directors and editors and involves many factors, including the number and type of competing stories, the amount of time available, and coverage area. The media report on only a small, carefully selected set of unusual events. This is epitomized in the phrase, "When a dog bites a man, that's not news. But when a man bites a dog—now that's news!"

In the media, and particularly in prime-time television, every second counts. News reports are edited down to a few concise minutes (or seconds). Context and background essential to understanding the story are frequently left out due to time or space considerations. What is left is a bare-bones recitation of the basic facts as the reporter understands them. Of course, this process isn't an insidious plot to bias and filter news. News directors, editors, and journalists themselves are in many ways victims of the news bias. But that doesn't mean they can't do better. After all, they have the power of the press. True, viewers can elect to change the channel, but this news-gathering process bias is so pervasive it does little good.

Local news is perhaps the worst in terms of relevance. Though there are occasionally some local news stories of import, much (perhaps most) of what is aired is filler. Typical local news stories one might encounter in an average week include house fires, car accidents, hit-and-runs, bank robberies, homicides, and the like. But very little of this is actually relevant to the vast majority of viewers. Take, for example, news of a store that caught fire across town. If you shop there, then you probably already know about the fire. If you don't shop there, then the story is almost certainly irrelevant to your life. The same goes for car accidents, abused-pet stories, robberies, and the like. Television news producers and directors do not help viewers decide what information is useful or helpful to the audience. Ultimately, their job is to increase ratings.

As I have mentioned, one of the main impediments to good journalism is a lack of airtime or newspaper space. Editors and producers are ever vigilant for ways to shorten articles and reports, hoping to squeeze in one more piece that may appeal to another reader or viewer. But even if reporters had all the time (or space) they wanted to present their stories, it is a mistake to assume that the coverage of news would necessarily be any better. According to David Altheide:

> One of the common criticisms made of TV news in general . . . is that they do not take enough time to investigate and thoroughly develop a story. . . . However, taking more time to develop a report does not guarantee that many of the problems [with television news biases] will be resolved. No matter how much time is devoted to an issue, if the options are predefined in order to make the story interesting or to comply with a reporter's persuasion about what is significant, then more time will make the report more detailed, but not necessarily more complete. Rather, the details will be used as evidence that research has taken place, and as supporting materials for the news angle.[7]

This glut of irrelevant news also applies on a wider scale. Charley Reese, in a commentary for Intellivu, presciently asked readers:

> As for news, do you really need to know about every accident and crime, many of which occur in faraway places? Of course not. That's the kind of information that is neither useful nor entertaining, except for sick people who enjoy other's misery. Do you really need to know trade news about trades you're not in, such as in-house awards and box office receipts for movies you didn't invest in? Does it really matter to you who some celebrity is sleeping with, marrying, or divorcing? Does it really matter to you if today is some performer's birthday? If it does, get a life.[8]

DISTORTING REALITY, OR WHERE TO FOCUS THE CAMERA?

Television, by its very nature, distorts the reality it claims to reflect and report on. Events are compressed, highlighted, sped up. Thus a person who occasionally watches sports highlights on TV will likely see more home runs and touchdowns than a person who attends local games regularly; television viewers are likely to see more murders than a police detective, more serious car crashes than a tow truck driver, and more plane crashes than a crash investigator.

The amount of time devoted to crime coverage is widely disproportionate to the amount of crime that actually occurs. Professor Joe Angotti of the University of Miami found that nearly 30 percent of air time is spent covering crime, courts, and cops. But air time is finite, of course, and less "sexy" (but more important) topics lose out: Education, for example, got just 2 percent of air time nationally in the newscasts surveyed. Race relations got just 1.2 percent. Angotti, formerly a senior vice president of NBC News, says of his findings, "It's unfortunate that body-bag journalism is what local news chooses to focus on at the expense of more important stories." Part of the problem is journalistic laziness. "Crime reporting is easy to do and doesn't require hardly any follow-up. Television journalists have to stand up and say we're here to tell people what they need to know," says Angotti. "Television news has abandoned its responsibility to do serious journalism in favor of sensational video."[9]

Another study, this one headed by Syracuse University professor Robert Lissit, found that of one hundred newscasts around the country, "nearly 30 percent of the news time was spent on crime and the courts. Ten percent was devoted to reporting calamities and natural disasters. Only 15 percent of the newscasts were devoted to government and politics. Health and medicine: about 7 percent. Race relations: 1.2 percent. Education: less than one percent." According to Lissit, crime gets a disproportionate amount of coverage not because it is important but because it is easy to cover: "A few shots of the crime scene, a quick interview with a police officer, or someone in the neighborhood, and a quick reporter-on-camera standup. Summary, and that's the end of story." Noncrime issues such as politics or education require more background and effort and usually can't be wrapped up in such a tidy, quick package.

Like Angotti, Lissit also dismisses the justification that news directors commonly give for such sanguineous fare: It's what the public wants. "Market-driven news is giving the viewers what the stations think they want. Some might ask if that isn't simply representative democracy at work: 'What could be more democratic than giving viewers what they want?' My answer: What could be more irresponsible, more cynical, and profoundly wrong?"[10]

Notice that the news media have, in a way, tied their own hands in trying to present "important" stories. Clearly, not everything that is reported on the news is newsworthy. But because viewers have been led to believe that what they see on the news *must* be important, news organizations can't be honest about their vacuous coverage without making liars of themselves. You'll never hear a journalist say, "We're still covering this story, but to be honest it's not very important." Instead, the rules of the profession require that each story be treated as important and relevant—otherwise why are they (and we) wasting time on it?

By and large, the news media (and entertainment media, for that matter) seek the broadest possible appeal. This makes sense; the more diverse the appeal, the larger the audience, and thus the more profitable a program is. But one side effect of this process is a dumbing-down and homogenizing of content. Programs that are too cerebral are doomed, while programs based on the basest instincts and interests—sex (*Baywatch*), violence (*World's Scariest Police Chases*), or sex *and* violence (*Jerry Springer*)—will thrive. Programmers frequently take this too far and insult the viewers' intelligence.

As *Newsweek*'s Jonathan Alter wrote, "When news oozes 24 hours a day it's not really news anymore. The TV becomes ambient noise. The newspaper becomes wallpaper. Finding patterns of importance becomes hard. It's easier—and more profitable—just to make the consumer gape."[11]

The Media Paradox

Another consequence of the news perspective that contributes to the public's fears is what John Ruscio, a social psychologist at Elizabethtown College in Pennsylvania, calls "the media paradox": The more we rely on the popular media to inform us, the more apt we are to misplace our fears. The paradox is the combined result of two biases, one inherent in the news-gathering process, the other inherent in the way our minds organize and recall information.

As Ruscio explains:

> For a variety of reasons—including fierce competition for our patronage within and across the various popular media outlets—potential news items are rigorously screened for their ability to captivate an audience. . . . The stories that do make it through this painstaking selection process are then often crafted into accounts emphasizing their concrete, personal, and emotional content.[12]

In turn, the more emotional and vivid the account is, the more likely we are to remember the information. This is the first element, the *vividness bias*: Our minds easily remember vivid events.

The second bias lies in what psychologists term the *availability heuristic*: Our judgments of frequency and probability are heavily influenced by the ease with which we can imagine or recall instances of an event. So the more often we hear reports of plane crashes, school shootings, or train wrecks, the more often we think they occur. But the bias that selects those very events makes them appear more frequent than they really are.

Imagine, for example, that a consumer group dedicated to travel safety established a network of correspondents in every country that reported every train and bus wreck, no matter how minor, and broadcast daily pictures. Anyone watching that broadcast would see dozens of wrecks and crashes every day, complete with mangled metal and dead bodies, and would likely grow to fear such transportation. No matter that in general trains and buses are very safe; if you screen the news to emphasize certain vivid events, accidents will seem more dangerous and common than they actually are. That explains, in part, why many people fear flying even though they know that statistically it's one of the safest modes of transport: Though crashes are very rare, the vividness and emotion of seeing dramatic footage of crashed planes drowns out the rational knowledge of statistical safety.

The homicide rate is another example. Many people are surprised to learn that the suicide rate is higher than the homicide rate: Nearly twice as many people die by their own hand than are killed by other people (the murder rate in the United States is 5.9 per 100,000; the suicide rate is 10.3 per 100,000). While murders make news, suicides are frequently ignored unless the victim is famous. This imbalance in news coverage leads many to believe that homicides are far more common than suicides, when in fact the opposite is true.[13]

The imbalance in media coverage is also due in part to the sensational nature of a murder. If a person is found killed by another, the story has only just begun: The police must look for the killer, determine a motive, find the weapon, arrest the killer, put him or her on trial, and so on. But when the killer *is* the victim, the story is over as soon as it starts.

There will be no dramatic arrests or jailhouse confessions, just grief and perhaps memorials or a short quest for motive.

As a society we throw money at things we fear in order to fix them. But when we misplace our fears, we run the very real risk of wasting time and resources on insignificant problems. As author John Ross states, "Are we then turning our backs on a raging inferno while we douse the flame of a match?"[14]

The news media do their best to raise alarm, even when no alarm is needed. The death of film director Alan Pakula is a good example. Pakula, director of many notable films, including *All the President's Men* and *Klute*, died in a freak freeway accident in November 1998. A vehicle in front of him ran over a piece of metal, which shot through his windshield, killing him. It was a sudden, horrific, once-in-a-million accident—yet the media reported it differently. While some reporters grudgingly admitted that the accident was very unusual, many others hyped the story. They tried to downplay the rarity of the accident, and rushed to air news segments revealing "hidden dangers on the highway." While trash on the roads is a threat, the number of drivers *ever* killed by road trash compared to, say, the number killed by falling asleep at the wheel or drunk driving in *a single month* is minuscule.

"A single death is a tragedy, a million deaths is a statistic," Joseph Stalin observed. The public and reporters latched onto Pakula's death because it was a single death of someone famous. And it's no accident that single deaths spark more outrage than many deaths. In 1994 more than eight hundred thousand people were killed in genocidal ethnic clashes in Africa. Yet Americans took little notice of the carnage in Rwanda; they (and the news media) were much more interested in the murders of just two people: Nicole Brown Simpson and Ron Goldman.

John Ruscio explains why the news media prefer testimonials:

> Producers are aware that a scientific analysis is not as emotionally compelling as one (carefully chosen) individual's personal experience. Why does a television news reporter stand in front of a courthouse when sharing a landmark verdict reached earlier that day? Why does a weather correspondent endure frigid temperatures, sleet, and harsh wind on camera to inform us that a severe storm is in progress? Even superficial background elements appear to add a sense of realism and concreteness to a story.[15]

Note that all this is done to promote the illusion of importance, and in the process the news media insult their audience's intelligence. Viewers are smart enough to know that a forecaster doesn't have to be actually standing outdoors to give them an accurate weather forecast.

Another example of the way in which the media emphasize the wrong risks is in health care and disease prevention. Though the news media like to run stories on both real and alleged carcinogenic dangers lurking in our environments—such as toxic chemicals, cell phones, power lines, and radiation—health experts say that poor diet may be more likely to cause cancers. At a conference sponsored in part by the National Institute of Environmental Health Studies, it was reported that a lack of vitamins found in fruits and vegetables could be damaging people's DNA, increasing their susceptibility to cancer.

A California study found that only one-third of California residents reported eating the minimum recommended amount of fruits and vegetables every day. This can lead to vitamin deficiencies, which has been shown to alter DNA. Bruce Ames, a professor of biochemistry at the University of California at Berkeley, said, "What is becoming clear is that there is a tremendous amount of DNA damage in people from not having their vitamins and minerals. People, when they think of cancer, they think of chemicals in the water or pesticide residue. I just think it's all a distraction."

Researchers have found that a lack of folic acid, a B vitamin, may influence a person's susceptibility to leukemia; vitamin B_{12} deficiency has been shown to damage chromosomes, and still other research suggests that zinc and iron deficiencies may also result in genetic damage.[16]

These problems can be solved by simply eating well or taking a daily multivitamin. Yet for the news media, this story isn't interesting. Telling people to eat right and take a vitamin just isn't eye-catching, not compared to showing footage of a leaking sewer pipe or pesticide spraying. Certainly there are real dangers from toxic chemicals and radiation. But the average news viewer has probably seen hundreds or thousands of reports on those dangers, and probably only a handful reminding them of the importance of eating a balanced meal.

The news bias causes us to misplace our fears in other ways as well. In his book *Creating Reality*, journalist David Altheide notes:

> [D]ifferent news sources produce different stories. Police radio monitors, for example, provide crime news involving street crimes which frequently involve lower-class and minority group youth. But the story of crime is incomplete if it is only learned about through these sources. The image is presented, albeit unintentionally, that certain kinds of crime are not only committed by certain groups of people, but that this is what the crime problem is about. White-collar crime and corporate rip-offs are not presented via police monitors, even though more money is involved than in dozens of $25–$100 robberies. Thus, the Phoenix media were reluctant to disclose that one of the area's largest banks was being investigated for passing illegal securities. If bank officials *are* eventually

> indicted, they will be interviewed in their plush offices. In all likelihood we will never see them "drug off" by police officers, handcuffed, disheveled, and looking ashamed.[17]

The white, middle-aged man or woman in a suit you happily sit across a business desk from is perhaps just as likely to rob you as the black youth you might cross the street to avoid—and they're likely to get much more money out of you than a mugger would.

Good News Is No News

First, a sampling of some good news. Pay attention, because some in the news media and advocacy groups would prefer you ignore or dismiss the following facts:

- Every major type of crime measured, rape or sexual assault, robbery, aggravated assault, simple assault, burglary, theft and motor vehicle theft, decreased significantly between 1993 and 1998. Violent crime affected 8.1 million Americans in 1997, the lowest number reported since the Justice Department began tracking figures in 1973.[18]
- The rate at which women were attacked or threatened with violence by husbands and boyfriends dropped 21 percent during the mid-1990s; the number of men murdered by wives and girlfriends dropped 60 percent from 1976 through 1998.[19]
- A survey of 6,529 teens, aged thirteen to eighteen, conducted in 1999 by the Partnership for a Drug-Free America found that drug use among teens is leveling off. Trial use of most drugs, including marijuana, crack, LSD, inhalants, cocaine, and methamphetamines were all down.[20]

Generally, good news doesn't get nearly as much airtime as bad news: As the news phrase goes, "If it bleeds it leads." Reports of mayhem in inner cities will always crowd out reports of kids getting off drugs and winning scholarships. But even when journalists and activists *do* report good news, they usually do so with gritted teeth, quickly following up with assurances that things really *are* bad after all.

A 1999 article by John Cloud in *Time* asks, "Is Hate on the Rise?" (with "hate" singled out in red to make sure we see it). The subhead seems to answer the question negatively, reading, "Racist groups may not be growing, but they're finding deadlier recruits." About halfway through the article Cloud admits, "To be sure, organized hate groups have not achieved great financial or political power; in fact, the old Aryan

Nation–style groups are struggling." The article went on to discuss how hate groups are recruiting on colleges and over the Internet, both of which were old news and not particularly relevant to the headline quote.[21]

The article appeared a week after racist Benjamin Smith killed two people in a weekend shooting spree. The event had already been thoroughly covered, so the author went looking for a new angle: Are racist groups on the rise? Apparently, after some research, the reporter concluded that the answer was no. No matter; the solution is to do a "No, but . . ." story, where a journalist glosses over a positive fact (hate groups are not growing) in favor of the usual general slant of alarm.

A Reuters story in 1999 titled "Study: Some Youth Violence Declines" began, "Some types of violent behavior are declining among teen-agers *but conditions that threaten youth safety remain unacceptably high overall . . .*" (my italics). The report, based on a survey from the CDC's Youth Behavior Risk Surveys, said that the incidence of guns being carried to school declined between 1991 and 1997, as did incidences of fighting and youth homicide.[22] With fewer murders, fewer guns brought to school, and fewer fights, the study's authors must have had to really dig to find the cloud of bad news.

On November 5, 1999, Amy Dickinson, a family columnist for *Time*, had good news to share with her readers: The National Center for Health Statistics concluded in a survey that girls ages fifteen to seventeen had the lowest birth rate in forty years, and 80 percent of the decline in teen pregnancy was attributed to an increase in the use of birth control.

The decline was something to congratulate ourselves about; changing sexual behavior is notoriously difficult, and the news was a real achievement. But sure enough, Dickinson adhered to the old newsroom rule: Let no good news go unblackened by some warning, to reassure the public that there are still problems to fix. Apparently desperate for bad news to taint the good, she looked hard and, sure enough, found something else to wring her hands about: oral sex.

She wrote, "Anecdotes and news reports from around the country suggest that oral sex is currently in vogue among schoolkids. In a recent survey by Planned Parenthood, 10% of self-described virgins admitted having oral sex—some in their early teens." Dickinson really had to stretch here. She relied on anecdotes (we know how reliable those are; good for telling a story, very questionable for generalizing) and news reports—the same news reports that systematically and routinely exaggerate the severity of virtually every problem or crisis. The best she could do was quote a survey that said that one out of every ten virgins admitted having oral sex, "some in their early teens." Translation: the vast majority of virgins surveyed, 90 percent, did *not* report that act, and of the few who *did*, most were in their mid- or late teens. This is the crisis that Dickinson used to cast a shadow over the much more robust, significant, and positive news.[23]

Similarly, when *NBC Nightly News* anchor Tom Brokaw reported a school shooting in Fort Gibson, Oklahoma, on the December 6, 1999, telecast, he duly noted that overall school violence was down. This is how he put it: "Overall teenage violence may be down, but the exceptions are coming all too often." The first six words of his introduction were quickly drowned out in the hundreds of alarmist words and images that followed.

A 1993 article on the ozone controversy further illustrates the way the press (and the public) treat good news. Boyce Rensberger, a respected veteran science reporter for the *Washington Post*, wrote an article that appeared in that paper on April 15, 1993. The article came out amid heated public debate about the threat of Earth's ozone depletion. Rensberger gave both sides of the issue, including the rarely heard, optimistic views of many knowledgeable scientists. He quoted, for example, an atmospheric scientist with the Environmental Defense Fund, who opined, "The current and projected levels of ozone depletion do not appear to represent a catastrophe." Many other scientists agreed, pointing out that ozone is a renewable resource, reliable data are sparse, and that the changes measured may well simply reflect normal fluctuations in ultraviolet light. Overall, the article could be taken as good news: The sky was not falling, and there was no need to panic.[24]

Rensberger described the reaction to his story in an article in *Skeptical Inquirer* magazine:

> The reaction to my ozone story was swift. Some readers were perplexed because they were under the impression that the amount of ozone depletion was approaching alarming proportions. My story didn't square with the prevailing public image of the problem. . . . There were letters, phone calls, and clippings of articles in environmentalist advocacy publications branding me an enemy of the planet. . . . [The Congressional environment caucus] was so startled by my story that they summoned a prominent atmospheric scientist at NASA to come in and please tell them what gives. . . . Well, the NASA scientist said (and I paraphrase): Rensberger's story is basically correct on the facts, but there is a problem with his tone.
>
> I was to hear the "tone" complaint many times. It puzzled me that a story could be factually correct and written in what I thought was a straight, unemotional style but be considered wrong in "tone." Eventually I figured it out, I think.
>
> Environment stories are usually written in an alarmist tone. That is to say, the stories deal with purportedly alarming developments and the sources are often people who wish to sound an alarm. A species is endangered. A chemical is toxic. The Earth is in peril. That's just the way

this kind of story is usually written in the news business. And, often enough, the facts are truly alarming. But it's become the norm in much environment writing to state things in this alarmist tone even if the facts are not well established.

As a science writer, coming out of a somewhat different journalistic tradition, I try to write my stories in a neutral, purely informational tone—and also to highlight the facts that strike me as posing the greatest challenge to conventional thinking. I suspect that people had become so used to alarmist stories on ozone depletion that my neutral story appeared, by contrast, to be unduly optimistic.[25]

In February 1994 Rensberger's article won the American Association for the Advancement of Science–Westinghouse Science Journalism Award for large newspapers.

Media critic Matthew Kerbel gives one last example from *NBC Nightly News*. Reporter Pete Williams provides "in-depth" reporting on the scourge of vehicle thefts in America. Williams's remarks are quoted verbatim, with the author's comments following.

> Pete: Car theft remains America's most expensive property crime, one every 23 seconds, adding up to almost one-and-a-half million stolen cars a year. And while that number is down over the past decade, police actually recover far fewer cars now.

Can we rewind the tape and listen to that again?

> Pete: And while that number is down over the past decade, police actually recover far fewer cars now.

It goes by quickly, but the on-screen graphic says, "Down about 19%."

> Pete: One-third of them are never found.

That's a scary way of saying two-thirds of them are.

In other words, car thefts are down nineteen percent over the past decade, and two of every three stolen cars are recovered. You could write the story that way, but why would you? The difference is just a variation in the way you interpret statistics, and everyone knows how easily manipulated statistics are.[26]

There is one common exception to the media's propensity to use scare tactics, and that's when they're going overboard exaggerating the benefits of a new medical device, drug, or procedure. In one study reported in the *New England Journal of Medicine*, an analysis of more than two hundred newspaper articles and television reports found the media's health coverage poor. The study found that 85 percent of the stories used statistics that exaggerated a drug's benefit, and more than half the coverage failed to mention potentially harmful side effects. The media's coverage also failed to include other important information such as potentially biasing financial links between drug companies and researchers.[27]

INTERVIEWING THE MIRROR

Reporters in the media tend to highlight those interview subjects who subscribe to their point of view. People who hold a contrary view generally don't get airtime, and this perpetuates the false impression that events have only one correct interpretation. The audience probably assumes that the reporter tried to get a representative sample, and that if there were competing views they would all be represented in the story. I refer here not to political stories, which are typically monitored for biased content, but another type of bias, the news bias.

Childrens' reaction to violence is a good example. Though *Time* reported on polls showing that—despite parents' fears and media hype to the contrary—most children weren't overly concerned about violence in schools or in general, *Newsweek*'s "My Turn" column on December 13, 1999, is typical of how the media portrayed kids' opinions and fears. Written by Beth Pollack, a junior in high school, the article was titled "How a Madman Changed Our Lives." It is an account of how the peace in an innocent, quiet, "peaceful suburb" of Chicago was disrupted when gunman Benjamin Smith wounded or killed nine people shooting at one black man, six Jews, and an Asian-American couple in July of that year. The account offers platitudes like, "Each act of violence chips away at our sense of safety" and the melodramatic ending, "With the whir of each approaching car, the unfortunate slogan of the '90s flashes through our minds: 'Which way do I run?'"[28]

If that's really how the author feels, and if *Newsweek* wants to publish it, the magazine certainly should, but readers shouldn't be left with the impression that Pollack's experience and fears are representative of all, or even most, young people's reactions to violence. Polls show that over 90 percent of kids feel safe in their communities and schools. The fact that one person doesn't—and writes her panicky story for *Newsweek*—does not a crisis make. The media's focus on this type of alarmist story (and *Newsweek* was just one of many such examples) implies to readers that the story is representative. After all, most readers probably assume that the media don't go out looking to emphasize the minority opinion—and they don't. They just look for the one that best fits their news bias.

Pollack's account is misleading: She says, "My parents chose my high school because they believed I'd be safe there," implying that her parents were wrong. But in fact, schools are among the safest places for children to be, much safer than in cars, at home, or at the mall.

There's a further irony in Pollack's piece. According to her, the violence shook her community's sense of security. The writer didn't, from her account, actually witness any of the violence or school shootings. And though a friend of hers was shot at, she wasn't a witness to either of the other two incidents she cites as shaking her sense of security: the Columbine attack and a workplace shooting. Thus, most or all of the information that robbed her sense of security came from the news media.

What we have here is a person who was basically justified in feeling secure before, during, and after the violence that she cites. Her fears (and loss of security) came not from firsthand experience with the violent acts, but from the sensationalized and alarmist reports in the news media—the very same kind she wrote for *Newsweek*. With TV anchors leading newscasts with misleading editorials like, "Another school, another tragedy . . . when will the violence stop?" it's no wonder that some of the public are scared. But the mistake is confusing increased *coverage* of crime for increased *incidence* of crime. They are two very different things, and Pollack, like much of America, confuses the two. In the process, she perpetuates the myth that crime is on the rise and that American youth are rightfully afraid.

The Ruined Fairy Tale Myth

The news media's penchant for framing the world's events in terms of narratives or myths is clear. Perhaps the most common myth is what I call the Ruined Fairy Tale: a news story that begins by setting up an idyllic family or person's life and proceeds to describe the horrors that followed. Build it up, then tear it down.

This device is most common among television newsmagazines such as *Primetime* and *Dateline NBC*. Typically, these reports start with a narration something like this: "Mary Beth had it all . . . two kids, a devoted husband, a successful professional career, and a beautiful house. Yet behind the couple's public smiles. . . ." This leads to the devastating teardown of the person's life, usually involving something sensational like murder or adultery or the discovery of a long-lost evil twin.

Yet while the basic facts of the story may be true, both of these polar depictions are at least partially fiction. How do we know how devoted her husband was or how idyllic their marriage was? Maybe the segment writers and producers consider being in a dead-end job for fifteen years as "a successful professional career." We don't know, but it seems unlikely that everything was as rosy before the bad events and as terrible after them as the writers want us to believe. Yet it makes for a good story.

In October 2002 columnist David Giffels of the *Akron (Ohio) Beacon Journal* wrote an article titled "Life Plays Mean Trick on D.C. Kids." In it, he discussed the then-recent sniper attacks in the D.C. area and his opinion of the effect on the children in the region. He begins, "What a strange season this is. You're a school kid inside the Washington Beltway. Your Pentagon was bombed by a jet plane last year. Your summer was tainted by Amber Alerts. . . . And now there's a lunatic in the woods with a rifle. Last Halloween, it was terrorism. Now, here it is again."[29]

Giffels weaves a melodramatic but unlikely account; I doubt that most kids in the Washington, D.C., area give much thought to the Pentagon building, much less take the attack on it personally and consider it "theirs."

He describes a child being told not to touch the mail (referring to the 2001 anthrax scare) and "sitting in the back seat at the gas station, watching your dad bob and weave to avoid some hidden, but very present danger." If the subject weren't so serious, this sort of exaggeration could be mistaken for humor. I wonder how many D.C.-area kids actually sat in the back of a car, terrified, watching their fathers fill the tank with one hand while bobbing and weaving as though trying to avoid a boxer's punch.

Giffels contrasts an idyllic child's life to the terrorism in the news. Yet his piece is entirely an alarmist straw man argument. Giffels writes, "You're a kid. You're supposed to be carefree." Yet Giffels's romanticized version of childhood has little basis in reality. Kids have never been carefree; they have always had to endure pains, cares, and scares, including school bullies, difficult math homework, unrequited crushes, abusive parents, and so on.

In fact, a survey taken around the same time (and in the Washington, D.C., area) found that children are more afraid of emotional violence (such as teasing and bullying) than physical violence such as shootings or terrorism.[30] The findings reinforce many studies that have found that, despite the media's myths and hype, children generally feel safe and secure.[31]

Giffels isn't comparing the modern loss of innocence caused by terrorism to the good old days, he's comparing an idealistic myth to reality and complaining that the real world comes up short. Giffels writes that anthrax scares, sniper scares, and terrorism are a "part of everyday life" and that kids "have lost the chance to live through these years like most kids do."

Yet the news media's overreaction to the threats shows exactly the opposite; the threats were and are very rare. We heard the same proclamations from the media after the spate of school shootings. In Giffels's piece, as during the September 11 attacks—and school shootings before that—we were told the myth that our children had lost their innocence, the world had been forever changed, and so on. Each time, the American spirit was underestimated and more resilient than the journalists and pundits gave credit for.

The world is not nearly as dangerous as Giffels makes it out to be. Despite the horrible crimes he lists, kids are far more likely to die in a car accident or be struck by lightning than be shot by a sniper or killed in an act of terrorism. There are many threats to children that are far worse and far more common than those he cites. The simple fact is that most kids are not scared, and to the degree that they are, it's because of alarmist news and pieces like Giffels's column. Fortunately, the snipers were arrested the following day, and Giffels's imaginary tykes had a terror-free Halloween.

Life after Terrorism

The same news bias was apparent in the news coverage of the aftermath of the September 11 attacks. In the months following the attacks, many people reported feeling depressed and anxious. News crews and cameras and reporters focused on the panicked, the alarmed, the devastated. Those who were sad but coping well were rarely seen on television.

You wouldn't know it from the news coverage, but many Americans were very resilient in their reactions to the attacks. An October 10, 2001, ABC News.com article reported a poll that found that "[n]early half of Americans surveyed—44 percent—say the attacks . . . had no lasting impact on their mental health."[32] By January 2002 almost 90 percent of Americans in a CBS News poll said that their lives had returned to normal or never really changed after the attacks.[33] According to a study in the *Journal of the American Medical Association*, six months after the September 11 attacks, nearly 95 percent of Americans living outside of New York City reported no significant, lingering symptoms related to stress from the attacks.[34]

Still, on the six-month anniversary of the tragedy, the news media dutifully and predictably emphasized those people who were still devastated. An article in the *New York Times*, for example, begins, "Linda Richard thought she would feel better by now. Instead, she is more anxious, more afraid, more paranoid. Six months after Sept. 11, she cannot sleep. She is overeating, taking the anti-depressants she had stopped using last spring. . . ." Linda's Brooklyn apartment is a mess, we're told, and she spends many Mondays hiding under the covers and ignoring telephone calls. She is terrified of another attack and is moving out of New York City. "The feelings, the hate, the fear, the insecurity are overwhelming," she says.

The article's author, Sarah Kershaw, tells us that "her story, a plunge from stability to fragility, from wellness to illness, is not an isolated case."

And perhaps it isn't isolated, but it is far from typical. Studies and polls showed that the vast majority of Americans' lives had returned to normal. Sure, there would always be a few people out of the millions who, for whatever reason, still hadn't readjusted to normal life. But the news media portrayed their devastation as typical when in fact it was very rare.

As before, the media's role in perpetuating the pain was clear. Kershaw notes that "[i]n most cases, these mental health professionals are treating patients who did not lose a relative or close friend, participate in the rescue effort or directly witness the attack but were nevertheless deeply affected." With little or no direct connection to the attacks, the source of their information and devastation is clear: the media. This holds true for the examples Kershaw gives, including one man who "watched the scenes from the attack over and over on CNN. . . ." Thus the media's relentless repetition of the devastation—and constant emphasis on those most damaged—begins the cycle anew.[35]

Following the Columbine High School shootings, the news media made the rounds talking to students. There were lots of images of group hugs, tearful recollections, and erecting memorials. Students who showed little emotion generally weren't interviewed. Those Columbine students who grieved on cue, in the "right" way, and to the right people were supported and seen on television; those who channeled their feelings with loud heavy metal and gothic clothes were left alone and not represented on television.

Apparently not everyone was as broken up as the teens shown on television. One man, Mike Smith, told reporters that he was a point guard for the Columbine basketball team. Journalists flocked to the young man as he proffered stories of the school's jocks, their antagonism toward the Trenchcoat Mafia, and how the school officials ignored it all. Several news media, including *USA Today* and the *Drudge Report*, ran the story. It eventually came out that the man was not who he claimed to be, the stories were made up, and in fact there was no Columbine student named "Mike Smith."[36]

One of the most pernicious—and least discussed—aspects of the media's love of hyperbole is the trivialization of important news events. The news media hype every story, every minor event (from O. J. Simpson's trial to shark attacks to anthrax scares), insisting that what they give us is very important and worth watching. Unfortunately, when a *truly* significant event happens (such as the September 11 attacks), the effect is muted because the press has already spewed its alarmist, panicky adjectives for years. Like the boy who cried wolf, the media has exploited tragedy and spectacle and pushed nonevents into prominence so many times that the September 11 adjectives and labels seemed hollow and clichéd.

JOURNALISM DEVOID OF CONTENT

> *The one function that TV news performs very well is that when there is no news we give it to you with the same emphasis as if there were.*
>
> —David Brinkley

Much has already been written about the excessive media coverage in the O. J. Simpson and Princess Diana spectacles, and there's no need to repeat the criticisms here except to focus on the meaningless facets of the media's response.

In the O. J. Simpson affair (the "trial of the century"—a phrase also applied to the trials of Roscoe "Fatty" Arbuckle, Bruno Hauptmann, Alfred Dreyfus, and others), the media presence was ubiquitous from the beginning. Simpson's televised highway chase on June 17, 1994, mesmerized millions and set the stage for the frenzy that was to come. Although not a particularly significant event in the spectrum of news, it's clear why it was so riveting: A famous former football star and actor was being chased by a dozen Los Angeles Police Department squad cars down a Los Angeles freeway. Anything could happen, from a shootout to a car crash to a suicide.

Yet once Simpson was caught, the same ultra-zoom lens was trained on everything he did, wherever he went. Perhaps the height of absurdity (although singling only one extreme absurdity isn't easy in this case) came when he was being transferred from a jail to be arraigned.

The coverage included live footage, shot from a helicopter, of the van Simpson was in snaking through the streets of Los Angeles. The trip took about twenty minutes, during which the camera followed every turn and stop. Of what possible relevance is this footage? It's as if the news directors were sure that Simpson would jump out the back or the van would explode. It was a simple transfer of a prisoner from point A to point B. There would be no glimpses inside the van, no confessions or comments—nothing that could possibly be meaningful or relevant was broadcast. How, where, and when O. J. Simpson, in police custody, was physically transferred between two buildings can hold no relevance to any viewers' lives and didn't need to be reported, much less aired live with running commentary from a trailing news helicopter.

The same sort of coverage without content was seen in the struggle for the Cuban boy Elián Gonzales: When the boy was driven to a neutral place to visit his Cuban relatives in late January 2000, a helicopter followed the car as it drove down the highway to the meeting place. Again, the footage of a car on the highway was wholly irrelevant to anything having to do with the case, as was video of Elián playing with a dog and walking around in his yard. But the case moved so slowly that the national media, in their desperate desire to air *something*, no matter how irrelevant or meaningless, were reduced to lining up to videotape a boy playing with his dog.

Ads following the *NBC Nightly News with Tom Brokaw* on Monday, January 17, 2000, plugged the newsmagazine *Dateline NBC*, appearing later that night. A television crew went to Cuba to get the "real story" behind little Elián's life back home. The voice-over promised "exclusive footage you've never seen before!"

What was this important footage *Dateline* had uncovered for the world? Hidden video of Elián being tortured by Fidel Castro himself? A sad glimpse at the squalor of life in urban Cuba? I had to tune in. The show, "Young Boy and the Sea," was reported by Keith Morrison on location in Cuba. It told the story of Elián's parents, how they split up, and what Elián's life was like back in Cuba. Finally the much-vaunted footage was shown, with the voice-over, "This video, obtained exclusively by *Dateline* and never before seen by anyone outside the family, is a record of Elián and his closest companion, his cousin, born shortly after he was." The footage was a homemade videotape of two kids in shorts gyrating to music on a small patio. This riveting "exclusive footage" aired for about twenty seconds.

That was it: two young kids spinning and dancing to Latin beats. It could have been any kid anywhere. It showed neither opulence nor deprivation, just a kid and his cousin dancing badly. The footage *Dateline* was so proud of added virtually nothing to the story. It didn't help us understand the political situation Elián was in, or what his life would really be like if and when he eventually returned. It was meaningless, essentially irrelevant fluff. It was a shiny, worthless trophy NBC could hold aloft to justify its hollow shout of "exclusive, never-before-seen footage!"

Another commonly uttered, meaningless media phrase is, "changed [his/her/my] life forever." What does that mean? Strictly speaking, *any* event in a person's life, no matter how insignificant, changes his or her life forever because it becomes a part of that person's irrevocable past. If the phrase is intended to mean that an event *deeply affected* the person, that's a meaningful phrase—and writers should say what they mean instead of using a meaningless cliché.

During the days of protracted legal wrangling between George W. Bush and Al Gore for the presidency in November 2000, Bloomberg News Service came up with what is perhaps a perfect example of a meaningless headline: "Bush, Gore Don't Know Outcome of Presidential Contest." This came on November 8, well into the second day of back-and-forth political maneuvering, when it was clear that there was no winner and likely wouldn't be one for at least several days.

This was news? That neither candidate knew who won? *Of course* neither knew; no one in the world knew, and the matter wouldn't be decided for weeks. The news media, chastened by early and serious election reporting errors, calmed down for a short time on the saturation coverage of the little news that trickled in. But soon the news media grew desperate for copy, desperate to put some sort of material, any material, out to the public.

Questioning the Straw Man

Another way that reporters provide their audiences with verbiage and meaningless news is through the use of straw man questions, asking leading questions designed to elicit a specific answer that the reporter (and frequently the audience) already knows.

NBC Nightly News anchor Tom Brokaw, introducing a report on January 30, 2000, that the governor of Illinois had decided to suspend the death penalty in his state, asked, "Is there any way to know how many people on death row may be innocent?" A second's thought would reveal that, if there were some foolproof way to distinguish the innocent from the guilty, the method would revolutionize the criminal justice system. The piece then went on to duly report the obvious: that no, there is no way to know how many people on death row may be innocent.

In December 1999 the border between the United States and Canada was the focus of increased scrutiny following the arrest of suspected terrorists. A man was arrested at the border entering Washington State, and traces of bomb-making residue were reportedly found in his vehicle. Authorities suspected that terrorists might try to disrupt millennium celebrations, and security along all borders was tightened. Pundits talked about how lax America's security was, and a New Year's celebration in Seattle was cancelled due to safety concerns.

During the media coverage, a senior national security spokesman was interviewed. One news reporter began by asking him, "Are our borders completely safe from terror?" As the reporter (hopefully) very well knew, the answer is no, our borders are not and will never be completely safe from terror. It's a stupid question: It is framed as an absolute, and no intelligent, responsible official is going to answer that question in the affirmative. What *would* be newsworthy is if the official had responded, "Yes, in fact we have come up with a way to completely seal our borders from terrorism."

I understand that asking such meaningless rhetorical questions is simply an easy way to begin an interview or report, but it is also a lazy, uninformative device that does a disservice to the audience. Precious airtime should be used to ask informative, probing questions of people who have specialized knowledge of the topic, not broad questions that anyone

Copyright © Ann Telnaes. Reproduced with permission.

with half a brain could answer. In the entire interview, in fact, there was precious little news that hadn't been reported: No, we can't totally secure our borders. Yes, we're on a state of heightened alert. No, we don't have any specific threats. With that, the reporter nodded as if anything new or meaningful came from the interview, and said, "Back to you, Tom."

Perhaps the news media's predeliction for pretending that answers from their interviewees actually mean something is most evident during elections and debates. When nonresponsive political candidates are given a chance to talk, frequently what they say is a canned position statement and not necessarily relevant to the question asked. Rarely do the the reporters return to the question, saying "That's a wonderful answer, but it had nothing to do with what I asked. Will you please answer the question?"

Since it's usually impractical to have ordinary citizens ask questions of public figures and candidates, the news media are there to represent the people. But democracy is not served when those supposed to be representing us allow those we are supposed to be informed about to weasel out of honest, legitimate—and sometimes pointed—questions.

Simplification and Misdirection

One of the news media's methods of analysis when reporting a story is to oversimplify complex issues. On one level, this is an important part of the journalistic process. There is always more material gathered than a journalist can use, and time and space constraints require distilling lots of information into a digestible (and hopefully informative) piece. This is especially true when the issues are technical or complex.

But too often the news media, in their quest for sound bites and quick slogans, rely on oversimplification. One example of such oversimplification is a caption in *Time* magazine's annual year in review for 1998. In an article titled "Black. Gay. And lynched for a label," a caption below the photos of Matthew Shepard and James Byrd Jr. read, "Shepard was killed because he was gay; Byrd died because he was black."

Hold on: As an editor myself, I know that copywriters sometimes get lazy, but those statements simply are not true.

Shepard's sexual orientation per se did not cause his death, nor did Byrd's skin color cause his death. It was *other people's beliefs and actions* that led to their deaths. The problem is not Shepard nor his sexuality; the problem is people like Russell Henderson and Aaron McKinney, his attackers. The problem is not James Byrd Jr. or his race; the problem is people like John King, Shawn Berry, and Lawrence Brewer, his attackers.

Imagine that Shepard, in fact, *wasn't* gay, but his attackers believed he was and beat and killed him. What would the papers say then? They'd probably still say that Shepard was killed because of homophobia and report on violence against gays in the area and nationwide. Yet that wouldn't be the case: In reality it wouldn't be a crime against a gay man. The crucial question, then, is what the attackers did and why, not Shepard's actual sexual orientation.

Both deaths were horrific and tragic, but neither can be reduced to a simple slogan, such as that Shepard was killed because he was gay. This may be a fine point, but the fact of the matter is that this sort of oversimplification occurs all the time and in many contexts. Antigay sentiments and racism are serious social issues that deserve more than perfunctory, oversimplified treatment.

Some may justify this as journalistic shorthand, claiming that while what is written or said is not literally true, most people understand what is meant. But I'm not sure that the public is sufficiently informed or conversant with the issues that the news media's shorthand is always understood.

OBJECTIVITY IN THEORY AND PRACTICE

David Shenk, author of *Data Smog*, notes:

> The proliferation of expert opinion has ushered in a virtual anarchy of expertise. To follow the news today is to have the surreal understanding that the earth is melting *and* the earth is cooling; that nuclear power is safe and nuclear power is *not* safe; that affirmative action works—or

> wait, *no it doesn't*. In the era of limitless data, there is always an opportunity to crunch some more numbers, spin them a bit, and prove the opposite. . . . With the widening pool of elaborate studies and arguments on every side of every question, more expert knowledge has, paradoxically, led to less clarity.[37]

And where is the press in all this, the journalists who are supposed to help us sift through the pounds and pounds of pundits and pablum?

All too often they are oddly silent, out of respect to "objectivity." Justin Lewis, a professor in the Department of Communications at the University of Massachusetts at Amherst and author of several books on the media, put it this way:

> [W]hile journalists profess their faith in this objective world, they have little confidence in their ability to recognize it. The norms of "objective reporting" thus involve presenting "both sides" of an issue with very little in the way of independent forms of verification. So, for example, a Republican will present one set of facts and a Democrat will present another set of facts. The objective journalist reports both, regardless of their veracity. We thus have the poignant irony that a journalist who systematically attempts to verify facts—to say which set of facts is more accurate—runs the risk of being accused of abandoning their objectivity by favoring one side over another. . . . [This model of reporting] also tends to promote a specific ideology. Lurking within this model is a specific philosophical assumption about where truth lies. Since the model tends to assume that both sides will always be speaking partial truths (a proposition that, however implausible, allows reporters to remain agnostic), it is easy to infer that the whole truth must lie somewhere in the middle.[38]

Writer Deborah Tannen points out another pitfall of the news media's bias: "The conviction that there are two sides to every story can prompt writers or producers to dig up an "other side," so kooks who state outright falsehoods are given a platform in public discourse. . . . Continual reference to "the other side" results in a pervasive conviction that everything has another side—with the result that people begin to doubt the existence of any facts at all."[39]

Most journalists would probably agree that objectivity is essential to good news reporting. Of course, reporters and editors are human, and they bring their biases, histories, and emotional baggage with them when they begin a story. But, one hopes, by and large they don't allow such bias to color their reporting.

But many in the modern media have a limited view of what objectivity is and what it means to be objective. Journalistic objectivity is not obvious. Many journalists apply a form of agnostic objectivity to their work, in which it's enough to simply let both sides of an issue have their say and leave it at that without much further comment.

This approach, though superficially appealing, is ultimately uninformative. If the journalist leaves key questions unanswered and points unchallenged, it is left to the audience to try to find out which view, set of facts, or assumptions is correct. Yet few in the public have the time or resources to research the claims from both sides and figure out who's right—and isn't that supposed to be the journalist's job, anyway?

What, then, does the audience come away with? At best, a thumbnail sketch of arguments and claims from both sides of the debate. Coke says it's better; Pepsi says it is. Democrats say Republicans killed a tax break; Republicans blame the White House. Amid all the finger pointing, contradicting experts, and duelling statistics, the journalist's role turns from claim analyzer to claim deliverer.

Ben Bagdikian discussed the objectivity doctrine in his book *The Media Monopoly*. He writes that objectivity

> contradicted the essentially subjective nature of journalism. Every basic step in the journalistic process involves a value-laden decision: Which of the infinite number of events in the environment will be assigned for coverage and which ignored? Which of the infinite observations confronting the reporter will be noted? Which of the facts noted will be included in the story? Which of the reported events will become the first paragraph? . . . The safest method of reporting news was to reproduce the words of authority figures, and in the nature of public relations most authority figures issue a high quotient of imprecise and self-serving declarations.[40]

This agnostic objectivity rests on several assumptions that may or may not be true. First, there is an implicit assumption of bipolarity. This is no doubt influenced by the familiar Democrat/Republican paradigm, but it gets applied to many other types of news stories. Who says that there are only two sides to an issue? The world is not black and white, and there may very well be three or more newsworthy and tenable positions. The traditional political paradigm of bipolarity doesn't always apply outside politics (or even within it).

Second, there is the assumption that the viewer has heard the best arguments from both sides. But the sound bites that are selected to run in a piece on the nightly news, for example, may be chosen more on the basis of brevity than relevance. Important points that the interviewee might consider essential to understanding her position may be left unseen because it was too long, or spoken too slowly, or the audio levels were jumpy—or any number of other factors having nothing to do with the strength of the argument.

Third, there is also an assumption that the viewer or reader can make an informed opinion or choice based (at least in part) upon the information in the news piece. Consumers can check some information and conflicting opinion for themselves, but in today's ever-specializing and complex world, consumers are more dependent on the media to inform them than ever before. Should you take aspirin daily to ward off a heart attack? Aspirin makers say yes. Others say that there isn't enough evidence that it's effective. Who do you believe? Presumably the journalist presenting a story will tell you—unless he is bound by agnostic objectivity, in which case you'll get both sides and a shrug.

No one expects journalists to have all the answers, much less a key to the truth. And there are many issues in which a journalist may honestly have no idea which side is right, and simply present both sides. But too often it seems that those in the news media just don't *want* to go that extra step to say who they, as informed and presumably impartial judges, believe to be correct. In their quest to simplify (partly for their own ease and partly, no doubt, to not confuse the viewers), journalists treat complex issues as if the points of view are obvious and in two distinct camps.

Obviously journalists can't cover every angle or canvas every opinion; for example, including a statement from the Flat Earth Society in a story about the moon walk is of dubious utility. But a reporter's job is to help separate the wheat from the chaff; instead, they usually just present two different piles of chaff for the viewer to look at and choose from.

In a segment for *ABC Nightly News*, religion correspondent Peggy Wehmeyer reported on the movement to introduce the Ten Commandments into Kentucky schools. "The idea," Wehmeyer said, "is the word of God might stop another event like the Columbine massacre." Reporting from Harlan City, she interviewed several people who held this view, then another person who held the opposite opinion. Yet she didn't ask or examine the obvious question behind that premise: Is there a link between religiosity and good conduct? If she had, she'd have found that studies have consistently shown that religious people are no more law abiding or ethical than the nonreligious. The evidence is pretty clear, compelling, and would presumably decide the matter: If more religion doesn't translate into better behavior (and it doesn't), then the entire question becomes moot.

It's like reporting on people who are fighting higher speed limits on the premise that they will lead to more highway fatalities and not bothering to do a little legwork to determine if their assertion is in fact correct. The obvious questions—the exact ones that need to be asked, the ones that get to the kernel of thorny assertions—are rarely brought up by the media, presumably to protect the veneer of objectivity.

The Columbine Story

While sticking cameras in pain-crumpled faces smacks of vulture journalism, it's also true that not all victims are reticent to participate in the coverage. This occurred in the wake of the Columbine tragedy. As Jessica Seigel wrote in the July/August 1999 issue of *Brill's Content*:

> [T]hese sources were teenagers, something that was perhaps easy to forget. In interviews after the first rush of terror, they seemed so self-possessed, looking directly into the cameras, spouting pithy sound bites. Garrulous and gossipy, the teens quickly warmed to the undivided attention of so many adults carrying microphones and pens, devouring their every thought and emotion. Soon the kids learned to query reporters, "Are you national or local?"[41]

Here's how one interview was described, when the *Today* show's Katie Couric interviewed prominent survivor Bree Pasquale:

> Couric, speaking from a studio in Washington, D.C., asked questions clearly intended to elicit a graphic blow-by-blow. Bree listened through an earpiece: "What kinds of sounds did you hear, and how did you feel when you heard them?" Couric asked. "They said something particularly callous after they shot Isaiah Shoels. Tell me what they said." . . . After pumping Bree for the gruesome particulars, Couric sounded especially sympathetic and intimate. "Bree, I can't imagine witnessing and hearing these things and being so terrified," Couric said. "How are you—how are you doing?"[42]

Couric's question is typical of much crime and crisis reporting: The question is rarely "What do you think about this topic?" but almost always "How did you *feel*?" While reporting on a subject's feelings may be legitimate and (slightly) newsworthy, it's also a lazy reporter's crutch. Feelings require no fact checking, no other sides demanding equal time. When there's little else to air, little forthcoming news, it's an easy way to fill airtime. Instead of reporting the truth—"We have nothing new to report, so we'll move on to other news"—reporter-wrung emotions are used as fodder to fill time.

There's also an ethical question to be addressed. Sobbing victims may make riveting television, but what about the real people being exploited for the camera? Haven't most survivors been through enough without being put on the spot in front of cameras and bright lights to describe how they felt in a moment of terror? It's one thing to intrude on a grieving person to get useful or important information; police must do it all the time. But it's quite another to intrude for the sake of ratings.

Beyond that, the question of feelings is a rhetorical question. Most people can pretty well guess how a woman would feel when her son or daughter is killed: numbness, pain, and sorrow, maybe mixed with anger. It seems distasteful to have a reporter stick a camera, light, and microphone in a victim's face to confirm what we already know: that crying victims are devastated and grief stricken. If the news media have such a surplus of airtime to run this pap, why don't they use a little of it to provide context and deeper content to more important news stories?

Edward Pinder, an ABC News producer, defends intruding on fresh tragedy: "It's sad that we have to approach these people and ask them to spill out their guts moments after their loss, but you have to do it."[43] Pinder's explanation, however, simply begs the question: *Why* do you have to do it? If you assume that in-your-face interviews with grieving relatives is necessary for responsible journalism, Pinder's answer is correct. But if you question that facile assumption, perhaps a different answer would come to light. What purpose is served? Who benefits from the interview, other than the news organization? And what real information is gained, anyway? Grief-chasing reporters seem oblivious to the contradiction inherent in talking about how devastated the mourners are. They are in enough pain to report on—but not so much pain that they can't spend time being interviewed about it for a live broadcast.

THE MYTH OF CLOSURE

The news media's obsession with public displays of grief in times of tragedy has occasionally drawn criticism. Responding to accusations of exploitation, the media often claim that though their grief coverage isn't particularly informative, it helps victims express their pain and provides a sense of closure. This, in turn, helps both the victims and viewers. But is it really true, or is it a self-serving media myth?

During the huge media-covered tragedies of the past decade or so, reporters have invariably brought up the question of closure. From international funerals to deaths of private people, it seems that no loss passes without calls for "healing" and "closure." This "closure movement," as some have called it, came about in part as a by-product of the victims' rights movement. Many people noted, quite accurately, that while the perpetrator or suspect in a crime makes the news and is (usually) treated fairly under the law, victims are forgotten or treated like "just another complainant" rather than as injured persons needing treatment and compassion. In addition to victim-assistance programs, measures were introduced to help victims deal with their ordeal psychologically.

On a more fundamental level, the idea behind the need to express emotions originally came, principally, from Sigmund Freud. Freud's theories of repression described many psychological problems as being rooted in painful memories that were repressed into unconsciousness. Indeed, much of psychoanalytical practice is based on this theory. It is ironic that, in a time when many of Freud's theories are being attacked and dismissed as sexist, dogmatic, unscientific, and antiquated, this facet of Freudian theory seems firmly entrenched—and reinforced—in the popular consciousness.

Yet despite the term's frequent usage in modern America, there is no agreed-upon definition of what "closure" is, nor is there really a way to define whether a person has closure or not. For some people, closure may come from burying a loved one. Others may have little need for closure and deal perfectly well on their own.

Sometimes the desire for closure seems to veer into the desire for vengeance. About a dozen states, including California, have enacted laws allowing victims' relatives the right to witness the killers' executions. This is done, many say, to bring closure. But does being present while a person dies in front of you really help bring closure? What sort of person gets satisfaction from watching the actual death of another person, regardless of the circumstances? Is this an activity that should be encouraged by our government? What if the survivors are sadistic and want the person tortured? That might also bring closure. But it's not the judicial system's job to make sure that families of slain people *feel* satisfied or achieve closure.

This point was seemingly lost on George W. Bush's newly appointed attorney general, John Ashcroft, when he agreed in April 2001 to televise Oklahoma City bomber Tim McVeigh's May 16 execution. The decision was made to show McVeigh's death on closed-circuit television to more than two hundred survivors and victims' families. Ashcroft said watching the execution "may help the group close this chapter on their lives," and that "the Department of Justice must make special provisions to assist the needs of the survivors and the victims' families."[44] The desire to watch a person die is thus deemed a "need," something *necessary* for those affected to experience. Clearly Ashcroft is wrong; some of the victims may *desire* to watch McVeigh die, but it certainly is not a *need*, nor is it a desire that the federal government must fulfill.

Apparently unaware of the irony in his words, Ashcroft said that, as an American who cares about our culture, he wanted "to restrict a mass murderer's access to a public podium." Yet Ashcroft himself provided McVeigh the podium he wanted through his death, last actions, and final words (though McVeigh suggested his death be televised nationally). As Salon.com writer Bruce Shapiro noted,

> The debate shows why any thought that McVeigh's execution represents closure is badly mistaken. Instead of recalling McVeigh's victims or encouraging violence prevention, the press and pundits are talking about how big the crowd will be that gets to watch McVeigh have poison dripped into his veins. Instead of fading into the anonymity of life behind bars, McVeigh is able to keep himself on the front page, to turn the chronicle of his last months and the video record of his death—whether closed circuit or telecast—into a martyrdom for the militia fringe.[45]

Adds Richard Small, a psychologist from Reading, Pennsylvania:

> I would expect that the people still looking for closure aren't going to find it. . . . This is becoming a public execution. Up to now, executions in no way have been a show. But now we're opening something up. If this is a catharsis for these survivors, why not for the rest of the city, the rest of the country. We should be cautious about seeing executions as therapeutic for the victims.[46]

The idea that events in people's lives have a finite, quantifiable beginning and end is a romantic one with only tenuous ties to reality. Each person deals with loss, grief, and tragedy in his or her own way. Americans, however, want instant gratification. Technology has allowed us to be more productive: conduct business faster, communicate faster, travel faster. But the mind, defiantly resistant to the ever-increasing pace of life, runs on its own time. In our desire for neat and tidy endings, the imposition of closure is in some ways a quest for control over the uncontrollable. Cardinal John J. O'Connor, speaking to survivors and families of victims of TWA Flight 800, cautioned, "The pursuit of closure is an elusive pursuit."[47]

To declare that a particular event, such as planting a commemorative tree or attending a funeral, will or should bring closure in many ways disrespects the individuality of each person's grieving process. You can no more tell a person to start being happy than you can suggest that he stop being sad. The event or memorial may or may not help bring closure, but the speed at which a person recovers is entirely individual, and to act as though closure is a panacea suggests otherwise.

As syndicated columnist Ellen Goodman noted,

> The American way of dealing with [grief] however has turned grieving into a set process with rules, stages, and of course deadlines. We have, in essence, tried to make a science of grief, to tuck messy emotions under neat clinical labels—like "survivor guilt" or "detachment." . . . Jimmie Holland, at New York's Sloan-Kettering Hospital, who has studied the subject, knows that "normal grief may often be an ongoing lifelong

> process." Indeed, she says, "The expectation of healing becomes an added burden. We create a sense of failure. We hear people say, 'I can't seem to reach closure, I'm not doing it fast enough.'"[48]

Edward Linenthal, a professor of religion and author of *The Unfinished Bombing: Oklahoma City in American Memory*,[49] agrees. He believes that the notion of closure is problematic in that it implies that closure has a finite duration. "There's no regularly predictable process," he says. "But we act like there's a kind of term limit on grief."[50]

To suggest that some painful episodes can somehow be boxed up and completely dealt with and put in the past is simply wrong. We are products of our past, and all significant experiences, both good and bad, will always be with us. Certainly people can deal with difficulties in their lives, but that is not the same as the putative "closure"; lingering feelings are never quite "closed."

There is incredible range in reactions to tragedy and grief. Some victims of violence and loss manage to deal effectively with their issues in a relatively short time and move on with their lives. Other people, perhaps less able to cope for one reason or another, may never achieve closure and always have difficulty functioning.

LETTING IT OUT

Another common myth is that the public and collective displays of grief seen on national television help those grieving. Viewers, so the argument goes, can see that the grief they're feeling is shared by others and are thereby comforted. It's a common assumption in America; it's also wrong.

Scientists have, in fact, found quite the opposite: "Letting it out" is not an effective strategy for coping with stress and grief. Recent scientific studies have shown that venting hostility can stir up hormones that could ultimately damage the heart and induce a heart attack. In a study published in the October 1, 1995, issue of the American Heart Association journal *Circulation*, Dr. Murray Mittleman and his colleagues at Harvard Medical School found that an angry outburst can more than double the risk of a heart attack in some people. The scientists found that the overall relative risk of heart attack during the two hours after an episode of anger was 2.3 times higher than among those who were not angry or upset. The paper notes that "several well-documented physiological effects of anger make the hypothesis of triggering of [heart attack] by an outburst of anger biologically plausible."

Richard Friedman, a professor of psychiatry at the State University of

New York at Stony Brook, concurs with the findings. This and many other studies, he says, leave little doubt that episodes of anger are dangerous: "The notion that letting it out is protective is not borne out in science."[51] Calming down is much safer and more effective than getting worked up, which is what happens when people express anger and grief.

A study published in the journal *Psychosomatic Medicine* found that those who suppressed their feelings and trauma may be healthier than those who pour their hearts out. The study, led by Karni Ginzburg of Tel Aviv University, studied 116 patients who were hospitalized following a heart attack and suffering anxiety. They took standardized tests for stress disorders and were compared with 72 people who had not had heart attacks. All were asked about their coping styles, whether they tended to ignore their anxiety or dwell on it. Those who tended to repress anxiety had the lowest levels of posttraumatic stress.[52]

In an effort to mollify their collective guilt (and placate critics) over their intrusive, emotion-wringing journalism, the news media use these arguments to explain why it's necessary to flood the airwaves with weeping victims instead of substantive reporting. For victims of tragedy who may not feel comfortable expressing their pain for millions in front of a news camera, there are legions of counselors and "grief workers" at the ready to offer another avenue for unspoken pain.

Following the Columbine shootings, columnist Charles Krauthammer observed:

> There is no good evidence that this "grief work"—talking out one's recollections and feelings about an experienced tragedy to one of these "experts"—makes any difference to the psychic outcome of the bereaved. Why then is grief work so popular? Why were packs of practitioners sent off to Littleton without the slightest hesitation? Or skepticism? Because the grief counseling business lives off the universal modern dogma that venting and openness, talking it out and letting it out, is good for the soul. But is it really? We did, after all, have 3,000 years of well-recorded human history before the advent of the grief counselor. Were people then more psychically disabled by tragedy (of which there was certainly more—routine infant mortality, death in childbirth, vulnerability to nature) than they are today? . . . [G]rief counseling is blindly accepted by a well-meaning public as a necessary response to America's Columbines—as necessary as SWAT teams and ambulances. We deem it unhealthy, even primitive, to bear our grief as our ancestors did, among friends, family, clergy.[53]

Krauthammer isn't alone in questioning the inherent value of expressing one's feelings. As columnist Christina Hoff Sommers writes,

> Jane Bybee, a Suffolk University psychologist, studied a group of high school students, classifying them as either "repressors," "sensitizers" (those keenly aware of their internal states), or "intermediates." She then had the students evaluate themselves and others using these distinctions. She also had the teachers evaluate the students. She found that the "repressors" were less anxious, more confident, and more successful academically and socially. Bybee's conclusion is tentative: "In our day to day behavior it may be good not to be so emotional and needy. The moods of repressed people may be more balanced."[54]

Sommers also discusses the research of psychology professor George Bonanno (formerly of Catholic University). Says Sommers:

> Bonanno's studies challenge the commonly held assumption that venting negative emotions like grief by talking about them openly is necessary for regaining mental health. His studies showed negative effects: grieving individuals who express strong negative emotions about their loss are worse off than the so-called repressors, who recover more rapidly. The ones who repressed their grief turned out to be considerably healthier than the strong emoters. More recently, Bonanno and a team of researchers at the National Institutes of Health have found that, among adolescent girls who have been sexually abused, those who showed emotional avoidance were doing better than those more openly expressive of their anger and grief.[55]

In the October 1997 issue of *Lingua Franca*, Emily Nussbaum also discussed Bonanno's work. Bonanno, Nussbaum writes, rails against "the 'bereavement industry,' a welter of professional bereavement therapists and support groups intended to help people through the grieving process. 'We've got all these therapists treating people for grief,' says Bonanno. 'And we haven't even defined what it is! We don't know what normal grief is, what pathological grief is, what psychological grief is. It's all very undefined, very unrigorous.'"[56] In one study Bonanno found that, contrary to popular wisdom, keeping grief and negative emotions in did *not* have a cumulative cost, and that instead those expressing less grief may instead be simply using an undervalued coping skill.

The article also cites the work of researchers Camille Wortman and Roxane Cohen Silver. The pair published an article titled "The Myths of Coping With Loss" in the *Journal of Consulting and Clinical Psychology*, which found that there was little evidence that "those who initially show minimal distress following loss are likely to become significantly depressed at a later point."[57]

Trying to bring closure to students following a suicide is especially fraught with difficulty. There is a risk, experts say, that talking to students about suicide to dissuade them can instead trigger copycat suicides. "When you're talking to a big class and saying a lot of things about suicide, different people listen to different words," says Dr. David Shaffer, head of the American Foundation for Suicide Prevention. "In disturbed kids, you probably reawaken bad thoughts and bad memories and set them off again."[58]

I do not want to give the impression that that reliving (or "reprocessing") past traumas is never therapeutic. Indeed, there is evidence that some treatments that force patients to confront traumatic stimuli can be helpful in treating conditions such as posttraumatic stress disorder.[59]

There is, however, a big difference between a pop-psychology, media-mandated public outpouring of grief designed to "let it out" and a sustained, professionally guided therapeutic intervention that allows people sufficient time to process their emotions. Simply bringing up painful emotions for the sake of bringing them up is unlikely to be cathartic.

The news media, of course, have a vested interest in perpetuating and reinforcing the notion that talking about emotions helps solve them. The more they can convince the emotionally wounded that they will be helping not only themselves but others by talking, the easier it is to get grief interviews—and high ratings.

In 2002 two teenage girls who were kidnapped but later recovered were besieged by the press following their ordeal. Reporters from all over the country bombarded the girls with interview requests—along with Hollywood producers seeking the rights to their story.

According to the *New York Times*, "the girls had initially planned to grant interviews with all three morning programs but . . . 'Today' persuaded them not to do interviews with its rivals." This made for a nice exclusive news coup for *Today*, yet the result was exactly the opposite of what the girls said they wanted. The reason they agreed to tell their story to the media was to reach as many people as possible and help other young women facing similar situations.[60]

NOTES

1. Bernard Goldberg, *Bias: A CBS Insider Exposes How the Media Distort the News* (Washington, D.C.: Regenery, 2002).
2. John Leo, "American Media Hobbled by Lack of Diversity of Thought," *Albuquerque Journal*, November 26, 1996.
3. Mike Pride, "On Second Thought," *Brill's Content* (October 1999): 45.
4. Ryszard Kapuscinski, "Reflection of the World," quoted in *World Press Review* (December 1999): 7.
5. David Altheide, *Creating Reality: How TV News Distorts Events* (Beverly Hills, Calif.: Sage Publications, 1974), p. 113.

6. Ibid., p. 25.

7. Ibid., p. 103.

8. Charley Reese, "Do All the Things We Do Really Matter?" *St. Augustine Record* [online], userpages.aug.com/frodo/matter.html [August 6, 2000].

9. Terry Jackson, "'Body-bag Journalism' Rules in Broadcast News, Study Says," *Miami Herald*, May 7, 1997.

10. "Ditching 'Body Bag Journalism,'" *Christian News Archives* [online], www.villagelife.org/church/archives/ucc_bodybagjournalism.html [October 22, 1997].

11. Jonathan Alter, "In The Times of the Tabs," *Newsweek*, June 2, 1997.

12. John Ruscio, "Risky Business," *Skeptical Inquirer* (March/April 2000): 24.

13. "Mortality," in *Time Almanac 2003* (Boston: Information Please, 2002), p. 132.

14. John F. Ross, "Risk: Where Do Real Dangers Lie?" *Smithsonian* 26 (1995): 42–53.

15. Ruscio, "Risky Business," p. 23.

16. Maggie Fox, "U.S. Poor Said Damaging Health with Lack of Vitamins," Reuters [online], www.thevitamindigest.com/news/2000/oct1900uspoorsaid.htm [October 19, 2000].

17. Altheide, *Creating Reality*, p. 191.

18. Cassandra Burrell, "U.S. Crime Numbers on Decline," Associated Press [online], www.beachbrowser.com/Archives/News-and-Human-Interest/July-99/US-Crime-Numbers-on-Decline.htm [July 19, 1999].

19. U.S. Department of Justice, "Intimate Partner Violence," *Bureau of Justice Statistics Special Report*, prept. no. NCJ 178247, May 2000.

20. Larry McShane, "Study: Teen Drug Use Leveling Off," Associated Press [online], wire.ap.org [November 22, 1999].

21. John Cloud, "Is Hate on the Rise?" *Time*, July 19, 1999.

22. "Study: School Violence Down, But Still Too High," CNN [online], www.cnn.com/US/9908/04/school.violence/.

23. Amy Dickinson, "Divided We Stand," *Time* [online], www.time.com/time/archive/preview/from_redirect/0,10987,1101991025-32769,00,html [November 5, 1999].

24. Boyce Rensberger, "Hard Time Dealing With Good News: Reaction to My Ozone Story," *Skeptical Inquirer* (fall 1994): 488.

25. Ibid.

26. Matthew A. Kerbel, *If It Bleeds, It Leads: An Anatomy of Television News* (Boulder, Colo.: Westview Press, 2000), p. 108.

27. Janice M. Horowitz, "Journalist, Heal Thyself!" *Time*, June 12, 2000.

28. Beth Pollack, "How a Madman Changed Our Lives," *Newsweek*, December 13, 1999.

29. David Giffels, "Life Plays Mean Trick on D.C. Kids," *Akron (Ohio) Beacon Journal* [online], www.ohio.com/mld/ohio/news/local/4339881.htm [October 22, 2002].

30. The survey, conducted by the Families and Work Institute, asked one thousand suburban Maryland kids in the fifth through twelfth grades about the violence that most affects their lives. Though the survey was conducted before the

sniper attacks in the D.C. area, it was done after the anthrax scares and the Pentagon attack. See Ellen Galinsky and Kimberlee Salmond, *Ask the Children: Youth and Violence Report* (New York: Families and Work Institute, 2002); and Kathy Slobogin, "What Are Kids Saying about Violence?" CNN [online], www.cnn.com/2002/HEALTH/parenting/07/30/young.bullies [July 30, 2002].

31. See, for example, Claudia Wallis, "The Kids Are Alright," *Time*, July 5, 1999.

32. "Lingering Emotions," ABC News [online], abcnews.go.com/GMA/GoodMorningAmerica/GMA011010Tipper_depression.html [October 10, 2001].

33. "Back to Normal?" CBS News [online], www.cbsnews.com/stories/2002/01/07/opinion/main323417.shtml [January 7, 2002].

34. Roxane Cohen Silver et al., "Nationwide Longitudinal Study of Psychological Responses to September 11," *Journal of the American Medical Association* 288, no. 10 (September 11, 2002).

35. Sarah Kershaw, "Even 6 Months Later, 'Get Over It' Just Isn't an Option," *New York Times* [online], www.nytimes.com/2002/03/11/nyregion/11PSYC.html [March 11, 2002].

36. Jessica Seigel, "Hugging the Spotlight," *Brill's Content* (July/August 1999): 84.

37. David Shenk, *Data Smog* (New York: HarperCollins, 1997), p. 91.

38. Justin Lewis, "Objectivity and the Limits of Press Freedom," in *Censored 2000*, ed. Peter Phillips (New York: Seven Stories Press, 2001), pp. 173–75.

39. Deborah Tannen, *The Argument Culture: Moving From Debate to Dialogue* (New York: Random House, 1998), p. 11.

40. Ben Bagdikian, *The Media Monopoly*, 5th ed. (Boston: Beacon Press, 1995), p. 180.

41. Seigel, "Hugging the Spotlight," p. 82.

42. Ibid.

43. Abigail Pogrebin, "Chasing Grief," *Brill's Content* (November 1998).

44. Jennifer L. Brown, "McVeigh Execution Telecast OK'd," South Coast Today [online], www.s-t.com/daily/04-01/04-13-01/a02wn016.htm [April 13, 2001].

45. Bruce Shapiro, "Killing McVeigh," Salon [online], archive.salon.com/news/feature/2001/02/04/mcveigh [February 24, 2001].

46. David Crary, "Experts Unsure What Impact McVeigh Execution Will Have on Viewers," *Salina Journal* [online], www.saljournal.com/stories/041301/new_ap.mcveigh2.html [April 13, 2001].

47. Ken Ellingwood, "Closure Talk Feeds Myth of Tidy Life," *Albuquerque Journal*, August 24, 1997, p. B-16.

48. Ellen Goodman, "Hurrying Healing," *Boston Globe* [online], members.bellatlantic.net/~vze2fjdu/EllenGoodman.htm [January 4, 1997].

49. Edward Linenthal, *The Unfinished Bombing: Oklahoma City in American Memory* (New York: Oxford University Press, 2001).

50. Peter Dizikes, "The End of Closure?" ABC News [online], abcnews.go.com/sections/us/DailyNews/Closure020311.html [March 11, 2002].

51. Jamie Talan, "Vented Anger May Actually Damage Heart," *Albuquerque Journal*, October 12, 1995, p. B-2.

52. Karni Ginzburg et al., "Repressive Coping Style, Acute Stress Disorder, and Posttraumatic Stress Disorder after Myocardial Infarction," *Psychosomatic Medicine* 64 (2002): 748–57.

53. Charles Krauthammer, "Public Airing of Private Pain Is No Panacea," *St. Louis Post-Dispatch*, May 9, 1999.

54. Christina Hoff Sommers, "The Republic of Feelings," *Free Inquiry* (fall 2000): 12.

55. Ibid.

56. Emily Nussbaum, "Good Grief! The Case for Repression," *Lingua Franca* (October 1997): 49.

57. C. B. Wortman and R. C. Silver, "The Myths of Coping with Loss," *Journal of Consulting and Clinical Psychology* 57 (1989): 349–57.

58. David Crary, "High Schools Face Trauma of Suicide," Associated Press [online], wire.ap.org [June 12, 2000].

59. One example is exposure and response prevention therapy, a type of exposure therapy in which an individual is exposed to their traumas and allowed to habituate to (and thus eventually control) the trauma-induced anxiety. This technique has also been used with other disorders, including obsessive-compulsive disorders.

60. Bill Carter, "Pastor Tells Why Abducted Girls Went on TV," *New York Times*, August 6, 2002.

4

ILLUSIONS OF PARTICIPATION AND INFLUENCE

Everyone likes to feel that their concerns are listened to and their opinions count. The media recognize this desire and capitalize upon it, creating an artificial global community where Princess Diana and Columbine massacre mourners could express their grief and pain publicly. From television newsmagazines such as *Dateline* to Internet service providers such as America Online (AOL), giving the public a voice on issues of the day has become a hot selling point.

A key promise of the Information Superhighway was that the World Wide Web would become a global village, where viewpoints would be shared and anyone with a computer could have access to information and opportunity. In some ways that promise has been borne out: Many ordinary citizens have their own Web pages, and people from all over the world can chat together in real time.

But in other ways the promised benefit to the common good has been a bust. AOL hosts "share your thoughts" chat rooms, message boards, and online polls, all ostensible avenues for fulfilling the educational promise of the Internet. Yet instead of serious venues for the exchange of ideas and information, many chat rooms are little more than opportunities for porn spammers to troll for e-mail addresses. Chat rooms seem to be the domain of crackpots and porn purveyors. What little genuine discussion ekes out of the morass is betrayed by the intellectual bankruptcy of most of the participants. The precious few who do participate with informed, earnest opinions, looking for intelligent discussion of serious topics, are quickly discouraged. Let's face it: Most informed people are busy working and have better things to do than chat for hours online. Who *cares* what JohnnyRocket1246 has to say about tax reform or relations with China?

Three hundred million voices with 300 million different opinions, biases, perspectives, and agendas make for a medium full of sound and fury, signifying nothing. In his book *Data Smog*, David Shenk discusses the effect the Internet has on us all:

> The more information we come upon, the more we narrow our focus. . . . Eleven billion words and 22 million Web pages bring us more information than ever before and, because of this, less information *shared*. Like niche radio and cable TV, the Net encourages a cultural splintering that can render physical communities much less relevant and free people from having to climb outside their own biases, assumptions, inherited ways of thought. This is perhaps best evidenced by the ominous emergence of so-called [computer] smart agents, which automatically filter out information deemed irrelevant to the customer.[1]

Polls, another venue for the public's opinions, are just as bad. Many of the stories on AOL News are merely short descriptions of the day's news, with two or more links below the text. One is "Details," for more information on the story; the other is frequently "Share Your Thoughts." The latter link is to a message board, a sort of huge Internet watercooler, where topics of the day can be discussed. But to what end?

On one randomly picked day alone (December 3, 1999), AOL users were asked their opinions on Webcams, adoption bans for unmarried couples, the Cuban boy Elián Gonzales, social promotion in schools, zero-tolerance policies for school misconduct, the federal college loan program, and whether researchers should treat teens for schizophrenia before they are diagnosed. That's an awful lot of topics for the average citizen to weigh in on! The issues are complex and entire books could be written on any one of them; to assume that the average AOL subscriber will contribute well-informed ideas and opinions seems a little idealistic.

The AOL poll for January 7, 2000, was: "Is breast milk best for babies?" Decades of research has indicated that the answer is clearly yes, so why is it the subject of an opinion poll? What's next, a poll asking people if they think smoking is good for you? On December 10, 1999, after the failure of a space probe, AOL posed to its users "Today's Poll: Where Is the Mars Lander?" The public was encouraged to send their opinion on the missing NASA lander. Somehow the fate of the Mars Lander became the subject of opinion, as if a consensus would clarify the Lander's fate. I can just picture a NASA press release: "The overwhelming majority of AOL users decided that the Mars Lander collided with a UFO, so we've settled on that as the official explanation for the loss of the unit."

Certainly, anyone can have an opinion on any subject, but uninformed opinions are nearly worthless. An opinion is just a statement of personal whim and preference, and need not be based in the slightest on logic, fact, intelligence, or good reason. We don't stop strangers on the street to ask their opinions about foreign policy or prison reform, so why should we care what the results are when AOL does it for us?

Critical thinking author Vincent Ryan Ruggerio has this to say about opinions:

> Is everyone entitled to his or her opinion? In a free country this is not only permitted but guaranteed. In Great Britain, for example, there is still a Flat Earth Society. As the name implies, the members of this organization believe that the earth is not spherical but flat. In this country, too, each of us is free to take as bizarre a position as we please about any matter we choose. When the telephone operator announces, "That'll be 95¢ for the first three minutes," you may respond, "No, it won't—it'll be 28¢." When the service station attendant notifies you, "Your oil is down a quart," you may reply, "Wrong—it's up three." . . . Free societies are based on the wise observation that people have an inalienable right to think their own thoughts and make their own choices. That fact in no way suggests that the thoughts they think and the choices they make will be reasonable.[2]

Some of these polls would be much more useful if we had an informed public, but by and large we don't. From the spelling of *potato* to naming the three branches of government, the American public is woefully misinformed. In an editorial in *Reason* magazine, Virginia Postrel lamented our poorly informed populace:

> In late December [1995], what used to be called the Times Mirror Center for the People and the Press released a compilation of six years of research on what news stories Americans followed, and how closely, and on what facts people know. . . . The results: People pay attention to disasters, natural and man-made, and wars involving U.S. troops. They pretty much ignore everything else. And they know precious few facts about national issues. . . . These results do not exactly suggest a well-informed American public.[3]

Or take, for example, the finding of a survey of twenty-one hundred college students in which 40 percent of the respondents thought that prehistoric people had to protect themselves from dinosaurs.[4]

The television newsmagazine *Dateline NBC* has a special feature called "*Dateline* Interactive," in which viewers are asked to contact the show during the program to give their opinion on the show's topic. The results of the viewers' opinions are shown at the end. A typical question might be, "Do you think the defendant is guilty?"

The premise ignores the fact that viewers would have to watch the *entire* show before making an informed choice. But if viewers waited until the end to make an informed decision, *Dateline* wouldn't have time to get the results, compute them, and put them on the air. Clearly many viewers feel justified in deciding twenty minutes into an unfolding story that they have enough knowledge to form an opinion and send it in to *Dateline*. This sort of knee-jerk, don't-bother-me-with-the-rest-of-the-facts attitude also doesn't bode well for an educated public—or their opinions.

A CASE STUDY IN THE USEFULNESS OF THE "AOL GLOBAL WATERCOOLER"

America Online touts itself as "a community of people talking to people" and says that "Message Boards offer a great way to gather information and share the experiences of others with similar interests." And just what sort of public service does AOL provide with its message boards? I decided to take a look on Tuesday, July 25, 2000, when a Concorde plane crashed in Paris, killing 109 people. Within minutes of the crash, AOL had set up a message board encouraging people to "talk about it." The first post appeared at 11:41 A.M. By 2:15 that afternoon five hundred messages had been posted; by 2:30 about ten posts per minute poured in; and by 3:20, the posts reached one thousand.

And what did AOL users do? Gather information, share experiences, and comfort each other? Not on your life! The majority of postings were racist: racism against Germans, French, British, blacks, and Scots. Several postings were like this one, replying to a request for respect for the dead: "Respect for whom? Germans whose parents were Nazis? And scummy French who collaborated with Hitler? . . . Good riddance to these bums." Another francophobe commented, "We have bailed them out of two wars and since Waterloo they've never won anything but a bicycle race." Yet another speculated that "the crash is very typical of a lone negro . . . a negro lit off a bomb in the bathroom."

Not all the messages posted were racist; others found the tragedy funny. In response to a posting that said Demi Moore had died on the plane and would be missed, one wag wrote, "Not by me . . . [signed] Bruce [ex-husband Willis]." That writer also said, in response to a post that asked if JFK Jr. was on board, "He was the pilot!"

Far from being a place to disseminate information, the message board quickly became a rumor mill. Leonardo DiCaprio was said to have been aboard the doomed plane, as were cycling star Lance Armstrong and Bob Dylan. Still others listed people they *wished* had been on the plane, including O. J. Simpson and Geraldo Rivera. Others swapped theories on why the plane went down, ranging from terrorist Osama bin Laden to God's retribution for Nazi Germany. One politically minded person started his post, "A vote for Al Gore is a vote for airline safety!" while another suggested that the crash was engineered by the White House to divert attention from the failed Middle East peace talks. Two others claimed to have predicted that the plane would crash, including one who suggested that "dreams [predicting crashes] should be reported or something, because who knows it could save a plane or hundreds of people."

I should note that the postings I read comprised only a small portion of the offensive remarks. Many others were removed immediately after posting for violating AOL's Terms of Service, which states that hate speech will be removed.

Those posting messages to the message boards had very definite opinions about each other, referring to each other variously and colorfully as "mutant idiots," "inconsiderate, uneducated, ignorant assholes," "nuts and fruitcakes," "emotionally ill dweebs," "moronic idiots," "retards," "imbeciles," and even one "total fucking embarrassment to Americans, West Virginians, and human beings everywhere." Ah, the joys of civil, AOL-facilitated discussion.

Not all AOL users thought that the message boards were appropriate, especially so soon after a tragic accident. "AOL joins media vultures!" read one subject line; the author went on to opine, "I couldn't believe it just hours later AOL is circling with the rest of the media vultures. Disgusting." Said another, "Must there be a written or spoken reaction to everything? This is so weird—is there anything wrong with just hearing the news for awhile and saying nothing about it—even for an hour? Wow!"

One contributor felt that

> AOL is very irresponsible to encourage this type of behavior by some of the writers, who take every opportunity to insult, degrade, and are apparently finding great humor in such a tragedy. Why have a post of this sort at all? AOL seems to bring out the worst in people. . . . AOL, every time there is a tragedy, you seem to delight in opening up a "talk about it" board, which seems to cause all the dregs of society to crawl out from under their rocks to make stupid, insensitive and often downright evil statements. I have seen this time after time, with celebrities who have died and other tragedies. Do you enjoy encouraging this sort of behavior?

A few others agreed, one writing, "Over a hundred people died, and all you can do is put down others because of their nationality?" Another put it more succinctly: "Talk about computer viruses! None worse than AOL when it comes to 'Speak Out.'"

No one is calling for censorship or the abolition of message boards.

But this example shows just how hollow and worthless such services can be. AOL perpetuates the myth that it is providing a useful, informative service for people to "gather information and share experiences." Much more frequently, however, message boards serve instead as a haven for cruelty, stupidity, racism, and hatred.

America Online, in its advertisements at least, promises its users a forum for meaningful exchange, and fails miserably at its task. The company isn't responsible for what its users post, of course. But what does AOL expect will happen when it puts up a message board within minutes, well before anybody knows anything substantive about an event? In this case, that it would serve as some sort of information clearinghouse for concerned families? If I thought a friend or relative of mine had been on board the plane, the last place I'd look for accurate information is on an AOL message board.

Though the Web was somewhat useful for disseminating news in the week after the September 11, 2001, attacks, many Americans weren't searching for useful information about what to do or how to help. The number one search term was not "Osama bin Laden," "blood donation," or "New York City"; it was "Nostradamus." The searches were in response to a flurry of messages circulated on the Internet claiming the attack had been foreseen by the French astrologer. A dozen or so Nostradamus verses were proffered; some were entirely fictional; others, partly embellished—but not one truly foretold the tragedy. Instead of useful information, many Americans used the Web to spread (and learn about) misinformation and myths.[5]

PARTICIPATING AFTER TERRORISM

In the weeks and months following the September 11 attacks on the Pentagon and World Trade Center, many Americans looked for anything they could do to help out. Millions donated blood or gave money to charities.

Other attempts to participate were just as well intentioned but poorly thought-out. For example, many chain e-mail messages zipped around the Internet asking the recipients to send cards or to light candles. On September 13, 2001, I received the following chain e-mail: "Friday night at 7 P.M. step out your door, stop your car, or step out of your establishment and light a candle. We will show the world that Americans are strong and united together against terrorism." I hate to be cynical about this sort of thing, as I understand the sentiment, but it makes no sense. First of all, how are a bunch of Americans lighting candles going to show the world that Americans are strong? Does it take strength to light a candle? What does that have to do with terrorism?

This sort of fluff patriotism was parodied in the *Weekly World News* on November 27, 2001, when the tabloid suggested a "Freedom Jump" during Monday Night Football on December 3. The idea was that if "Americans jump up and down at the same time it will cause an earthquake on the other side of the world in Afghanistan—flushing terrorists out of their mountain caves." (Says an unnamed MIT physicist, "It's so crazy, it just might work!") It would certainly have no less effect than lighting candles at 7 P.M.

Another chain e-mail, this one circulated in early December 2001, was not only useless but in fact almost certainly counterproductive:

> Let's start a Card Writing Campaign. Go out to your local Hallmark or whereever [*sic*] it is you buy your greeting cards. Buy a card that reflects what your feelings are about the workers heroic efforts and send it to the New York Fire Department. Just think how powerful an influence you might become. Please send this e-mail to everyone you know or copy it and share it with all of your coworkers, friends, and relatives. They need to know that we, the American people, believe in them! Let's start our own miracle. Let's show these brave men and women how we feel about them. DO IT, DO IT, DO IT—Forward this e-mail, send those cards!

Again, I understand and sympathize with the sentiment, but I'm worried it did more harm than good. Here's why: In the months after September 11, individuals (and especially schools) across the country sent literally tons of gifts, teddy bears, flowers, photos, drawings, notes, letters, cookies, gloves, and so on to Ground Zero. Schoolchildren in Texas sent a thousand pairs of gloves; Miami schoolchildren sent twenty-six thousand teddy bears. Hundreds of other schools sent similar contributions.

This is a touching idea, but the workers there couldn't use or even look at all this stuff. The police and firefighters weren't sitting around playing with teddy bears and looking at schoolchildren's letters and drawings; they were busy working hard in dangerous conditions. There were just too many contributions, and resources had to be taken away from the recovery effort to get rid of the tons of gifts, letters, and cards.

Many other items were donated for people left homeless. But hold on: The World Trade Centers were office buildings. Though some people were temporarily displaced, no one was left homeless by the attacks. Everyone who survived the attacks had a home they could return to, clothes they could wear, and so on. What were police and firefighters going to do with thousands of new and used jackets, gloves, and shirts?

The firefighters and police were appreciative, but the misguided efforts turned into a logistical problem. Most of the donations were given to local children's shelters, which is great. But the workers couldn't look at most of what was sent even if they wanted to. Red Cross media director Nancy Retherford said that those sorts of donations were pouring in, and that "[w]e have bags that are as yet untouched in this room because the volunteers have not been able to get through in a day more than what's coming in."[6] This is a case where people's good intentions caused more problems.

The basic truth is that there was very little that the average American could do to help out after the terrorist attack. Many people made trips to Ground Zero but were rejected because their skills simply weren't needed. Unless volunteers were experienced metalworkers or firefighters, or had one of a handful of specialized recovery skills, they were turned away or asked to help in other places.

Even those who generously donated blood didn't end up helping the victims of the attacks. According to the *2002 World Almanac*, a grand total of five people were pulled alive from the World Trade Center rubble.[7] The *Washington Post* reported that the American Red Cross collected hundreds of thousands of blood donations, knowing that the blood could not be used for the victims of the attacks. All the blood Americans donated was not needed; there was easily enough on hand at any local hospital to cover the five victims. Certainly, at the beginning it was unclear how much blood would be needed. But within a few days it was evident that they already had much more blood than they could use. Yet the Red Cross still asked for more blood, still ran commercials asking people to donate.[8]

Though some of the actions taken following the attacks were of dubious value, other responses were appropriate and helpful, in particular those that directly helped victims in need. People's efforts to help also benefited themselves: Researchers found that people who employed "active coping strategies" following the attacks (such as giving blood or attending memorial services) had lower stress levels than those who didn't.[9]

In November 2001 California Governor Gray Davis announced that a terrorist threat had been made against the Golden Gate Bridge. Davis suggested that well-known California bridges might be bombed or attacked in the days or weeks to come. In response, a San Francisco man began a daily four-mile walk across the Golden Gate Bridge while carrying the American flag. He did it, he said, as an act of defiance, a message to terrorists that "you're not going to do that to the Golden Gate Bridge."[10]

The man was right: Terrorists weren't in fact going to attack the bridge. Soon after Davis made his statement, the FBI announced that Davis had been mistaken and that the bridge threat was "not credible." The threat that had sparked such anger and outrage was never real. The man's patriotism is admirable, and I'm sure the exercise did him good, but he was responding to a threat that didn't exist. In early 2003 a more credible threat was made against the Golden Gate Bridge. An anonymous caller allegedly phoned 911 four times on March 10 to say he had placed explosives on the bridge. Police eventually arrested a suspect: not a foreign terrorist but a San Francisco construction worker.[11]

Another way in which Americans acted before thinking was in the distribution of relief funds to the families of the victims. A tremendous outpouring of support followed the attacks, with hundreds of separate funds set up to help those affected. But soon the question came up about who was to get what, and by what criteria. In fact, the distribution of funds hit a snag with the Internal Revenue Service (IRS) in early November 2001. The IRS quite reasonably asked that those who benefit from the public's money be, in fact, poor or distressed. Steven Miller, the director of the IRS division that oversees charitable donations, pointed out in congressional testimony that "merely being present at the scene of a disaster does not establish a need for assistance." As the *New York Times* reported:

> The I.R.S. typically requires tax-exempt charities like the Twin Towers Fund to serve people who are in dire financial need: those who are struggling to afford mortgages, grocery bills, and other basic necessities. Yet many of the families of the lost police officers and firefighters have already received tens of thousands of dollars in charity and all have considerable pension and death benefits. In certain cases, their family income is actually higher than it was before Sept. 11.[12]

Many people contributed to a Twin Towers Orphan fund, which was set up to help children left orphans by the attacks. The *New York Times* said that thousands of children were left without parents; on National Public Radio Sen. Hillary Rodham Clinton set the number at closer to ten thousand. Fortunately, though, there were in fact *no* children left orphans by the attacks. Nina Bernstein of the *New York Times* writes that there is "not a single child who needs foster care or adoption by strangers. Not a single documented case of a child who lost both parents."[13] These children certainly need care, but that is a far cry from the image that most people have of orphans. The money that was donated to help children left without a parent might have been better spent helping others in need. Or, as Bernstein points out, those who have offered to adopt the mythical orphans might do more good by taking in some of the thousands of *real* children in state custody whose parents have lost the right to keep them.

TESTIMONIAL JOURNALISM

With the growing popularity of Internet message boards, it was just a matter of time before "news" articles were written with material largely culled from Internet respondents. A good example of this pseudojournalism is a piece by Eileen Livers that appeared on iVillage on May 5, 2000, titled "Boys Do Cry." The article discussed why and how men show emotion. It is filled with phrases like, "As iVillager Tabitha puts it, 'men who cry are brave . . .'" and "iVillager Lana is onto something. . . ."[14] This quasi-anonymous forum allows just about anyone to say just about anything. In this milieu, facts are irrelevant, with personal opinion and whim the coin of the realm.

There's nothing inherently wrong about writing an article on Internet participants' opinions on certain topics. But it's also a bit disingenuous to call it journalism. There are few facts to be checked; much of the text is written by and about everyday people who might or might not know what they are talking about. Most of the information in the piece is correct because it is inviolable opinion, and, as we have seen, opinion need have no basis in reality. If (fictional) iVillager Betty says that "most men cry all the time in public," that's certainly her opinion, presumably worthy of being quoted, and no more or less valid than anyone else's. The sources could be lying about anything, even their names, and/or fabricating their accounts.

Contrast this to mainstream journalism, which, by its very nature, deals with supposedly verifiable facts and interviews with knowledgeable sources. Even the results of opinion polls (of which this sort of story is a variant) are necessarily grounded in reality: Either the claimed number of people expressed certain opinions or they didn't. Methodologies can be examined and questioned; pollsters' biases can be uncovered—but the inherent difference is that between testimonials and science.

It is exactly this sort of "testimonial journalism" that runs along a slippery slope and lends itself to fabrication. This allegedly happened in the case of Julie Amparano, a columnist dismissed by the *Arizona Republic* newspaper in August 1999. Amparano wrote a column titled "Conversations," which ran three times a week in the Life section. The column featured interviews with average people, expressing their concerns and highlighting their achievements. *Republic* editors tried to trace some of the people Amparano quoted, finally concluding that "we can't find them or prove they exist. Nor has Amparano been able to substantiate those sources to date."[15]

But just because you're telling one person's opinion, experience, or tragedy is no excuse to spin tales, make up quotes, embellish stories, and tell lies. The readers have a right to expect that the columnists and writers whose work they read and admire are not passing off fiction as truth. Writers who feel the need to do so should put a disclaimer at the beginning of each piece, warning the reader that what they read may or may not be accurate, depending on how much effort the writer felt like putting in that week.

Other cases of fabricated journalism have come to light, including fictional articles and letters to advice columnists in teen and women's magazines. The June/July 1995 issue of *YM: Young and Modern*, for example, ran a letter to "Love Crisis" advice columnist Sally Lee from "Mortified," a young woman who, she said, "got trashed and had sex with three guys." The only problem was, there was no "Mortified"; the letter was a fake. The reason it came to light was that the young model whose photo accompanied the letter sued the magazine for violating her privacy rights by implying that she was "Mortified."[16] *Cosmopolitan* magazine ran an article in the "His Point of View" column titled "Why Watching a Sex Flick with My Girlfriend Is Good." Freelance writer Christopher Hunt took the assignment, wrote it up, and turned it in to the editors. When he got his piece back, it had been rewritten by several editors—not just edited but spiced up, and with fictional elements put into it. The piece had turned from a nonfiction account into a heavily fictionalized one without the author's consent or knowledge. Hunt eventually had his name removed, and the piece ran under the pen name "Ben Edison."[17]

OTHER ILLUSIONS OF INFLUENCE

E-movements

E-mail petitions, which make many citizens feel that they are influencing others, are generally worthless and disregarded. This is because anyone with a modicum of computer programming experience can easily generate lists of e-mail addresses to affix to cyberpetitions. Those who receive such petitions know that, and thus the petitions hold very little weight or credibility. Some e-petitions actually endanger the person or group they are designed to help. In early 2003 an e-mailed petition from the human rights group Amnesty International circulated on behalf of a Nigerian woman who was sentenced to death by stoning for having a child out of wedlock. Recipients were asked to add their names to the list and forward the petition to others, presumably to be presented to the Nigerian Supreme Court in an appeal for clemency. The e-mail was widely circulated, drawing protests from across the globe.

Unfortunately, the efforts were in vain; much of the inflammatory information in the e-mail was incorrect. The Amnesty International logo had been forged, and the group said it had nothing to do with the e-mail campaign. Nigerian advocates for the woman issued a request to stop the petition, saying that the efforts were in fact doing far more harm than good: "The information currently circulated is inaccurate, and the situation in Nigeria . . . will not be helped by such campaigns." Ndidi Ekekwe, a program officer for the Nigerian advocacy group, cautioned e-mail petition recipients that "before anyone signs anything, they should take the extra step of confirming the facts, because it could just do more harm."[18]

Well-intentioned Westerners with little grasp of the facts can in this way express their moral indignation with a few keystrokes and congratulate themselves on their humanitarian efforts. Meanwhile, the problems remain unaddressed—and sometimes are made worse. In this way the Internet provides its Netizens only the illusion of influence.

In late 1999 America Online created the "AOL.com PACT to Stop Violence." The introduction stated:

> Since the tragedy at Columbine High School, AOL's chat rooms, message boards and polls have reflected sadness, as well as a determination to make a difference. The recent school shooting in Georgia had made all of us even more concerned about violence in our schools and communities. After hearing from families and educators who want to stop the violence we worked with experts to create PACT (Parents And Children Together).

It went on to request that the reader take the pledge, and offered three sets of pledges, one each for adults (sample: "I will talk with my children and listen to the issues they think are important . . . ," "I will get more involved in my community and our schools."); teenagers ("I will not put other kids down by labeling them with names . . . ," "I understand that violence is real and has permanent consequences . . . "); and kids ("I understand that not all kids are the same . . . ," "I will look for ways to settle disagreements without violence.")

The PACT stated that (as of April 2001) 272,565 people had signed, including Britney Spears, the band Hootie and the Blowfish, and Steve Case, chairman and CEO of AOL. Aside from sleeping better at night knowing that Britney Spears pledged that she understands that violence is real and that the chairman of AOL will keep his guns locked up, I'm not sure that the PACT had much impact. It was a "let's-all-pretend-to-make-a-difference" quick-fix, fast and easy to sign—and just as easy to forget.

Furthermore, the PACT's very raison d'être was flawed: violence both generally and in schools has not been increasing but rather dropping for many years. Whether AOL as a company is "concerned about violence" or not is irrelevant; what's relevant is that a spate of blemishes on an otherwise very good safety history does not constitute a crisis.

"But," one might say, "whether violence is truly on the rise or not, kids are scared, and that's enough reason to do something." But that's simply not true: Kids themselves aren't anywhere near as scared as adults expect them to be. A few weeks after the Columbine High shootings, pollsters Penn, Schoen & Berland Associates polled 1,172 kids ages six to fourteen, in twenty-five cities across America. When asked how safe they feel in their schools, 93 percent said they feel "pretty safe" or "very safe." While parents felt that crime, youth violence, and peer pressure were the worst things about being a kid, the kids themselves felt that getting bossed around at school and homework were their biggest problems.[19]

It appears that amid all the scary headlines, worrywarts, and hand wringing, people forgot to listen to the kids. What was that pledge in the PACT about "I will talk with my children . . . and listen to the issues they think are important"? Apparently the parents only want to hear it if it's bad news and confirms their fears. The AOL.com PACT typifies the illusion of influence. The PACT eventually fizzled out and, as of October 2002, its Web site was inactive.

Schoolchildren Buying Slaves

Actions fueled by good intentions but blinded by emotion and ignorance are easy to find. One example is a class of fourth-graders at Hughline Elementary School in Aurora, Colorado. The children held fund-raisers and saved their lunch money to buy slaves.

This effort was suggested by their teacher, Barbara Vogel, and eventually the group raised more than $50,000. The idea came about during a discussion of slavery, when children were shocked to learn that an active slave trade still existed in some parts of the world.

The money was funneled to a group called Christian Solidarity International (CSI), which actually does the hands-on work of going to Sudan to purchase slaves. After the slaves are paid for, they are given a medical check and returned home. The Arab slave traders, known as *murahaleen,* frequently take slaves in raids conducted in southern Sudan. CSI pays about fifty dollars per slave, some of the money coming from schoolchildren's fund-raisers. The number of slaves CSI claims to have emancipated since 1995 varies widely, from eight hundred to sixty thousand.

Apparently the idea of encouraging fourth-graders to buy other human beings sat well with others, because eventually at least one hundred schools around the country had joined the effort, auctioning off art, selling candy, and holding fund-raising car washes and bake sales.

The effort to end slavery by purchasing slaves met with criticism from many groups, including UNICEF, which pointed out that the payments only encourage more slavery. The freed slaves usually aren't monitored after their release, so there is little guarantee that the slaves won't simply be recaptured and enslaved again. Said Jemera Rone of Human Rights Watch, "Even fifty dollars a head is a lot of money in Sudan—if you talk about 1,000 heads, that's a lot of bucks. . . . You have to assume this kind of money will attract people who are profit-motivated. It will cause more raiding."[20]

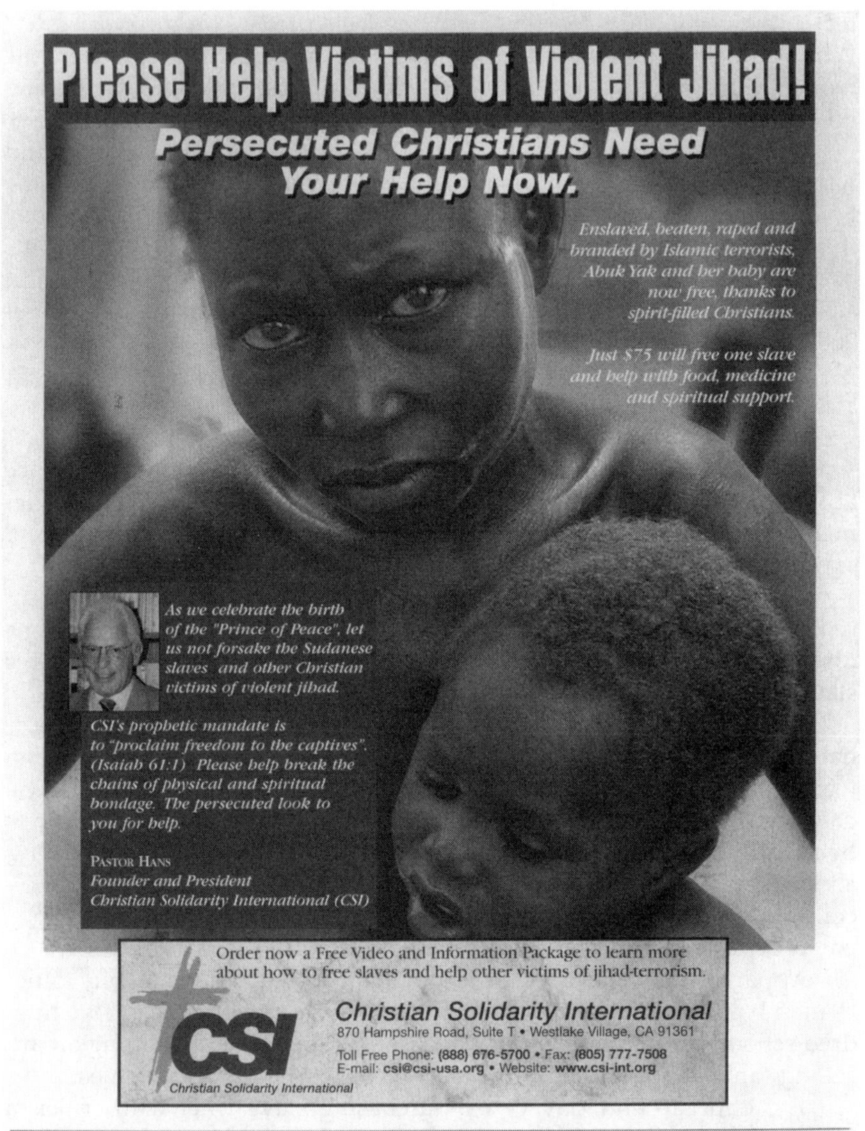

An advertisement for Christian Solidarity International, a group that has received money from American schoolchildren to buy slaves.

CSI's American branch split away in 1998 and changed its name to Christian Freedom International. James Jacobson, former head of the American branch, visited Sudan and found evidence of massive corruption in the program. Free children were pretending to be slaves to attract Western donations, and a Reuters reporter interviewed one boy who spun a completely implausible story of his life in the north, then abruptly changed his story when translators were swapped. Jacobson now believes that the effort is flawed, has abandoned the effort to buy slaves, and has returned donors' money. As he explained to Reuters, "It has turned into a circus. The problem now is that Western dollars are making the situation worse, both in terms of abductions and in terms of corruption."[21]

According to a *Washington Post* article, aid workers and human rights monitors confirm that the practice of buying slaves is rife with corruption:

> Insiders say that . . . officials have pocketed money paid to buy captives' freedom and in some cases stage-manage the transactions, passing off free southerners as slaves. . . . [I]n some cases, according to witnesses and rebel officials, the slaves weren't slaves at all but people gathered locally and instructed to pretend they were returning from bondage.

This not only fuels more slaving but artificially inflates the price that the families of actual slave children must pay for the return of their loved ones. Making it all the more tragic, it is American children who are helping perpetuate the slavery and misery, manipulated by uninformed and misguided teachers and activists. Asks Samson Kwaje, a Sudanese rebel spokesman, "The money comes from those American kids, [but] who gets the check?"[22]

In June 1999 the United Nations withheld the accreditation of Christian Solidarity International because the group let a rebel Sudanese leader speak on his own behalf at a conference, in violation of UN rules.[23]

Buying slaves to set them free is like buying drugs only to burn them: it benefits the seller, encourages the practice, and does nothing to address the underlying causes of the problem. On an emotional, visceral level, and at first glance, the idea might seem like a good one. Seeing images of sad, chained black children being given food and set free is moving and inspiring. One can understand why such a simplistic and misguided solution might have appeal for a classroom of fourth-graders. But for adults and teachers to promote the slave trade under the aegis of ending it demonstrates a profound and tragic misunderstanding of the nature of the problem.

The Phantom Slave Ship

An international crisis arose in April 2001, when stories came out of Cotonou, Benin, that a Nigerian ship carrying hundreds of child slaves was lost at sea. The children, the stories said, were on a rusting and decrepit hulk that lacked fresh food and water and was bound for slave work on cocoa plantations. Nicolas Pron, a program manager of UNICEF in Benin, announced that his organization was "concerned about the health, nutrition, and psychological welfare of these children. . . . They are very likely in unsanitary circumstances. We don't know about food. We don't know about water." Esther Guluma, another UNICEF official, added that they were "quite worried because from what we know of the condition of the boat, it is not seaworthy."

The story made nightly news broadcasts around the world, and alarmed politicians, journalists, and aid workers scrambled to rescue the poor children. The National Association for the Advancement of Colored People issued a statement praising the international efforts to find the ship and urging President Bush and the UN to "take every step to return these children to normal lives and punish those responsible for this horrific traffic in human life." For several days the fate of the ship was unclear: Had it sunk? Had it returned to ports in Cameroon or Gabon? Government authorities said they did not have the resources to search for the missing ship, and appealed for help from Britain and France, both of which had navy ships in the area.

Finally, the dangerous slave ship docked in Cotonou port on Monday, April 16. Relief workers rushed to the ship to rescue the malnourished slave children. Instead of a ramshackle boat in danger of sinking, they found a clean ferry in good condition, with a fresh coat of paint and adequate drinking water. Where were the hundreds of slaves? Douglas Farah of the *Washington Post* Foreign Service explained, "There were perhaps a dozen teenagers on board who were not on the ship's passenger manifest and were called unaccompanied minors, sources said, but the young men were in good health and apparently were job hunters, not slaves."[24]

Refusing to believe that the ship didn't hold slaves, rumors—some started or repeated by Pron of UNICEF—circulated that the captain may have drowned the children while at sea (the passengers and crew on board denied this), or that a second, unknown mystery ship was really the slave ship and was still to be found (no evidence of a second ship ever appeared). In a classic example of rumormongering, the story apparently changed from a (mistaken) consul report claiming that the ship was in poor condition; to a story of a few children on board the rusting boat; to an account of hundreds of slave children on a dangerous ship without water. It was not even clear who introduced the slavery element into the story.

The panicked reports by Beninese officials, UNICEF, and relief organizations were wrong in almost every respect. Embarrassed and discredited officials put the best spin they could on the events. Said one, "This appears to be a fiasco, but if it brings attention to a very real problem then it is not a bad thing." There is no doubt that modern slavery exists throughout the world, including child slavery in West Africa. But crying wolf with bad information is ultimately counterproductive, and misinformation and lies in the service of truth are still lies.

In many cases it appears that some children in West Africa may be in more danger from the aid workers themselves than child slavers. In 2001, refugee children in Liberia, Guinea, and Sierra Leone accused dozens of relief workers of exploiting and sexually abusing them. In some cases, girls reported being forced to give sexual favors in return for food, shelter, or medicine. One refugee in Freetown, Liberia, reported that "the secretary-general of our camp once told me that if I did not make love to him or give him one of my seven girls . . . they would not supply us with food." Said another refugee, "If you do not have a wife or daughter to offer . . . it is hard to have access to aid."[25] The allegations of widespread abuse name more than forty well-established relief agencies and nongovernmental aid organizations, according to the United Nations high commissioner for refugees. Paul Nolan, child protection manager for the aid group Save the Children, said the investigation uncovered "possibly endemic" abuse, and that "there is a serious problem of child exploitation."[26]

Relatively few journalists bother to write more than a superficial treatment of the issues involving modern African slavery. One of the few who did, Norimitsu Onishi of the *New York Times* Service, wrote on African boys working in the Ivory Coast. Trying to verify information circulated by the Western news media that thousands of foreign children (UNICEF estimated fifteen thousand) worked in slave conditions on cocoa plantations, Onishi went to look for himself. During a weeklong investigation he found only a handful of working children, not the hundreds or thousands claimed in news reports: "The discovery of just a few foreign children during visits to dozens of plantations suggests that children who are smuggled by a stranger for profit do not make up a significant share of the cocoa force here." Onishi points out that "child labor retains deep roots in Africa but it is hard to measure, and the line between slave trading and the bondage of poverty is sometimes unclear. . . . Much of the confusion stems from the working conditions here. Backbreaking work for 50 cents a day is part of everyday life in much of Africa. Indeed, that wage puts plantation workers at a very low rung, but hardly at the bottom rung, of the ladder in Africa."[27]

Onishi describes the problem of child labor in its context, instead of from a patronizing Western point of view. The issues and causes are complex and do not lend themselves to short sound bites demonizing landowners as inhuman and parents (willing to send children to work) as greedy and uncaring.

Meanwhile, those looking to find children in slavelike conditions need not look as far as Africa; a five-month Associated Press investigation in 1997 found nearly three hundred thousand children working illegally in the United States, many in dangerous jobs in poor conditions. In many states, children as young as twelve or thirteen work long hours farming, one of the most dangerous occupations. Many of those worst off work in fields that produce America's food. Reporters found children as young as six in fields picking crops in many states, including New Mexico, Michigan, Tennessee, Texas, California, and Pennsylvania. Underage workers were found in farms that supply such major food and restaurant companies as H. J. Heinz, Campbell Soup Company, and Chi-Chi's, a Mexican food chain. According to the National Institute for Occupational Safety and Health, at least 40 percent of children killed on the job are doing work prohibited by federal child labor laws. And the agency in charge of enforcing child labor laws, the U.S. Department of Labor, rarely tracks, prosecutes, or fines those who exploit child laborers.[28]

Faulty Famine Relief Efforts

Year-round, but particularly during the holiday season, charities hit the airwaves and newspapers asking for a few dollars a month to feed and clothe "Rosa" or "Miguel," a wide-eyed, hungry child dressed in rags in a Third World country. The images are heart-tugging—and counterproductive.

Philanthropy experts warn that such campaigns mislead donors by suggesting that the way to end hunger is to hand food out to starving children rather than fund development projects. Kathleen McCarthy of the Center for the Study of Philanthropy points out that the problem with focusing on a single child is that "all you're doing is taking care of the symptoms. Generally, what is needed is a better sewage system, a well, maternal and child health programs." Stacey Mihaly of Childreach (formerly Foster Parents Plan) agrees: "What we have found, and this has been substantiated by government organizations . . . is the best way to help people is through more of an empowerment model, working with communities so they are active participants in lifting themselves out of poverty."[29]

The problem is that donors give money out of an emotional connection to photos of a sad-eyed girl, but have no emotional connection to a deeper community well or a new bridge. The money given to clothe one girl could be better spent toward building a water treatment system, perhaps saving several hundred lives. Diarrhea is the primary killer of children in developing countries, and potable water is essential for preventing it. Once again emotions lead us away from what's best.

The struggle to alleviate African famines in Sudan, Ethiopia, and Somalia captured American hearts and opened our pocketbooks in the 1980s. Fundraising events such as U.S.A. for Africa and Live Aid in 1984 raised over $50 million for famine relief. The hit single by Band Aid, "Do They Know It's Christmas?" raised millions (though the Eurocentrism of such a "global" song was lost on many—Sudan and Somalia are overwhelmingly Muslim countries, and don't celebrate Christmas anyway).

Yet, as with the slavery problem, most Americans poorly understand the famine situation. The widely held, simplistic view is that all we need to do is buy lots of food, load it onto planes, and hand it out to the needy. But the causes of famine are much more complex than that, and the difficulty is more of a political problem than an agricultural one. For the most part, the problem is not that there is no food available for the starving; instead, local infighting and petty warlords stem the flow of readily available food. The route between the airport or dock and those in need may pass through several towns or territories, each controlled by local chieftains wanting to know what's in it for them to allow the food through.

Don't think of it as charity. Think of it as hope for one little child.

Like so many deprived children in Kenya, little Buchi depends on the kindness of others.

You can sponsor Buchi or a child like her through Children, Inc. Just $24 a month will help provide food, clothing, school and health needs. And we'll send you a picture, story and address.

Please contact us soon. Because hope can work miracles in a child's life.

Write to: Mrs. Jeanne Clarke Wood, Children, Inc., P.O. Box 5381, Dept. NG9B2, Richmond, VA 23220 USA
www.children-inc.org

- ❑ I wish to sponsor a ❑ boy, ❑ girl, in ❑ USA, ❑ Latin America, ❑ Middle East, ❑ Africa, ❑ Asia, ❑ Greatest need.
- ❑ I will give $24 a month ($288 a year). Enclosed is my gift for a full year ❑, the first month ❑. Please send me the child's name, story, address and picture.
- ❑ I can't sponsor, but I will help $______.

Name

Address

City

State Zip

❑ Check ❑ American Express ❑ Visa ❑ MasterCard

Card No. Expiration Date

Signature

1-800-538-5381

CHILDREN, INC.

Serving Needy Children Since 1964

U.S. gifts are fully tax deductible. Annual financial statements are available on request.

Most aid organization advertising focuses on helping "one little child."

Frequently supplies, medicine, and food must be tithed to these warlords (and/or the military) to assure safe passage. Theft and banditry are common problems as well, with tribal and ethnic rivalries compounding the difficulties.

Efforts to simply buy food and ship it off (images the public at large likes to see) are well intentioned but grossly inefficient. What little success such quick fixes provide are short lived, as they do not address the root of the famines. When the television news cameras pack up and the story is over, the food shipments fall back to a trickle and the cycle starts anew.

According to Kevin Toolis of London's *Guardian*:

> When Clare Short, Britain's international development secretary, criticized [an appeal for money to save starving children] as unnecessary and misleading, stressing that the cause of the famine was war, not drought, she was howled down by outraged members of Parliament and bewildered aid agencies. . . . But the history of recent disaster emergencies such as those in Somalia, Rwanda, and now Sudan proves that the aid world's simplistic mantras are very far from the truth.

Toolis sums up the paradox of aid in Sudan:

> The aid agencies are the silent allies of the principal aggressor and, to guarantee access to that same aggressor's victims, are prepared to make a pact with the Sudanese devil. In order to aid the poor, the international community must also feed [the government's] besieged garrisons in the south of the country—garrisons that would have fallen years ago without World Food program aid.[30]

Tajudeen Abdul-Raheem, the general secretary of the Pan-African Movement based in Uganda, had this to say about nongovernmental aid organizations (NGOs):

> The first problem with NGOs is that they have become sacred cows that cannot be touched. Anyone who wishes to criticize Western NGOs is likely to meet with accusations of ingratitude, churlishness, inhuman cynicism, or lack of sympathy for the victims of disasters. . . . No doubt many are involved in the charity business out of moral and political commitment. But it is also true that there are many who are doing it only for career purposes. Our misery is their job. If you are a disaster manager, what will you do if there are no more disasters? This is particularly true when more and more NGO money is going into emergency operations rather than long-term development work.[31]

Christina Neal, a geologist at the Office of Foreign Disaster Assistance at the U.S. Agency for International Development (AID), believes that the deeply flawed approach to aid that has been dogma for decades is slowly being revised. "I think at AID there has been a learning process and a cultural shift in the past few years that mitigation is increasingly the important way to approach problems and that by running in after an earthquake or merely saving bodies and providing first aid, we don't do anything for the long-term problem."[32]

Ironically, even the more direct methods of relief intervention may end up exacerbating the problem. On a 1996 flight to Khartoum, the capital of Sudan, I was seated next to a young relief worker who described the work she was doing in remote villages. She told of extraordinary efforts she and others made to stem the high infant mortality rate. It was a struggle, she said, to get anything done among the byzantine regulations, poor communication, local corruption and infighting, and low supplies.

While I commended her efforts, it also occurred to me that every baby she saved from death would need more and more food as it matured, thus indirectly perpetuating the famines. More mouths to feed do not help in the long run, and in fact might lead to more deaths. What good does it do to save a baby from starvation if it dies as an adolescent, after taking food from the living? She acknowledged the problem, agreed, and shrugged, saying she could only do her part.

The AIDS situation in Africa is another example. AIDS and HIV infection has been at crisis levels for years; in Zimbabwe, the National AIDS Coordination Program estimates that between one in four and one in five people carries the virus. Although foreign aid has helped to provide free condoms, education programs, and other anti-AIDS measures, one of the main obstacles is the Africans themselves. Despite widespread AIDS education programs, AIDS continues to ravage the continent.

AIDS is not transmitted through casual contact, but primarily through sexual activity. This is, of course, a behavior, and changing sexual behavior is the hardest part of the struggle against AIDS. Prostitution and infidelity are rampant, and women are hesitant to suggest their partners use condoms. Folk beliefs also help spread the disease: Many men are said to believe that having sex with a virgin can cure them of AIDS. Says one African woman of the epidemic, "We are taking too long to change our behavior. We are still under a lot of denial."[33] No amount of foreign aid will force Africans to practice safe sex; it is a cultural and social problem, and one that is virtually immune to a financial solution.

Clearly, efforts to relieve famine and AIDS in Africa should not be stopped; instead solutions should take the larger, long-term, complex picture into account. Knee-jerk, emotional quick-fixes will only make the problems worse. And, once again, most public relief efforts are better at giving the *illusion* that the problem is being addressed than actually making real, lasting improvements. They perpetuate the myth that famines are sporadic and solved by sending food, when in fact famine has been endemic in northeast Africa for centuries. Many people are moved to contribute when they see news footage of sacks of grain being given out. However, more useful efforts to end famine may be made in a laboratory to grow hardier or more nutritious grains or through political means.

THE *EXXON VALDEZ* SPILL

Following the 1989 *Exxon Valdez* oil spill in Alaska, wildlife rehabilitation experts were flown into Prince William Sound to clean the oil-coated sea otters and seabirds. Volunteers arrived to join the effort, and donations were sought and accepted for the cleanup. Much of the resources (and attention) were devoted to cleaning the oiled animals. However, as Karen Schmidt wrote in *New Scientist* magazine, the efforts were notable more for their public relations value than actual effect:

> After the Exxon Valdez oil spill in 1989, 357 sea otters were brought in for treatment, and 197 were returned to Alaskan waters. Each survivor cost Exxon more than $82,000. But radio-tracking studies of 45 of the released otters found that, eight months later, 12 were dead and nine were missing. Around 1,600 sea birds were also captured and treated. Half of them were returned to the sea at a cost of nearly $32,000 per bird. After assessing that effort, the Pacific Seabird Group of Stinson Beach, California, concluded that rehabilitation is generally labor-intensive, costly, and has a low probability of success.[34]

Certainly, most people have no problem with Exxon footing the bill for cleaning up the mess they made. But the money spent on cleaning animals that are likely to die soon anyway could have been spent to design additional safety systems, invest in oil containment research, or pay for additional EPA personnel. Yet the public prefer the hands-on, emotionally satisfying method of rehabilitating individual birds, though in the long run such a method may cost more, both in animal lives and in dollars. Schmidt notes the emotional appeal: "Tighter regulations on the shipping industry, stiffer enforcement of laws to prohibit dumping, and campaigns to reduce the public's appetite for petroleum products would probably never be as popular as caring for oiled wildlife."[35]

Once again, the public is provided the illusion of progress and effectiveness. According to biologist Dee Boersma of the University of Washington, "Washing birds gives people the impression that we can mitigate oil spills, that we can fix the damage. That's a very insidious view because people think if we just wash more birds or do it better, we could solve the problem."[36]

NOTES

1. David Shenk, *Data Smog* (New York: HarperCollins, 1997), p. 125.
2. Vincent Ryan Ruggerio, *Beyond Feelings: A Guide to Critical Thinking* (New York: Mayfield Publishers, 1998), p. 35.
3. Virginia Postrel, "Clueless," *Reason* (March 1996): 4.
4. Survey by John Cronin and Alan Almquist, cited in David Shenk, *Data Smog* (New York: HarperCollins, 1997), p. 138.
5. "Web Search Activity Indicates Pop Culture Has Not Changed Since September 11," Terra Lycos, Inc., press release, September 5, 2002.
6. Michael James, "Return to Normalcy" ABC News [online], abcnews.go.com/sections/living/DailyNews/wtc_schools011004.html [October 5, 2001].
7. "Facts about the Sept. 11 Attack," *World Almanac 2002* (New York: World Almanac Books, 2001), p. 35.
8. Raymond Hernandez, "Getting Too Much of a Good Thing," *New York Times*, November 12, 2001.
9. Roxane Cohen Silver et al., "Nationwide Longitudinal Study of Psychological Responses to September 11," *Journal of the American Medical Association* 288, no. 10 (September 11, 2002).
10. "Flag Man Waves Goodbye," *San Francisco Examiner* [online], www.examiner.com/examiner_ga/default.jsp?story=n.QA.0704W [July 4, 2002].
11. Stacy Finz, "S.F. Bomb Hoax Suspect Gives Himself Up," San Franciso Chronicle [online], sfgate.com/cgi-bin/article.cgi?f=c/a/2003/04/02/BA291831.DTL [April 2, 2003].
12. Diana Henriques and David Barstow, "Victims' Funds May Violate U.S. Tax Law," *New York Time*s, November 12, 2001.
13. Nina Bernstein, "Thousands of Orphans? An Urban Myth," *New York Times*, October 26, 2001.
14. Eileen Livers, "Boys Do Cry," iVillage [online], www.ivillage.com/relationships/features/membersolutions/articles/0,189190_66624,00.html [October 9, 2001].
15. Joe Strupp, "Amparano Fired from *Arizona Republic* for Fake Sources" [online], www.unc.edu/~haman/ariz.html [August 26, 1999].
16. Rachel Taylor, "Signed, Whoever," *Brill's Content* (July/August 1998): 71.
17. Katherine Rosman, "The Secret of Her Success," *Brill's Content* (November 1998): 105.
18. Somini Sengupta, "When Do-Gooders Don't Know What They're Doing," *New York Times*, May 11, 2003, p. WK3.
19. Claudia Wallis, "The Kids Are Alright," *Time* [online], www.time.com/time/archive/preview/from_redirect/0,10987,1101990705-27434,00.html [July 5, 1999].

20. Simon Denyer, "Aid Group Tries to Break Sudan Slavery Chain," Reuters [online], www.vitrade.com/slave_trial/990712_csi_reuters_eibner.htm [July 12, 1999].

21. Ibid.

22. Karl Vick, "Ripping Off Slave 'Redeemers,'" *Washington Post*, February 26, 2002, p. A1.

23. Nicole Winfield, "Anti-Slavery Group May Lose Support," Associated Press [online], wire.ap.org [June 18, 1999]; Leslie Miller, "U.S. Group That Purchases the Freedom of Slaves in Northern Africa Attracts Criticism," *Buffalo News*, May 30, 1999, p. A-7.

24. Douglas Farah, "Officials Probe 'Inflated' Slave Ship Report," *Washington Post* [online], www.washingtonpost.com/ac2/wp-dyn?pagename=article& node =contentId=A28049-2001Apri17 [April 18, 2001].

25. Quoted in Sarah Coleman, "Sex-for-Food Scandal," *World Press Review* (May 2002): 29.

26. "Aid Workers Accused of Child Sex Abuse," Associated Press [online], www.sexcriminals.com/news/12281 [February 27, 2002].

27. Norimitsu Onishi, "African Boys Are Lured to Toil on Ivory Coast's Cocoa Plantations," *International Herald Tribune*, July 30, 2001, p. 2.

28. David Foster and Farrell Kramer, "Underage Kids Still Toil in U.S.," *San Francisco Examiner*, December 14, 1997, p. A-20; Christopher Sullivan, "Many Kids Killed Each Year Trying to Do Grown-Up Jobs," *Albuquerque Journal*, December 28, 1997, p. B-9; David Foster and Farrell Kramer, "Thousands Slave in America's Secret World of Child Labor," *Albuquerque Journal*, December 21, 1997, p. B-1; Verena Dobnik and Ted Anthony, "All Work and No Play . . ." *Albuquerque Journal*, December 21, 1997, p. B-12; Martha Mendoza, "Agency Lax on Enforcing Tough Child Labor Laws," *Albuquerque Journal*, December 23, 1997, p. A-1.

29. Julia Lieblich, "Images of Starving Kids Raise Ethical Issues," *Albuquerque Journal*, December 6, 1997.

30. Kevin Toolis, "Feeding the War in Sudan," *Guardian*, reprinted in *World Press Review* (December 1998): 40.

31. Tajudeen Abdul-Raheem, "Impact of Angels" [online] www.peace.ca/afimpactangels.htm [August 2000].

32. Marguerite Holloway, "The Killing Lakes," *Scientific American* (July 2000): 98.

33. Carol Ezzell, "Care for a Dying Continent," *Scientific American* (May 2000): 104.

34. Karen Schmidt, "Saving Face—Not Birds," *World Press Review* (August 1997): 41.

35. Ibid.

36. Ibid.

5

TEARS IN THE CAMERA EYE

For many people, the public airing of anguish and pain (such as the deluge that followed Princess Diana's death in 1997) may help them feel part of a larger whole. Yet given the media's predeliction for overkill coverage of tragedy, it is a fair question to ask just how genuine the elicited emotions really are.

Is it really in the public's interest when the news media manipulate their audiences, push their buttons, and jerk their tears? There was something slick and hollow about seeing huge crowds reduced to tears during the idealized, manipulative, sappy "tributes" to Princess Diana. They were filled with sad music and slow motion replays of her shy smiles, intercut with plenty of shots of grieving adorers. No one expects an objective, detached funeral, especially for a person as universally regarded as Princess Diana. But hours and days and weeks of emotional gush serves no one. A loss of life is a tragedy regardless of how well photographed and documented that life is. Did all the slick manipulation truly serve a purpose? If the saturation news coverage of Diana's funeral allowed an additional half billion people around the world to feel even worse about Diana's death, is that some sort of achievement in journalism or public service?

The death of John F. Kennedy Jr. a few years later had many of the same hallmarks. Many people spoke of their feelings of loss. Yet I suspect that most of the people who were so broken up hadn't given JFK Jr. a second thought when he was alive. Before Kennedy died, most of his notoriety centered around his magazine, *George*, and his status as "America's most eligible bachelor" and "the sexist man alive"; after he died, he became "America's son," as Garrison Keillor wrote in an article in *Time* titled, "Goodbye to Our Boy." To America he was, in effect, whatever myth the media wanted him to be for their purposes.

Relatively few people met either Princess Diana or John F. Kennedy Jr. They traveled in circles with the rich and famous, and though both were lauded for their work with us common folk, the truth is that most of their time was spent in pursuits that fit in with their well-off lifestyles. There's nothing wrong with that, but it does point up the apparent contradiction of masses of people brought to tears for people they'd never met and had heard of only casually, peripherally, and through the media. Most wept not for John Kennedy Jr. himself (who they didn't know), but for the loss of the media's image of him—whichever image they liked best.

As one critic noted,

> This sort of false intimacy isn't new. . . . It's natural and in most ways harmless to identify with the famous. But today's combination of busy lives, fragmented families and saturation media coverage of celebrities means this is the only intimacy many of us experience outside our immediate family. And that's unhealthy, because these celebrity relationships are not two-way.[1]

Part of the reason for the excessive attention is that both Diana and Kennedy were mythologized. Diana's was the original real-life "fairy-tale wedding," and millions were smitten with the continuing marital (and extramarital) saga of Diana and Prince Charles. JFK Jr., of course, drew on the Kennedy tragedy and Camelot mythos and traditions, well told and repeated (as any good mythology is) in the press for decades.

In this sense as well the grief and loss that millions felt were somewhat manufactured; the media created the stories for the public, modern-day epic tales of power, true love, money, beauty, and tragedy. When the bubbles burst, the media gleefully covered that as well. The public played their role through the outpouring of grief, much of it scripted and staged by the media.

Former *Baltimore Sun* columnist Roger Simon, for his part, refused to participate in the grief hysteria: "I refuse to be part of this mania of making people bigger in death than they were in life. That does not honor people; that diminishes them. The nation truly mourned the death of John F. Kennedy in a way that it is not going to mourn the death of his son."[2]

The parade of manufactured feelings was seen ad nauseum after Diana's and JFK Jr.'s deaths. As one commentator put it at the time, "Most of the Diana grief . . . wasn't the personal grief we feel when something bad happens to ourselves or someone we know or love. This was 'event' grief, in which emotion is the glue that fastens people to an event played out in the papers or on television. Emotions of this sort hardly count as feelings at all; they're a form of participation. They're like screams at a pop concert, which don't signify love or even admiration but just exuberance at being part of the show."[3]

James Poniewozik, in an essay published in *Time* magazine, describes one process by which heroes are shoehorned into convenient and popular myths. He discusses a book by Jere Longman, titled *Among the Heroes,* about the heroes of the September 11, 2001, attacks.

Regarding Todd Beamer and the driven, rebellious passengers of Flight 93, "Longman describes the passengers as if they were job candidates. They were 'self-directed, independent thinkers,' he writes, 'people who could assess a situation and work in teams.' . . . Longman is explaining these heroes using the terms by which the world measured them."

Poniewozik catches Longman doing some mythmaking of his own: "Of course you're going to find Type A, goal-oriented people flying cross-country on an 8 A.M. Tuesday flight. But what's to say that a planeload of weekend vacationers wouldn't have fought for their lives too?"

This mythmaking, Poniewozik points out, is in service of trying to reconcile a paradox that became apparent in the post-attack soul searching:

> Since Sept. 11, we've told ourselves that facing our mortality changed our attitudes toward work and life. Yet here we are, still working in those office towers, still catching those planes. . . . Our way of life is predicated on our *not* taking stock; *not* getting off the career-overtime-promotion hamster wheel; *not*, God forbid, living each day as if it might be our last. Because who would spend that day in an airless cubicle or on the 8:30 to Denver? We needed to believe that civilian, commuter-consumer life is heroic.[4]

THE EMOTIONAL "WHY?" QUESTION

The news media commonly react to news of many tragedies, and school shootings in particular, with shock, horror, and disbelief. But it is in many ways an act, a false disbelief, a pretend shock. After all, few actions will alienate viewers as much as a reporter coming across as jaded and unsympathetic to the tragic story he or she is covering. Yet news reporting is perhaps among the most jaded and cynical of professions; longtime reporters have seen it all, from horrific death in Cambodia and Rwanda to cult suicides to presidential sex scandals. It's not that they don't care about the events they are covering, it's just that if reporters got emotionally involved in every tragedy and scandal they were assigned to cover, they would burn out quickly.

Though phrases such as "struggle to understand" and "make sense of this tragedy" are peppered throughout coverage of tragedies, they are simply glib news shorthand, meaningless phrases meant to fill airtime and to emphasize to viewers just how grievous a tragedy has unfolded—in case they missed it.

A CBS News reporter covering the February 3, 1996, incident in which a U.S. military plane sliced through a cable car full of skiers in Italy talked of "investigating why twenty people died for no reason on the mountain."[5] What does that mean? The reason the skiers died is that a plane cut through the cable supporting them and they fell to their deaths: They didn't die "for no reason." Presumably the reporter was trying to imply that the accident was preventable, but in any event, even preventable events occur for a reason.

In his April 21, 1999, coverage of the Columbine school shootings, veteran NBC News reporter Roger O'Neil told of the "students' struggle to make sense of the senseless" as close-ups of crying students filled the screen. Later that night, Deborah Norville of *Inside Edition* introduced their take on the story with, "How did it happen, why, and how can the town ever recover?" An interview subject said that a wounded boy's brothers were safe, "but, like the rest of us, they are still trying to understand." In an April 1999 article, a *New York Times* reporter discussed how a woman affected by school shootings "has spent the last year trying to make sense" of the killings.[6]

"Joaquin Phoenix says he'll never understand his brother's death, but he's close to accepting it." So begins a story in the February 3, 1998, *Albuquerque Journal*, quoting from an interview in *Movieline* magazine. Joaquin Phoenix's brother, actor River Phoenix, died outside the Viper Room, a Hollywood nightclub, on Halloween 1993. The twenty-three-year-old actor died of a drug overdose, his body full of cocaine, heroin, Valium, and cold medicine. Many of the dead actor's fans shared Joaquin's stubborn refusal to understand River's death, yet there seems little to "understand" about it: River Phoenix died because he wanted to get high and took too many illegal and dangerous drugs. There's nothing remotely puzzling or incomprehensible about his death. Young film and rock stars die all the time of drug overdoses.

Many times the notion that a death is beyond understanding is used to sanctify or deify a person. The unspoken implication seems to be that the perplexed person doesn't understand why the otherwise common phenomenon of death inexplicably applies to such a great/famous/talented person. Presumably Joaquin Phoenix (and others who don't "understand" a loved one's death) understand it when it happens to *someone else*. Yet it is made to seem almost disrespectful to the dead to point out that the great and talented are just as mortal and vulnerable as the rest of us.

Following the August 10, 1999, shootings at a Los Angeles Jewish community center by racist Buford Furrow Jr., President Clinton urged the nation to "intensify our resolve to make America a better place," and called the shootings "another senseless act."[7] Yet Furrow's act wasn't senseless at all; it was a logical extension of his racist Christian Identity religion and ideology.

Just because an act is *wrong* does not mean that it is *senseless*, and we as a nation ignore the distinction at our peril. When Clinton and news reporters refer to acts of violence as "senseless," the implication is that no one who is sensible would commit such an act, and not only is that notion simply not true, but it is dangerous. Something that is senseless is therefore incomprehensible, and a racist shooting at Jews and foreigners is perfectly understandable. As Alan Lipman, professor of clinical and criminal psychology at Georgetown University sees it, the "senseless" label "casts a veil" that discourages attempts to identify volatile individuals. "In every situation, what you hear from the community is the following phrase: 'I can't believe it would happen here.' But it's not an entirely different community from which these actions emerge. These things happen with and to and among people like us."[8]

Those who dare to say that such deaths or violent acts are understandable risk being labeled unsympathetic, and no one wants to be seen as gloating over a person's death or supporting mass murderers. We haven't progressed enough as a society to recognize that an action can be deplorable and yet still be understandable.

THE MYSTIFICATION OF SEPTEMBER 11, 2001

There was an odd tendency in the media to mystify the September 11 terrorist attacks, to claim they were incomprehensible, as if they were somehow beyond human understanding. A September 24 ABC News report by Dave Roos called the attacks "a series of unthinkable events that changed everything." The *Buffalo News* referred to the World Trade Center attacks as "utterly unimaginable," but declared that, with some thought, they could be "vaguely comprehensible."[9] An ABC News report by Amanda Onion on October 10, 2001, quoted Geoffrey Nunberg, a Stanford University linguist, who stated that "these events defy description."

But the attack was not unimaginable, nor did it change everything. Certainly, the particular, horrific method the terrorists used was shocking. But the idea of Muslim terrorists attacking thousands of Americans in the World Trade Center was hardly unthinkable; it had happened eight years earlier, on February 26, 1993. In fact, there had been several attacks on America in the previous decade. The idea that we would be a target of further attacks was quite the opposite of unimaginable; it was, in fact, to be expected. It was only unimaginable to those with a very poor understanding of current events and recent national and international history.

The Culture Shock That Wasn't

Another media myth that sprung up after the September 11, 2001, attacks was that American's tastes in entertainment would be forever changed: Americans would yearn for nonviolent, wholesome family programming. *Entertainment Weekly* devoted much of its September 28 issue to, as the cover put it, "The challenge to our culture." The magazine joined in the media chorus talking about the death of irony and the dramatic impact terrorism would have on nearly all facets of the entertainment industry. Jeff Gordinier wrote that "it's hard to believe that we'll ever see anything the same way. . . . it took only an instant of excruciating reality to render our old [entertainment] appetites moot, piddling, even nauseating." The effect was so profound, Gordinier wrote, that "the mere glimpse of a quippy sitcom was enough to induce a sour grind of physical revulsion."[10]

Entertainment Weekly filled pages and pages with well-intentioned but mawkish commentary second-guessing America's taste in entertainment—nearly all of which turned out to be overstated or flat-out wrong. Less than two months after the attacks, *Entertainment Weekly* began backpedaling, reporting, "'Nothing is ever going to be the same,' showbiz experts intoned on Sept. 11, predicting that in a newly threatened and threatening world, pop-culture junkies would now avoid all things violent, dark, and cynical." Yet the article cited an online poll of more than twenty thousand people showing that 75 percent of the respondents said that their taste in films and television had not changed in the two months since the attacks.[11]

Susan Whiting, president of Nielsen Media Research Company, confirms that the "everything changed" myth just didn't pan out: "All of the pundits who said this would happen were wrong. Shows like *The Osbournes* became wildly popular, along with shows like *Fear Factor*."[12] A look at the films released in the year following the attacks showed that the filmgoing public didn't shy away from horror, violence, or even terrorism-themed entertainment.

Geraldine Sealey, writing for ABC News on the anniversary of the attacks, pointed out that "we have not changed as drastically as many once imagined." Among other trends that were much touted but that never materialized, "a religious awakening leads the pack . . . polls show the number of Americans who say religion is 'very important' to their lives hardly changed." In fact, Sealey reports, less than one-third of Americans said the terror attacks actually transformed the way they live.[13]

Following the September 11 attacks, many in the media claimed that the attacks would profoundly change American life and culture.

Dozens of television shows and films were delayed, altered, or scrapped because producers were worried about offending the public's sensibilities. Logos, artwork, and film scenes depicting the World Trade

Center were changed; one poster for the film *Spider-Man* was pulled because it showed the two towers in a reflection.

The myth seemed to have two polar-opposite theses: On one hand, the idea was that references to (and images of) the Twin Towers should be removed because they might remind audiences of the loss and tragedy connected with them. In this view, it is best to simply remove the image to avoid the association. On the other hand, hundreds of images appeared specifically featuring the buildings (on hats, shirts, posters, etc.), for the express purpose of reminding people that the towers were there.

The Twin Towers, as symbols of freedom, New York City, or America, meant anything and everything to Americans, and their image (or lack thereof) served as Rorschach blots. For some the towers were symbols of tragedy; for others they were hope, patriotism, defiance, defeat, apocalypse, or unity. There was no consensus on the right thing to do, the right interpretation to embrace.

Randy Cohen, ethics columnist for the *New York Times Magazine*, discusses how David Letterman handled tragedy on his talk show: "Whenever there was an airplane crash, Dave would refrain from jokes about, say, airplane food. His intention was not to add to people's suffering, but I always found it odd. For whose benefit was he doing it? Would anybody be comforted by a shift in his monologue?"[14]

On the anniversary of the attacks, despite extensive programming and coverage of the terrorism, the public was largely indifferent. Television audience shares were about typical, and in fact viewership was down from the previous week, when 22 million viewers tuned in to see *American Idol*.[15] The same held true for books about the attacks; despite a deluge of more than two hundred September 11–themed books, sales were disappointing. The public had simply reached grief fatigue and weren't interested in reliving the attacks.

Aaron Schatz, writer for the Lycos 50 (a list of the top fifty searches on the popular Web search engine Lycos) found that Americans' interests and thoughts, as reflected in what information they searched out online, did not change drastically: "Based on Internet search traffic, it appears that American pop culture has returned to where it was prior to September 11. At the end of 2001, a lot of news reports stated that pop culture searches on the Internet dropped significantly after September 11, but that's really not true." A year later, Fox television's series *American Idol* got thirty times as many searches as "anthrax," and buxom blonde model "Anna Nicole Smith" got twelve times as many searches as "Afghanistan."[16]

The *New York Times* reported that academic and news media pollsters at the fifty-seventh annual meeting of the American Association for Public Opinion Research "repeatedly reacted skeptically to the aphorism that 'everything has changed'" in the year following the September 11 attacks.[17]

This American refusal to understand death, to understand attacks against our country, comes at a great price. We need to be aware of the world around us and acknowledge that in the real world angry students will sometimes kill others in schools, people we love will die, and terrorists will claim American lives. It seems almost a childlike protection of innocence, an unwarranted assumption that if we just ignore death and pain (or shrug and call them incomprehensible) maybe they will go away. This is no way to run a country—or to be informed citizens of it.

WHY?: THE BLAME GAME

After tragedy, the question arises as to why it happened. Sometimes this is essential, especially in cases of accidents or intelligence failures. But often the "Why?" question is applied to motive, and the question becomes rhetorical instead of investigative. It should be self-evident that the emotional "Why?" question is, in cases such as school shootings, a dead end, a road that leads inquirers into the black box of an individual's mind. "Why?" seeks to find a cause of an action, which leads to an individual's motives. No one, not even the person himself, ever knows *absolutely* why he committed a certain act. The "Why?" question leads to blame throwing, and the bigger the perceived threat, the more blame there is to go around. The *real* "Why?" question is, Why do the media and public refuse to accept the answers they are given when they pose the rarely answerable question "Why?"

Sometimes very clear answers are given as to why a tragedy occurred. This was true in the case of Seth Trickey, the boy who wounded four students at Fort Gibson Middle School in Oklahoma. When he was asked why he did it, his answer was, "I don't know." The self-evident truth—that if the boy himself doesn't know why he did something, then certainly no one else will, either—was seemingly lost on the press, who pored over the "Why?" question interminably.

Five years after he shot three classmates, school shooter Michael Carneal was still unable to answer the "Why?" question: "People want one simple answer—I can't give it," he said in a 2002 interview.[18]

When a ten-year-old boy burned down a historic 147-year-old church in Southbridge, Massachusetts, the community was shocked. Fire officials said that the boy admitted to excusing himself from Sunday school class to visit the bathroom, but instead set a fire in a wastebasket, then returned to class and waited, he said, "just to see what would happen." Fire Chief Leonard Laporte was quoted as asking rhetorically, "What makes a 10-year old do this? I don't know. Is it a craving for attention? Who knows?"[19] Well, the boy knew, and he openly explained it to the police and the fire department. Laporte, like many people, apparently refused to believe the very clear and simple explanations offered by the perpetrator himself.

Undoubtedly, the most prevalent "Why?" questions in recent years concerned Columbine High School. Responding to the question, shooting survivor Nick Foss stated that, during the shooting, "Finally I started figuring out these guys shot to kill for no reason." But the press didn't want the question answered so simply.[20] The truth didn't fit with the news media's assumptions and news bias, so Foss's comment was drowned out by another round of asking "Why?"

Peter Blauvelt, president of the National Alliance for Safe Schools, presciently noted that it's nearly impossible to find quick or meaningful answers to a tragedy like Columbine. "I think one of the things we are suffering from is trying to rationalize what was really an irrational act," he said.[21]

In many ways the "Why?" question turns into a sort of witch-hunt, with inquisitors from all sides (the police, parents, peers, etc.) demanding to know why a person did something. When the individual does offer his answer, it is set aside by reporters and others looking for an arcane conspiracy or smoking gun. They want a clear, definable target to focus on so that the story can continue. If the boy says he did it because he listened to Marilyn Manson or played Dungeons and Dragons, that lets parents, reporters, and politicians affix quick and easy blame.

In 1995 three boys killed a fifteen-year-old girl in San Luis Obispo. The local police found that the killers, like many teenagers, listened to heavy metal bands such as Slayer, Iron Maiden, and Ozzy Osbourne. Despite a lack of indication of ritual sacrifice, police determined it was a case of devil worship, and the murdered girl's parents filed a lawsuit against the band Slayer for inspiring the killings. The boys deny that they were satanists or inspired by any Slayer song. When asked, then, why the satanic story stuck, one of the boys said simply, "It was a small town and a big murder. They needed to know why it happened."[22]

ATTACKING ENTERTAINMENT

Following the death of Princess Diana, the paparazzi and the press in general were attacked as having caused the princess's death. Various American celebrities, including Madonna, George Clooney, and Tom Cruise, used the opportunity to chastise the ever-pursuant press. Even Earl Spencer's eulogy for his sister contained a few select swipes at the media. It soon became clear, however, that the proximate cause of Diana's death was her chauffeur, Henri Paul. The driver had consumed about eight glasses of wine during the hour before the accident and was legally drunk when he sped down the street. Still the public demanded that the paparazzi were largely responsible; there was even talk of sweeping legal reforms limiting freedom of the press.

It seemed that the cause of her death was too easy, too graspable. Sporadic complaints about invasion of privacy by photographers solidified after Diana's death into the form of a scapegoat. It wasn't until September 3, 1999, two years later, that charges were finally dropped against nine photographers and a motorcycle driver in connection with the accident. To the best of my knowledge, Diana's image hasn't been used in any anti–drunk driving campaigns. That seems odd, as alcohol abuse clearly and directly contributed to her death. It was easier to attack the press than address the problem of drunk driving.

Entertainment media are an easy target for policymakers and parents. Gradually, over the past two decades, nearly all forms of entertainment have been rated, ranked, and slapped with warning labels. Films have long been rated by the Motion Picture Association of America (MPAA). Ranging from G (general audiences) to NC-17 (no children under seventeen allowed), they are intended to serve as guides for parents to help them monitor what their children watch.

The idea seems to be that, as long as certain forms of entertainment are sanitized or warned about, fragile young minds won't be corrupted. The reality is, of course, that real life has violence, strong language, and mature themes.

Many film critics, including Roger Ebert of the *Chicago Sun-Times*, complain that the NC-17 rating is ineffective and "crippled with the curse of pornography." (All the film ratings are copyrighted by the MPAA except X. The XXX rating, as well, is not used by the MPAA; it was adopted by the adult film industry, hoping to signify to the public that the material was somehow three times as naughty as an X-rated film.)

Many people are concerned about protecting children from arts and entertainment. Among the evils waiting to corrupt America's youth are dirty words. Roger Ebert summed up the issue of rating films for bad language this way: "The MPAA should concede the melancholy fact that every teenager has heard this and most other nasty words thousands of times."[23]

Music labeling and rating has long been a contentious issue, driven in large part by a music clean-up campaign started by Tipper Gore in 1985. Her efforts culminated in the infamous Parents' Music Resource Center hearings, in which Gore claimed that 14 million children were "at risk" and in need of counseling due to the "graphic brutality marketed to these kids through music and television."[24] In the wake of the hearings, the music industry decreed that record companies would monitor their releases for offensive content and, where appropriate, label some albums with "Parental Advisory: Explicit Lyrics." Fifteen years later, the labels remain.

Like music, television shows now also carry labels to help parents choose the suitability of broadcasts for their children. A 1996 telecommunications law required that all new televisions thirteen inches and larger be equipped with v-chip technology. This system allows the user to block out shows that contain violent content.

Yet according to a report to the Henry J. Kaiser Family Foundation, there's an 80 percent chance that a television show containing violence did not carry the required "V" content label between 1997 and 1998, and a 90 percent chance that a television show containing adult language or sexual themes did not carry the required content labels.[25] It's probably just as well, since most parents themselves aren't concerned enough to actually use the v-chips and Internet filters anyway. A study by the Annenberg Public Policy Center at the University of Pennsylvania found that only 40 percent of parents surveyed reported having a v-chip or other device on their television sets that can block programs with violent or sexual content and crude language. And only half of those parents actually use the devices. Parents aren't much more worried about their childrens' Internet browsing habits either; though half of American families have Internet access at home, only a third of them activated software filters before allowing their children to surf the Web.[26]

The fact that the average parent (and child) isn't terribly concerned about Internet filtering suggests that, for the most part, the "terrible dangers" are a myth perpetuated by advocacy groups and politicians who hype the dangers and then proudly proclaim they can solve the problem to garner support and votes.

In response to complaints about violence in video games (again, largely by politicians and lobbyists), a rating system was initiated using ratings from the Entertainment Software Ratings Board. The board rates games on a scale from EC (early childhood; suitable for persons three and older) to AO (adults only). The ratings are the products of a byzantine set of criteria, with specific categories such as "mild animated violence," "comic mischief," "animated blood," "realistic blood," "mature sexual themes," "gaming," and "use of drugs."

When New York State Senator Mary Lou Rath wanted to look into the link between violent video games and youth crime, she surveyed residents in her district about their opinions on the effects of video games on young people. Rath's point of view is clear from this quote, which appeared in the *Buffalo News* on January 1, 2000: "With the number of incidents of school violence which have occurred in our country in the last few years, it is imperative that we take steps to prevent this situation from perpetuating itself."[27] The link between school violence and video games was assumed. I don't know what the results of her survey were, but I expect she found what she was looking for.

Rath seems to miss the fact that the public's perception about whether violent video games are harmless or not is irrelevant. Hopefully, laws are not simply popularity contests, where, if the majority of people feel that video games are to blame, then they should be held responsible. Scientific evidence, not opinion polls, should carry weight in drafting effective legislation. Opinions on the topic of those in her district are relevant only if the goal is to garner that public's votes, not to actually address or solve the problem. The truth or falsity of a claim is not subject to a majority vote.

When I inquired into Senator Rath's findings, I was told that the senator had held public hearings on the topic, and that "to a person, everyone agreed that juvenile crime has become more brutal and violent. Statistics bear this out: Although the overall youth crime rate is on the decline, arrests for violent juvenile crime including murder, rape, robbery and assault with a weapon shot up 72 percent in New York from 1986–1996."[28]

There are several logical problems with this response. One is that an increase in the arrest rate among youths almost certainly has more to do with better policing than an increase in youth violence. And why would information on youth arrest rates in New York reflect the rest of the country? Do New Yorkers play more violent video games than other states? Without answers to these questions, a statistic like this is worse than meaningless, it is deceptive. One could even use Rath's logic to claim that violent video games make kids *less* likely to commit crime!

Second, even if the arrest rate did reflect more crime, it has little relevance to violent video games. Senator Rath tries to make the argument that video game playing is somehow related to the youth crime rate (which she admits is on the decline). Yet it would be nearly impossible for the violent video games Rath is worried about to have caused the supposed increase in arrests, as most of the games were not released until the mid-1990s.

Among the most often cited examples of violent video games are Mortal Kombat, Doom, Quake, Duke Nukem, and Carmageddon. Duke Nukem was released in 1991, Mortal Kombat and Doom came out in 1992, Quake came out in 1996, and Carmageddon came out in 1997. How then do violent video games, most released between 1992 and 1997, account for a rise in youth arrests between 1986 and 1996?

It should give Americans pause that, over the course of the last thirty years or so, nearly all manner of entertainment has gradually become prescreened, examined, classified, rated, and, in some cases, censored. This is largely a reaction to sensationalized media coverage of scary myths and knee-jerk legislation.

Blaming entertainment for social ills is nothing new, of course; Elvis Presley was accused of corrupting America's youth with lewd hip gyrations in the 1950s, for example, and in 1880s London the play *Dr. Jekyll and Mr. Hyde* was blamed for encouraging Jack the Ripper in his crimes.[29]

In science, outside the agenda enclaves, the effects of violent video games on behavior is very much an open question. If we're not sure there's a problem, how, then, can we work to prevent it? One wonders how we ever got along before all our television shows, movies, music, and games were screened and rated for appropriateness.

Amid all the concern over the violence that teens and kids see in their video games, television shows, and films, one simple fact is often overlooked: Violence and murder is considered mainstream entertainment by most Americans. Aside from the obvious violence in action and some drama films, multiple murders are entertainment every single night. Top-rated television drama shows routinely involve killings and death, from *Law & Order* to *CSI* to *The Sopranos* to *ER*. Just about any police, detective, or medical drama will, by definition, often involve violence and killings.

While many of the murders that entertain us are fictional, others aren't. Newsmagazine shows such as *Dateline NBC* and *48 Hours* regularly feature real-life murders packaged as entertainment mysteries. There's nothing new here, but it's odd to see the finger wagging and hand-wringing over the violence that kids and teens watch, while adults settle down for a night of entertainment fueled by murderous storylines.

Public overreaction followed the spate of school shootings and the perceived trend in increasing violence in America. Parents, police, psychologists, and politicians all have a laundry list of theories about why crime is on the rise (never mind that it isn't): too many guns, violent video games, violent rap lyrics, violent television programs, violent films, "antisocial personality" (ASP) disorder, single-parent families, school bullies, lack of parental control, drug use, teen sex, lack of religion in school, a "crime gene," truancy, teen isolation, divorce, inattentive parents and teachers, the list goes on.

With all these possible culprits, one might assume that research could single out a few true causes, or exonerate others. Certainly, some of the above *may contribute* to an act of violence, but surely not all of them do; and besides, regardless of which factors are found to be important, the insurmountable problem of free will remains. It doesn't matter if every teenager carries a gun or watches violent and gory films. Whether Johnny turned to crime because he watched too much television or he's just an excitable boy, the choice was still his. The ultimate choice to act, the ultimate responsibility, lies with the individual. No matter which agenda advocates promote, which hot button they want to push, they will end up at the same place: personal responsibility. But that doesn't stop them from trying to play the blame game.

A quote by Suzanne Wilson, who lost a daughter to school shooters, is typical of the assumptions about violence and video games: "We teach our children, 'Thou shalt not kill,' and then we let them play hours and hours of the most violent video games."[30]

While a few studies claim that violent entertainment may be linked in some way to violent behavior, many other studies contradict that assertion. One study commissioned to examine the link between television and violence, the *UCLA Violence Monitoring Report*, noted that "when the impact of television is discussed or when television is blamed for having caused something to happen, it should never be suggested that television alone is a sufficient cause." Another study, the *National Television Violence Study*, underwritten by the cable industry, found similar results: "It is also recognized that televised violence does not have a uniform effect on viewers. The outcome of media violence on viewers depends both on the nature of the depictions and the sociological and psychological makeup of the audience."[31]

Where did the assumption that there are mountains of evidence pointing to the media's culpability in fomenting real-life violence come from? Richard Rhodes, a writer for *Rolling Stone*, tackled this question and found that the alleged mountains of evidence are really molehills—and shaky ones at that. The approximately two hundred studies on media violence are remarkable primarily for their inconsistency and weak conclusions. Some studies show a correlation between television and violence; others don't. Some find that watching violent programming can increase aggressiveness; another finds that watching *Mister Rogers' Neighborhood* does. Several studies, including the most cited ones, are deeply flawed methodologically. In one case, a graph presented in Senate testimony apparently showed a dramatic link between violent television watching and violent crime later in life. Yet what neither the public nor the Senate was told was that the graph held true for just 3 boys out of a sample of 145, hardly representative of the general population. Nonetheless, those fighting media depictions of violence happily cite the studies, blithely unconcerned about the lack of scientific validity to their examples and arguments.

Rhodes notes that "the research no more supports the consensus on media violence than it supported the conclusions of the eugenics consensus eighty years ago that there are superior and inferior 'races,' with white Northern Europeans at the top."[32]

The assertion that video games make people violent got a boost in May 2000, when the American Psychological Association (APA) issued a press release saying that violent video games can increase aggression. That conclusion was taken from a study by two researchers, Craig Anderson of Iowa State University and Karen Dill of Lenoir-Rhyne College in North Carolina, who claimed they had found a link between violent video games and aggression.

The claim was widely reported and touted by the anti–video game lobby. Amy Dickinson's May 8, 2000, column in *Time* began with the subheading, "New studies link violent video games to violent behavior." She wrote:

> Two studies released last week go beyond anecdotal evidence and find that playing violent video games can contribute to aggressive and violent behavior in real life. . . . These [video] games teach kids to connect gore and glory in a fantasy world in which the most vicious killers are the winners.[33]

Dickinson apparently relied heavily on the press releases and made no effort to get an alternative viewpoint or an expert's take on the study (or, if she did, it never made it into her column).

An examination of what the researchers actually found shows how tentative their conclusions are. The study appears to show some association between the playing of violent video games and concurrent aggressive behavior and delinquency. Yet, as any social sciences or psychology student can tell you, correlation does not imply causation. One critic of the study, British psychologist Guy Cumberbatch, noted:

> [F]inding that people who enjoy violent media may also be aggressive is tantamount to observing that those who play football also enjoy watching it on television. "The correlational nature of [this] study means that causal statements are risky at best," the authors admit. . . . All in all, Anderson and Dill's new evidence is exceptionally weak, and in its one-sided approach it has a depressingly familiar ring to it. . . . [S]tudies to date have been notably biased towards seeking evidence of harm. This "blame game" may be fun for some researchers to play, and knee-jerk reactions such as the APA's press release may be media-friendly. But we deserve better.[34]

We also deserve better journalism than Dickinson provided in her column. The study itself contradicted one of Dickinson's points, that "the researchers found increased delinquency among those who had played violent video games throughout their high school years." If Dickinson read the study, she missed the fact that the researchers apparently did not ask the participants whether the games they had played "throughout their high school years" were violent. For all Anderson and Dill know, those in the study might have played nonviolent games such as Pac-Man or Space Invaders.[35]

Politicians pushing their constitutionally challenged quick-fixes and alarmist agendas often don't even recognize the contradictions in their rhetoric. How is it, for example, that American teens on one hand are said to be desensitized to real violence through playing video games and watching violent films, yet in the next breath we are told that those same students are shocked and stunned by the violence in their schools and communities? If young people don't think much of killing because they see gore and violence in the video games Doom and Mortal Kombat and watching *The Matrix*, they presumably don't need the phalanx of psychologists and counselors that floods into schools after each shooting.

The antigaming lobby has perpetuated the image of legions of young, violent malcontents playing violent, gory video games for hours on end, then heading to school to carry out their grisly mission. The reality, however, is quite different. A 2000 survey of more than sixteen hundred households found that most people who play video games do so as a way to interact with their friends and family. As Associated Press writer Gary Gentile reported:

> Sales numbers tend to support the notion that family-oriented and non-violent games are popular. The top two best-selling computer games in 1999 were "MP Roller Coaster Tycoon" and "Sim City 3000"—games which allow players to build simulated parks or cities. . . . Only one of the top 25 video games was what the industry calls a "first-person shooter" such as the Doom or Quake games.[36]

The common claim is that youth have a hard time distinguishing real-life violence from fiction. Ironically, in the post-Columbine era, it is the adults (teachers, parents, and police) who seem to have difficulty making that distinction.

The news media reported that the Columbine shooters listened to music with explicit lyrics about violence. That was enough for Wisconsin Senator Gary Drzewiecki to propose a bill that would make it illegal for minors to buy music with explicit lyrics. In his reasoning, the senator employs the logical fallacy of *post hoc ergo propter hoc* ("after this, therefore because of this"). But just because the pair may have listened to violent song lyrics *before* committing the crime does not imply that they did it *because* of those songs. One or both of the killers probably drank sodas and watched television in the days before the killings; presumably those didn't cause their rampage. In any event, hundreds of thousands of people also listened to the same music without committing any crime. As Michael Moore noted in his Academy Award–winning film *Bowling for Columbine*, the killers went bowling the morning of the shooting, yet no one is blaming bowling alleys for the violence.

Charles Manson listened to the Beatles's "Helter Skelter" before some of his crimes; Mark David Chapman read *Catcher in the Rye* before gunning down John Lennon. By Drzewiecki's logic, perhaps such classic songs and books should be made illegal for minors to buy as well.

The courts, incidentally, also take a dim view of the claim that fictional violence instigates real violence. In April 2000 a federal judge threw out a lawsuit brought by the families of three victims of a 1997 school shooting. The lawsuit named twenty-five defendants, including the makers of the violent film *The Basketball Diaries* and the producers of video games such as Doom and Quake. The judge ruled that the shooter's actions were unforseeable, and that product liability law did not extend to ideas contained in movies and games.[37] In 2001 a federal judge dismissed lawsuits brought by family members of Columbine victims against a Colorado school district, ruling that the killers "were the predominant if not the sole cause" of the massacre. The following year, U.S. District Judge Lewis Babcock dismissed a similar lawsuit filed against several video game and movie makers, claiming that they shared the blame for the massacre.[38]

Entertainment Weekly writer Kristen Baldwin summed up the controversy nicely (though not without hyperbole):

> What happened at Columbine High was a tragedy, an unearthly glimpse into hell—but it was not Marilyn Manson's fault. Nor was it caused by [musical artists] Rammstein or the videogame *Doom*. . . . Is vilifying the videogame really the answer? For the *Dateline*s of the world, yes. There's only so much footage of weeping teens and bloody victims available; blaming Marilyn Manson means you can slap a clip of the shock rocker on screen. Condemning [the film] *The Basketball Diaries* is even better—producers get to run an image of Leo DiCaprio. It fills time, it looks provocative. More important, it feels good to place blame. But it doesn't get us any closer to understanding the horrific event. Maybe nothing will. One Columbine student, asked why this happened, just shook his head: "There's no why."[39]

NOTES

1. Michael Lemonick,"Love for Strangers," *Time*, August 2, 1999, p. 100.
2. Roger Simon, "A Nation Mourns?" AOL News, July 22, 1999.
3. Kenneth Auchincloss, "The Year of the Tear," *Newsweek*, December 29, 1998/January 5, 1999, p. 40.
4. James Poniewozik, "The White-Collar Warrior," *Time*, August 5, 2002, p. 74.
5. *CBS Nightly News*, January 4, 1998.
6. Timothy Egan, "Violence by Youths: Looking for Answers," *New York Times*, April 22, 1999, p. A27.
7. "Police Close in on LA Gunman," BBC News [online], news.bbc.co.uk/2/hi/americas/416922.stm [August 10, 1999].
8. David Foster, "Shootings Erode Sense of Peace," Associated Press [online], wire.ap.org [November 5, 1999].

9. "Aftermath: Finding the New Center," Ask First Sunday, *First Sunday* (supplement), *Buffalo News*, November 4, 2001, p. 7.

10. Jeff Gordinier, "How We Saw It." *Entertainment Weekly*, September 28, 2001, p. 11.

11. Josh Wolk, "How Much Is Too Much?" *Entertainment Weekly*, November 2, 2001, p. 32.

12. Interview on *Good Morning America*, cited in "Guilty Pleasures," ABC News [online], abcnews.go.com/sections/GMA/GoodMorningAmerica/GMA 020917TV_viewing_habits.html [September 17, 2002].

13. Geraldine Sealey, "This Sept. 11, the Nation Carries On," ABC News [online], abcnews.go.com/sections/us/DailyNews/sept11_lifechangeupdate.html [September 11, 2002].

14. Benjamin Svetkey, "Appropriate Action," *Entertainment Weekly*, October 5, 2001, p. 20.

15. David Bauder, "9/11 Shows Drew Moderate Ratings," Associated Press [online], www.softcom.net/webnews/wed/da/Asept-11-tv-ratings.RmUN_CSC.html [September 12, 2002].

16. "Web Search Activity Indicates Pop Culture Has Not Changed Since September 11." Terra Lycos, Inc. press release, September 5, 2002.

17. Adam Clymer, "U.S. Attitudes Altered Little by Sept. 11, Pollsters Say," *New York Times*, May 20, 2002.

18. "Ky. School Shooter Has No Answer," Associated Press [online], www.gaypasg.org/Press%20Clippings/September%202002/Ky.%20School%20Shooter%20Has%20No%20Answer.htm [September 13, 2002].

19. Trudy Tynan, "Boy Set Church Fire Out of Curiosity," South Coast Today [online], www.s-t.com/daily/12-99/12-21-99/a03sr021.htm [December 20, 1999].

20. Robin McDowell, "15 Dead in Colorado School Shooting," Associated Press [online], wire.ap.org [April 21, 1999].

21. Michelle Locke, "After Shooting Many Wonder Why," Associated Press [online], wire.ap.org [April 21, 1999].

22. Allison Hope Weiner, "Facing the Music," *Entertainment Weekly* (fall 2001 double issue): 10.

23. Lori Tharps, "Foul Plie?" *Entertainment Weekly*, October 27, 2000, p. 23.

24. Christopher Taylor, "Warning labels: A Comparison of Two Opinions," *Anthology of the William C. Banks Award Winners* [online], www.class.uidaho.edu/banks/1999/articles/warning_labels.htm.

25. "Ticker," *Brill's Content* (December 1998/January 1999): 140.

26. Jesse Holland, "Study: V-Chips, Filters Not Used," Associated Press [online], www.apnic.net/mailing-lists/apple/archive/2000/06/msg00027.html [June 26, 2000].

27. "Rath Surveys Video Game Effects," *Buffalo News*, January 1, 2000, p. B-6.

28. John Emery, communications director for Sen. Mary Lou Rath, personal correspondence with the author, October 30, 2002.

29. Paul Begg, Martin Fido, and Keith Skinner, *Jack the Ripper A to Z* (London: Headline Books, 1991), p. 294.

30. Timothy Egan, "Violence By Youths: Looking for Answers," *New York Times*, April 22, 1999, p. A27.

31. Nick Gillespie, "Missing Links," *Reason* (May 1996): 18.

32. Richard Rhodes, "The Media-Violence Myth," *Rolling Stone*, November 23, 2000, p. 55.

33. Amy Dickinson, "Video Playground," *Time* [online], www.time.com/time/magazine/article/0,91871,1101000508-44031,00.html [May 8, 2000].

34. Guy Cumberbatch, "Only a Game?" *New Scientist*, June 10, 2000, p. 44.

35. Ibid.

36. Gary Gentile, "Survey: Computer Games Are Family Activitiy," Associated Press [online], www.canoe.ca/CNEWSTechNews0005/12_games.html [May 11, 2000].

37. "Parents of Students Killed in Kentucky Lose Suit," CNN [online], www.cnn.com/2000/US/04.07/prayer.circle/index.html [April 7, 2000].

38. "Columbine Family's Lawsuit against Video Game Makers Dismissed," Associated Press [online], vigilant.tv/article/1068 [March 4, 2002].

39. Kristen Baldwin, "There's No Why," *Entertainment Weekly*, May 7, 1999, p. 9.

6

TRAGEDY AS LICENSE TO ABANDON RESPONSIBLE JOURNALISM

Many ethical reporters and journalists who would ordinarily be loathe to stray from their prized objectivity use tragedy as an excuse to throw in emotional reporting and loaded words that would be wholly unacceptable in any other type of news story.

When Walter Cronkite passed on the tragic news that John F. Kennedy had died, he did it with composure and without loaded words or emotional hyperbole. He surely felt a loss, yet he understood the need to separate himself from the news. Cronkite is one of the most beloved and respected news anchors in history, yet few felt his professional detachment was wrong or inappropriate.

Emotion in news media can bias reporting and manipulate audiences, but there is another reason it pops up so frequently. Emotion is easy, while getting the facts right takes work. It is much, much easier to get a crying person's tearful (but possibly baseless) testimonial than to ask probing questions and uncover solutions. Testimonials often focus on one or two people to illustrate and give focus to broader trends. When digesting news about layoffs, people have an easier time following an interview with Joey, the laid-off Detroit machinist, as he sadly ponders his fate, than hearing a litany of statistics about unemployment trends.

There is nothing inherently wrong with using testimonials—as long as they are used in context, with a balance of broader facts and issues. But what happens when the testimonial (and its personal power) contradicts reality or is not representative of the general public?

Crime reporting provides a good example: Though crime has been steadily dropping for decades, the amount of news time devoted to crime has gone up since the early 1980s. Much of that crime reporting includes emotional testimonials from victims about what they experienced. But if a reporter spends two minutes and fifteen seconds letting a crime victim tell how horrible crime is and closes the report with "Of course, her plight is rare; violent crime is down 30 percent since 1982," the audience will easily remember the emotional, anomalous testimonial and forget the relevant, quick statistical caveat undermining its importance.

The problem is not just in the news content, but also the words and tone the reporters and news anchors use. As John Stossel of ABC News reported in his "Give Me a Break!" segment on *20/20 Friday* on October 22, 1999, journalists and anchors reporting on school shootings veered perilously close to outright fabrication in their tragedy hyperbole. With a high school behind him, veteran CBS News reporter Bob McNamara began a story, "It has become an American nightmare that too many schools know too well." NBC anchor Tom Brokaw, meanwhile, referred to shootings as "a dark stain on American life."

This sort of pathos-laden hyperbole may rivet viewers' attention, but it also misleads them. Dr. Frank Farley of the American Psychological Association says that "American schools are not violent. . . . American schools in fact are safer than most communities and most homes. I don't know why there is all this press coverage other than the need for a story."[1]

PRINCESS DIANA AND JOHN F. KENNEDY JR.

According to Nielsen estimates, 26 million households watched Princess Diana's funeral, and print media was prevalent. As Jacqueline Sharkey wrote in "The Diana Aftermath":

> Print media found coverage of Diana so profitable, both before and after her death, that *Newsweek* media critic Jonathan Alter wrote, "Lady Di launched at least a thousand covers, and hundreds of millions of newspaper and magazine sales. When Diana died, magazines such as *Time* and *Newsweek* scrambled to redo their covers and devote dozens of pages to stories about the princess. As reporters started to question what *Time* contributor Martha Smilgis called the "media gush" about Diana, *Time, Newsweek, People,* and *TV Guide* all published special commemorative editions."[2]

Each television network had its own packaged "mourning show" titles, such as "The Final Farewell" or "The Death of Diana." No matter the title, Diana: The Show was a sad affair indeed. By mid-September, two weeks after Diana's death, even *Entertainment Weekly* had had enough, and ran an excellent cover article by Mark Harris titled "Television Is Relentless," in which he noted:

Time magazine ran several cover stories on John F. Kennedy Jr.'s death

> During a week in which scant teaspoons of fresh information were used to flavor 55-gallon barrels of repetition, it was hard to deliver good journalism. . . . What a creepy debasement to see Barbara Walters announce that she was barely able to bring herself to spill the beans about her friendship with Di (somehow she managed), or Diane Sawyer, glowing with the news that *PrimeTime Live* would be re-creating Diana's last day, or Dominick Dunne letting NBC viewers know that Di thought O. J. Simpson would be acquitted, which must mean . . . something.[3]

Coverage of John F. Kennedy Jr.'s death wasn't quite as bad, though *Time* magazine, for example, devoted least two front-cover stories to John-John, the first in a "commemorative issue" on July 26. This issue devoted nearly half (thirty-eight) of its eighty-eight pages to Kennedy's life and death, lavishly illustrated with photos. It included one double-page photo spread of him and his father, a full page each of the young JFK Jr. in the Oval Office and saluting at his father's funeral. And to sate those who preferred the "hunk" angle, it ran a full-page photo of him, brawny and bare-chested, on a boat.

Apparently *Time*'s editors felt they hadn't profited enough from Kennedy's death, eulogized him enough, or both, and ran an "In Memoriam" the next issue (August 6). Once again we saw the photo of him saluting as a boy, with the words, "Ask Not . . ." on the cover. This time we got even more photos, including two three-page fold-out photos, one of father and son in a boat on a beach, the other a blurry telephoto shot of the bow of the USS *Briscoe*, where the Kennedy family had gathered to cast JFK Jr.'s ashes to sea. (The ceremony was private, thus necessitating the use of telephoto lenses.) We had six full pages, nearly four square feet of space that could have been used to report on important current events, showing the readers that John spent time with his dad and how his ashes were cast away. The blurriness of the USS *Briscoe* photo might cause viewers some faint unease, a reminder that they were privy to private grief against the family's wishes, that the little privacy afforded the Kennedys was enforced not out of respect but by police patrols.

The anniversary of JFK Jr.'s death provided the media with a new excuse to run more photos of Kennedy, and just about everyone was in on the act. *People* magazine's July 24, 2000, cover featured JFK Jr., with the headline "Scenes From a Marriage." *Us Weekly* magazine did a cover photo spread titled "JFK Jr.: The Forgotten Photos." The carrion frenzy is sure to go on, surfacing on the fifth and tenth anniversaries of his death.

TIME'S COLUMBINE REDUX

Time magazine gave lots of ink and cover space to the April 20, 1999, massacre at Columbine High School—so much in fact that when they did yet *another* cover article on December 20, 1999, *eight months* to the day after the killings, the editors felt the need to justify their tragedy-milking coverage. They did it on page six with a message from Managing Editor Walter Isaacson. The piece, titled "To Our Readers: Why We Went Back to Columbine," begins, "I want to explain why we returned to Columbine this week, running a chilling cover photo and stories about killers we would rather forget. Although we worked hard last April to report the news in the days following the shootings, we felt there were questions that still needed to be answered." Furthermore, Isaacson writes, they "had to wrestle with whether running a picture of [the killers] might seem, perversely, to glorify them to other twisted minds or give them the publicity they wanted, even though they are dead. Indeed it would be nice if we could always avoid showing evil people on our covers. 'It's not our tendency to sensationalize crime or do covers on the crime of the week,' says editor-in-chief Norman Pearlstine."[4]

In this both disingenuous and self-serving piece, they claim that, as journalists, they would "rather forget" what happened. The assertion is ridiculous: If they really thought that the public would rather forget (and

TO OUR READERS

Why We Went Back to Columbine

HEALING THE WOUNDS: Columbine celebrates its recent state championship

I WANT TO EXPLAIN WHY WE RETURNED TO COLUMBINE THIS week, running a chilling cover photo and stories about killers we would rather forget.

Although we worked hard last April to report the news in the days following the shootings, we felt there were questions that still needed to be answered. So six weeks ago, we sent a team back to Littleton, Colo., to investigate what actually motivated the killers and find out what they were really like. What could we learn about how to spot—and deal with—the demons that can lurk inside the souls of seemingly average kids? What was the community doing to heal its wounds and prevent such shootings in the future?

In the course of our reporting, correspondent Tim Roche was allowed to view the five videotapes made by Eric Harris and Dylan Klebold before their massacre. In them, they explain their insecurities, hatreds, worries, desires and motivations. When you read what was going on in their minds, you will be frightened and sickened, but you will understand better the twisted motives that drove them. We were also given access to much of the evidence collected by investigators, including videotape of the gunmen taken by a school security camera, which provides a clearer picture of what actually happened.

Assistant managing editor Dan Goodgame, who led our team, is the father of three schoolkids and the husband of a teacher, and he was sympathetic to the concerns of the survivors and others in the community. "Family after family told us what they wanted most was to know everything about what happened and why, so that the deaths would have some meaning and might help others stop such things," he says. "What we have uncovered is far more than any of them have been told. While they won't be happy to see the killers back in the news, they'll have more of the answers they've been seeking."

Klebold and Harris say on the tapes that they did not want to be seen as copycats and that they were planning their own horror before other school shootings made news. Nevertheless, we had to wrestle with whether running a picture of them might seem, perversely, to glorify them to other twisted minds or give them the publicity they wanted, even though they are dead.

Indeed, it would be nice if we could always avoid showing evil people on our covers. "It's not our tendency to sensationalize crime or do covers on the crime of the week," says editor-in-chief Norman Pearlstine. "Sometimes, however, a shocking picture—of a wartime execution, a brutality, a kid with a gun—along with an analysis of the tale behind it serves to focus our eyes on things we would prefer to ignore but instead should try to understand. I think it is worth the pain if it forces us to confront the issues of guns and violence and hidden anger in our schools, communities and families."

This story is not so much about kids seeking glory as it is about grownups not looking and seeing, about people who preferred to sugarcoat rather than confront reality. We're likely to get letters from people saying they had to hide the issue from their children. I understand. Some of us may be hiding it from our own little kids as well. But I don't think we should hide the shocking images and stories from ourselves. The concept of a kid in a school cafeteria with a gun is one that should disquiet us.

Before you make a judgment, please read the stories, written by Nancy Gibbs, Andrew Goldstein and Sam Gwynne. I think you will find them sensitive, and I hope you will agree that they provide a new level of insight into what happened at Columbine. You will also learn how the parents in that community have tried to find ways to help others avoid a similar tragedy. If it makes you want to join their cause, you can do so by contributing to the fund they are supporting: the HOPE Columbine Atrium and Library Fund, c/o The Denver Foundation, P.O. Box 24035, Denver, Colo. 80224-0035 (*www.hopecolumbine.org*), which has announced its drive to raise at least $3.1 million to build a new library for the school.

Walter Isaacson, Managing Editor

6 TIME, DECEMBER 20, 1999

After extensively covering the massacre at Columbine High School, *Time* magazine devoted another cover and special issue to the killings a year later.

therefore wouldn't buy yet more "news" about) the Columbine killers, they wouldn't have run the story. A major reason *Time* went back to Columbine, to sell more magazines, wasn't mentioned.

A quick review of past issues of *Time* show that Pearlstine's indignation over the perception that *Time* sensationalizes crime and death is vacuous. There's the two-page spread close-up photo of a child's gruesome skull, complete with flies eating away at the flesh ("Crimes of War," June 28, 1999); the cover photo of a dead body being put into an ambulance—reprinted on page 23 in case anyone missed it on the cover—and another body on page 24, and still, on the following page, a clear photo of the dead gunman with blood coming from the gunshot wound on his head ("The Atlanta Massacre," August 9, 1999); and a photo of a wounded earthquake victim in Turkey, a mother half-buried under cement and rubble, with the left foot of her dead child sticking out from under her ("Buried Alive," August 30, 1999).

Although Pearlstine may feel that running more photos of the Columbine killers is a public service, many parents and families of their victims felt otherwise. Sue Petrone, whose son Daniel was killed, said, "It would do all of us a lot of good if we did not have to look at the two individuals who destroyed and shattered so many lives."[5]

KOSOVO CRISIS THE AWFUL TRUTH

A team of TIME reporters discovers chilling evidence of Serbia's well-organized, vicious killing machine. It's even more horrific than you imagined

CRIMES OF WAR

By JOHANNA MCGEARY

THE HORROR IS STILL LOCKED IN GENTIANA GASHI'S MIND. HER eyes are red-rimmed holes in a pinched, exhausted face. She came home safely to Cuska last week, but she is still harrowed by the unspeakable memories of May 14, the day she left. Back then, she stood beside her weeping mother, too terrified to cry out, as she watched the Serbs march her father away with the other men, hands clasped behind his neck. He looked back once, tears streaming down his face. Gentiana's mother wept silently too as she watched her husband's retreating figure until laughing Serbs herded the women out of the village, elbowing them with sly smirks, singing obscene songs. That night when the women slipped back into Cuska, it was Gentiana who picked through the charred pieces of bodies inside three smoldering

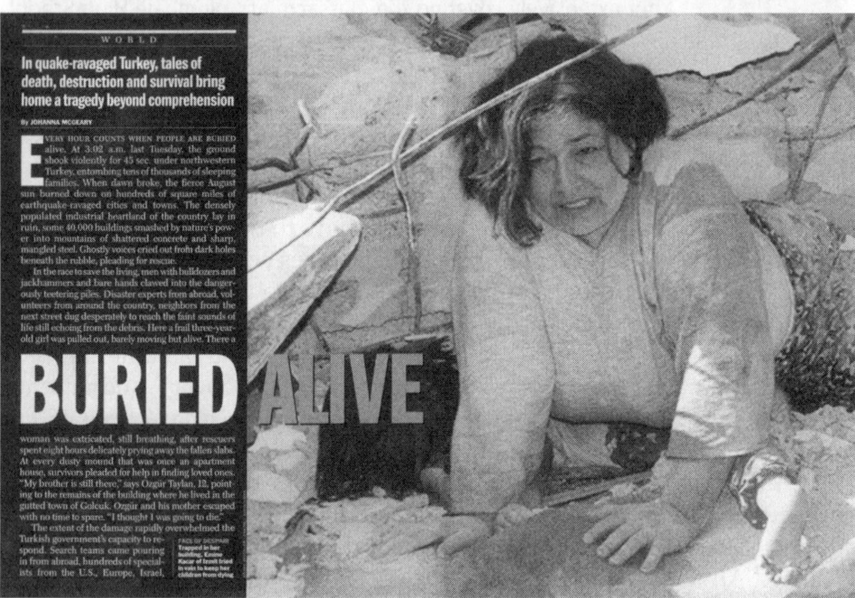

WORLD

In quake-ravaged Turkey, tales of death, destruction and survival bring home a tragedy beyond comprehension

By JOHANNA MCGEARY

BURIED ALIVE

EVERY HOUR COUNTS WHEN PEOPLE ARE BURIED alive. At 3:02 a.m. last Tuesday, the ground shook violently for 45 sec. under northwestern Turkey, entombing tens of thousands of sleeping families. When dawn broke, the fierce August sun burned down on hundreds of square miles of earthquake-ravaged cities and towns. The densely populated industrial heartland of the country lay in ruin, some 40,000 buildings smashed by nature's power into mountains of shattered concrete and sharp, mangled steel. Ghostly voices cried out from dark holes beneath the rubble, pleading for rescue.

In the race to save the living, men with bulldozers and jackhammers and bare hands clawed into the dangerously teetering piles. Disaster experts from abroad, volunteers from around the country, neighbors from the next street dug desperately to reach the faint sounds of life still echoing from the debris. Here a frail three-year-old girl was pulled out, barely moving but alive. There a woman was extricated, still breathing, after rescuers spent eight hours delicately prying away the fallen slabs. At every dusty mound that was once an apartment house, survivors pleaded for help in finding loved ones. "My brother is still there," says Ozgur Taylan, 12, pointing to the remains of the building where he lived in the gutted town of Golcuk. Ozgur and his mother escaped with no time to spare. "I thought I was going to die."

The extent of the damage rapidly overwhelmed the Turkish government's capacity to respond. Search teams came pouring in from abroad, hundreds of specialists from the U.S., Europe, Israel,

Graphic double-page photos of tragedy in *Time*.

Far from helping to heal the Littleton community, the *Time* article sparked further pain and outrage. Following publication of the issue, Jefferson County Sheriff John Stone was asked by angry parents of Columbine victims to resign. Stone apologized for what he conceded was a mistake in allowing *Time* to see videotapes made by the two gunmen. He claimed that *Time* had broken an agreement not to quote anything the killers said on the tapes.[6] As one reporter noted, "[The *Time*] article about the videos was published shortly before the Christmas holidays, causing fresh grief for the victim's families."[7] One letter that appeared in the January 1, 2000, issue read:

> I am the parent of two students at Columbine High. Do you think that looking at Harris and Klebold on the cover of your magazine holding the automatic weapons that killed or physically or mentally maimed our children will give us a sense of resolution? It's more like pouring salt on the wounds. To release your story just before Christmas . . . shows a shocking lack of compassion. . . .[8]

THE NEWS BIAS TOWARD EMOTION

At times, emotional and wrenching images are important and appropriate; other times they are superfluous and irrelevant. What informative purpose is served, for example, when we see people grieving following a tragedy such as Diana's death or the Columbine shootings? What is the point in shoving a camera in a woman's face as she recounts how her beloved son died?

In the absence of any real news, the news media push the emotion buttons, hoping viewers won't notice that they have nothing to add to a slowly unfolding story. They run footage of sobbing people hugging each other over and over, in case any viewers were still unsure that what occurred was indeed a tragedy.

Notice that the media's emotion bias also exists in the choice of who is interviewed. Following a tragedy, those seen dealing with it well or not outwardly affected by it don't make the news. The reporter's biased mindset is clear: The event was a tragedy, and the public's reaction is part of the story—*yet not all reaction to the tragedy is equally newsworthy*. The reporters and cameras seek out the most emotional subjects, and if you are connected to a tragedy but aren't sobbing, screaming, or protesting, you will likely be ignored. This, in turn, reinforces the weight of the tragedy in the public's mind, though that impression is likely to be based on an emotional (and vocal) minority.

Matthew A. Kerbel discusses this type of selective reporting when he provides advice for potential news interviewees in his book *If It Bleeds, It Leads*:

> There are a couple of things you should know so you're prepared when that microphone is raised to your mouth. The first is that what you say matters. Nobody ever made it on the air because they weren't worried about uncertainty and danger. The second is the time it takes to say it matters even more. Anything important can be expressed in less than four seconds.
>
> Imagine you're approached by a local news reporter who tells you there was a murder in your neighborhood and the suspect is still at large. She wants to get your reaction for "Live at Five." You agree. She asks you how you feel. You say something like, "Crime is so random that I can't be bothered to torment myself fretting over the possibility that I'll be next."
>
> Wrong answer.
>
> It's not an unreasonable answer. But it's the wrong answer. Skilled reporters are likely to find it to be too measured and rational. . . . So the reporter will need something emotional, something hysterical, something like, "It's scary. This is a quiet neighborhood. Nobody's safe anywhere."
>
> Acceptable responses might also refer to your intention to lower the blinds, bolt the door, keep a weapon by your bed, or shop for enough canned goods so you don't have to leave the house for a month. Say it in four seconds or less, and you're on the air.[9]

In another example, following the September 11 attacks, ABCNews.com asked those who visited its Web site to answer questions about how they were affected by the attacks. Titled "Trouble Working?" the short polling piece asked, "Have you had difficulties—emotional, physical, logistical—at work since the events of Sept. 11? Does the fear of terrorism or other related problems prevent you from going to work at all? Do you have trouble concentrating? If you're experiencing these problems, you are not alone, and we'd like to hear from you."

Notice the loaded question, designed to elicit a particular response: "If you're experiencing these problems, . . . we'd like to hear from you." Those adjusting well or simply not experiencing these or similar problems were not invited to respond and were unlikely to be heard. ABC News essentially predefined the story and was seeking confirmatory anecdotes to build an article around. Comments that did not fit the "all of America is devastated" news angle were not encouraged, thus biasing the resulting news reporting toward an emotional angle.

Children as Social Barometers

America's children are often presented in the news media as agenda-free barometers of American zeitgeist. After just about any tragedy of national

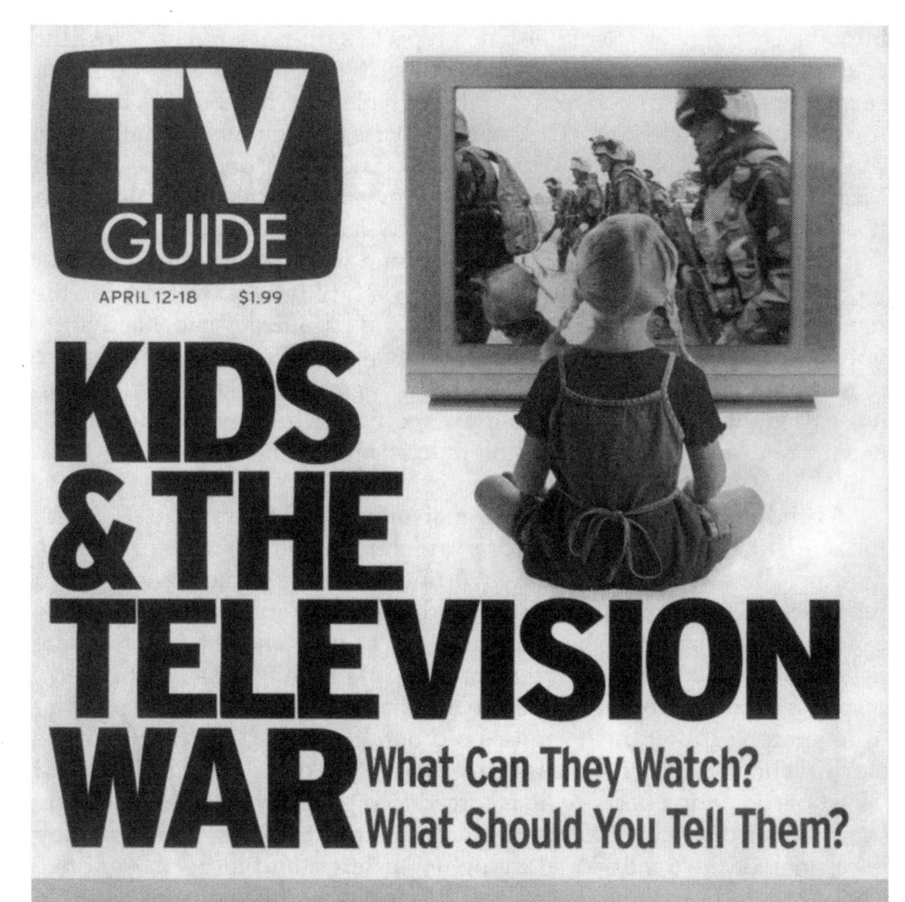

Crises and tragedies often spawn questions of what to tell children about the news.

importance, the news media dispatch reporters into classrooms across the country to report on how kids are coping. News reports show children "expressing their fears and feelings" through pictures, hand-drawn banners, songs, and other activities. Whether the topic is the Columbine High School shootings, the space shuttle *Columbia*, the war with Iraq, or even the death of Mister Rogers, the same questions arise: How are the children dealing with it? What do we tell the children? How much *should* we tell them?

Teachers and reporters pretend they (and we) are glimpsing the inner worlds of children, but this is largely a morality play put on for the reporters and teachers. These are staged and organized school activities, not spontaneous expressions of children's fears or wishes. Children are required to participate in forced solidarity, regardless of their actual opinions, thoughts, or feelings. Children should be informed about world events, and instilled with suitable patriotism, but not forced to act out adults' ideas of their reactions.

Without a hint of skepticism or real journalism, the reporters go with the predefined news story: Children are in turmoil. The nonstory notion that most kids might be coping just fine is not a productive angle that reporters wish to pursue. When children are interviewed, they know exactly what responses the teachers want to hear and the reporters are fishing for. It would be interesting to know how many children's responses are cut from the final broadcasts or articles because a reporter or an editor felt that the responses did not reflect the "right" tone of the story. A child who admits he isn't really upset about a given tragedy and is just participating because he is forced to probably won't get on the air.

Aside from the vacuous journalism, this trend is also troubling because children's individual thoughts, feelings, and ideas are ignored. They are told how they are supposed to feel, what they are supposed to think, how they are supposed to interpret the events around them.

This approach ignores the fact that children take cues from the adults around them and often act as they are expected to act. Many kids exhibit fear because they think they are *supposed* to. Parents and teachers see them as fragile, hypersensitive, and unable to deal with reality. The adults coerce children to enact what they think society wants them to feel or express. Thus they are photographed making memorials, sending messages, and concocting political statements in response to events they little understand or care about. Concerned parents might do far better to try to control their own reactions than worry about their children's.

National, impersonal tragedies simply have far more emotional weight for adults than children. Instead of fretting over a war in Iraq or the loss of the two tallest buildings in Manhattan, most kids, I suspect, are far more interested in what's going on in the latest pop star's love life, music videos, or the latest video game for Playstation 2. Simply put, the lives of kids and adults are quite different. Because most kids don't spend hours watching the news about whatever scares or tragedies are being hyped that week, they don't work themselves into a pubescent funk worrying about them. This is clearly reflected in polls that ask kids what *they* are concerned about: Studies consistently show that the issues kids worry about are very different than those their parents and teachers worry about.[10]

The news media fill pages and airwaves offering advice on what to tell children about the news. It is ironic that American adults, who themselves are largely ignorant of national and global issues, suddenly take such a keen interest in making sure that their children have at least a superficial understanding of each new crisis. If the news media itself wasn't geared toward sensationalizing crime and tragedy, this would likely be far less of an issue.

In some cases the activities and emotions portrayed by the media may be genuine and self-generated, but more often they seem imposed on children. Helene Guldberg, writing for *Spiked* magazine online, pointed out that

> [d]espite all the concern, there is a distinct lack of evidence that children have been adversely affected or distressed by [the September 11 attacks]. . . . A colleague's eleven-year-old brother described how his classmates discussed among themselves (in gory detail, as many adults did) what they had watched on TV on September 11: "We were saying to each other: Did you see those people jumping out of the windows?!" But the horror of the event didn't stop them [from] inventing a new playground game called "Blow up Bin Laden": "We started screaming and running every time a plane passed, but the teachers asked us to pray for peace and stop messing about."[11]

A recently retired schoolteacher in upstate New York told me about the reactions of her former students to the September 11, 2001, attacks: "I can't speak for all the kids, but I can tell you what most of the kids [I taught] would be thinking when they saw the planes hit the [World Trade Center] buildings: Cool! Look at that!"

Following the September 11 attacks, one teacher described how she "watched in horror" as her fifth-grade students made three-foot high stacks of books and then toppled them with makeshift airplanes: "My first instinct was to yell at them. I thought how could they be so insensitive but then I realized they were trying to tell us something in the only way they could. Even though they were smiling and laughing, I knew they were hurting inside."[12]

In another news report, Associated Press writer Sara Kugler began:

> With crayon drawings and building block toys, children in the New York area are still resurrecting the World Trade Center. Then they ignite the drawings in scribbled orange flames, and topple the blocks with their small fists. Nearly a year after the nightmare of Sept. 11, children are still struggling to understand what they went through that morning. . . . Parents say their children show signs of stress in their play, building and then destroying towers of blocks.[13]

This sort of reporting reflects little more than adults' projection of their own fears onto children. If kids aren't playing, that's a sign of stress. If kids are "smiling and laughing" while playing and knocking down towers of blocks, that's a sign of stress. While it's true that children (and many adults, for that matter) can't always express their emotions, that doesn't give adults license to impose their own thoughts and feelings on children. It is misleading to the public, disrespectful to the children, and poor journalism.

Superfluous Sensationalism

When a reporter covers a tragedy or other emotionally charged issue, emotions are bound to come up, but the reporter doesn't have to actively seek them out. Sometimes journalists find ways of injecting emotion into what would ostensibly be a neutral, objective news piece. There are several ways to do this; one can be seen in the similar way two different news outlets reported a story.

A Phoenix, Arizona, man claimed he was sleepwalking when he killed his wife in 1997. He was found guilty and received a life sentence. Two articles on the story were released on January 10, 2000, one by David Schwartz of Reuters and another by Jolyn Okimoto of the Associated Press. Each story emphasized slightly different aspects of the case and trial, but both reporters dutifully noted that the defendant, Scott Falater, "showed no emotion" as the sentence was read.

This practice of carefully noting a defendant's reactions is a staple of courtroom reporting. Millions watched a tight close-up of O. J. Simpson as he heard the verdict that exonerated him, and it was endlessly replayed on television news. The minute nuances of a defendant's facial reaction to his sentence simply is not newsworthy. Yet it is ubiquitous, perhaps because the public is curious in a voyeuristic, vindictive sort of way. People see it as a glimpse of the defendant's feelings; the accused may remain stoic throughout a trial, but when a decision about the rest of her life is read, she usually has some sort of strong emotion about it.

Accounts of executions are even more journalistically dubious. Occasionally newspapers will run gruesome, second-by-second accounts of an executed person's final minutes. When convicted murderer Terry Clark was executed in Santa Fe, New Mexico, in 2001, the *Albuquerque Journal* ran several articles on his death. Certainly, it's possible that the final minutes of a person's life might be newsworthy, for example, if the prisoner gave a last-second admission of guilt or information about other crimes. But that's not why the reporters were there.

Associated Press reporter Barry Massey carefully noted all the lurid, morbid details as he and others gathered around to watch a person die: "Clark swallowed hard. His cheeks puffed as he expelled a breath with a low gasp. Clark pinched his face together, grimacing as if he felt the drugs taking control and shutting down his body."[14]

Is this sort of reporting something to be proud of? What journalistic purpose is being served? Does the story somehow help inform the public, give them useful information, or help them understand the issues? Is using newspaper space to tell readers about Clark's final facial and finger movements really serving the public interest?

In news media coverage of a young woman who was attacked with a brick in New York City, emotionally loaded words and violent verbs were used to describe the attack. Associated Press writer Larry McShane wrote that the woman was clinging to life after an attack by a homeless man who "*smashed* a 6-pound brick *into her skull*," and "*slammed* the 8-inch gray paving stone into the back of [her] head" in front of "several *horrified* witnesses" (all italics mine).[15]

Another AP writer, Beth Gardiner, described the victim as "*bashed* in the head" (italics mine), though a few sentences later she states the victim was simply "struck from behind."[16]

The violent verbs used to describe the attack, as well as the detailed description of the weapon (a 6-pound, 8-inch gray paving stone) and the back story of the young woman's recent move to the big city from Texas ("we were just starting to feel comfortable here," her roommate said), leave no doubt that the story was spiced up. Simply reporting that a woman was hit in the head with a brick and in critical condition was too bland; reporters want readers, and they assume that readers want emotion and sensationalism.

Following such emotional reporting and the public outrage it helped fuel, New York City mayor Rudolph Guliani announced a crackdown on street people, forcing them to accept help, move along, or face arrest. This was met with protest from homeless advocates, and the effort was toned down after it was discovered that the man accused of the crime was not, in fact, living on the street after all. It seems unlikely that the mayor would have gone to such measures (and the case gained such notoriety) had reporters simply reported the facts objectively and without loaded words.

Even the PBS series *Frontline*, usually a bastion of levelheadedness, jumped on the hysteria bandwagon with its January 18, 2000, profile of teen killer Kip Kinkel, titled "The Killer at Thurston High." *Frontline* correspondent Peter J. Boyer gave in to hyperbole with material like:

> Schoolyard shootings. A violent choreography that in the course of a school year became stunningly commonplace. In homes across America, there was an awakening to a most unwelcome thought: Our schools are not the safe havens we had come to assume them to be. . . . What would you find if you opened the door into a young life that had produced an unspeakable horror?

Despite Boyer's breathless prose, statistically schoolyard shootings were—and are—anything but "stunningly commonplace."

For a story on road rage, Associated Press reporter Erin McClam recounted a terrifying ordeal:

> Two-year-old Anthony Grimes was asleep as his father's 18-wheeler rushed down the interstate, carrying the family home to Alabama for Easter. Then a complete stranger fired a bullet that ripped through Anthony's shoulder and the side of his face, leaving him clinging to life. Now his father, Jeremy Grimes, spends hours staring through the glass of a children's intensive-care unit, at the tubes twisting out of his son's little body. . . . This is what Grimes remembers: His wife, panicked, calling out to the boy. His other son, 4-year-old Joshua, screaming: "Pull over! Pull over!"
>
> Blood everywhere.[17]

This account was clearly hyped for sensationalism; the last line, "Blood everywhere," was placed on its own paragraph to draw attention and weight to the words.

The incident is certainly a tragedy, and the family and little boy deserve all the support and compassion they can get. But it's already a tragedy without McClam "juicing up" the story with loaded words. In this particular article, this use of sensationalism was used to help draw attention to what McClam believes is a serious and growing national problem.

Reporters' motives aren't always altruistic: If they can make their article seem more universal, more relevant, it raises the profile of both the reporter and the piece. Framing this case as symbolic of a growing epidemic of road rage instead of a nearly unique freak occurrence bolsters the article's newsworthiness—at the expense of accuracy.

McClam asserts that "road rage—random violence committed by infuriated drivers—is becoming more common each year." Somewhat paradoxically, McClam later states that the most recent American Automobile Association study was conducted in 1996 and found "an average

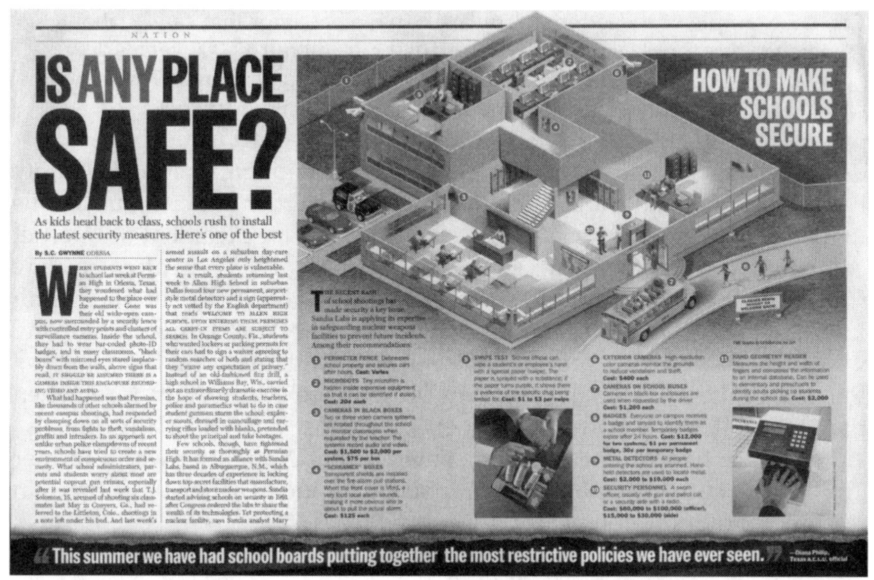

NATION

IS ANY PLACE SAFE?

As kids head back to class, schools rush to install the latest security measures. Here's one of the best

By S.C. GWYNNE ODESSA

When students went back to school last week at Permian High in Odessa, Texas, they wondered what had happened to the place over the summer. Gone was their old wide-open campus, now surrounded by a security fence with controlled entry points and clusters of surveillance cameras. Inside the school, they had to wear bar-coded photo-ID badges, and in many classrooms, "black boxes" with mirrored eyes stared implacably down from the walls, above signs that read, IT SHOULD BE ASSUMED THERE IS A CAMERA INSIDE THIS ENCLOSURE RECORDING VIDEO AND AUDIO.

What had happened was that Permian, like thousands of other schools alarmed by recent campus shootings, had responded by clamping down on all sorts of security problems, from fights to theft, vandalism, graffiti and intruders. In an approach not unlike urban police clampdowns of recent years, schools have tried to create a new environment of conspicuous order and security. What school administrators, parents and students worry about most are potential copycat gun crimes, especially after it was revealed last week that T.J. Solomon, 15, accused of shooting six classmates last May in Conyers, Ga., had referred to the Littleton, Colo., shootings in a note left under his bed. And last week's armed assault on a suburban day-care center in Los Angeles only heightened the sense that every place is vulnerable.

As a result, students returning last week to Allen High School in suburban Dallas found four new permanent, airport-style metal detectors and a sign (apparently not vetted by the English department) that reads WELCOME TO ALLEN HIGH SCHOOL. UPON ENTERING THESE PREMISES ALL CARRY-IN ITEMS ARE SUBJECT TO SEARCH. In Orange County, Fla., students who wanted lockers or parking permits for their cars had to sign a waiver agreeing to random searches of both and stating that they "waive any expectation of privacy." Instead of an old-fashioned fire drill, a high school in Williams Bay, Wis., carried out an extraordinarily dramatic exercise in the hope of showing students, teachers, police and paramedics what to do in case student gunmen storm the school: explorer scouts, dressed in camouflage and carrying rifles loaded with blanks, pretended to shoot the principal and take hostages.

Few schools, though, have tightened their security as thoroughly as Permian High. It has formed an alliance with Sandia Labs, based in Albuquerque, N.M., which has three decades of experience in locking down top-secret facilities that manufacture, transport and store nuclear weapons. Sandia started advising schools on security in 1998 after Congress ordered the labs to share the wealth of its technologies. Yet protecting a nuclear facility, says Sandia analyst Mary

Alarmist news stories fuel the myth that schools are dangerous and children are threatened.

of nearly 1,500 incidents each year."[18] If the latest figures are four years old and indicate that about the same number of incidents occur annually, upon what basis can McClam conclude that road rage is "becoming more common each year"?

The truth is that road rage is in fact very rare, and the Grimes shooting, while tragic, is far from representative of the typical case of road rage. Barry Glassner, a professor of sociology at the University of Southern California, examined reportage of the road rage phenomenon for his 1999 book *The Culture of Fear*. He found

> only one article that put [the 1997 AAA study's] findings in proper perspective: a piece in *U.S. News & World Report* noted that, of approximately 250,000 people killed on the roadways between 1990 and 1997, the AAA attributed 218 deaths, or less than one in a thousand, directly to angry drivers. And of the 20 million motorists injured during that period the AAA attributed less than 1 percent of those injuries to aggressive driving.[19]

Glassner notes that road rage, like other "pseudodangers," allows opportunities to divert attention from social problems we don't want to face:

> An example of the latter is drunk driving, a behavior that causes about eighty-five times as many deaths as road rage (about 17,000 versus 200). . . . [Yet] polls taken on the eastern seaboard during the late 1990s found people more concerned about road rage than drunk driving.[20]

When a story doesn't seem juicy or sexy enough, the media rarely have compunctions about latching onto irrelevant or superfluous details for sensationalism. Patrick Naughton, a former vice president of Internet company Infoseek, was arrested on September 14, 1999, after he flew from Seattle to California to have sex with a young girl he met in an Internet chat room. At the time of his arrest, the Walt Disney Company was in the process of acquiring Infoseek, and Naughton had been fired by the time of the final acquisition. Why is all this relevant? It isn't. Yet when the story hit the press, virtually every article mentioned (incorrectly) either in the headline or the first sentence that Naughton was a former "Disney executive." One Reuters report mentioned Disney three times in its three-paragraph-long story.

The Disney angle was pure, irresponsible hype and lurid sensationalism. Nothing Naughton did relating to the charges had anything remotely to do with Disney: the meeting didn't take place at Disneyland, on Disney company time or property, or anything else. The reputed link between family- and kid-friendly Disney and Naughton's charges is notable for its shock value, but not its accuracy or relevance.

When a bedridden double amputee and his elderly mother were found dead of natural causes in Avon, Ohio, Associated Press reporter Thomas Sheeran sought out the ghoulish, sordid details:

> Richard Donaldson, 37, may have been able to see the body of his dead mother down the hall before he died several days later of dehydration, Lorain County Coroner Paul Matus said Tuesday. . . . "All he had to do (to see her body) was to sit up in bed and lean forward," Matus said.[21]

Of what possible relevance is that morbid detail? Isn't the story sad enough, a double amputee dying of dehydration all alone, without going into whether or not he could see his dead mother on the floor? Perhaps he could smell her rotting flesh while he rolled in his own sticky feces for weeks. Is that relevant? Does knowing what he *might* have seen, or felt, or thought, help readers understand what happened? We will never know if he did or didn't see his mother's body, and such lurid conjecture has no place in responsible journalism.

Sometimes reporters claim that reporting the grisly details of a person's death somehow honors his memory. A case in point is *National Post* newspaper columnist Christie Blatchford, who covered the trial of

Ken Murray. Murray served as the lawyer for convicted torture murderer Paul Bernardo in St. Catharines, Ontario. Bernardo and his wife, Karla Homolka, kidnapped, raped, and tortured two teenage girls in 1995. Videotapes made by Bernardo showed him and his wife attacking the girls, and the trial was filled with lurid details of sexual assault and torture. Murray found the videotapes—and withheld them from police. During the trial, the tapes were played, and reporters heard "the words the girls were forced to say, their sobs and their doomed pleas." Writes Reuters reporter Lydia Zajc, "Blatchford, who covered Murray's trial, feels it was necessary to air every detail to keep alive the memory of the dead. 'The best way to honour, in my view, those girls who were so horribly tortured and killed is to remember them.'"[22]

But is that the case? Would the girls want to be remembered for the descriptions of the violations done to their bodies and their sobs for mercy, or might they prefer to be remembered for their musical talents, sports abilities, or good social works? Might they not prefer to be remembered as whole people instead of as violated victims?

JOURNALISTS CROSSING THE LINE

At times, journalists cross the line from embellishing stories with heart-wrenching—but true—facts to outright fabrication.

One example was a story that emerged from a plane crash on August 16, 1987. Northwest flight 255 crashed at Detroit Metropolitan Airport, killing all on board except four-year-old Cecelia Cichan, whom news reports described as being spared only because she was "clutched in the lifesaving arms of her dead mother." The story made headlines worldwide. As folklorist Jan Brunvand describes,

> In mid-December, however, when files of the National Transportation Safety Board's investigation of the accident became available, it was revealed that the girl had been found thirty-five yards away from the body of her mother and six to eight feet away from any other bodies. Trained journalists working on the scene were at a loss to explain how the fantasy details crept into the reports, though once the anecdote was *printed*, journalists were reluctant to publish the truth.[23]

David McCullough, in his book *The Johnstown Flood*, relates an identical incident (and other embellished and fabricated journalistic details) in the reporting of the 1889 flood in Johnstown, Pennsylvania.[24]

One of the dangers of emotional reporting is that it lends itself to fabrication and journalistic fraud. The venerable and respected *New York Times*

Times Reporter Who Resigned Leaves Long Trail of Deception

A staff reporter for The New York Times committed frequent acts of journalistic fraud while covering significant news events in recent months, an investigation by Times journalists has found. The widespread fabrication and plagiarism represent a profound betrayal of trust and a low point in the 152-year history of the newspaper.

The reporter, Jayson Blair, 27, misled readers and Times colleagues with dispatches that purported to be from Maryland, Texas and other states, when often he was far away, in New York. He fabricated comments. He concocted scenes. He stole material from other newspapers and wire services. He selected details from photographs to create the impression he had been somewhere or seen someone, when he had not.

And he used these techniques to write falsely about emotionally charged moments in recent histo-

CORRECTING THE RECORD

An accounting: The journalistic deceptions in 36 articles, Pages 22-23.

The Times for nearly four years, and he was prolific. Spot checks of the more than 600 articles he wrote before October have found other apparent fabrications, and that inquiry continues. The Times is asking readers to report any additional falsehoods in Mr. Blair's work; the e-mail address is retrace@nytimes.com.

Every newspaper, like every bank and every police department, trusts its employees to uphold central principles, and the inquiry found that Mr. Blair repeatedly violated the cardinal tenet of journalism, which is simply truth. His tools of deceit were a cellphone and a laptop computer — which allowed him to blur his true whereabouts — as well as

The *New York Times* reports on journalistic fabrications and plagiarism in its own pages.

---

admitted in an unusual front-page article on May 11, 2003, that one of its reporters had continually and purposely deceived its readers for years.[25]

The article began by stating, "A staff reporter for the *New York Times* committed frequent acts of journalistic fraud while covering significant news events in recent months. . . . The widespread fabrication and plagiarism represent a profound betrayal of trust and a low point in the 152-year history of the newspaper." The reporter, Jayson Blair, wrote "falsely about emotionally charged moments in recent history," including the Washington, D.C., sniper attacks and "the anguish of families grieving for loved ones killed in Iraq."

An investigation by *Times* reporters uncovered a widespread and longstanding pattern of deception, fabrication, factual errors, and plagiarism. Despite a history of reprimands and warnings for repeated errors, Blair was kept on staff and eventually promoted. The *Times* said that Blair's deceptions were allowed to continue for so long because of several factors, including Blair's devious use of technology to disguise his location and "a failure of communication among senior editors." Blair, who wrote for the newspaper for nearly four years, resigned on May 1, 2003, citing "personal issues."

The *New York Times* has demonstrated a commendable (if at times belated) willingness to issue corrections. Three years earlier the *Times* printed a lengthy editorial about its flawed and biased coverage of Chinese scientist Wen Ho Lee (see pp. 290–93). At the end of the article on Blair, *Times* editor A. M. Rosenthal is quoted: "When you're wrong in this profession, there is only one thing to do. And that is get right as fast as you can."

Five years earlier, another reporter, Stephen Glass, was also discovered to have concocted a series of fabrications under the guise of journalism. Glass, who had been a reporter for the *New Republic* magazine, tried to turn his notoriety into success with a semiautobiographical novel released in May 2003.[26]

Readers of the *Washington Post* were used to articles describing the crime and drug problems in the nation's capital. But even they were shocked at the depravity surrounding them when they read "Jimmy's World," a Pulitzer Prize–winning article by *Post* reporter Janet Cooke. The article described the life of an eight-year-old addicted to heroin by his ex-prostitute mother's drug-dealing boyfriend. Cooke described the scene as the man, "Ron," "grabs Jimmy's left arm just above the elbow, his massive hand tightly encircling the child's small limb. . . . The needle slides into the boy's soft skin like a straw pushed into the center of a freshly baked cake. . . ." Cooke's story went on to describe further squalor and horrible abuse.

The public's response to the article was swift, and police launched a citywide search for "Ron," Jimmy, and his mother. After three weeks, the police concluded that they were unable to find anyone matching Cooke's descriptions. Later, when confronted by her editors, Cooke denied she had fabricated any sources or quotes. She claimed that she couldn't break confidentiality agreements with her sources and that she had received death threats to keep silent (this last tactic was also claimed by those surrounding the allegedly abused boy Anthony Godby Johnson; see pp. 172–73).

Doubts about Cooke's work were further bolstered when Vassar College notified the *Post* that Cooke had dropped out after a year, a far cry from the graduation with magna cum laude distinction Cooke had reported on her resume. Cooke had also lied about her undergraduate degree, having earned a bachelor's degree, not a master's as she had claimed. Finally Cooke admitted that Jimmy and the characters in her article didn't exist, and resigned. Washington mayor Marion Barry, himself no stranger to drugs, said, "I was very firm in my conviction that Miss Cooke's article was part myth, part truth."[27]

In 1997 Patricia Smith, a columnist for the *Boston Globe*, was a finalist for the Pulitzer Prize. She later resigned after admitting she made up characters and quotes in her columns.[28]

Even the prestigious *Journal of the American Medical Association* was duped into publishing at least one falsified article. The piece, by Shetal I. Shah, was published in the October 18, 2000, issue, and gave an emotional, first-person account of an elderly Alaskan man walking out into the frozen arctic to commit suicide. Shah described his conversation with a toothless, ninety-seven-year-old Inuit villager as he prepared to kill himself in the way of his people.[29]

This story came as a surprise to several people familiar with Inuit culture, including Shah's former supervisor, who wrote to the journal to report that Shah's account was fictional. Shah later admitted that the account was not something he personally had experienced, but instead was based on stories he had been told. The journal's editors said that Shah had presented the essay as fact.[30]

In 2000 one of Germany's most prestigious newspapers, the *Sueddeutsche Zeitung*, fired the editors of a weekly color supplement for publishing fabricated interviews with Hollywood stars. Los Angeles–based freelancer Tom Kummer had filed made-up interviews with Sharon Stone, Ivana Trump, and other celebrities over the past few years. Kummer defended his fabrication as "conceptual art," while the editors issued a two-page apology that said, in part, "Whoever fabricates interviews or knowingly prints fabricated interviews, drives press freedom as a democratic idea into bankruptcy."[31]

"I'm going to die! I'm going to die!" wrote Kim Stacy, a columnist for the Owensboro *Messenger-Inquirer*. "I have terminal brain cancer. I was told I had about 10 months to a year to live." Stacy wrote a series of five articles for the rural Kentucky newspaper about her experience, recounting painful, moving details of her cancer diagnosis and treatment. Many readers followed her columns closely, and were shocked when Stacy admitted that the disease and treatment were lies. The admission came after being confronted with suspicions by another newspaper she worked at previously, where she also lied about having cancer. "We let our hearts overrun our reasoning," *Messenger-Inquirer* publisher Ed Riney admitted. "We were, in retrospect, emotionally involved in a story and unconsciously failed to apply our normal standards of skepticism."[32]

A letter to the editor of the *Los Angeles Times* from Josh Nelson, a twelve-year-old boy, claimed that when he asked New York Mets catcher Mike Piazza to autograph a ball, Piazza demanded fifty dollars. This letter provoked anger toward the multimillionaire pitcher, the incident clearly demonstrating that Piazza was just an overpaid, spoiled athlete with no time for kids. Piazza denied it, but it wasn't until a sports columnist talked to Nelson that the truth came out. According to syndicated columnist Richard Reeves, "The kid told three different stories of what happened. . . . Finally he admitted, 'Piazza never exactly asked me for $50.' Oh? Josh Nelson said he had to 'juice up' the letter a bit to make sure it got published."[33]

While there are many responsible journalists, when the press blow it, they tend to blow it big. A 1999 Associated Press report on a supposed massacre at No Gun Ri during the Korean War won a Pulitzer Prize despite numerous documented inconsistencies and the fact that the main source was shown to have fabricated much of his story.[34] In 2002 many news outlets reported a World Health Organization study that claimed blondes were dying out of the population because of a recessive gene. The WHO never did such a study, and the source of the hoax was never located.[35]

Who, Rigoberta Menchu?

In some cases emotions have been substituted for truth, especially in emotionally moving literary works. False and misleading information has been excused or overlooked by some academics and the public as being irrelevant if the text "serves a larger truth." In fact, the highest honors in the world have gone to storytellers with little regard for truth. The common thread: vivid, emotional stories presented as fact yet partly or wholly made up.

The 1992 Nobel Peace Prize was awarded to a Guatemalan Indian woman, Rigoberta Menchu, following the publication of her autobiography, *I, Rigoberta Menchu*.[36] In it, she describes her struggle as a poor, uneducated, and oppressed Quiche Indian. She became an international spokeswoman for the rights of indigenous peoples, in large part because of her book. Menchu was given honorary doctorates and served on several Latin American panels and commissions. Her book is required reading at many American colleges as a true, firsthand account of native Indians' struggles in Guatemala.

Unfortunately for Menchu, an anthropologist, David Stoll, found some of Menchu's claims suspect. He spent nearly a decade conducting archival research and interviewing over one hundred people, including Menchu's relatives, friends, former classmates, and neighbors. He found that significant sections of Menchu's "true" account were largely made up. Stoll's conclusions were later independently verified by a *New York Times* reporter.

When Stoll's allegations came to light, Menchu dismissed the criticisms as part of a racist political agenda, an unfair and baseless charge. (She eventually admitted that there were "inaccuracies" in her book.)

In truth, however, the problems with Menchu's story go beyond "inaccuracies." She lied about some aspects of her past. She claimed to have spent much of her youth away from home working on distant plantations for low pay, though it's likely she never did; she claimed to witness many events that she never saw; she claimed she had no schooling when in fact she had unusually good schooling; she claimed that her father struggled against wealthy landowners when in fact her father was a landowner himself, struggling against other Indians. She fit the facts to accommodate her politics as it suited her. As Stoll writes in his book *Rigoberta Menchu and the Story of All Poor Guatemalans*, "The story she told in 1982, the one that launched her career, had been told with the fervor of a convert. Now she was famous, but the fervor had passed, and words transformed into a book had defined her, apparently forever, as someone she was not."[37]

There is no question that much of what was written in *I, Rigoberta Menchu* is mostly true, and the reasons for Menchu's fabrications and omissions are voluminous, understandable, and too complex to detail here. But understanding an author's motivations to bend the truth does not excuse the conduct.

When questions about the book arose, Menchu at first blamed inaccuracies on Elisabeth Burgos, who transcribed Menchu's spoken words into the book. A subsequent examination of a portion of the original interview tapes confirmed, however, that in fact Burgos had faithfully and accurately reported what was told to her. Menchu later declared of the book that made her famous, "That is not my book."

The director of the Norwegian Nobel Institute said in 1998 that despite questions raised about the book, revoking the prize was not an option and that the award was not based solely on the book. Stoll himself has stated that he doesn't believe that Menchu's low regard for truth should necessarily disqualify her from the prize.

The fact that Rigoberta Menchu falsified her story is only a small part of the issue. The Nobel Institute, as bestower of the highest honor in literature, should have confirmed Menchu's story instead of immediately championing her as a hero and her story as a textbook case in the oppression of native peoples. Yet it was sucked in, let emotion cloud its judgment, and allowed fabrication to be passed off as truth under the respected Nobel imprimatur.

What does it say to struggling writers and activists who see the money, prestige, and support Menchu garnered (through her Rigoberta Menchu Foundation), despite her unmasking? The case can only encourage dishonesty and exaggeration. It is unfair to those who struggle honorably and tell their stories truthfully, without embellishment. They may see that, if you just make up details of a brother's death or recast a family squabble as government oppression, you can attract international attention and donations to your cause.

It is certainly true that many indigenous peoples have been and continue to be oppressed, both in Latin America and throughout the world. Their struggles are honorable and should be supported. But lies cannot be used as shortcuts to the truth. We set a dangerous precedent if we show indifference to people in positions of authority and prestige who lied and fabricated their past and achievements to get there. One false history is as good as another, yet there is only one truth.

The Ordeal of Kaycee Nicole

On May 14, 2001, a young woman named Kaycee Nicole died after a long illness. A blonde nineteen-year-old in Kansas, she had endured a long string of health crises, including a blood clot lodged in her brain, high fever, seizures, an aneurysm in the artery that fed her liver, blood clots in her arm, and a ruptured vein in her esophagus. But it was complications from leukemia that finally ended her life. Throughout it all, Kaycee was not alone in her pain; for two years she had shared her ordeals, loves, fears, dreams, and pain, with hundreds of people through her online diary, "Living Colors." She wrote a Web log ("blog"), with her online friends cheering her on and grieving with her when she was in pain. Kaycee wrote poetically and bravely about overcoming adversity, displaying a maturity and intimacy that many found inspirational.

She was soon being promoted around the Web. Radio station 91X in San Diego, California, selected Kaycee to be highlighted as an inspiring person in honor of Dr. Martin Luther King. The station posted a notice on its Web site telling listeners that "the person who writes 'Living Colors' has never led a march or spoken in front of congress. She has never won a Nobel prize or been arrested for her beliefs. But reading the day-to-day thoughts of Kaycee Nicole is perhaps the most inspiring pursuit of dreams on the Web or anywhere."

Her death stunned hundreds of people. Most had gotten to know Kaycee well, reading her diary and hearing about her through word of mouth. They exchanged e-mails, shared inspiring stories and poems, and sent her get-well gifts. Some people, including Randall van der Woning, a Canadian Web designer living in Hong Kong who hosted her Web site, spoke with Kaycee regularly by telephone. Kaycee wrote about her friends, the handsome doctor who had taken a liking to her, and her heroes. She in fact had a whole section on her Web page titled "Hero's [*sic*] of my Heart." Prominent was a tribute to her mother: "My mom is the one who taught me kindness and love and compassion. She taught me strength by example. She has always gone out of her way to help anyone she could. . . . She taught me to look beyond what I saw on the surface and see the hidden beauty within. There has never been a time when my mom hasn't supported me."

Kaycee's mother, Debbie Swenson, the recipient of the glowing praise, also began posting an accompanying diary. In it she wrote lovingly of Kaycee and helping her daughter through medical setbacks. Both their diaries were very descriptive and emotionally compelling. Kaycee originally asked van der Woning not to publish any photos of herself, wanting, she said, to be known for her words and not judged by her face. Eventually, though, she sent a photo of herself to post on the site. It revealed a pretty blonde girl with a nice smile.

On April 24, Kaycee sent van der Woning an e-mail admitting a terrible secret she had been keeping from her mother: she was dying of liver damage. This panicked him, and he insisted on flying out to be with Kaycee. He was unable to contact either Kaycee or Debbie for a time afterward, and on May 15 van der Woning got a call from a sobbing Debbie who told him the bad news that Kaycee had died.

After a few weeks, readers' suspicions were aroused that something was amiss. There was no funeral for anyone to attend, and Debbie wouldn't provide an address for Kaycee's friends to send flowers. The question was raised as to whether Kaycee existed at all.

When confronted, Debbie Swenson told several different stories before finally admitting that Kaycee had never existed. She had written all the e-mails and Web diaries, made up all the health emergencies. The voice on the other end of the phone pretending to be Kaycee was probably Debbie Swenson all along, who had written all those wonderful things about herself on Kaycee's Web page. Kaycee's photo turned out to be that of a local high school basketball star who didn't know anything about the deception. It was all a long-lived, elaborate hoax fueled by people's goodwill and desire to believe.

This hoax was hardly a harmless prank. Many people were deeply hurt by the deception, and felt both foolish and used. One person, calling Kaycee the "epitome of bravery and spirit," wrote that "many of us pray for her survival and well being, I am doing the best I can but being what I thought was an agnostic for so many years I but lately have returned to belief."[38] If Kaycee inspired a change from nonbelief to religion, one can only imagine the damage done to this person's faith after such a betrayal.

For van der Woning, the cost was emotional as well as financial. He had lost both parents to cancer, most recently his father in 1999. This, along with a trusting nature, had made him especially vulnerable to Kaycee's story. When he was told that Kaycee was dead, he relived much of the pain of his father's death. While worrying about the person he thought was his dear friend, van der Woning was on an emotional roller coaster. According to his online recap of the whole case, "The End of the Whole Mess," for two years van der Woning worried about Kaycee, fearing for her life. He describes the time after he heard about Kaycee's aneurysm as "a period of high stress and anxiety." He grieved with her, was "sick inside" when she was ill again, and was stunned and "totally numb with shock" when he heard that she had died.

"She used me," he writes, "knowing that I was putting myself out to serve her and Kaycee. I made myself available. I altered my schedules. I lost sleep. I devoted my time to help other human beings in need, or so I thought."

Van der Woning felt horribly betrayed and manipulated. He writes, "I'm dealing with embarrassment, betrayal, anger, resentment, regret, and disappointment. I felt worry, anxiety, fear, dread, sorrow, and grief. . . . I invested huge amounts of emotional and spiritual energy in the belief that somehow I was helping . . . I have the shakes. I have headaches. I'm physically, mentally, and emotionally exhausted." This cruel emotional manipulation went on for months and years, not only to van der Woning but to hundreds of other people.

One person who had turned to Kaycee had a best friend whose mother died of leukemia. In a sad and angry post to Swenson, the person wrote, "You basically just took the knife and twisted it for him and for everyone else here who found themselves in a deep, dark place and needed something to help them up."[39]

In an article posted following the revelation, one writer noted that "most people believed that Kaycee was real because no one would attempt such a massive ongoing hoax. That was the stuff of outlandish conspiracy theories. Supporters assumed that the family just wanted to maintain an appropriate level of privacy." The evidence that Kaycee was fictional began to add up. Among the reasons cited: (1) "People began to realize that no one had actually met Kaycee in real life, even those who had frequent phone conversations with her over the course of several years time"; (2) "Kaycee often quoted song lyrics in her posts, 1960s and 1970s song lyrics. And her posts seemed to be written by someone older than 19"; (3) No one could find an obituary; (4) "No one could show that anyone named Kaycee Nicole had lived in Oklahoma or Kansas."

Those who were duped by Swenson are not gullible fools. Kaycee's journals were very believable and detailed, and few want to question the truthfulness of a sick person who they find inspiring. But in the end hundreds—perhaps thousands—of people were emotionally used and manipulated. And why? Some have suggested that Swenson gained financially by the hoax, though since the loss is probably less than a thousand dollars the FBI declined to investigate. More likely it was simply done for attention and ego. Swenson got to be a hero and have legions of people eagerly awaiting her next journal.

In some respects, this sort of desire for attention is similar to the psychological condition Munchausen's by proxy, in which a caregiver, usually the mother, purposely inflicts or exaggerates the child's medical problems to gain sympathy and attention. Whatever the reasons, many people who let their emotions cloud their judgment were taken advantage of and emotionally abused.

The Strange Case of Anthony Godby Johnson

When it comes to tragic stories, Anthony Godby Johnson's is without equal. According to his 1993 book, *A Rock and a Hard Place*,[40] his parents beat him, allowed their friends to rape him, and denied him food and a bed. In 1989, when he was eleven and on the verge of suicide, Tony fled from his horrific abuse and into the arms of a New York city couple who adopted him. Yet there was more tragedy lying in wait: Tony soon found out that he was dying of AIDS. Tony's book garnered much acclaim, with *USA Today* calling Tony a "boy with a powerful will to love"; and book reviews posted on Amazon.com gush of this "powerful" and "incredible" story.

Tony's book may be the true story of a brave young man against incredible adversity—or one of the longest-running modern literary hoaxes. *Newsweek* reporter Michele Ingrassia tried to track Tony down to verify his story, but found not a sick, tragic boy but a byzantine Chinese puzzle:

> Paul Monette, the award-winning author who wrote the foreword to the book, has never met Tony in person. . . . Tony's agent has never seen him, nor have . . . Tony's editor and publicist. The litany of Tony non-sightings could populate an Elvis convention: Norma Godin, executive director of the New Jersey Make-A-Wish Foundation, which gave Tony a computer, has never met Tony. Neither has her son Scott, who installed the computer in his house. . . . The only person *Newsweek* could find who says she has seen Tony is his adoptive mother, and she ferociously guards every shred of information.[41]

Following the publication of that article, an Associated Press reporter said she was granted an interview with Tony, though she refused to divulge any quotations or details of the meeting. Tony's adoptive mother said she has received death threats and fears for Tony, and that is why she refuses to grant access to him. (Note that this excuse has been used before to cover up faked stories.)

Nearly ten years after Tony's book came out, there is still no evidence that the "author" even exists. Contacted in 2000, Ingrassia says that, to her knowledge, Tony has never been seen publicly, despite making an "appearance" on *Oprah*, interviewed with both his identity and face obscured. And there's another reason to doubt his story: According to his book, Tony contracted AIDS in the very early 1990s. That means he has been dying from AIDS-related illnesses for more than a decade. And since drug cocktails to slow the progress of AIDS have been available only in the past few years, that means that we're being asked to believe that a boy with an already compromised immune system is still alive and (fairly) well after being ravaged by unchecked AIDS for at least a decade. Yes, there are people living with AIDS who are in seemingly good health; they are the lucky people who started taking the drugs in the early stages of their disease, not after many years.

He has suffered from an amazing variety of health problems, including immune problems, tuberculosis, a stroke, recurring pneumonia, syphilis, and shingles, as well as losing a leg, his spleen, and at least one testicle. One doctor at Northwestern University School of Medicine, and an expert on the life expectancy of AIDS patients, expressed doubt that Johnson could live this long with all the health problems he claims to have had: "This is one unique individual."

A person claiming to be Tony's adopted mother sounded exactly like Tony on the telephone (and an expert in voice analysis concluded they were the same person). Searches for Tony's birth certificate have come up empty. Though Tony claims his parents were tried for abusing him (and his police officer father was supposedly killed in prison) no one at the Manhattan district attorney's office or the New York Department of Corrections has heard of the case. A young woman who fits the description of Tony's sister said she'd never met him. And so on. Over and over, Tony's facts just don't check out. The remarkable story is far too complex to go into here; readers are invited to read Tad Friend's excellent article in the *New Yorker*.[42]

A quote Tony provided *Newsweek* hints at his disregard for truth and reliance on feelings: "It's a book about my feelings and perceptions." But the setting and framework for those "feelings and perceptions" are supposedly real events: Either they happened or they didn't.

Apparently, in the rush to defend Tony's book (and avoid tarnishing the reputation of a vocal AIDS advocate), those surrounding Tony abandoned even a modicum of skepticism. In follow-up letters to the editor in the June 21, 1993, issue of *Newsweek*, both the senior editor at Tony's publishing house and the executive director of Northern Lights Alternatives (an HIV/AIDS support organization) vociferously defended Tony's reality. Wrote Amy Amabile of Northern Lights,

> [M]any so-called journalists are willing to expose and exploit people with AIDS and victims of child abuse for the sake of a story. . . . This is

> not the first time a child prodigy's words have met with skepticism. . . . Fortunately, Tony has enough self-esteem to believe in himself, whether or not *Newsweek* does.

The issue is thus framed as an attack on an abused child's self-esteem, not a legitimate inquiry into the reality of an author and the truth of his story.

When I posted my suspicions about Johnson in a review of his book on Amazon.com, many readers jumped to his defense, some quite angrily. They said that Tony doesn't meet people because he is concerned about his privacy. I was accused of being "intimidated" by Johnson's talents, called "a conspiracy theorist with an axe to grind," and my suggestion that Johnson may not exist was characterized as "an effort to destroy Tony and, by association, anyone else who was moved by Tony's book." Another writer compared me to a Holocaust revisionist, saying that "There are people who still choose to belief [*sic*] Auschwitz didn't happen. Deny reality and it disappears."

Curiously, though all the writers claim friendships with Tony, not one of them claims to have actually met him *in person*. They mention e-mails, letters, and telephone calls, but no face-to-face meetings. The public's reluctance to closely examine its heroes insulates them from honest criticism.

A sampling of reviews from Amazon.com for *A Rock and a Hard Place* show that many readers, though apparently believing Tony's book, seem to suspect that perhaps the real author is someone older than the fourteen-year-old the author claimed to be:

- In a review posted August 25, 1998, a New Hampshire reader wrote, "Anthony Godby Johnson has the wisdom of some one [*sic*] twice his age."
- A review posted January 20, 1999, by a chaplain from Altus, Oklahoma read, ". . . [N]ever have I been so taken by the words of one so much wiser than his years."
- A reader from Carmel, California, posted a review on June 5, 1999, saying, "Anthony Godby Johnson was one extraordinary youngster and his book reads like an adults [*sic*]."
- Says a reader from Fort Collins, Colorado, in a posting on November 8, 1997, "I had to look again to verify that a fourteen-year-old wrote this book."

Indeed.

Journalists, editors, and average citizens use emotion to blind us to their duplicities while they garner prestige and awards for their fictions passed off as truths. What message does it send to honest, hard-working reporters who verify sources and do solid journalism when they are in competition with others who pass fiction off as serious journalism—and win?

When writers fudge the line between fiction and nonfiction, journalism suffers, and we all suffer. A reporter who adds minor but colorful details to his articles steps into muddy waters. It also, in a way, shows a lack of imagination and laziness. Surely the real world is interesting and colorful enough to stand alone without fiction and sensationalism; if it's not, perhaps it's not the subject but the source that needs attention. A journalist who can't make a story good without embellishing facts isn't doing a good job and should find another line of work.

NOTES

1. John Stossel, "Give Me a Break!" *20/20 Friday*, October 22, 1999.

2. Jacqueline Sharkey, "The Diana Aftermath," in *The Media and Morality*, ed. Robert M. Baird, William E. Loges, and Stuart Rosenbaum (Amherst, N.Y.: Prometheus Books: 1999), p. 105.

3. Mark Harris, "Television Is Relentless," *Entertainment Weekly*, September 19, 1997, p. 24.

4. Walter Isaacson, "To Our Readers; Why We Went Back to Columbine," *Time*, December 20, 1999, p. 6.

5. Holly Kurtz, "Moment of Silence for Columbine," *Denver Rocky Mountain News* [online], denver.rockymountainnews.com/shooting/0324aprl1.shtml [March 24, 2000].

6. Michael Janofsky, "Columbine Parents Ask Sheriff to Resign over Tapes of Gunmen," Associated Press [online], wire.ap.org [December 21, 1999].

7. Jeff Kass and Tillie Fong, "Columbine Report to Be Edited," *Denver Rocky Mountain News* [online], denver.rockymountainnews.com/shooting/0328coll.shtml [March 28, 2000].

8. Joanne Abel, "Letter to the Editor," *Time* (January 1, 2000).

9. Matthew A. Kerbel, *If It Bleeds, It Leads: An Anatomy of Television News* (Boulder, Colo.: Westview Press, 2000), p. 138.

10. Claudia Wallis, "The Kids Are Alright," *Time*, July 5, 1999.

11. Helene Guldberg, "Are the Kids All Right?" *Spiked* [online], www.spiked-online.com/Articles/00000002D292.htm [October 25, 2001].

12. Michele Norris, "Troubled Emotions," ABC News [online], abcnews.go.com/sections/living/DailyNews/wtc_childrencope010924.html [September 24, 2001].

13. Sara Kugler, "NYC Schools Prepare for 9/11," Associated Press [online], www.softcom.net/webnews/wed/cv/Aattacks-schools.RJYA_CaD.html [August 13, 2002].

14. Barry Massey, "Reporter Gives Firsthand Account of Final Minutes," *Albuquerque Journal*, November 7, 2001.

15. Larry McShane, "Texan Fights for Life after Brick Attack," *Laredo*

Morning Times [online], www.lmtonline.com/news/archive/1118/pagea10.pdf [November 18, 1999].

16. "Brick Attack Victim Heads Home with Family," *Laredo Morning Times* [online], www.lmtonline.com/news/archive/1218/pagea13.pdf [December 18, 1999].

17. Erin McClam, "Tiny Road Rage Victim Clings to Life," Associated Press [online], www.roadrageiq.org/articles/showarticle.asp?faq=11&fldAuto=35 [May 1, 2000].

18. Ibid.

19. Barry Glassner, *The Culture of Fear* (New York: Basic Books, 1999), p. 5.

20. Ibid., p. 8.

21 Thomas Sheeran, "Bodies of Mother, Son Go Unnoticed," Associated Press [online], wire.ap.org [March 8, 2000].

22. Lydia Zajc, "Brutal Sex Killings Again Haunt Canada," Reuters [online], www.reuters.com [May 24, 2000].

23. Jan Harold Brunvand, *The Truth Never Stands in the Way of a Good Story* (Chicago: University of Illinois Press, 2000), p. 166.

24. David McCullough, *The Johnstown Flood* (New York: Simon & Schuster, 1968), pp. 214–20. Thanks to Mike Dennett for this reference.

25. "*Times* Reporter Who Resigned Leaves Long Trail of Deception," *New York Times*, May 11, 2003, p. A-1.

26. Stephen Glass, *The Fabulist* (New York: Simon & Schuster, 2003).

27. Bob Tamarkin, *Rumor Has It: A Curio of Lies, Hoaxes, and Hearsay* (New York: Prentice Hall, 1993), p. 105.

28. Abigail Pogrebin and Rifka Rosenwein, "Not The First Time," *Brill's Content* (September 1998): 12.

29. Shetal I. Shah, "Five Miles From Tomorrow," *Journal of the American Medical Association* 284, no. 15 (2000): 1897–98.

30. Lindsey Tanner, "JAMA Editors Say They Were Duped," Associated Press [online], jama.ama-assn.org/issues/current/ffull/jlt0822-6.html [August 21, 2001].

31. "German Editor Sacked Over Hoax Star Interviews," Reuters [online], www.reuters.com [May 30, 2000].

32. "Reporter Fired for Cancer Tales," Associated Press [online], www.medserv.dk/health/1999/05/12/story07.htm [May 11, 1999]; "Kentucky Newspaper Fires Reporter for Hoax Illness," Reuters [online], www.reuters.com [May 11, 1999].

33. Richard Reeves, "Jaded America Indifferent to Truth," *Albuquerque Journal*, May 15, 1996.

34. Robert L. Bateman, *No Gun Ri: A Military History of the Korean War Incident* (Mechanicsburg, Penn.: Stackpole Books, 2002).

35. Lawrence K. Altman, "Stop Those Presses! Blondes, It Seems, Will Survive After All," *New York Times*, [online], www.nytimes.com/2002/10/02/health/02BLON.html?ex=1054267200&en=b3acf391d00a3793&ei=5070 [October 2, 2002].

36. Rigoberta Menchu, *I, Rigoberta Menchu: An Indian Woman in Guatemala* (New York: Verso, 1987).

37. David Stoll, *Rigoberta Menchu and the Story of All Poor Guatemalans* (Boulder, Colo.: Westview Press, 1999).

38. "Bravery and Spirit" [online], at bastion.diaryland.com/332.html [November 24, 2000].

39. "The End of the Whole Mess" [online], bigwhiteguy.com/mess.php [May 25, 2001].

40. Anthony Godby Johnson, *A Rock and a Hard Place: One Boy's Triumphant Story* (New York: Signet, 1994).

41. Michele Ingrassia, "The Author Nobody's Met," *Newsweek*, May 31, 1993, p. 63.

42. Tad Friend, "Virtual Love," *New Yorker*, November 26, 2001, pp. 88–99.

7

THE CHANGING FACE OF NEWS

The media's selective coverage of the news is in some ways a threat to democracy. This was perhaps most apparent in recent years during the coverage of the 1999 global summit of the World Trade Organization (WTO). The meeting, which took place in Seattle in November of that year, was covered by all the mainstream news media.

The summit was most notable not for its accomplishments but the protests it sparked: Scenes showing armed police using tear gas and pepper spray against unarmed protesters were shown around the world. There was coverage of the WTO, the protests, the methods of the protesters, the city's reactions to the protests, the public's reaction to the city's reaction to the protests, and so on. Yet there was one topic that most of the news media were conspicuously silent about: what, exactly, it was that was being protested *against*. Very few reports in the mainstream news media bothered to detail the reasons that thousands of people marched in the streets, blocked traffic, and led chants. For all the news media bothered to report, it could have been a slacker rebellion against overpriced Starbucks lattes.

A quick examination of the WTO's nature sheds some light on why the organization makes many people uneasy. The WTO was established in 1994 to help guide global commerce between trading partners; it also, critics say, exists largely to promote the interests of multinational corporations. In 1996 the WTO decided that the Clean Air Act was unacceptable because of the restrictions it put on pollutants in imported gasoline. That ruling meant that provisions in the Clean Air Act would be circumvented by the auto industry and auto exhaust emissions would increase. The Clinton administration decided to voluntarily comply with the

WTO's decision, effectively undermining air quality and public safety because the Clean Air Act put a crimp in the plans of multinational companies. Norman Solomon, a nationally syndicated columnist, described the WTO as "a supremely undemocratic institution, [whose officials] deliberate in secret and issue edicts that deem local or national laws to be unfair 'trade barriers' if they impede the pursuit of profits. Laws that protect workers or the environment or human rights are supposed to get out of the way."[1]

Many of the protesters demanded that the regulations address social concerns such as human rights and exploitation of Third World environments and labor. Many developing countries aren't thrilled with the WTO either, claiming that they are forced into unfair trade arrangements that open their markets with little direct benefit.

The protesters' arguments and their points of view were given very short shrift in the mainstream news media. Pro-WTO voices were heard everywhere, but little attempt was made to get the other side of the story, the other point of view. Protesters were, for the most part, demonized, depicted as blindly antigovernment paranoids, and summarily dismissed. Maybe the protesters have valid points; maybe not. But their voices, right or wrong, should have been better heard so the American viewers could decide for themselves.

Although the World Trade Organization is frequently seen as a lapdog of huge corporations, and corporate America specifically, it is true that the United States doesn't always get its way. In August 2002, for example, the WTO ruled that the European Union could impose up to $4 billion in penalties against the United States because its tax breaks for exporters amounted to an illegal subsidy under international law. It was the largest trade penalty ever approved. Oddly, though the news made headlines around the world, very little coverage of the penalty was reported in the American press and it was not mentioned on any of the nightly news broadcasts that evening.[2]

Another, perhaps even more egregious, example was the television networks' collective coverage (or, rather, noncoverage) of the Telecommunications Act. Signed into law by President Clinton in 1996, the act has far-reaching implications for corporate ownership of the mass media. For the first time, it allows television networks to own cable systems and lets a single company own television stations that reach as many as 35 percent of American households. This may not seem like much, but it was a giant step toward the centralization of media outlets under megacorporations. Robin Anderson, in a piece titled "Who Is Killing the Press?" noted that one of the few news shows that covered it, *Nightline*, couldn't get information from a tight-lipped press: "It's possibly the most important communications bill in history, and here's what the networks had to say about it. NBC said, 'No comment.' ABC suggested that we talk to CBS, who told us 'No comment.' And Fox? 'No comment.'"[3] Some mainstream newspapers (not directly affected by the Telecommunications Act) dutifully reported on the bill's passage and implications.

Similar noncoverage occurred in 2002 when campaign finance reform legislation finally passed the Senate after nearly a decade of effort by senators John McCain and Russ Feingold. Among the provisions were bans on soft money (much of which would end up in broadcasters' pockets through ad revenue) and a measure that would require that broadcasters give nonpreemptible time to candidates and national parties at the lowest rate they charged advertisers for the preceding 180 days. Senator Robert Torricelli, sponsor of the measure, said that broadcasters (following years of criticism of the campaign finance system) were "lobbying using the same influence of big money to undermine the legislation so that their profits are protected."[4]

Through the National Association of Broadcasters (NAB), broadcasters lobbied hard against the measures, which by some estimates could cost them $300 million in political advertising each year. The broadcasters vowed to fight through both lobbying and lawsuits to remove the provisions.

The NAB, aware that the political climate and public opinion at the time were not in its favor, was careful not to appear to be too aggressive in opposing the reform bill. Whether explicitly directed or implicitly understood, the broadcasters' wishes were reflected in the way their news departments reported the news. The nightly news broadcasts at the time carried very little coverage of the campaign finance reform efforts, and virtually no mention of the fierce lobbying the networks were doing to stop the bill. The scant coverage the issue did receive was seen in print media.

MEDIA CONGLOMERATES AND THE THREAT TO INFORMATION

As the nation's television networks and newspapers are owned by fewer and fewer parent companies, the quality and breadth of news coverage has been compromised. Due to the incestuous nature of the various media outlets, companies tend to be reluctant to cover or criticize corporations with which they are affiliated.

In his book *The Media Monopoly*, Ben Bagdikian found the problem of advertisers trying to influence the news to be pervasive. He cites a 1992 Marquette University poll in which the vast majority of newspaper editors—93 percent—claimed that advertisers tried to influence their news. Worse,

> a majority said their own management condoned the pressure, and 37 percent of the editors polled admitted that they had succumbed. A recent Nielsen survey showed that 80 percent of television news directors said they broadcast corporate public relations films as news "several times a month."[5]

Bagdikian puts the crux of this problem concisely:

> It is normal for all large businesses to make serious efforts to influence the news, to avoid embarrassing publicity, and to maximize sympathetic public opinion and government policies. Now they own most of the news media that they wish to influence.[6]

Not only do corporate decisions influence what gets on the news, they also influence what doesn't get on the news. Mark Crispin Miller, professor of media ecology at New York University, discussed former *60 Minutes* producer Lowell Bergman's comments on the media in an issue of *Free Inquiry* magazine. Miller wrote:

> Bergman offered a wry commentary on the kinds of revelation that the TV news will *never* bring us, regardless of how many ratings points they might rack up. From the journalists of General Electric, Disney, News Corporation, Viacom, and AOL/Time Warner, there will never come a word of troubling news about the ownership of any franchise in the National Football League because that game is simply worth too much to TV's own proprietors.[7]

Media critic and activist Ronnie Dugger wrote in a 2001 article that

> on the Sunday morning political talk shows, according to a recent study, topics loosely related to corporate power made up only four percent of the discussion topics. When your employer is owned by a just-indicted worldwide price-fixer, how much airtime do you give the story, if any? When your boss is a weapons merchant, what do you report, if anything, about the case against the war?[8]

Disney chairman Michael Eisner is clear on his policy about Disney media (such as ABC) covering Disney interests: "I would prefer ABC not to cover Disney," he said on National Public Radio's September 29, 1998, program *Fresh Air*. "I think it's inappropriate. . . . ABC News knows that I would prefer them not to cover [Disney]." Presumably this policy is intended to facilitate, not stifle, objective reporting, but of course it doesn't work that way. When Eisner speaks of ABC not covering Disney, that obviously does not apply to ABC covering Disney media and promotions, and likely does not apply to positive news about the company.

A report studying the content of the network morning shows conducted by the Project for Excellence in Journalism found that much of the content was infomercials, frequently for products of parent companies. Shows such as CBS's *The Early Show*, NBC's *Today*, and ABC's *Good Morning America* were heavily commercialized. On average, a third of the content is devoted to selling a film, television program, book, or music CD. In one example, the project found that nearly a third of the products promoted on CBS's *The Early Show* are owned by communications giant Viacom—which also own CBS, as well as Paramount Pictures. As Associated Press reporter David Bauder found, the morning show producers are unapologetic:

> I think that Jennifer Lopez being on the "Today" show to talk about her concert on NBC is a completely legitimate view of what morning television is all about, and I don't think you should be criticized for it," said Steve Friedman, a morning show executive producer.[9]

True enough, in our day of ever-larger media companies, some cross-promotion is not only unavoidable but to be expected. Morning shows would be remiss to ignore talent that happened to be working for a parent or sister company. But this approach can also be taken too far, and the lines between legitimate news and in-house promotion easily blurred.

This is not just an academic problem; corporations are becoming more and more powerful and important in our society. With billions of dollars in assets, huge companies can rival small governments in the power and influence they can wield. Many of the protests against the World Trade Organization (mentioned earlier) address this very issue. One of the complaints against the WTO is the enormous power it has, in some cases the power to effectively nullify the laws of a sovereign country. The organization can ignore inconvenient laws restricting environmental pollution, minimum wages, labor laws, and other such regulations that might limit profit, trade, and commerce.

Each year, Project Censored, an ongoing investigative sociology project at Sonoma State University, publishes a book of the previous year's top twenty-five censored news stories. These are news stories that were largely ignored by the mainstream press for various reasons, but that have important implications for the public and solid documentation to back them up. Though a distinctively liberal bias sometimes emerges from their works, it is an invaluable project, and essential reading for anyone interested in media criticism.[10]

At times the corporate influence on local news is more subtle. Even when corporations have no direct power over the news media, they can still manipulate the news in other ways. In 1994 the computer chip maker

Intel was fined for allegedly violating its air pollution permit at its largest plant in Rio Rancho, New Mexico. Intel agreed to pay $40,000 in fines to the New Mexico Environment Department.

The company, long accused by locals of contributing to respiratory and health problems because of its toxic pollution, had a public relations problem on its hands. In a blatant and preemptive attempt to divert attention from the news of its fine, Intel pulled an inspired media sleight-of-hand trick.

Instead of addressing the fact that it was found guilty of pollution for months on end during 1992 and 1993, Intel basked in a well-publicized "Intel Appreciation" event put on by business bigwigs from throughout the Albuquerque metropolitan area. The luncheon was held Wednesday, January 26, 1994, and Intel's press releases to the media stated that the purpose was "to thank Intel for bringing 3,000 construction jobs and 1,000 permanent jobs to the Albuquerque and Rio Rancho areas."

Intel also placed large newspaper ads thanking itself for bringing jobs to the area and listing dozens of locals who expressed their appreciation, including the governor, two senators, and two local mayors. To counter local activists who protested Intel's environmental record and lack of paying gross receipts or property taxes, Intel employees were given signs with slogans like "Intel is a safe place to work" and "Thank you for our jobs!" and held a counterprotest.

Two days later the fine against Intel was quietly announced. The media effort was clearly orchestrated to use corporate clout to drown out bad news with praise and accolades. *Albuquerque Journal* writer Christopher Miller covered the story in an article titled "Applause for Intel," and began with, "It was a show of appreciation seldom witnessed in Albuquerque."[11]

CORPORATE LAWYERS AS NEWS EDITORS

Another impediment to independent journalism is the legal dangers and threats of lawsuits by powerful and litigious corporations. The corporate reminder to keep an eye on the bottom line makes some news departments wary of running in-depth stories that may incur potentially monumental legal bills if their subjects are unhappy with the way they are portrayed.

One of the highest-profile cases of this was the controversy surrounding a *60 Minutes* segment featuring a former Brown and Williamson tobacco company scientist. The scientist, Jeffrey Wigand, was one of the first to publicly confirm what many had suspected for decades: Tobacco companies knew that their product was addictive, and they conducted research into ways of manipulating the nicotine content in cigarettes.

The evidence was solid and corroborated. Yet the problems with airing the piece came not from editors but from lawyers. Concerned about protracted and very expensive lawsuits that might be incurred if *60 Minutes* ran the story, the decision was made to air the segment without Wigand's damning testimony. The fact that the story was essentially gutted by the excising was apparently of little consequence. The story was later made into the Academy Award–nominated film *The Insider*.

Certainly, the lawyers themselves were just doing their jobs, and any news department should be concerned about the potential for lawsuits, making sure that anything that airs is factually correct and legally airtight. The larger issue is the decision not to air important, accurate, and damaging information about a public health threat. *60 Minutes*, in many people's eyes, backed down.

Spiking the Milk: The Fox/Monsanto Story

Another notorious case in which corporate pressure was brought to bear on a news story occurred in the late 1990s when two investigative reporters in Tampa, Florida, began looking into a controversial growth hormone used on dairy cows. The hormone, called rGBH and manufactured by the Monsanto Corporation, was being widely used across the United States as a way to increase milk production. The hormone had been tested and approved by the Food and Drug Administration (FDA), though questions remained about safety for those who consume the milk. Scientists in other countries were sufficiently concerned about the questions surrounding rGBH that the United States was the only major industrialized nation to approve of the drug's use.

The veteran investigative reporters, Jane Akre and Steve Wilson, discovered troubling information regarding the drug's safety testing, including that the longest tests for human toxicity lasted only ninety days and were performed on thirty rats. Worse yet, about a third of those rats developed cysts and lesions. Akre and Wilson also raised questions about lax safety standards and an FDA approval process that, according to several experts, frequently gave cursory approval. The reporters also interviewed health regulators who claimed that they had been threatened then offered a bribe by Monsanto to fast-track the drug's approval.

The four-part series was to air on the local Fox station on February 24, 1997. But just days before the airdate, the station received a letter from a New York law firm representing Monsanto. The letter claimed that the reporters had "no scientific competence" to report the story and that the report contained reckless and misleading allegations.

The report was delayed while the station's general manager reviewed the report. He found no major errors or problems, and it was agreed that Akre and Wilson would offer Monsanto another interview to reply to the allegations. Monsanto refused the interview and sent another letter that referred to "dire consequences for Fox News" if the report aired. Fox, instead of supporting its reporters on an important and well-researched public health story, pressured them to change their story. The report was further delayed, and lawyers presented Akre and Wilson lists of items they wanted changed before the report could air. The reporters did dozens of rewrites, but refused to change the essential facts of the story. The changes, Akre and Wilson knew, "would result in broadcasting what we knew to be false and misleading information to the public." They were repeatedly threatened with termination if they did not change the news story to suit Monsanto's dictates.

One Fox lawyer, Akre said, "could never understand why we insisted on investigating Monsanto's glowing claims about its product. 'While some say this, Monsanto says that' was her approach. Just let the viewers sort it out."[12] (This is a good example of the agnostic objectivity I discussed in chapter 5.) Finally the reporters were fired on December 2, 1997. The following year Akre and Wilson filed suit under a whistleblower law, claiming they suffered retaliation for their refusal to broadcast inaccuracies and distortions.

During the trial Fox attorneys found themselves in the uncomfortable position of suggesting that veteran *CBS Evening News* anchor Walter Cronkite, as an expert witness, was not sufficiently qualified to give testimony on the prebroadcast review of a news story. One attorney, apparently reflecting Fox News's position on the topic, argued that "there is no law, rule, or regulation against slanting the news."

Akre and Wilson eventually won their case, though the appeals process will likely take years. Both journalists have received journalism awards, but are still saddled with staggering legal fees.

These are only a few of the better-known incidents; we will never know how many journalists were unable, for emotional, financial, or legal reasons, to fight back and let the truth be known about corporate attempts to censor and manipulate news.

NEWS AS WIDGET: TED KOPPEL, DAVID LETTERMAN, AND MICKEY MOUSE

In early 2002 executives at the Disney-owned American Broadcasting Company (ABC) approached late-night talk show host David Letterman to try to lure him away from CBS, where he had worked for several years. ABC, hoping to raise its flagging ratings, was looking for a way to capture a younger demographic, which in turn would bring higher advertising revenues. If Letterman accepted the $31-million offer to jump networks, he would run in approximately the same time slot—thereby jeopardizing the venerable and award-winning hard-news show *Nightline,* hosted by Ted Koppel.

ABC made it clear that *Nightline* (widely recognized as one of the best broadcast news shows, with a twenty-two-year history and a shelf full of journalism awards) would be happily pushed aside if David Letterman wanted the slot. Thus arose a near-perfect example of how entertainment programming can drive out news programming and of the corporate mindset applied to news reporting.

The *Washington Post* ran an insightful commentary by Tom Rosenstiel and Bill Kovach in which they point out that "what Disney executives are really arguing is that journalism is just another kind of content; that communication is communication."[13]

To the corporate mindset, television content itself is far less important than who will watch that content, and in what numbers. From *Seinfeld* reruns to *60 Minutes*, from *Wheel of Fortune* to *Nightline,* all programs are essentially identical and interchangeable blocks of time. News is turned into widgets. It is not that the networks are actively against programs that serve to inform and educate the public; perhaps worse, they are indifferent.

Frazier Moore of the Associated Press wrote that "after years of media consolidation, concepts like 'market niche,' 'branding,' and 'multiple platforms' are what matter to the bosses in the content they dispense. A thoughtful, older-skewing newscast has become a marketing albatross, not a public trust and a source of pride."[14]

ABC tried to justify its decision by claiming that *Nightline* was losing money (an assertion since proven untrue). Even more disturbing was a quote from an unnamed Disney executive that *Nightline* was no longer relevant. Ted Koppel answered his anonymous critics with a statement in the March 5, 2002, *New York Times*:

> I would argue that in these times, when homeland security is an ongoing concern . . . when, in short, the regular and thoughtful analysis of national and foreign policy is more essential than ever—it is, at best, inappropriate, and, at worst, malicious to describe what my colleagues and I are doing as lacking relevance.[15]

In the end, Letterman decided to stay with CBS, though ABC was widely and rightfully criticized for its inability or unwillingness to recognize the value of *Nightline* when the opportunity arose to replace it.

Ed Bishop, editor of the *St. Louis Journalism Review at Webster University*, writes that

> NBC, CBS and ABC—where most people get most of their news—are all owned by conglomerates which make more money in jet engines, theme parks and movies than they do delivering the news. In fact, the corporate bosses of the network news departments often see their employees more as pitchmen than journalists.[16]

SEXING UP AND DUMBING DOWN

In the shift from news as a public service to news as an advertising vehicle, the quest for high ratings has led in many cases to a dumbing down of news. The news is largely homogenized, with reporters from different media telling pretty much the same story—and from the same perspective—with only slight variation in phrasing and images.

A 2000 poll conducted by the Pew Research Center for the People and the Press found that 40 percent of journalists say they have purposely avoided newsworthy stories or softened the tone of stories to benefit their news organization. The main reason for this was market pressure, which causes news organizations to avoid stories that the public might find too boring or too complicated. The poll included nearly three hundred local and national reporters and news executives.[17]

James R. Smith, a media professor in New York, believes that recent cable news wars have contributed to a trend in which the news business is more like show business. He writes:

> Notice the number of AOL Time Warner magazine staffers doing segments on defense, health, money, law, and politics. It doesn't take sophisticated research to reveal that recaps, studio interviews with in-house experts, news analysis, anchor cross-talk and loosely identified opinion units have pushed out some hard news.[18]

Many of the news shows, particularly those on cable networks, have redesigned their sets to be more informal, with younger and more attractive reporters. As well, the sound-bite nature of modern news can be seen in the pollution of the broadcast screens. Many, such as those on MSNBC, have multiple sources of information displayed at the same time. While a ticker running across the bottom gives the latest sports and entertainment news, an icon in the corner tells what's coming up next while below that is a regional weather report. Somewhere amid the clutter a news anchor asks a rhetorical question of an in-house expert, who, coincidentally, happens to be the host of the show to follow, turning the session from a news broadcast into a promotion.

THE DEARTH OF FOREIGN NEWS

In newsrooms across America, there is less emphasis on informing viewers and more on entertaining them. One area that has been particularly hard hit is foreign news. If Americans are poorly informed about current events and politics in their own country, they are almost uniformly ignorant about foreign matters.

According to an article by Peter Arnett in the November 1998 *American Journalism Review*,

> Foreign news is disappearing from many of America's newspapers. Today, a foreign story that doesn't involve bombs, natural disaster, or financial calamity has little chance of entering the American consciousness. This happens at a time when the United States has become the world's lone superpower and "news" has so many venues that it seems inescapable. So how is it that Americans are less informed than ever about what's going on in the rest of the world? Because the media have stopped telling us. In the *Indianapolis Star*, for example, in the 30 days of November 1977, there was a total of 5,100 inches of foreign news. In the same month in 1997, foreign news accounted for just under 3,900 column inches, a 23 percent drop over two decades. . . . Television news, during the heyday of Walter Cronkite, John Chancellor, and Frank Reynolds, contained at least 40 percent international coverage. The figure today is 7 to 12 percent and dropping.[19]

According to the *Harper's* magazine index, eighty-eight nations got less than ten minutes' coverage on U.S. network evening news in the 1990s.[20] Less than ten minutes of news coverage on multiple news shows over the course of ten years is abysmal. No wonder many Americans are oblivious to world events.

Each year the editors of *World Press Review* (a magazine that reprints news stories from around the world) collects lists of the top ten news stories compiled by U.S. and overseas editors. The purpose, writes managing editor Margaret Bald, is to "take the measure of U.S. media and public interest in the wider world and highlight the international perspectives we are missing as resources devoted to foreign news continue to diminish in America's newsrooms."[21] In the March 2001 issue, she noted:

> As has been the case in recent years, few of the international news stories that dominated the headlines abroad received the same level of attention in the U.S. media. . . . The international relief organization Doctors Without Borders, which issues its own annual top-10 list of the most underreported humanitarian stories, blamed the intense focus of the American media on the presidential election for what it described as a "virtual blackout of

> international news." Said Joelle Tanguy, executive director of the [organization's] U.S. office, "News of human suffering, from Chechnya to Indonesia, has been obscured by election coverage all year. It is unconscionable that in three presidential debates, including one ostensibly devoted to foreign affairs, not one of the issues on our list surfaced."[22]

Some in the news media lament the status of their profession. ABC's Ted Koppel, in remarks made at the 1997 Committee to Protect Journalists' International Press Freedom Awards ceremony, compared the risks that journalists in other countries face to those American journalists deal with:

> In some respects, journalism in America today may be in greater peril than in some of the more obviously dangerous places that are so clearly inhospitable to our profession. We celebrate the men and women whose dedication to the collection and distribution of facts threatens their very existence. When they antagonize those with money, political power and guns, they risk their lives. We, on the other hand, tremble at nothing quite so much as the thought of boring our audiences. . . . Our enemies are far more insidious than that. They are declining advertising revenues, the rising cost of newsprint, lower ratings, diversification and the vertical integration of communications empires. . . . They are the fading lines between television news and entertainment. There is, after all, a haunting paradox in the notion that, even as we honor journalists abroad for "risking personal and political peril in upholding the highest standards of their profession," their own stories and the stories they cover are increasingly unlikely to lead any of our broadcasts or appear on any of our front pages. We celebrate their courage even as we exhibit increasingly little of our own. It is not death or torture or imprisonment that threatens us as American journalists, it is the trivialization of our industry. . . . We need to help our readers and viewers find their way through the blankets of fog laid down by spin doctors and press secretaries, media advisers and public affairs officers. We react too much and anticipate too little. We struggle to be first with the obvious. The most important events of the past couple of years have not been the O. J. Simpson trial and the death of Princess Diana.[23]

Koppel brought important news about terrible and ongoing civil wars in Africa's Congo in a five-part *Nightline* series titled "Heart of Darkness." In his introduction to the series, Koppel admitted that his profession had failed to give the story the attention it deserved: "How can two and a half million people die over a three-year period and we don't even notice? . . . These are events you should have heard about on *Nightline* years ago." The series had the bad luck of being originally slated for broadcast the week of September 11, 2001, when the World Trade Center and Pentagon were attacked. The voices and stories of genocide in Africa were shuffled around once again, lost in the din of more pressing matters and more urgent news. The series finally aired in January 2003.

The news media's bias against foreign news was also apparent in other areas. *Brill's Content* magazine compared coverage of the 1994 outbreak of genocide in Rwanda in which hundreds of thousands of people were killed to coverage of a kidnapping in Uganda in which eight tourists, including two Americans, were killed. *Time* and *Newsweek* both devoted about twice as much space to the eight foreigners killed than to the eight hundred thousand Africans killed. Daily newspapers such as the *Washington Post* and the *New York Times* gave about comparable coverage to each. If amount of coverage is a measure of importance, American news media feel that a handful of non-Africans equals several hundred thousand Africans.[24]

The consequences of the dearth of foreign news can perhaps most readily be seen in the reaction to the September 11, 2001, attacks. In an ABC News article a week after the attacks, Romy Ribitzky wrote, "prior to last week's attacks, the idea that Americans are all potential targets was completely foreign to them."[25] Many Americans were apparently ignorant of world events, having missed the August 7, 1998, American embassy bombings in Kenya and Tanzania, and the 2000 attack on the USS *Cole* in Yemen. The real world can be a dangerous place, and the insular, cozy illusion that Americans get from ignoring the rest of the world can come back to haunt us. The shock and surprise that many Americans felt on September 11 is the price of wilful ignorance and remarkably poor international coverage by the American news media.

Shortly after September 11, the *Buffalo News* ran an article discussing the lack of foreign news in America. Author Anthony Violanti writes that

> until Sept. 11, hard news and foreign news were out of fashion. Until Sept. 11, the media gave us celebrity culture disguised as real life. . . . What passed for news before, that steady diet of gossip and celebrity, is not going to cut it anymore. In a world that now seems much smaller, more interconnected, and more dangerous, the public has been brutally awakened from its news coma.[26]

Violanti is correct, but conveniently glosses over the fact that the *Buffalo News* itself had done a very poor job of covering international news up until then. The paper's dearth of foreign news is not surprising given managing editor Margaret Sullivan's editorial emphasis. In a 1999 article for *Brill's Content*, writer Charles Kaiser noted:

> Another force drives Sullivan's thinking about page one: Reader surveys consistently show that consumers want as much local news as possible. . . .

> [T]he story that dominates every front page and is always accompanied by a large photograph . . . is supposed to be local whenever possible. . . .[27]

It's somewhat hypocritical of the *Buffalo News* to publish an article wringing its journalistic hands about how poorly informed the American public is regarding international matters. The paper's own editorial decisions (only one example in a national trend) helped fuel American ignorance and "news coma."

Many, both in the public and in the news media, pointed to September 11, 2001, as a turning point in journalism, where fluff stories and soft news would be replaced by useful fact. The effect seems, alas, to have been short lived. According to the Project for Excellence in Journalism, news coverage immediately after the attacks was based on solid sources and hard facts, but soon slipped. Among the findings: the factual coverage dropped from 75 percent in September to 63 percent three months later; 82 percent of print accounts were factual, compared with only 57 percent of the televised stories; and that news coverage heavily favored American and Bush administration policy.[28]

A report issued by the Project for Excellence in Journalism found that the terrorist attacks did not cause any long-lasting changes in the way evening news programs cover the news. The study found that the amount of hard-news coverage returned to about what it was before the attacks.[29]

On a superficial level, one might mistake the marked increase of news shows over the past two decades for an increase in quality journalism. After all, the dictum goes, increased competition should lead to better quality. Yet this has not borne out. The presence of more news shows doesn't necessarily lead to a broader spectrum of topics being covered; instead there is more repetition as more news shows cover the same material.

As Tom Rosenstiel and Bill Kovach wrote in the *Washington Post*, "Television journalism increasingly becomes defined by talk shows, celebrity and consumer segments and soap-operatic episodes on, say, 'Dateline.'"[30]

Newsweek reporter John Schwartz also points out that

> the proliferation of news shows . . . has heightened pressure to get stories and ratings. And, laments CBS News executive producer Andrew Lack, it has changed the way some journalists do business. Many young TV reporters rate the success of their stories by the overnight ratings: "I don't hear a lot of discussion of the journalism of the stories the next day," Lack says.[31]

"Investigative reporting," writes Kristina Borjesson, in her introduction to *Into the Buzzsaw: Leading Journalists Expose the Myth of a Free Press*, "is dwindling, particularly at the major networks, because it is expensive, attracts lawsuits, and can be hostile to the corporate interests and/or government connections of a news division's parent company. News operations tend to avoid these hassles. Big, sensitive stories that can't be ignored are often covered by dutifully telling the public what appointed spokespeople and spinmeisters have to say about them."[32]

NOTES

1. Norman Solomon, "The Media Battle of Seattle," in *Censored 2000*, ed. Peter Phillips (New York: Seven Stories Press, 2001), p. 216.
2. Edmund L. Andrews. "U.S. Rebuked: Slapping the Hand that Fed Free Trade," *New York Times* [online], www.uscib.org/%5Cindex.asp?documentID=2283 [September 1, 2002].
3. Robin Anderson, "Who Is Killing the Press?" in ibid., p. 169
4. Jim Abrams, "Broadcasters Lobbying Ad Rates," Associated Press [online], www.aef.com/channel.asp?ChannelID=7&DocID=1918&location=Government%20Regulation [February 11, 2002].
5. Ben Bagdikian, *The Media Monopoly*, 5th ed. (Boston: Beacon Press, 1995), p. 138.
6. Ibid., p. 26.
7. Mark Crispin Miller, "Censorship Inc.," *Free Inquiry* (spring 2000): 12.
8. Ronnie Dugger, "Corporate Takeover of the Media," *Free Inquiry* (winter 2001/2002): 24.
9. David Bauder, "Study: Shows Peddle Products," *Albuquerque Journal*, November 29, 2001.
10. Project Censored is online at www.projectcensored.org.
11. Christopher Miller, "Applause For Intel," *Albuquerque Journal*, January 27, 1994.
12. Jane Akre, "The Fox, The Hounds, and the Sacred Cows," in *Into the Buzzsaw: Leading Journalists Expose the Myth of a Free Press*, ed. Kristina Borjesson (Amherst, N.Y.: Prometheus Books, 2002), p. 48.
13. Tom Rosenstiel and Bill Kovach, "'Nightline' Island of Intelligent Fare," *Albuquerque Journal*, March 10, 2002.
14. Frazier Moore, "'Nightline' Remains Along With a Problem," Associated Press [online], www.augustachronicle.com/stories/031402/fea_1246669.shtml [March 14, 2002].
15. Ibid.
16. Ed Bishop, "They Were Only Half Right," *St. Louis Journalism Review at Webster University* 32, no. 243 (February 2002). Available online at www.stljr.org/pages/archives/february2002.htm.
17. *Self-Censorship: How Often and Why?* Pew Research Center for People and

the Press [online], people-press.org/reports/display.php3?pageID=218 [April 30, 2000].

18. James R. Smith, "Cable News Wars Pit Substance, Hollywood Fluff," *Albuquerque Journal*, March 4, 2002.

19. Cited in Phillips, *Censored 2000*, p. 45.

20. "Harper's Index," *Buffalo News*, January 24, 2002.

21. Margaret Bald, "Top 10 Stories of 1999," *World Press Review* (March 2000): 16.

22. Margaret Bald, "Top 10 Stories of 2000," *World Press Review* (March 2001): 22.

23. Ted Koppel, "Journalism Under Fire," *Nation*, November 24, 1997, p. 23.

24. Leslie Heilbrunn, "Measuring the Coverage: Rwandan Genocide vs. Ugandan Tourist Massacre," *Brill's Content* (May 1999): 38.

25. Romy Ribitzky, "Innocence Lost," ABC News [online], abcnews.go.com/sections/us/DailyNews/WTC_longterm_affects_010920.html [September 20, 2001].

26. Anthony Violanti, "The End of the News Coma," *Buffalo News*, November 4, 2001, p. 26.

27. Charles Kaiser, "Making Page One," *Brill's Content* (December 1998/January 1999): 121.

28. Jennifer Loven, "Study: Fewer Facts in Media Coverage," Associated Press [online], home.earthlink.net/~mjohnsen/Post_911/fewer_facts_study.html [January 28, 2002].

29. David Bauder, "Report: 9/11 Didn't Change TV News," Associated Press [online], www.softcom.net/webnews/wed/d9/ASept-11-tv-ratings.RmUN_CSC.html [May 23, 2002].

30. Tom Rosenstiel and Bill Kovach, "*Nightline*'s Island of Intelligent Fare," *Albuquerque Journal*, March 10, 2002.

31. John Schwartz, "No Scandal, No Story," *Newsweek*, February 22, 1993, p. 42.

32. Kristina Borjesson, introduction to *Into the Buzzsaw: Leading Journalists Expose the Myth of a Free Press* (Amherst, N.Y.: Prometheus Books, 2002), p. 13.

Part 3

PROFITING FROM FEAR AND MYTH

8

CASHING IN ON CRISES AND MANUFACTURING MARTYRS

There are few things that the news media like more than a crisis. Crises are, in a way, the raison d'être of the news media. Crises draw huge audiences, and news organizations are not oblivious to this fact. And sometimes, when there really is no pressing crisis, the media create one.

The summer of 2001 was an especially busy time for creating crises. Instead of a made-up crisis of dangers on the highways or store shelves, beaches and sports stadiums were the settings. A shark scare started when eight-year-old Jesse Arbogast was attacked while swimming in Florida. His arm was torn off and the news media gave his ordeal heavy coverage. A few other reports of attacks surfaced over the next two months, most of them garnering high profiles. In its July 30 issue, *Time* magazine dutifully contributed to the panic with a front-cover photo of a great white shark, its mouth open and terrifying teeth bared. The caption warned readers that it was the "Summer of the Shark."

Amid all the attack footage, warnings, and "wake-up calls," the voices of reason were largely ignored. Shark experts calmly and repeatedly pointed out that the number of shark attacks was not unusual or cause for alarm. More people are killed annually by dogs, bees, venomous snakes, and lightning than by sharks. A report released in 2002 by the University of Florida's International Shark Attack File found that shark attacks were actually down from the previous year, despite the media's hype. The group found seventy-six unprovoked shark attacks in 2001, down from eighty-five the previous year. Fatal attacks also dropped, from twelve in 2000 to five in 2001.[1]

Those who avoided the dangerous beaches faced a silent killer on the nation's football fields as players succumbed to the summer's heat wave.

In July 2001 a University of Florida freshman collapsed from heatstroke and died. The following month several football players (including Korey Stringer of the Minnesota Vikings) collapsed during games and practices, and nightly news stories voiced concern over whether America's kids were being pushed too hard by themselves and their coaches.

Though many of these incidents were attributed to heat-related illness, it soon became clear that only a few of the injuries were actually caused by heat. In one case, for example, fourteen-year-old Leonard Carter Jr., widely reported to be a victim of the heat, was found to have died from complications of an enlarged heart. The Center for Catastrophic Sports Injury, which tracks sports injuries, found only three confirmed heatstroke deaths reported as of late August, about the same number as the year before.[2]

Like the shark attack scare, the heatstroke scare fueled panicky news reports and the public's fears, then slowly died out. Shortly afterward, the terrorist attacks on the World Trade Center and the Pentagon provided the news media with an actual crisis to report on.

The public's fears about crime and safety also feed security firms: the more fearful people are, the more they buy devices and services to make themselves feel safe. Whether it's stun guns, handguns, alarm systems, or armed guards, fear sells.

When the public believes crime is rising, that perception also triggers more spending on police and prisons. In an article in the *Atlantic Monthly*, Eric Schlosser discussed the rise of what he calls the prison-industrial complex,

> a set of bureaucratic, political, and economic interests that encourage increased spending on imprisonment, regardless of the actual need. . . . It is composed of politicians, both liberal and conservative, who have used the fear of crime to gain votes; impoverished rural areas where prisons have become a cornerstone of economic development; private companies that regard the roughly $35 billion spent each year on corrections not as a burden on American taxpayers but as a lucrative market; and government officials whose fiefdoms have expanded along with the inmate population. Since 1991 the rate of violent crime has fallen by about 20 percent, while the number of people in prison or jail has risen by 50 percent.[3]

Thus we see another set of people lining up to profit from Americans' fear of crime. Fueled by literally decades of alarmist media reports, Americans demand a reduction in the crime rate (whether it's high or not); politicians, in turn, get votes by spending the public's money on get-tough-on-crime measures of dubious utility (such as the notoriously expensive and ineffective D.A.R.E. program) and imposing long sentences for nonviolent drug offenses. The result is a high rate of incarceration—by far the most expensive form of punishment—for nonviolent criminals, the very type of crime that the public is *least* concerned about. America imprisons more people—and a higher ratio of its population—than any other country in the world.

The cashing-in on fear occurs on a smaller scale, too. Following a December 6, 1999, school shooting in which four students were wounded, Steve Wilmoth, superintendent of schools in Fort Gibson, Oklahoma, complained that he had "gotten numerous brochures, pamphlets, e-mails and phone messages from companies hawking everything from high-tech security systems to firearms training." Wilmoth said, "I'm a little offended when someone wants to take a crisis and turn it into a profit." One organization (presumably affiliated with the NRA) offered free firearms training to teachers, but Wilmoth passed, saying, "That's just what we need—more guns at school."[4]

The missing-children panic in the 1980s spawned an entire industry feeding on concerned parents. Firms such as Ident-A-Kid and Saf-T-Child marketed identification kits and cards, along with safety tips, to help prevent abductions. These days, cell phones have become common security items for parents to purchase for their children. While the utility and safety afforded by a cell phone can't be denied, again the question is, What are the kids being protected *from*? They are still in more danger at home than in a mall or at school.

When advocates bend the truth for their own gains, they frequently do it through fear mongering, alarmist rhetoric, and dubious statements. The distinction between hype and genuine alarm becomes blurred. In our proactive mindset, we feel the need to run around stomping on all the little fires, just in case one of them really is a threat. But when you can't tell the heat from the light, problems ensue.

Frequently, the justification for many alarmist reports and campaigns is that their intention is to "raise awareness." Yet usually the issues—violent crime, school shootings, road rage, and the like—are ones that already have a high profile. Many dangers do merit awareness-raising campaigns: drowsy drivers, suicide, and heart disease, to name a few. But campaigns to alert people to these dangers don't get much attention; they aren't sexy stories that lend themselves to riveting footage.

Just because the public (wrongly) believes that crime is on the rise does not mean that more money is needed to stem the phantom rising crime rate. Laws are enacted, money is allocated, and important decisions are made based upon what the public *believes* to be true. This is done despite clear evidence that such fears are frequently unfounded. When neutral, objective information contradicts their agendas, proponents and advocates stubbornly refuse to hear the evidence and instead resort to opinions and feelings to support their positions.

Those who resort to public opinion to justify their agendas tread on shaky ground. At one time in America popular opinion held that slavery was acceptable; in some places people have the opinion that blacks or gays are inferior. Many people today believe that extraterrestrial aliens have contacted humans and, in some cases, abducted and experimented on them. Sincere, strongly held belief and opinion are no substitutes for empirical evidence about the world.

PROFITING FROM PAIN AND PATRIOTISM

Crises and tragedies create second-generation profiteers, those who make money off the hype created by the media. In the wake of Princess Diana's death, the world was flooded with books, calendars, coins, ornaments, figurines, collector's plates, coffee mugs, stamps, and trashy trinkets of every imaginable kind cashing in on Diana. Both established companies (e.g., the Franklin Mint) and fly-by-night firms jumped at the marketing potential.

Some entrepreneurs went all the way to Africa to capitalize on JFK Jr.'s death. A commemorative JFK Jr. ten-dollar coin was minted in 2000, with television ads touting that the coin is "destined to be a collector's item" and is "legal tender"—and it is, in Liberia. The money is apparently valid currency in the West African nation, a country slightly smaller than North Carolina. Numismatists call such coins "noncirculating legal tender," and tend not to be impressed or take such "collector coins" seriously. As Bill Gibbs of *Coin World* explains: "Countries learned many years ago that there is a collector market for just about anything. . . . Many times, these coins never reside within the borders of the nations they're supposedly from; they rarely, if ever, circulate locally. Numismatists and serious collectors tend to look down upon them."[5]

Although some projects—notably, Elton John's single "Candle in the Wind 1997," which benefited the Diana, Princess of Wales Memorial Fund—provide funds for charities, much of the money made by selling such collectibles goes to private companies. O. J. Simpson's drama was marketed by everyone from street vendors hawking "Loose The Juice" T-shirts to a slew of "insider" books written by lawyers, jurors, witnesses, and various media and legal hangers-on.

Selling September 11

The terrorist attacks of September 11, 2001, provide an excellent example of the way many people exploited the emotions surrounding the tragedy to turn a profit. From legitimate, grieving families to insurance fraud

Vendors at Ground Zero in New York City lined up to sell September 11–related items. (photo © 2003 Benjamin Radford)

artists, from airline industries to the mafia, everyone had their hands out to get a chunk of the billions of dollars raised and earmarked for victims of the attacks.

A month after the attacks, more than two dozen people applied for trademarks related to the terrorist attacks. Seeing money to be made in the marketing of T-shirts, mugs, bags, jackets, hats, and nearly every other imaginable item, people deluged the Trademark Office with applications. One man who tried to trademark the phrase "World Trade Center" told a reporter that "he was not trying to exploit a national tragedy—in fact he said he wanted to stop others from doing so."[6]

In December 2001 the New York Fire Department had to send cease-and-desist letters warning dozens of small retailers to stop selling counterfeit goods displaying the popular "FDNY" logo. Many people wanted to show their support for the firefighters, but counterfeiters ended up profiting. Only the profits from the real, authorized items (purchased at Bloomingdale's) go to fire education funds.[7]

Other entrepreneurs rushed to sell everything from inflatable anthrax-proof shelters to "executive parachutes," for any businessman unlucky enough to be trapped in a burning high-rise building. I can just see the ads: A businessman preparing for a meeting goes through a checklist: "Let's see—got the Powerpoint presentation, proposal, Palm Pilot—oh yeah, almost forgot my parachute!"

It wasn't just small businesspeople who hustled to make money from America's newly replenished patriotism. Spurred by President Bush's repeated requests to spend money to stimulate the economy, many Americans consumers heeded the call. Big business jumped on the bandwagon, with Ford adopting its "Ford Drives America" slogan. General Motors wanted a piece of the patriotic pie and launched its own campaign to "Keep America Rolling." True, these efforts were backed by low financing that cut into the companies' profits, but the smell of opportunism still surrounded such efforts. Bob Garfield of *Advertising Age* magazine stated that "[i]t's an emotional time for everyone and advertisers—like everyone else—want to do something and reach out this way. That's fine, but when you start exploiting the situation to promote your brand, it becomes gross opportunism."[8]

Many politicians took advantage of the push to spend billions to jump-start the economy to serve their special interests. Among them, as ABC's Linda Douglass reported,

> [C]ongressmen and senators from such vacation-popular states as Hawaii and Arizona want the federal government to subsidize up to $500 of personal travel for every American. . . . Sen. Frank Murkowski [of Alaska] argues more energy may be needed for the war against ter-

> rorism and wants Congress to fund an oil and gas pipeline. And Sen. Robert Torricelli wants billions of dollars to upgrade Amtrak trains.[9]

Senators, in fact, ended up adding nearly $400 million in pet projects to a bill designed to rebuild the damaged Pentagon and fight terrorism.[10]

Politicians quickly took advantage of the public's patriotism and fears. According to a study by the Campaign Media Analysis Group, candidates in the November 6, 2001, elections spent more than $10 million on commercials relating to terrorism. The focus of the ads was protection, and what the candidates promised to do to protect the public. This is largely misdirection, though: For the most part, measures that protect the American public come from the federal government, and few mayors or sheriffs realistically have the purview or resources to protect the public from international terrorism. Nonetheless, local political candidates with little or no connection to terrorism-struck cities (such as Baton Rouge, Louisiana, and Birmingham, Alabama) made use of images of waving flags, police officers, and firefighters.[11] In this way, politicians who had done little or nothing about crime or violence exploited a national tragedy to get elected. They offered easy solutions to a fearful public battered by scary news reports.

Major industries had their hands out as well. The airlines received a $15-billion bailout that included a guarantee of billions of dollars in loans and protection from lawsuits by victims' families. If the litigants agreed to not sue the airlines, they were eligible for money from a victim's fund partially paid for with taxpayer dollars. In October 2001 a leaseholder of the World Trade Center also lobbied Congress to shield him from similar lawsuits. Thus, instead of wealthy companies paying the debts they incur due to unfortunate circumstances, American taxpayers get to foot the bill.

Lawyers lined up to represent those victims' families who wanted to sue. Some lawyers worked on proving the psychological pain and suffering of those who knew that death was coming. If someone trapped in flames survived for twenty minutes, for example, his survivors might be entitled to thousands or hundreds of thousands of dollars for the amount of time he grieved over his impending death. This may be a legitimate basis for a claim, but it also flies in the face of what happened in other cases. For example, there's the well-publicized case of Todd Beamer, a thirty-two-year-old businessman who died on the hijacked flight 93. Knowing that they were all going to die, he and others tried to overtake the hijackers. His famous last words were, "Let's roll!"

Following the "imminent death psychological suffering" model, Beamer's wife should get nothing for his pain. His knowledge of impending death didn't stop him from being heroic; he was (apparently) not overcome with grief and psychological suffering. He was, by all accounts, calm and collected, not panicking and grieving over his mortality. Should Beamer's widow get less compensation because her husband was more courageous than others?

Within weeks of September 11, quickie books on the World Trade Center were rushed to stores. Though not all were necessarily exploitative (a few authors donated some of their profits to relief funds), it is worth raising the question: Why were they produced at all? Americans had been barraged with constant images of lost family members, twisted wreckage, and wrecked lives for months. During a time when many Americans were trying to heal and get on with their lives, did we really need to see even *more* photos of pain, destruction, and devastation?

In November 2001 a dozen workers at the Port Authority's cafeteria at the World Trade Center were charged with defrauding the Red Cross out of $14,000 in emergency cash. Despite the fact that their jobs were safe, they claimed to be unemployed and in need of funds.[12]

Thousands of New York City residents used the terrorist attacks to loot $15 million from the Municipal Credit Union. When a computer failure caused by the collapse of the World Trade Center allowed credit union members access to money in automatic teller machines, they took full advantage of the situation to overdraw their accounts. About four thousand people were investigated by the Manhattan district attorney's office, all of whom stole at least $1,000; more than seventeen hundred people overdrew their accounts by at least $3,000. As Susan Saulny of the *New York Times* noted, "A frenzy of wrongful withdrawals began almost immediately after the terrorist attacks." Police Commissioner Raymond W. Kelly said that "people tried to profit from the confusion. They made a calculated decision to take money that was not theirs, and for a while, they got away with it."[13]

Some people even stooped so low as to pretend that loved ones perished in the attacks to ask for charity. One Canadian woman, Maureen Curry, scammed thousands of dollars from benefactors, telling them that her daughter had died in the World Trade Center and that she needed money to go visit her grandchildren.[14] Another Canadian woman was charged with falsely claiming her husband had been killed in the attacks, and in the United States, at least a half dozen people in separate cases were charged with claiming that family members had died.[15] I suspect that in the years to come at least one case will surface in which a person used the tragedy to fake his death and start a new life.

The Internet helped many people exploit tragedy as well. In October 2001, in the midst of anthrax scares and hype, a seller on the online auction site eBay tried to sell the rights to the domain name "anthraxvaccinations.com" for a thousand dollars (there were no takers). A month later, on November 4, I received an e-mail titled "Chemical and Biological Safety Alert," which read in part:

> As we all know, our world has now changed since the September 11 attacks on the Pentagon and the World Trade Center. . . . We do not know what they may try next, but Attorney General John Ashcroft says there is 100% chance that they will try something in the future. . . . As we all know, there is a threat, that these terrorists may try to attack next with chemical or biological weapons. . . . We now offer Gas Masks that are 100% Certified by the Israeli Army. . . . Please, think about the safety of yourself and your family. Is it worth the risk not too [*sic*]?

According to another Web site, gasmask.com, "If you live anywhere near a major city and you receive word that a terrorist has slammed into a nuclear power plant, exploded a nuclear weapon, or released biological or chemical warfare agents, then gas masks are the only things that will protect you and your family from certain death."

Medical and safety experts who are not trying to make money from the sale of gas masks have a different point of view. They state that people should not bother to get gas masks because they are expensive, using them correctly takes training, not all of them work well, by the time you knew to put one on you would likely already be affected, and to be effective the mask would have to be carried around all the time.

Religious groups were also quick to make their presence felt at the site of the attacks. Amanda Onion, writing for ABC News, wrote:

> Representatives of Baptists, born again Christians, Jews for Jesus, scientologists, Episcopalians, Hare Krishna, and other followings were present in significant numbers near Ground Zero and at memorial sites on the days following the attacks. Some churches took out full-page advertisements in area newspapers, announcing their services. Within two hours of the attacks, the American Tract Society had begun designing a new pamphlet advertising their faith in light of the tragedy.[16]

AWARENESS CAMPAIGNS

A 1997 article in the *Albuquerque Journal* epitomizes a call for action based upon unfounded opinion. The piece reported on a survey mailed to six thousand students, faculty, and staff at the University of New Mexico (UNM) by Cyndie Tidwell, a fifty-two-year-old graduate student. The article begins, "A University of New Mexico survey shows many students believe crime is a big problem at the school and the campus is a frightening place at night." Tidwell, who became an activist for campus safety after a 1995 parking lot confrontation with a menacing stranger, said she hoped her survey would spur an increase in money for campus security. "This campus is scary," she said. "It terrorizes people." The reporter, however, noted that, "UNM's official campus crime report shows few serious crimes since 1993: one murder, 10 rapes, 13 robberies and 20 weapons violations. But Tidwell said her survey reveals something that won't be found in a crime report—the fear factor."[17]

Here Tidwell seems to acknowledge that campus crime is in fact low, but that if people *think* there's a problem, then there must be one. Gil Berry, then associate director of facility planning, falls into the same logical fallacy: "They [the survey respondents] are the users of the campus, and if they don't feel safe, we're not doing our job." It's a popular sentiment, and a common one to hear from a person who serves the public, but it's not rationally sound. The university police's job is not to make people *feel* safe—though one hopes that would happen—it's to make the campus safe in reality.

If simply making the public *feel* safe is the appropriate criterion, then Tidwell should not be bothered by what happened in the Philadelphia Police Department in the 1980s and 1990s. Thousands of crime reports, including those of rapes, were taken by police, shelved, and not reported or followed up on. "The way we solved crime was with an eraser," said Capt. Rich Costello, president of the local chapter of the Fraternal Order of Police. This resulted in a lower reported rape rate for the city; surely the lowered "official" incidence of rape made the citizens of Philadelphia feel a little safer.[18] Yet it was not true; it was a myth. Again, the notion of predicating police success on the public's feelings and perceptions, instead of reality, is simply misguided.

Tidwell's methodology may also have led her to inaccurate conclusions. The article states that many of the respondents reported what they heard about campus crime: "They reported hearing of numerous rapes, sexual assaults, beatings, and even abductions on the campus." But hold on: Just because many people report *hearing* of such crimes does not necessarily mean that that many incidents occurred. This is due to multiple reporting of the same incident. If a man is stabbed on campus and it makes the local news, ten thousand students may hear about it. If those students are later surveyed, most will report that they *heard* about a stabbing, but that doesn't mean that ten thousand people were stabbed.

UNM security officials pointed to the low crime rate and a list of recent improvements in campus security, including annual campus safety walks to identify areas that need more light, installation of security cameras, an expanded night escort service, and student patrols at night.[19]

The survey (and article) may also be self-perpetuating: Students who were otherwise not particularly fearful may get the impression that most of the people around them are afraid, and use that inference to reinforce or justify their own fears. After all, the person may think, there must be *some* reason so many people think the campus is "scary."

It is also a fair question to ask whether it is ethical to exaggerate a risk in the name of "raising awareness." The article's title is "UNM Campus 'Scary,'" a designation that can only increase readers' fear of crime. But aren't people scared enough about crime as it is, without feeding the fear with emotional testimonials and misleading information? If a person's risk of assault is really one in ten thousand, but an awareness campaign implies the risk is much higher, is that really doing anyone a service? Such exaggeration might arguably be useful or appropriate if the public underestimated their real risk (as in auto accidents), but in the case of crime most people dramatically *overestimate* their risk, in large part because of awareness campaigns and media hype.

In the world of alarmist activism, there is no such thing as good news. No problem is significantly solved or alleviated, and any claims that a cause is progressing receives jeers and dismissals. At the University of Virginia, the University Police Department's 1995 crime index reported no rapes on campus during that year. Good news? Something to celebrate? Absolutely not! Soon after the report was made public, Dean of Students Robert T. Canavari warned that "[n]obody should take comfort in that. We shouldn't drop our guard."[20]

A police spokeswoman cautioned that just because no rapes were reported doesn't mean that none occurred, and of course she's correct. But that's just stating the obvious: Of course crime statistics reflect only reported crime; how could they possibly report unreported crime? And though it's true that rapes are more likely to go unreported than other crimes, that still doesn't necessarily mean that any rapes occurred. Certainly, no one was suggesting that women should become complacent about personal safety. But doesn't the fact that no rapes were reported warrant at least *some* positive acknowledgement? If not, then what could possibly qualify as good news? For many activists, bad news is bad news, and good news is bad news.

Activists and advocates set a trap for themselves when they fear good news and treat those bearing it as enemies. Their wars will never be won because they are too busy protesting how bad the situation is to acknowledge even small victories.

The "My Turn" column in *Newsweek* magazine mentioned in chapter 5 is another good example of how the media help to legitimize the public's fear of crime. The author emotionally recounted her (and, by implied extension, her community's) fear of crime following the Columbine shootings. No mention was made of the fact that the author's fears were unfounded and her views unrepresentative of other teens.

One consequence of both the public's and the media's emphasis on the importance of emotions is that at times emotions are substituted for action. Instead of advocacy groups actually *doing* something positive for their cause, they frequently give only the illusion of progress and influence.

At the University of New Mexico, the Student Health Center promoted a "Week Without Violence," an annual project first begun in 1995 by the YWCA. A tree was planted in front of the entrance to the Student Services Center, representing "peace and freedom from violence." The next day at noon, whistles were distributed and blown to commemorate victims of violence. Jesus Hernandez, chairman for the Campus Safety and Security Committee and the master of ceremonies, noted, "This is not by any means a violent or high-crime campus."[21] It's fortunate that the campus is already fairly safe, because dozens of people blowing whistles together at noon isn't going to make it any safer. Whistling and planting trees is all very warm, unifying, and symbolic, but it ultimately does little to reduce the already low crime rate. It's easy to do, takes a few minutes, and lets everyone feel that they're making a difference. Yet *real* changes are brought about through hard work, better policing, planning, and effort.

The frequent battle cry to "take back the night" can have dangerous repercussions. It may sound inspiring, but on the occasions when there actually *is* a serious threat on the street, those who have the night may not want to give it back. Greg Miles of Buffalo, New York, found that out the hard way in August 2001. Miles is a neighborhood watchdog, the leader of a club formed as a first-line defense against street crime. One afternoon a young woman started damaging a curb planter filled with flowers. Miles confronted her and demanded she stop. He was immediately surrounded by eight people, including the woman, who beat him to the ground. "Do you think you own this street?" someone yelled as blows rained down on him. Miles ended up in the emergency room, unable to eat solid food for a week.

In another part of Buffalo, block club leader Judson Price was shot in the jaw and chest by young toughs trying to impress a local gang leader. Price survived, but still carries a bullet lodged near his heart, his reward for "taking back the night." Other people trying to clean up Buffalo streets have been victims of death threats and arson threats, as well as vandalism and harrassment.[22]

In October 2002 a Baltimore, Maryland, woman and five of her children were killed when their house was firebombed. The woman was a neighborhood activist who had tried to drive drug dealers away from the corner in front of her home. Police believe that the family was killed in retaliation for her efforts to clean up the streets.

According to journalist Wendy McElroy, the "Take Back the Night" movement was organized in response to a hoax, a nonexistent threat. McElroy writes that "in New York . . . when a porn movie was purported to be a snuff film, feminists had almost rioted outside the theater in which it played. This incident was the beginning of the 'Take Back the Night' movement, under whose banner feminists still march through the streets of major cities to protest violence against women."[23] Violence against women (or men, for that matter) is a serious and legitimate issue that deserves support, but hoaxes and misunderstandings make a poor basis for outrage.

It's easy to call for action, hold vigils, and sell T-shirts to raise awareness of women's safety issues and street crime. But when the simplistic slogans are gone, it's others who face the very real dangers of actually making a difference.

Attracting the Spotlight

One of America's cottage industries is manufacturing martyrs. In earlier days, heroes and martyrs were typically revered because of grassroots enthusiasm. These days martyr packaging comes with slick press kits and book tours. Clearly, not every incident, crime, or tragedy is cause for alarm, memorials, picketing, and protest. Yet just about any cause can be turned into an event—provided those advocates have the money and means to attract the media's attention. As a consequence, causes seen in the media are highlighted because of their advocates' access to the media, and not as a measure of inherent injustice. But causes, as we have seen, are just like any product: Those promoters with bigger budgets will get their message across. Advocates for unpopular—yet legitimate—issues such as drug policy reform or prison rape have difficulty getting money and attention.

JonBenet Ramsey's death got lots of front-page ink, while the death of a homeless man may warrant only a paragraph-long account buried deep inside the paper. But people's lives (and deaths) should not be measured by how notorious their deaths are or how well they fit into our mythos and social causes. All men may be created equal in theory, but they clearly are not equal in the media.

This is perhaps the most troublesome aspect of the media's selective focus; they implicitly tell the audience that some lives are more important than other lives. Certainly, some people's lives and deaths are more interesting; that's why people tune in to stories about famous and infamous people instead of anonymous teen store clerks from Trenton. But those who confuse media attention for an imprimatur of validity or significance profoundly misunderstand our media.

Few people know this better than Donna Raley, whose stepdaughter Dena has been missing since 1999. She has done all she can to find Dena, but says that the police refuse to follow up on leads she has given them and warn her not to investigate them herself. She is frustrated and seeking ways to put pressure on the police. Chief among them: get the media's attention. But this is hard to do, and it is much more difficult and frustrating when competing with the coverage of the disappearance of a young woman named Chandra Levy.

In a July 2001 interview with Dean Schabner of ABC News, Raley told of trying to get people to listen to her story, to look for her daughter: "I was out on the street. We put out our own press release to the TV stations, but we didn't get any coverage. You feel like you're beating your head against the wall, especially when you see what Chandra Levy's getting after two months." Raley said she's not jealous or angry, just frustrated with the inequity of the situation.[24]

Schabner pointed out something that was largely overlooked among all the accusations, innuendo, and denials in the Levy case: that Levy's parents were able to keep interest in their daughter's disappearance largely through implicating Rep. Gary Condit as having some devious role in her disappearance. The case wasn't necessarily about Condit at all—Levy's body was found in May 2002, with no evidence at all linking Condit to her murder—but by bringing the congressman up at every opportunity, the Levys assured that their story would stay in the spotlight. Schabner discusses how the Levys skillfully spun the story to further their agenda:

> The family has effectively controlled the flow of information regarding their daughter, creating the promise of a scandal that lifted the story back from the obscurity that befalls most missing persons stories as police run out of leads and news organizations move on. Even though, as has become clear, Chandra Levy's parents knew weeks before she disappeared that she was having an affair with the congressman, for weeks they restricted themselves to repeatedly calling on Condit to come clean with what he knew.[25]

It appears that the Levys' public relations tactic was actually counterproductive. If, as the evidence suggests, Condit had nothing to do with the murder, then much of the attention they worked so hard to drum up was misdirected. Instead of pursuing other leads, the police, pressured by the Levys, wasted time interviewing Condit and searching his apartment.

These days nearly any event or tragedy can, with a little spin doctoring, be turned into a simplified, tearjerking mythological narrative complete with hero, villain, and social agenda. The heroes tend to be young innocents suffering or dying due to a dread predator. The martyr's accomplishments, of course, don't stop at their deaths. Fueled by a mission and self-righteousness, the promoters write books about their heroes (Misty Bernall's *She Said Yes*), launch Web sites and national organizations, television shows (*America's Most Wanted*), and get laws passed in their names (Megan's Law).

Matthew Shepard's death inspired a three-act, three-hour play titled *The Laramie Project*. Eighteen months in the making, the play was performed by the Tectonic Theater Project, a New York–based theater troupe. The play's author, Moises Kaufman, interviewed scores of Laramie residents and friends of Shepard's. Kaufman said he considered Shepard's death "one of history's watershed moments." A film based on *The Laramie Project* was released in 2002. A film was also made about the hate-crime death of Teena Brandon, a young transvestite, *Boys Don't Cry*, for which Hilary Swank won an Academy Award.

Having books, plays, and films written about martyrs is nothing new. But in recent years it seems that the body is barely cold before advocates scramble to find a way to claim the departed as a martyr for their cause. This opportunistic co-opting of the dead should make at least some people uncomfortable. What if Matthew Sheppard didn't *want* to become a gay rights icon? What if he didn't want to be known for his death but instead for his *life*?

People recast victims into posthumous activists because of the circumstances of their deaths. But people are more than just the circumstances of their deaths, and if anyone would know that it should be those closest to the victims. Many gays claim that their sexuality doesn't define who they are. Yet by making Matthew Shepard into a martyr, Kaufman and others ensure that he will be remembered in the public mind as "the gay hate-crime victim in Wyoming." Perhaps some martyrs would be comfortable with their postmortem advocacy roles. But, with few exceptions, we'll never know. I'm sure that if someone had asked Shepard what he wanted to be remembered for, it wouldn't have been that.

Martyrhood reduces a complex person into a stereotype, demeaning her into merely a victim's role. Parents and friends of those who have died in tragedies frequently aren't shy about injecting their own personal agendas into the memories of the dead. The implicit message seems to be that the martyrdom is done for a good cause, and helps the dead person's life have lasting meaning. But that's a disrespectful argument; hopefully their lives were meaningful quite apart from the circumstances of their deaths.

Awareness du Jour

Awareness days are everywhere—even Valentine's Day has been coopted by those with agendas. As Donna Laframboise of the *National Post* explains:

> Forget flowers, chocolates and romantic dinners. A U.S.-based campaign, now in Canada, is linking St. Valentine's Day instead to rape, bat-

> tery and sex abuse. Dubbed V-Day—it stands for "vagina, anti-violence and victory"—the movement turns a day traditionally devoted to celebrating romantic love into an opportunity to dwell upon violence against women.[26]

The V-Day campaign includes a performance of *The Vagina Monologues*, a play whose themes include violence and abuse. Among the celebrities founding and participating are Winona Ryder, Glenn Close, Lily Tomlin, Susan Sarandon, Whoopi Goldberg, and Calista Flockhart. *Variety* reviewer Steven Oxman found *The Vagina Monologues* inchoate, pretentious, and the performance more cathartic for the performers than effective for the audience: "This is a performance that seems more for the benefit of the actors than the audience."[27] A performance I attended in 2002 reflected this assessment.

According to writer Christina Hoff Sommers in a *Wall Street Journal* article, the information given at V-Day isn't very reliable: The V-Day Web site claims that "22% to 35% of women who visit emergency rooms are there for injuries related to on-going abuse," though the U.S. Bureau of Justice Statistics puts that figure at 1 percent.[28]

Another tactic for raising awareness of a cause is to simply proclaim a day or month a time of awareness or remembrance. This ridiculous trend may have begun when someone noticed that Mother's Day skyrocketed when Hallmark Cards promoted it to sell more cards. Ironically, one of the founders of a national Mother's Day, Anna Jarvis, grew disgusted with the commercialization of the day and actually sued to stop a 1923 Mother's Day festival. "I wanted it to be a day of sentiment, not profit," she said.[29]

In 2000 a group called Morality in Media trumpeted October 29 through November 5 as Pornography Awareness Week, denouncing "illegal obscenity" and vowing to "uphold standards of decency in mainstream media." (Ignore for a moment the redundancy in denouncing something that's already by definition illegal.) Not to be outdone, the conservative Family Research Council proclaimed the entire month of May Victims of Pornography Awareness Month. The group produced a thirty-second commercial aired nationwide to "help people find a way out of pornography addiction as well as raise awareness of the issue."

Tobacco company Philip Morris celebrated May 2000 as Older Americans Month, and vowed to "pay tribute to older Americans" (older than what?) not only that month but throughout the year. Lee jeans proclaimed that October 6, 2000, was National Denim Day. April 22 is TV Turnoff Day, according to *New Internationalist* magazine, and then-Texas governor George W. Bush proclaimed June 10, 2000, as Jesus Day.

Pam Johnson, founder of a group called the Secret Society of Happy

People, tried to get all fifty U.S. governors to declare August 8, 1999, National Admit You're Happy Day. Of those, only fifteen agreed, and many of those who did not were given the title "stick in the mud" or "parade rainer" by Johnson.[30] On and on the special days go, from Birthmother's Day (celebrated on the eve of Mother's Day), to Single Parents' Day (March 21, invented by Janice Moglen, a single mother of two). There's Breast Cancer Awareness Month, something called Math Awareness Month, even an Ultrasound Awareness Month (presumably for those unaware of ultrasounds).

October is Disability Employment Awareness Month; it is also Domestic Violence Awareness Month, Vegetarian Awareness Month, Wisconsin Energy Awareness Month, Celiac Sprue Awareness Month, Islam Awareness Month, and National Home Indoor Air Quality Action and Awareness Month. If you're already aware of all these causes, don't fret, because October is also Spina Bifida Awareness Month, National Electrology Awareness Month, Down Syndrome Awareness Month, AIDS Awareness Month, Learning Disability Awareness Month, Liver Awareness Month, Sudden Infant Death Syndrome Awareness Month, Lupus Awareness Month, Lead Awareness Month, and Brain Injury Awareness Month.

Trying to be aware of all these causes is impossible; the promoters have polluted the calendar with their pet causes. When one or two causes claimed a week or month, it was novel and noticed. Now that dozens of individuals and organizations do it, their awareness campaigns are just advertisement—more noise to ignore.

The gates have been opened, and now anyone could have his own awareness Web site and press releases, announcing his own day, week, or month (or even year) for his pet cause, such as Arthritic Goat Appreciation Day or Toenail Hygiene Awareness Month.

Many "cause" projects are similar to some self-published books; their authors love their own work, and the effort serves more as an agendized vehicle of catharsis than an informed discussion of the issues. Anyone can have a cause célèbre but not everyone's pet cause is a national crisis that warrants a movie of the week, play, book, or special day of recognition. Any death, insult, or injury can be tweaked to further a cause. Many tragic events have been proclaimed a "wake-up call to America." But America is wide awake, thank you, and busy pouring attention and resources to all the other "crises" and causes wailing for coverage and funds.

Yet Americans are tolerant and accommodating, perhaps feeling it unseemly, insensitive, or undiplomatic to tell someone to take a hike—and take their pet cause and martyr with them.

MYTHMAKING AND SOCIAL AGENDAS

Cassie Bernall

I wonder if the people who were so eager to cash in on Diana's death would be comfortable selling "I Survived Columbine" T-shirts in Colorado after the April 20, 1999, school massacre. Presumably not, although the parents of Cassie Bernall weren't reluctant to capitalize on the tragedy to promote both their daughter and their religion. Bernall is the young woman who gained posthumous fame when a friend claimed she defiantly affirmed her belief in God when the shooters threatened her, and was killed for it.

Cassie's mother, Misty Bernall, wrote a book titled *She Said Yes: The Unlikely Martyrdom of Cassie Bernall.*[31] The book recounted Cassie's journey from a troubled youth obsessed with death rock and vampires to an upstanding Christian. It had all the elements of a good Christian redemption story: a lost child who found her path in Jesus, only to be killed for defending her faith before Satan's merciless thugs. After the book's publication, the Bernalls made the media rounds, giving interviews and even appearing on televangelist Robert Schuller's Sunday television show, telling their story to millions. As it turned out, Cassie's martyrdom *was* in fact unlikely—and unlikely to be true. Investigators showed that Cassie was almost certainly *not* the young woman who had this exchange with her killers, but that it was a girl nearby, Valeen Schnurr. The shooter asked if Schnurr believed in God; she said yes and the gunman spared her. Instead of Bernall dying for affirming her faith, Schnurr lived by affirming hers.

Prior to publication, questions regarding the book's accuracy were brought to Plough, the small Christian publishing house that handled the book. Although the very premise of the book was in substantial doubt, both Plough and the Bernalls decided to release it, and it soon became a *New York Times* best-seller. Making money and promoting their faith were apparently more important than telling the truth.[32]

The Bernalls weren't the only ones exploiting the Columbine tragedy out of religious zeal: A Halloween display at a Texas church featured a reenactment of the massacre. The attraction, the "Hell House" at Trinity Church in Cedar Hill, featured a skit in which trenchcoated youths reenacted the killings, including a scene in which a girl prays to God before the gunmen kill her. Jesus appears and rewards the girl, and in the end the pair of killers are sent to hell. One mother of Columbine students was "repulsed by it," and said, "I don't know what purpose it serves. My family will live with this forever." Trinity's youth pastor, Tim Ferguson, defended the skit, calling it "tasteful" and saying that he had to scare teens in order to save them from sin.[33]

Kimberly Bergalis

In 1991 the U.S. Congress heard tearful testimony from twenty-three-year-old Kimberly Bergalis, who showed up to beg for legislation requiring all health care workers in America to be tested for HIV and to prohibit HIV-positive medical workers from practicing their professions. Bergalis, carrying the AIDS virus, claimed to have been infected by her dentist, Dr. David Acer. She swore she was a virgin and that the HIV-positive dentist was the only way she could have been exposed to the virus. Yet a medical exam prior to the hearings found signs of prior sexual contact and that she had another sexually transmitted disease. She had sued the then-dead dentist's estate and insurance company for damages.[34]

The legislation Bergalis lobbied for never passed, due in part to intense pressure and lobbying from privacy advocates and heath care workers. "Because there is mass hysteria, and because this is a fatal disease, and because people don't know very much about this, people's common-sense reaction, including Senators', is to act first and think later," said Geri Palast, a lobbyist for the Service Employees International Union, which represents 350,000 health care workers. The senators also realized that there is a vastly higher risk of a health care worker becoming infected from a patient than the reverse. "The risk of getting AIDS from your doctor is lower than the risk of dying in a car crash on the way to the hospital," says Dr. James Mason, assistant secretary for health at the Department of Health and Human Services.[35]

Although we will likely never know the whole truth about the case, it is very plausible that Bergalis lied to cover up her own risky sexual behavior, as one Centers for Disease Control investigator suspected at the time. If that's true, it should give Americans pause to consider that, had Bergalis's testimony not been overcome by level heads, one young, pitiful, photogenic girl might have launched a serious, nationwide violation of privacy based on lies. Such emotional testimony, though heartrending and compelling, cannot be taken at face value, without some skepticism, and used as the basis for enacting legislation. If the threat was as serious and dire as Bergalis claimed, it is remarkable that there has not been an explosion of patients infected with AIDS by their doctors in the past decade.

As we have seen, activists thrive with bards, and the Bergalis family was no exception. They commissioned a play about her struggle. The play, *Patient A,* was written by Lee Blessing and performed off-Broadway in 1993.[36]

Ringing False Alarms

Often the goal of emotional manipulation isn't to gain money but instead sympathy for a cause. That appears to be what happened in the small Texas town of Johntown in 1992. The town became the epicenter of an AIDS epidemic when a counselor claimed that thirteen teenagers were found to be infected with HIV, a rate six times higher than the national average. The claim was made by AIDS counselor and activist Dona Spence, a forty-year-old nurse whose husband had died of AIDS. In December 1991 Spence alerted the local school board that six students at Rivercrest High School (population 197) were infected with AIDS, as were seven other kids in two nearby schools.

Spence's numbers and credibility were questioned by Superintendent David Anthony. Anthony pointed out that Spence was in the process of applying for a grant to open an AIDS clinic in Johntown, and had incentive to exaggerate (or invent) an AIDS outbreak. Spence ended up going into seclusion, apparently unable to substantiate her claims.[37]

In Oregon, a group called Oregon Citizens Alliance pushed for a measure on the voting ballot that would bar public school teachers from promoting or sanctioning homosexuality in class. The head of the group, Lon Mabon, said that many parents were concerned that their children were getting the wrong message in sex education classes. Teachers, he said, "are establishing in young people's minds that homosexuality and bisexuality are acceptable and normal."

The claim that many parents were outraged over teachers promoting homosexuality was news to Larry Austin, a spokesman for the Oregon Department of Education. He said that his agency hadn't received any complaints at all about the topic: "It seems like a non-issue. We hear comments and complaints all the time about class size, school funding, and teacher quality. But our phones have been silent on this issue."[38] It seems that Oregon Citizens Alliance created a crisis where there was none in order to get an antigay initiative on the November 2000 ballot.

Even former president George Bush wasn't above manipulating the public's fears to shore up continued support for his war on drugs. In September 1989, during a televised speech from the Oval Office, Bush held up a sealed bag of crack cocaine marked "EVIDENCE." "This is crack cocaine seized a few days ago by drug enforcement agents in a park across the street from the White House. It's as innocent looking as candy, but it's murdering our children," Bush said.

But, as Barry Glassner writes in his book *The Culture of Fear*:

> There was little drug dealing of any sort in that park, and no one selling crack. With Bush's speech already drafted to include a baggie prop, the

> [drug enforcement] agents improvised. In another part of town they recruited a young crack dealer to make a delivery across from the White House (a building he needed directions to find). When he delivered the crack the DEA agents, rather than "seizing" it, as Bush would report, purchased it for $2,400.[39]

A bust was staged just to produce the infamous bag of crack so that Bush could wave it around as a threat to Americans of the importance of the continued support (i.e., funding) of the war on drugs. Bush, in effect, created a myth to lend legitimacy to his cause.

A sample of other recent cases include:

- Antigay hate-literature flyers with a "hit list" appeared at Eastern New Mexico University in July 1997, threatening that "a queer a week" would be killed. Posters were distributed around the city of Portales urging people to "beat up a queer" and "kill a queer." Miranda Prather, a lesbian graduate student and president of the Alliance, a gay and lesbian support group on campus, reported being attacked in her home. Police later determined that Prather faked the attack, and surveillance video showed her distributing the hate flyers.[40]
- In 1998 South Carolina Senator Darrell Jackson, trying to get lawmakers to support his hate crimes bill, recounted the story of Regan Wolf, a lesbian who claimed that she was beaten twice by an intruder in her home. Wolf was found on her porch with her hands and feet tied and abrasions across her back. She said a stocky, red-haired man attacked her, and the phrase "Jesus weren't born for you, faggot" was spray-painted in red on her porch steps. Police later determined that the event was staged. Investigators grew suspicious when a local man came forward and admitted that Wolf paid him to hit her with a belt to simulate the attack.[41]
- Milo John Reese, an antiprostitution crusader, disappeared in November 1999, leaving behind his bloodstained car. Police searched for Reese for nearly two weeks, until an automated teller machine videotape captured him withdrawing funds from his account. Reese, the leader of the group Nevada Against Prostitution, claimed that he faked his own death to bring attention to his cause.[42]

The "Just One" Fallacy

Frequently advocates say that "if just one person is saved" (from dying from drugs/getting involved with gangs/getting kidnapped/etc.), then "it's all worth it." That's an admirable sentiment, but those expressing it are usually holding purse strings to bags of other people's money, whether donated or public.

Is it really true that no matter what the cost, if one life is saved, then it's all worth it? Let's say that the war on drugs effort has cost $5 billion. Is it really all right with you, as a taxpayer, if "just one" life is saved for that kind of money? Should the rest of us give a blank check to any cause that promises to save "just one" life? I would hope not; "just one" life saved would be a terrible record in any context. That money could instead go to safety programs and campaigns that have demonstrated their effectiveness in saving lives—and not just one life, but dozens or thousands of lives.

What if an auto manufacturer installed a special device in its cars that was expected to save just one person's life—say, a special harness for very short people involved in rollover crashes that end up underwater. The device would add five thousand dollars to the price of each car. Would that be acceptable? Presumably those who subscribe to the "just one" belief would be happy to spend whatever it took to save that one person's life. The rest of us, however, might have better things to do with our money.

NOTES

1. "'Summer of the Shark' in 2001 More Hype Than Fact, New Numbers Show," press release, University of Florida [online], www.napa.ufl.edu/2002 news/sharks02.htm [February 18, 2002].

2. "Heat Ruled Out in One Football Death," ABC News [online], abcnews. go.com/sections/US/dailynews/football_death010820.html [August 20, 2001].

3. Eric Schlosser, "The Prison-Industrial Complex," *Atlantic Monthly* (December 1998): 51.

4. "From Shooting to Sales Pitches," *Bremerton (Wash.) Sun* [online], www. thesunlink.com/news/2000/january/0110say.html [January 10, 2000].

5. Bill Gibbs, personal correspondence with author, August 22, 2000.

6. Sabra Chartrand, "Trademarking Symbols from a Disaster," *New York Times*, November 12, 2001.

7. Peter Viles, "N.Y. Upset By Knockoffs of Hot Fire Department Logo," CNN [online], www.cnn.com/2001/US/12/16/rec.fdny.logo/index.html [December 16, 2001].

8. Catherine Valenti, "Patriot Games," ABC News [online], abcnews.go. com/sections/business/DailyNews/patriotic_ads_011019.html [October 12, 2001].

9. Linda Douglass, "Pork Barrel Patriotism?" ABC News [online], abcnews. go.com/sections/politics/DailyNews/WTC_Congress_economy011004.html [October 4, 2001].

10. "Senators Load Nearly $400 Million in Pet Projects onto Anti-terrorism, Defense Bill at Last Minute," *San Francisco Chronicle* [online], sfgate.com/cgi-bin/article.cgi?f=n/a/2001/12/14/national1619EST0670.DTL&nl=fix [December 14, 2001].

11. Richard Berke, "Local Candidates Everywhere Focus on Terrorism," *New York Times*, November 5, 2001.

12. "WTC Staff Charged with Cheating Red Cross," ABC News [online], abcnews.go.com/sections/US/DailyNews/homefront011109.html [November 9, 2001].

13. Susan Saulny, "Credit Union Says ATM Users Stole Millions after 9/11," *New York Times*, August 6, 2002.

14. Ian Bailey, "Politician, Co-workers Taken in by Woman's Bogus Trade Center Tale," *National Post*, September 27, 2001.

15. "Two Accused of False Reports," *New York Times*, September 28, 2001, p. B9; "Ohio Man Arrested for WTC Death Hoax," *New York Times* [online], www.nytimes.com/aponline/national/AP-Attacks-Deception.html [November 14, 2001]; Robert Worth, "Sept. 11 Death Faked, Police Say," *New York Times*, November 29, 2001.

16. Amanda Onion, "Change in Faith," ABC News [online], abcnews.go.com/sections/living/DailyNews/WTC_religion011003.html [October 3, 2001].

17. Pat Butler, "UNM Campus 'Scary,'" *Albuquerque Journal*, April 26, 1997.

18. Frank McCoy, "Listening to the Victims" *U.S. News and World Report*, April 24, 2000.

19. Butler, "UNM Campus 'Scary.'"

20. Ellen Traupman, "Officials Say Rape Statistics Mislead," [University of Virginia] *Cavalier Daily*, January 18, 1996.

21. Jen Barol, "Campus-Community Members Promote Safety, Awareness at Week without Violence Events," *Daily Lobo*, October 19, 1998, p. 1.

22. Sandra Tan, "In the Line of Fire," *Buffalo News*, August 24, 2001, p. A1.

23. Wendy McElroy. *XXX: A Woman's Right to Pornography* (New York: St. Martin's Press, 1995), p. 7.

24. Dean Schabner, "Looking for Attention: Without Controversy Hunt for Missing a Lonely Task," ABC News [online], more.abcnews.go.com/sections/us/dailynews/missing_families010711.html [July 11, 2001].

25. Dean Schabner, "Spinning Out of Control," ABC News [online], more/abcnews.go.com/sections/us/dailynews/levy-pr010720.html [July 20, 2001].

26. Donna Laframboise, "It's V-Day Today, But Not in the Way You Thought," *National Post* (Canada), February 14, 2000.

27. Steven Oxman, "The Vagina Monologues,' *Variety* [online], www.variety.com/index.asp?layout=review&reviewid=VE1117778679&categoryid=33&CS=1 [February 15, 2000].

28. Laframboise, "It's V-Day Today."

29. Alison Krieg, "A Modern Mother's Day," ABC News [online], abcnews.go.com/sections/us/DailyNews/mothers_day990507.html [May 7, 1999].

30. Megan Stack, "Governors Waffle on 'Happiness' Day," Associated Press [online], wire.ap.org [July 26, 1999].

31. Misty Bernall, *She Said Yes: The Unlikely Martyrdom of Cassie Bernall* (Farmington, Penn.: Plough Publishing, 1999).

32. Hanna Rosin, "Legend of Columbine Martyr Poses Dilemma," *Buffalo News,* October 18, 1999, p. A-1; Dave Cullen, "Who Said Yes?" Salon [online], www.salon.com/news/feature/1999/09/30/bernall/index.html [September 30, 1999].

33. "Hell House Scene Offends Some in Columbine High Community," *Jeffernson City (Mo.) News Tribune* [online], www.newstribune.com/stories/102799/wor_1027990037.asp [October 27, 1999].

34. Stephen Barr, "The 1990 Florida Dental Investigation: Is the Case Really Closed?" *Annals of Internal Medicine* 124 (1996): 250–54.

35. Christine Gorman, "Should You Worry About Getting AIDS from Your Dentist?" *Time,* July 29, 1991.

36. William A. Henry III, "Asking Who Is Innocent," *Time,* May 17, 1993.

37. Jerry Adler, "A Hard Lesson or a Hoax?" *Newsweek,* March 2, 1992, p. 77.

38. Brad Cain, "Oregon Considering Anti-Gay Measure," Associated Press [online], www.youth.org/loco/PERSONProject/Alerts/States/Oregon/measure 3.html [August 4, 2000].

39. Barry Glassner, *The Culture of Fear* (New York: Basic Books, 1999), p. 134.

40. Mike Taugher, "Gay 'Hoax' a Mystery to Portales," *Albuquerque Journal,* July 25, 1997, p. A-1.

41. "Police Say Lesbian Arranged Her Own Beating for Publicity," Seattle Gay News Online [online], www.sgn.org/archives/sgn.10.2.98/Archive/sgn.7.17.98/news/associatedpress.htm [July 17, 1998].

42. Scott Sonner, "Anti-Prostitution Man Faked Death," Associated Press [online], www.ainews.com/Archives/Story72.phtml [November 18, 1999].

9

EMOTIONAL LEGISLATION

solutions without problems

"Hey, mister, what are you looking for under that light?"
"My keys."
"Where did you lose them?"
"I lost them across the street."
"Then why don't you look for them across the street?"
"Because the light's better over here."

It's an old joke, but it applies well to modern American politics. Politicians and activists look in the wrong places for easy solutions to complex problems. Instead of tackling the hard tasks with practical, logical efforts, they look for quick fixes in the wrong places. The light may be better where they are looking, but that's not where the solutions are.

Without a good idea of what the real problems our society is facing are, politicians eagerly endorse measures that, while likely of dubious real value, will make them look good to voters.

In many cases, the problems that activists and politicians hype are real enough; however, they are frequently greatly exaggerated and mischaracterized, and the solutions proposed to fix those problems do little or nothing to address the issues.

JUMPING TO SOLVE PROBLEMS

America has become frenetically reactive to crises and tragedies. Nothing seems to "just happen"; events such as school shootings and celebrity deaths are framed by the media (and, by extension, most Americans) as riddles to be picked apart and explained. They are rarely seen as the isolated and uncommon events that they are, but instead as harbingers of heretofore unrecognized impending doom.

While the effort to make sure recent tragedies aren't repeated is admirable, it is also in some ways misguided. It fosters a mindset that sees everything as a crisis, demanding action, marches, and legislation.

The 1993 asbestos scare serves as an example. American schools were required to have asbestos insulation from 1940 until 1973, when the Environmental Protection Agency (EPA) banned its use. In 1982, at the EPA's directive, all schools were inspected for friable (easily crumbled) asbestos. As the American Council on Science and Health noted,

> By 1990 it was estimated that the cost of [abating the asbestos hazard] was over $6 billion. The public health benefit from all this was unclear, as asbestos experts have estimated that the lifetime risk to schoolchildren exposed to 0.001 fibers of chrysotile asbestos per milliliter of air for a minimum of 10 years is one additional death in 100,000 (that's three times less than being struck by lighting)—and most schools had asbestos levels far lower than 0.001 fibers per milliliter.[1]

The American Medical Association also found that the low level exposure found in schools did not pose a health hazard.

The nature of asbestos and the method of its removal compounded the problem. The EPA found that postremoval asbestos levels in schools were often higher than preremoval levels, indicating that shoddy removal practices may have actually *increased* health risks by releasing more particles into the air. In general, leaving asbestos undisturbed is safer than removing it.[2]

One day after a dormitory fire claimed three lives at Seton Hall University in January 2000, New Jersey governor Christine Todd Whitman said she would consider legislation requiring sprinklers in all state college dormitories. Six months later, Whitman returned to the site for a photo op to sign the law. In March 2000 Sen. Frank Lautenberg of New Jersey and Sen. John Edwards of North Carolina introduced legislation to provide $500 million in grants to install sprinklers in college dormitories, fraternities, and sororities.

Yet sprinkler legislation doesn't address the more salient causes of the fatalities. Among the preliminary findings: the fire may have been intentionally set; students ignored fire alarms; resident assistants hadn't conducted detailed fire drills for the students; thirty-five safety violations were found at the time of the fire; and the last fire inspection prior to the 2000 fire occurred in October 1988. The government, in fact, fined Seton Hall University $12,600 for failing to have a fire plan in place to protect its employees and students. The Occupational Safety and Health Administration issued three citations to the university in July 2000.[3] Problems such as these should be addressed *before* spending a half billion dollars to add sprinklers to college dorms.

Sprinkler legislation, though appealing to voters, may be a case of killing a fly with a (very expensive) sledgehammer. Retrofitting dormitories with $500 million in added fire protection is an expensive measure, when simply fixing current fire alarms and teaching students not to just ignore them when they do go off might do the trick. (Said one hospitalized student, "When I first heard the alarm, I thought 'I'm not leaving.'") In any event, it seems that suggesting legislation before investigators had even found the cause of the fire was a bit premature. The causes of any tragedy should be soberly analyzed before politicians rush to suggest expensive legislative quick fixes that may not address the problem.

What we have seen is that many laws are spearheaded by the public groups of special interests powerful (or media savvy) enough to put pressure on legislators. Yet it is precisely the public that is poorly informed about the issues to begin with. As David Shenk points out in his book *Data Smog*, "While critics carp that government is unresponsive to the people, the problem is in fact precisely the opposite: Government is all *too responsive* to a citizenry that neither grasps the precise nature of our problems nor has the will to make the hard choices to solve them."[4] This is surely one of the main roots of our bad laws. A poorly informed public, prompted in part by manipulation by and through the media, pressure lawmakers to enact laws that don't solve the problems.

Sometimes politicians and legislators actually address (and battle against) problems that simply do not exist. There are perhaps few things more amusing in politics than watching as ill-informed politicians sputter in moral, indignant outrage over a fictional story or urban legend. For example:

- On August 4, 1998, two young virgins were scheduled to have sex for the first time on a live Webcast from the Internet. This world's first real-time pornographic coupling could be seen at www.ourfirsttime.com for a five-dollar charge. News of this impending event sparked renewed efforts to pass antipornography legislation. Senate Commerce Committee Chairman John McCain specifically cited the Webcast as evidence that children need protection from online pornography. The whole thing was a hoax, however, and the big event never took place—nor was it really planned to.[5]
- In 2000 Sacramento, California, Assembly Member Thomas Calderon proposed a bill that would ban the sale and possession of "snuff" films. (A snuff film is a movie in which actors are suppos-

edly intentionally killed onscreen.) In a press release from his office, Calderon expressed his outrage at the existence of snuff films. "I'm appalled that legislation is needed to put a halt to the filming of these sorts of activities, but unfortunately this is a reality," the press release said. "In fact, the activities depicted in these videos are prohibited by state and federal laws, and while it seems logical that possession or sales of videotapes of these heinous acts would be illegal—they're not. [His bill] AB 1853 closes that loophole."[6]

A year earlier, Australian Communications Minister Richard Alston also raged about the dangers of pornography and snuff films. He specifically cited the films as a reason to censor Australians' access to the Internet: "It's not impossible to find bomb recipes or pedophile lists, indeed if it's totally unrestricted there's nothing to stop snuff movies . . . coming through on the Internet."[7]

Fortunately, Calderon's and Alston's worry and outrage is misplaced: Snuff films do not exist. They are an urban legend, and despite decades of searching by law enforcement, not a single snuff film has ever been found.[8]

The legislation was proposed a year after the film *8MM* came out, starring Nicolas Cage as man trying to avenge the death of a person killed in a snuff film. Calderon apparently believed the urban legend and took up the cause against the myth.

EXPLOITING EXPLOITED CHILDREN

No politician or government official ever lost votes by proposing or endorsing laws that protect children. The effort to protect children from predators is in many ways a business, and business is good. Whether or not children actually need the protections created in their names is a frequently ignored question.

Images of children are routinely used for political purposes. Politicians and legislators know that supporting and proposing bills helping children will benefit them, and voting against any bill that might affect children is inviting attack from others. In an article in *Newsweek* magazine, Kenneth Auchincloss noted:

> At a time when the electorate neither expects nor asks much from government, anyone with a favorite piece of legislation faces a hard time mobilizing public support. One way of doing so is to frame a proposal that will tug at the heart. That's just what's happened this year [1997]. Have you noticed how many government measures have been put for-

> ward that would benefit children? President Clinton wants a new program to help parents pay for child care. This year's tax bill offers credits for children and for education. Joe Camel ads are banned because they appeal to kids, V-chips are proposed to keep TV violence away from our kids and the government may even get into the school-uniform business. Our politics has become kiddie politics—if you want a new government program, hitch your wagon to a child.[9]

Perhaps it's time to stop treating the children of America as bait or bargaining chips for political ends. Whether the agenda is television violence, school safety, or any other cause, America's children have become the silent sacred cow, unable to vote or speak for themselves. They are propped up as exhibit A to defend all sorts of agendas. Since very few people are explicitly antichildren, it's disingenuous to frame arguments in such a way that either you support children or you're "against them," whatever that would mean. Stephen Schulhofer, a law professor at the University of Chicago, said of this trend, "Policy issues are reduced to poster children and you have an up-and-down emotional vote as if you're choosing between the killer and a particular child."[10]

Loaded questions such as "Do you support the children or do you support gun violence/Internet pedophiles/etc.?" pop up frequently in political and private interest rhetoric, though rarely are they so blatant. Who benefits from scaring parents into believing that their children are likely to be abducted by strangers who might violate and kill them? Lots of people.

Cynthia Crossen, in her book *Tainted Truth*, notes that "[s]ince bigger numbers almost always mean bigger allocations or more attention, most of the numbers flying around policy debates exaggerate on the high side."[11] Many advocates and activists happily inflate their crises for attention. Denny Abbott, former national director of the Adam Walsh Child Resource Center, has stated that "[i]n my twenty-five years in social services, I have never seen an issue as exploited as the problem of missing children."[12]

In 1995 Attorney General Janet Reno formed a new federal task force to coordinate the delivery of federal services to missing children and their families. The effort enlisted the aid of many federal agencies, from the FBI to Customs and several Justice Department offices.

The Department of Justice estimated that 440,000 children were lost or otherwise missing each year; such numbers are alarming but very misleading. David Finkelhor of the University of New Hampshire conducted a study that found that the 440,000 figure includes children missing for any amount of time, ranging from a few minutes to overnight to weeks or months. Another analysis of the Justice Department figures (this one done by the Statistical Assessment Service) found that 12 percent of the "lost" children simply forgot the time while 19 percent misunderstood parental instructions. In all, nearly three-quarters (73 percent) of the "lost" children were home within twenty-four hours.

While the term "missing child" may conjure up visions of malevolent, trench-coated men luring children into their cars with candy or Pokémon cards, the reality is much different. The vast majority of "missing" children are taken by family members, often when one divorced parent absconds with a child during legally sanctioned visitation. The child may not be where he morally or legally should be, but it is a far cry from being in a dangerous stranger's clutches. This puts the term "missing" in a whole new light, since at least one parent knew exactly where the child was. "Missing," then, is used as more of a legal word regarding the child's status than a descriptive one designating the child's whereabouts.

Between 1990 and 1995 the National Center for Missing and Exploited Children (NCMEC) handled only 515 stranger abductions, 3.1 percent of its caseload. Just as a child fifteen minutes late for dinner can be considered a "missing or lost" child to inflate the figures, so, too, can runaways be counted among the missing. Though a child or teenager leaving home voluntarily may be in trouble, he or she isn't quite "missing or lost" in the usual parlance.[13]

University of Southern California sociology professor Barry Glassner wrote of the fallacious missing children panic in his book *The Culture of Fear*:

> In national surveys conducted in recent years three out of four parents say they fear that their child will be kidnapped by a stranger. They harbor this anxiety, no doubt, because they keep hearing frightening statistics and stories about perverts snatching children off the street. What the public doesn't hear often or clearly enough is that the majority of missing children are runaways fleeing from physically or emotionally abusive parents.... According to criminal justice experts, a total of 200 to 300 children a year are abducted by nonfamily members and kept for long periods of time or murdered. Another 4,600 of America's 64 million children (.001 percent) are seized by nonfamily members and later returned.[14]

Two to three hundred abductions per year certainly constitute a tragedy, but the figure is off by several orders of magnitude from the Justice Department's figure of nearly a half million. In 1985 the *Denver Post* won a Pulitzer Prize for a series of articles investigating the child abduction scare. The investigation found that the numbers had been grossly exaggerated, frequently by child advocacy groups. One child-safety expert, Gavin De Becker, pointed out that compared to a stranger kidnapping, "[a] child is vastly more likely to have a heart attack, and child heart attacks are so rare that most parents (correctly) never even consider the risk."[15]

Child abductions made the news in mid-2002, fueling panicky headlines and parental hysteria. When seven-year-old Danielle van Dam was kidnapped from her San Diego, California, home at night in February of that year, it made national headlines. She was found dead, and a neighbor was later convicted of her murder. In July Samantha Runnion, age five, was also abducted and killed by a friend of her family.

The media reinforced the image of the threat to children being the evil man lurking in the shadows, waiting to reach out and snatch away our children. Yet the van Dam and Runnion cases are only two of the higher-profile abductions; for a more balanced picture, let's examine cases that didn't get as much attention. In my research I found a total of seven notable kidnappings between February and August 2002 that made the news as part of the "rash of abductions." In addition to van Dam and Runnion, there was also the July 26 abduction of six-year-old Cassandra Williamson of St. Louis, Missouri; the August 14 abduction of one-month-old Nancy Crystal Chavez from an Abliene, Texas, parking lot; the August 1 abduction of teens Tamara Brooks and Jacqueline Marris from Los Angeles; the August 11 kidnapping of four-year-old Jessica Cortez from a park in Los Angeles; and the abduction of nine-year-old Nicholas Farber in Palm Desert, California.

Nicholas Farber was kidnapped at gunpoint from his father's California home. After an Amber Alert was issued for the suspect's motor home, an attentive security guard spotted the vehicle. Farber was found with his mother and a male companion in an RV park eighty miles away.[16]

When little Jessica Cortez was abducted from a Los Angeles park, news reports alerted the public to watch for her with a black male suspect. Cortez was recovered several days later when her kidnapper brought the girl to a clinic to treat a sore throat. Though Cortez's appearance had been changed, the staff recognized her and called police. The abductor, a thirty-four-year-old woman, was arrested.

Margarita Chavez had just finished placing her three children in her minivan in a parking lot when her infant daughter, Nancy, was kidnapped. As Chavez turned her back, a woman snatched the infant from the seat and sped off. Margarita Chavez screamed at the woman to stop, and was dragged forty feet behind the vehicle. A nearby teenager, Robert Gann, rushed to stop the car, pounding on the passenger window and finally breaking the glass. Eventually the abductor, Paula Lynn Roach, was arrested and charged with aggravated kidnapping.[17] Abilene Police Sergeant Kim Vickers called the abduction a "classic infant abduction case," and said that "the surveillance video shows this woman circling around the parking lot. We counted at least five to seven times. She had been looking for an opportunity and when it afforded itself, she seized it."

About half of these abductions were committed by women, and in only two cases was the abductor a male stranger. More children were abducted by female strangers than male ones, yet the media did not send out warnings for parents to watch out for women in parking lots and parks snatching their children. Jessica Cortez's abductor was not a black male but a white female; the mistaken race and gender both reflected the public's stereotypes of child abductors. The media's myth of stranger-male abductors misled both police and the public. Despite all the hysteria and publicity, law enforcement officials reported that stranger abductions actually declined in 2002, and have been falling every year since 1999.[18]

Not all abduction claims that appeared during the kidnapping panic were even true; in some cases they were simply made up. On September 9, 2002, three teenage girls from Palm Beach, Florida, disappeared from a beach south of Key Biscayne. Police searched the area as the news media broadcast alerts for the missing girls. The girls later reappeared and said that they had been forced into a car at gunpoint by men who threatened to kill them.

But rather than victims of a kidnapper, the three were in fact part of an armed robbery plot. They had lured a sixteen-year-old boy to the beach, where they threatened him with a gun, beat him, attacked him with pepper spray, and stole his wallet, car, and cell phone. The girls admitted to faking their abductions to hide their armed robbery.[19]

On July 16, 2002, a young woman in Memphis, Tennessee, reported that her Honda Civic had been carjacked with her five-year-old daughter, Samantha, inside. Dozens of police officers spent hours searching for the car and child; when the car was located, the child was gone, setting off further alarm. The woman then admitted that she did not have a daughter; she had told the police the abduction story to make them search harder for her car.

Some cases are even worse. In April 2002 a California woman abducted her two young daughters from day care. She kept them hidden for six months while their father searched for them. She later told a judge that she had given the girls to strangers and did not know where they were. When the girls were finally found, it turned out that their mother had left them in the care of a convicted child molester.[20]

One study published in the journal *Pediatrics* found that, though parents are most commonly responsible for the abuse or neglect of a child, abuse was nearly nine times more likely to be recorded on a death certificate if the perpetrator was unrelated to the child. This suggests that police tend to believe the media-perpetuated myth that parents are unlikely to abuse or kill their child. It also suggests that child abuse deaths are sharply underestimated.[21] In fact, a 1999 study found that the number of children killed by their parents or caregivers is underreported by nearly 60 percent. Caregivers commit 85 percent of the homicides of children ten and under, compared to just 3 percent by strangers.[22]

The news media also unnecessarily alarm parents by emphasizing negative stories about children. For example, much of the time when a child makes national news it is because something horrible happened to her: She was killed, or abducted, or fell down a well. A 2001 study from Children Now, a child advocacy group, found that over a third of all stories about children depict them as victims of crime. Nearly half (45 percent) of all stories about children focused on crime, usually violent crime. This in turn contributes to "a climate of fear for children's safety by portraying them in grave danger."[23] Only rarely do happy, healthy, safe children make the news.

Bad Numbers and Bad Journalism

Bad science and flawed statistics surround us all the time, and part of the journalist's role is to help separate the good information from the bad. But when dubious science combines with poor journalism, the results are far worse than either alone. On September 10, 2001, University of Pennsylvania professor Richard Estes called a press conference to announce the results of a three-year investigation into child sexual exploitation. Many of Estes's findings, such as that most children are abused by someone they know, fit well with what was already known on the subject. But it was his most shocking finding that made headlines and drew the crowd: As many as four hundred thousand children each year are victims of childhood sexual exploitation.

The study's findings made international news, partly because the number was much higher—anywhere from two to ten times higher—than any previous studies had indicated. Estes referred to the widespread exploitation he found as "the nation's least recognized epidemic."

The figure Estes came up with is important because up until that time, estimates of the number of children involved in the commercial sex trade were sketchy at best. The three-year, $400,000 Estes study was the strongest evidence to date on the subject. A spokeswoman at the American Bar Association's Center for Children and the Law was quoted in a *USA Today* article, saying, "This looks like it's the most comprehensive study yet."[24] So it wasn't just a new study; it was touted as the *best* study to date.

Estes himself said he was stunned by the numbers he and his coauthor, Neil Weiner, came up with: "That figure just blew our minds. We never . . . thought we would encounter so many children in this predicament," he told a Reuters reporter.[25]

The number Estes found came as a surprise to other researchers as well—including the researchers from whose studies Estes derived his data. David Finkelhor called the numbers "terribly flawed" and said that "there are serious questions about whether the study's findings have been greatly exaggerated." Finkelhor should know, as the Estes report was based largely on studies he had done ten years earlier.

Soon after the Estes report was made public, Finkelhor issued a short news release commenting on the study. It read in part:

> The new report . . . relies extensively for its estimates of the national scope of the problem on data gathered in earlier studies by ourselves and some of our colleagues. Unfortunately we do not think that the data from our studies support the estimates that have been extrapolated in this new study. Overall the estimates in the new study have been generated making assumptions that are very speculative, in some cases mistaken, and not well supported by national research. Sometimes estimates derived from very different and incompatible populations have been combined to reach a conclusion. In addition, the new report makes an obvious mistake of counting many children two or more times.[26]

Finkelhor went on to cite several specific examples of errors, such as assuming that youth who were gone from their homes for a week or more were in shelters or on the streets, and therefore very vulnerable to exploitation. Yet Finkelhor's study found that most runaways stay with friends or relatives, and only a small number end up in shelters or on the streets. "Since the new study is likely wrong in this assumption, the number of victims of commercial sexual exploitation could easily be half of their estimate or less." The statement concludes:

> [W]e are of the opinion that at the present time we do not have adequate research to make an accurate national estimate, and certainly not using the speculative assumptions in the new study. It is important for everyone concerned about the well-being of children that we have numbers that are scientifically defensible and cannot be dismissed by skeptics.[27]

The basic problem, according to Finkelhor, was "a lack of experience and a lack of understanding on how to deal with epidemiological data."

When I asked why he was nearly the lone voice in publicly questioning the inflated findings, Finkelhor suggested that many researchers fall for the "greater good" argument: They may feel that, though the data and findings are deeply flawed (and may eventually be disproven), at least the subject is getting some attention. "A lot of people in a position to critique it feel that, well, 'I support the work but don't want to get into a fight with an ally.'"

One might think that a shockingly high number such as nearly a half million child victims, dramatically higher than any previous estimates, would have set off alarm bells that perhaps something was wrong with the study or its data. Though he did not publish the findings in a peer-reviewed journal, Estes claims that the study was subjected to peer review. Regardless, Finkelhor says that Estes and Weiner never consulted with him about the use of his data. Finkelhor adds that the Estes report is not without some merit, calling the information on child exploitation pathways "very useful" and the policy recommendations excellent. His main complaint is what the story's hype was all about: The big numbers were "entirely premature and without scientific basis."

In science, as in the rest of life, mistakes can be made, methodologies can be flawed, and numbers can be miscalculated. Perhaps Estes should have been more cautious with his conclusions, especially given the long and spotty history of inflated threatened-child numbers. But that's only part of problem. Ultimately, Finkelhor blames the news media for their lack of skepticism: "The biggest failure was the journalists' failure to question the findings."

Journalists know—or should know—enough to dig a little deeper than skimming press conference materials for their stories, especially when the results are so widely at variance with previous estimates and studies. Reporters should have asked if the results had been published or peer reviewed and sought commentary from others in the field.

Yet out of all the news outlets that covered the story, apparently only one or two sought out and published comments from researchers critical of the study. The Associated Press and ABC News duly reported the results of the Estes study—and quoted Finkelhor's rebuttal.

The reporting on the whole, however, was abysmal. Not only were skeptical and informed researchers not questioned, but at least one of the very few experts cited as endorsing the study claims to have been misquoted. Remember the woman from the American Bar Association, quoted in *USA Today* as supporting the study? She flatly states, "I did not make the statement attributed to me in *USA Today* and I never endorsed the study. I regret that the reporter chose to mischaracterize our conversation."[28] The reluctance of other experts to endorse the study should have raised questions in journalists' minds.

The results of the study were very quickly overshadowed by the September 11, 2001, terrorist attacks, but the damage had been done. Six months later, an Internet search turned up more than fifty articles and Web pages citing the Estes study and his claims of three hundred thousand to four hundred thousand annual child victims. Of those sites, fewer than a dozen mentioned Finkelhor's criticisms. The inflated numbers will almost certainly be cited and repeated in the years to come, one more dubious factoid to muddy the waters. As of May 2002, Estes had not publicly revised the estimates, but had revised the report to include Finkelhor's criticisms.

Megan's Law

On July 29, 1994, seven-year-old Megan Kanka was raped and killed by paroled sex offender Jimmy Timmendequas. The New Jersey girl's death led to a proposal requiring police to notify neighbors, schools, churches, youth groups, and the media within forty-five days of a convicted offender's move into a neighborhood. The law was eventually passed and was given the name Megan's Law in her memory. Since then, every state has enacted some type of sex offender law modeled after Megan's Law.

Such laws, however, have been fraught with charges of unconstitutionality and violating the double jeopardy clause by civil rights advocates. Ed Martone of the American Civil Liberties Union claims that in states where Megan's Laws have been in effect for a few years, they haven't worked:

> What you've seen in other states, for example, that have this is that half or more of the sex offenders don't register, and many who do register at park benches and vacant lots and abandoned buildings because they're not crazy. They know what happens to them when their neighbors know about them.[29]

In some cases, Megan's Law has actually *hindered* police investigations. Eight-year-old Xiana Fairchild vanished on her way to school in Vallejo, California, on December 9, 1999. Curtis Dean Anderson, a career criminal with a history of abusing women, admitted involvement in Xiana's disappearance. At the time, Anderson was not questioned, despite the fact that he lived in the area, drove a cab for the same company as Xiana's mother, and had just been released from prison. Why didn't the Vallejo police suspect Anderson? According to police lieutenant JoAnn West, "We focused initially on high-risk registered sex offenders and moved on to examine all sex offenders in the area."[30]

Despite his history, Anderson was never registered as a sex offender; the time the police spent questioning the three hundred released offenders in Vallejo on the registration list was wasted. Anderson was charged with kidnapping and sexually assaulting another eight-year-old girl at a later date. Had the police not begun their investigation looking in the wrong place (using Megan's Law), perhaps Anderson would have been apprehended before he could attack his second victim.

There have also been several cases of vigilantism and inaccurate registry information. In 1999 a twenty-seven-year-old Dallas man was beaten by vigilantes. The victim, a disabled man with the mental capacity of a sixth-grader, had four teeth knocked out. The four men who beat him thought he was a child molester—because he happened to live at an address a sex offender called home months before. Similar incidents have occurred in New Jersey and other states.[31]

Such incidents have also occurred in England (where a law similar to Megan's Law is in effect), and the problem has gotten so out of hand that British Labor MP Robin Corbett urged the government to prosecute a newspaper for inciting mob violence. In July 2000 *News of the World*, Britain's best-selling newspaper, published the names, pictures, and details of dozens of registered sex offenders. Hundreds of protesters took to the streets to harass suspected pedophiles, and the protests continually turned violent. Many people not connected with the offenders in any way were harassed and threatened, including four families who asked to be rehoused. Corbett warned that the public naming of pedophiles actually puts more children in danger: "What it means is that some of those convicted of serious sexual offenses simply disappear, and the police and other agencies do not know where they are."[32]

As we have seen, the abduction, rape, and killing of children by strangers is very, very rare. The vast majority of crimes against children are committed not by the trench-coated, recently released sex offender across the street, but instead by the victim's own family, church clergy, family friends, and others the victim knows. Strangers are far less dangerous to children than their own friends and families. A 2000 report on abductions by the Office of Juvenile Justice and Delinquency Programs reported that over three-quarters of kidnappings were committed by family members or acquaintances of the child. The study also found that children abducted by strangers were in fact harmed *less frequently* than those taken by acquaintances (16 percent versus 24 percent).[33]

In March 2000 the U.S. Supreme Court refused to reinstate Pennsylvania's sexual predator law, which was thrown out by that state's highest court as a violation of defendants' rights. Previously, Pennsylvania Supreme Court Justice Stephen Zappala invalidated key provisions of the law, finding that the law's presumption that a person is a sexually violent predator and that the offender must rebut that assumption was "constitutionally repugnant." For her part, Megan's mother, Maureen, apparently frustrated by legal minutiae such as the Bill of Rights, feels that "[o]ur judges have gone from what was a basic concept, to putting procedures in place that have really strangled the law."[34]

In some cases, inmates who finished their prison sentences and were released were rearrested simply because they didn't have a place to live upon release and therefore couldn't comply with the registration requirements of Megan's Law. Many advocates of reform contend that the policy is unconstitutional and unfair to inmates who have few or no resources after being in jail for years. One former inmate, a Matthew Dix, was convicted of rape in 1983 and served a seventeen-year sentence. He was released on October 3, 2000, and was soon rearrested because he had no residence to list. A month later, he was still in jail, unable to raise the $5,000 bail.[35]

There's also the issue of the cost of implementing Megan's Law. This is especially onerous when a sex offender moves from one state to another. Ann Dawley, a member of the Massachusetts Registry Board, says:

> The problem for us is trying to figure out if that crime is identical or similar to one of ours. So there is a review mechanism by which we look at the history of the case, police reports, psychiatric evaluations. . . . We spend a lot of time on this.[36]

Diane Moyer, a public policy attorney with the National Sexual Violence Resource Center, agrees:

> I don't think anybody was aware of what the cost of Megan's Law would be. Like anything in the criminal justice system, people don't realize that it eventually has a fiscal impact.[37]

The real problem with Megan's Laws is that they simply don't work. They do not provide protection from sexual predators; worse, they give a false sense of security. It is perhaps the best example of a well-intentioned but misguided public safety measure ever introduced in America.

Proponents of Megan's Laws have a hard time trying to marshal any evidence at all that the laws work. Usually they rely on the fallacious argument that Megan's Laws don't hurt, and that we will never know how many lives have been saved because the child killers and molesters were prevented from attacking in the first place. Laura Ahearn, executive director of Parents for Megan's Law, admits that proving the law's effectiveness has "created a challenge" for groups like hers. "You can't prove a negative," she told me, but "you can look at anecdotal evidence."[38] This argument is reminiscent of an old story about a father who notices his young son blowing a whistle every night before bed. He asks his boy why he blows the whistle. The boy says, "It keeps tigers away while I sleep." The father says, "Son, that's silly. There are no tigers within a thousand miles of here"—to which his boy replies, "See? It works!"

While we can't know how many attacks, if any, have been prevented by Megan's Laws, we *can* work backward and see how many attacks were *not* prevented. And here is where the ineffectiveness of Megan's Laws becomes clear. Seven-year-old Danielle van Dam was kidnapped the night of February 1, 2002, and killed by her abductor, David Westerfield. Westerfield was not on any sex offender registry. A few months later, on July 15, 2002, five-year-old Samantha Runnion was abducted in

Stanton, California. She was assaulted and killed; her abductor, Alejandro Avila, also was not on any sex offender registry. In fact, of the half dozen or so high-profile abductions between February and August of 2002, not a single person who was charged with any of the abductions was affected by Megan's Laws.

In his book *The Limits of Privacy*, Professor Amitai Etzioni of George Washington University examines Megan's Laws and finds them to be deeply flawed. Etzioni writes that "Megan's Laws, even if fully implemented, do not protect children sufficiently." Furthermore, Etzioni notes that "Megan's Laws generate a false sense of security: People tend to believe that they will be notified about all sex offenders who move in next door, and that is not the case."[39]

The obvious and fundamental flaw is the assumption that simply knowing that a sex offender is in the area will somehow make children safer. There is little or no evidence that this is true. Just because a sex offender lives nearby doesn't mean that he stays in the area; most people regularly travel some distance on a daily basis.

So you are told a sex offender lives somewhere in the neighborhood. What then? Tell your children not to accept rides from strangers? Hopefully you've already done that. Tell them to be careful around a certain person or neighborhood? Fine, but the chances are that if your child is attacked, the abductor or molester will not be the registered sex offender you are focusing on but instead a family member, friend, or someone not on any offender registry.

Etzioni recognizes this problem as well, saying that the laws will fail "unless the whole of community life is modified so that children are not left alone on playgrounds and not allowed to walk to school or to a friend's house unchaperoned."

The mother of one child who was abducted and killed pointed out that constantly sheltering children is not the solution to avoiding kidnappings. Erin Runnion, the mother of Samantha Runnion, told Larry King that "I don't think there's a way to prevent this . . . you have to let your children be the people that they are, and there's no sense in boarding them up. That doesn't make any sense. That's no life."[40]

I've only been able to find one other case similar to Megan Kanka's in the wake of her notification law. In Connecticut, convicted sex offender Jose Torres was charged with killing an eleven-year-old girl on August 13, 1998. At the time, a version of Megan's Law was in effect, but the law did nothing to prevent the killing. The police chief kept the required sex offender registry; he said that prior to the killing, only two people in three years had looked at the list. Even if they had, it wouldn't have helped much: The address the defendant gave was out of date, and was more than a mile away from where he was living at the time of the girl's death.[41]

As of August 2000, New Jersey was home to 5,408 registered sex offenders. Since Megan's Law notification began in January 1998, residents have learned the location of only 118 offenders—just over 2 percent.[42] An investigation by the Associated Press found that California had lost track of nearly half of that state's convicted sex offenders, according to 2002 data. At least 33,296, or 44 percent, of California's 76,350 sex offenders were unaccounted for.

Even groups that support Megan's Law admit that the registrations are badly out of date: A survey released in 2003 by the advocacy group Parents for Megan's Law found that states on average were unable to account for nearly a quarter of the sex offenders who were supposed to be in the databases. Eighteen states said they were unable to track how many sex offenders were failing to register. The law is clearly not an effective tool for notifying the public. In 2002 the state of Tennessee passed a law that extended Megan's Law to cover college campuses across the state. It's not clear what the rationale is behind applying a law intended to protect young children to a campus of adults, nor how effective it could be.

And even the original Megan's Law in New Jersey underwent revisions because U.S. District Judge Joseph Irenas said that the state failed to implement consistent standards on how notifications are conducted and because the old system violated privacy rights. The revised guidelines require that anyone notified that a sex offender lives near their home or school sign papers agreeing not to disseminate the information. To her credit, then-governor Christine Todd Whitman initially balked at Megan's Law, and wanted community notification only when an inmate is "really at risk of committing these kinds of offenses again," arguing that too broad a law risks deluging the police with paperwork.

Is this a case of pro-pedophile judges conspiring to protecting child abusers? No. This is a case of fundamentally bad laws proposed more on emotion than logic or a respect for civil rights. And because of the social climate, nearly ten years have passed and still the issue is being fought back and forth. The law clearly violates civil rights laws and has proved worthless in protecting children in the one case it had any effect at all.

Bad laws in turn lead to convictions being thrown out and prisoners released. Yet when convictions are overturned, rarely—if ever—are the lawmakers held responsible for hastily crafting laws only tenuously based in reality. Instead, the public blames the justice system for protecting criminals' rights and trampling victims' rights. The cause-and-effect relationship between bad laws and bad results seems lost on both the public and proponents of such legislation. The activists may mean well, but they become so focused on their crusades that they ignore larger issues. Politicians, in turn, have little to lose and much to gain by promoting these laws; it's a low-risk venture.

In what is perhaps the final irony, it's unclear that Megan's Law would have even saved the girl whose death brought the law about. As *Newsweek* reporter Matt Bai noted, "It wasn't clear, however, that Megan would still be alive if neighbors and schools had known about Timmendequas. A lot of people on Megan's street already knew that at least one child molester—one of Timmendequas's roommates—lived among them."[43] The Kankas' claim that no one knew molesters were in the area—and that's what led to Megan's death—is simply not true.

Compare Megan's Laws to the Amber Alert system. The Amber Alert sends out information on recent area kidnappings to television, radio stations, and electronic traffic signals. In this way, ordinary motorists can become eyes and ears of police and search for a fleeing suspect or vehicle. As of September 2002, seventeen states and several cities had the systems in place. The system was named for a nine-year-old Texas girl who was kidnapped and murdered in 1996.

Unlike Megan's Laws, the Amber Alert system at least has a track record of success: The National Center for Missing and Exploited Children claims that, as of 2002, at least seventeen children have been recovered using the system.[44]

There are, however, concerns that the Amber Alert system may become less effective the more it is used. Joann Donnellan, who manages the Amber Alert system for the national center in Virginia, points out that, by some estimates, nearly two thousand children are reported missing every day. (It is important to realize that "missing" is not the same as "abducted," and applies to a child missing for a few minutes as well as voluntary runaways.) Donnellan says that "this alert should not go off 2,000 times a day or the system will make the public unresponsive."[45] There are also other issues to be worked out, as well as the question of what sorts of missing cases warrant an Amber Alert. As Cynthia Gorney, associate dean of journalism at the University of California at Berkeley, writes, "What's the age cutoff for these alerts? What's the rationalization for limiting them to children? What about the Alzheimer's patient who goes missing, or the bank robber with hostages in his car, or the woman last seen being forced from the house at gunpoint by her estranged husband? . . . What will we say the day federal authorities want to borrow AMBER for a terrorism suspect alert?"[46]

There have also been many false reports. In April 2003 a Maryland woman reported that her two young children had been kidnapped, triggering the activation of the statewide Amber Alert system. Police later determined that the report was false, and she was charged with lying to detectives. According to the *Baltimore Sun*, the Maryland Amber Alert was activated three times in the first six months of operation; all three turned out to be false reports.[47]

Christina Long and Kid-Friendly Web Domains

Although Megan's Law is probably the best known of the "victim laws," new ones are proposed all the time, often just as ill-conceived. A good example is the case of Christina Long, a thirteen-year-old girl from Danbury, Connecticut. Long was an altar girl and a cheerleader at St. Peter School.

In late May 2002 Christina disappeared after her aunt dropped her off at a local mall. Police searched her home computer and found that she had exchanged risqué e-mails with Saul Dos Reis, a twenty-five-year-old Brazilian man from nearby Greenwich. Dos Reis was arrested, confessed to Christina's murder, and led police to her body. She had been strangled and dumped in a nearby ravine.

Stories about the dangers lurking on the Internet were rampant in the news media at the time. Politicians, ever eager to champion a vote-getting cause, jumped on the case within days.

Two pieces of legislation were proposed. The first, versions of which were sponsored by Rep. John Shimkus of Illinois, Sen. Byron Dorgan of North Dakota, and Rep. Fred Upton of Michigan, directed the federal government to set up and oversee a special domain on the Internet for kids. The domain, "kids.us," would contain only material appropriate for children under thirteen. Participation would be voluntary, and parents would theoretically be able to limit a child's access to only that domain area. The bill's supporters claimed that the new domain would "reduce the chance of accidental exposure to pornography and to other Web sites considered harmful to children."

The second bill was proposed to expand wiretap authority to target Internet predators. That bill was sponsored by Rep. Nancy Johnson of Connecticut, and provided "federal authorities greater power to wiretap suspected predators." In both cases, the death of Christina Long was specifically and repeatedly cited as evidence that the new laws were needed.[48]

The politicians, however, seem to have jumped the gun. If they had looked a little deeper into the circumstances of Christina Long's death, they would have found that the measures they proposed in her name have little or no relevance to the circumstances of her death. For example:

- The politicians suggested that Christina Long had been lured away from her home by a stranger she met on the Internet. In fact, Long and Dos Reis had a relationship and the two had met for sex on several occasions. While it is apparently true that they first met online, the two were friends before the killing and it seems that Long could just as likely have been in that situation with a man she'd met at a party, through friends, or in a mall.

- Saul Dos Reis would not have been arrested or stopped from meeting his victim by Representative Johnson's bill. Dos Reis was not a "suspected sexual predator" and in fact had no criminal record.[49] The law might even have applied to Long herself, who, on her Web site, allegedly mentioned luring other teens into sexual encounters.
- The "kids.us" domain would have material only for kids twelve and younger. Long was thirteen, so the domain wouldn't have applied to her anyway. Aside from that, there's little need to establish a special kid-friendly domain on the Web; the Web is full of existing kid-friendly sites that are "free from pornography and dangerous material," hosted by everyone from Disney to Nickelodeon to Sesame Street to the U.S. government. In fact, the vast majority of Web sites do not contain pornography at all. Ironically, Long's own Web page would not have been allowed in the domain; it contained many sexual references and what Police Chief Robert Paquette called "some pretty graphic stuff."[50]
- Christina Long wouldn't have used the "kids.us" Web domain; she was actively searching adult chat rooms for the purpose of finding men to have sex with. The problem is not that Long wanted kid-friendly material on the Web but couldn't find it. No matter how many Web sites are designed for children, if a teen is searching for sex instead of Snoopy, he or she will find it.

In pushing for the passage of her bill, Representative Johnson mentioned Christina Long's death and shouted, "The threat to our children is real!"[51] While there is no doubt that the threat of Internet predators is real, it is also very remote. Despite all the political grandstanding, alarmist activism, and media myths that suggest that teen girls are lured to their deaths by Internet predators on a weekly basis, Long's case was in fact the first of its kind.

Long was described as "streetwise" and, according to her aunt, was well aware of the dangers of meeting people in chat rooms.[52] Rather than being lured away from her home for sex, she actively sought out sexual partners on the Web, and one of them happened to kill her during sex. It is a tragic story, but Christina Long would hardly seem to be a good example of why kids need more under-thirteen Web sites or wiretapping laws should be expanded.

In December 2002 President George W. Bush signed the Dot-Kids Implementation and Efficiency Act into law, creating an Internet "neighborhood" for children. Almost immediately questions were raised about the law's effectiveness. Elliot Noss, president of Internet address registrar Tucows Inc., said that the domain has "absolutely zero" chance of being effective. It is, he said, "an exercise in making politicians who don't understand the medium feel good."[53]

It seems that measures such as these stem less from a genuine desire to protect children than a blind quest for political benefit. Instead of suggesting workable solutions to real problems, politicians exploit a real-life tragedy so they can point to their legislation as protecting America's kids.

Megan's Law is far from the only law enacted in memory of child victims. There's also Aimee's Law, Kieran's Law, and Lizzie's Law, just to name a few. Lizzie's Law is a good example of a law enacted to remedy a very specific problem, with little applicability to other situations. The law, named for a girl named Lizzie Thompson, prohibits judges from requiring children to visit parents convicted of the first-degree murder of the other parent. The law seems very esoteric: how many people could this law possibly apply to? Besides, there's no demonstrable damage in *not* having the law; just because one child was killed in an unusual circumstance such as Lizzie Thompson's doesn't mean that all, most, or even some children in similar situations would necessarily be in danger. There are already laws in effect that deal with parents attacking their children. Once again, we see legal policy being made based on rare, unrepresentative—though emotional—events. Perhaps one day advocates and politicians will learn that they don't need to go to such lengths "to make sure it never happens again."

Kendra's Law was named after Kendra Webdale, a woman who was pushed into the path of an oncoming subway train and killed in January 1999. Her killer was a schizophrenic named Andrew Goldstein. In the usual fashion, the Webdale family took up a cause in her memory and is suing and lobbying to reform the medical and hospitalization system that allowed Goldstein to slip through the cracks and go untreated. The interesting question, however, is *which* cause they chose to attach to Kendra's memory.

For example, the family could have sued the transit authority and subway for not providing adequate security, starting an organization lobbying to provide more police and cameras in the subways. Or their cause could have targeted the pharmaceutical companies that manufactured the antipsychotic drugs Goldstein was supposed to be on for not having a way to ensure medication is taken on time and in proper dosages. Or they could have been advocates for providing guard rails, barriers, and other safety measures to prevent other people from falling or being pushed onto the rails. Just about any reasonable angle could have been tailored to pursue an agenda in Kendra's name. The claim that Kendra's death is a rallying cry (or, in alarmist parlance, a "wake up call") for the psychiatric community is certainly one way to spin the circumstances of her death, but it is far from the only one.

Ironically, the Webdale family's high-profile efforts in their daughter's name may have contributed to another person nearly being killed. In April 1999, three months after Kendra's death, a man named Julio Perez pushed Edgar Rivera into the path of an oncoming subway train. Rivera lived, but the train severed his legs. Assistant District Attorney Peter Casolar said Perez was seeking attention by copying Goldstein's killing of Kendra Webdale following the widespread publicity.[54]

We all have little pet causes that we'd like to see turned into law and imposed on other people; I personally would like to require left-turn signals at every intersection. Not as important as saving a life, you say? Well, in fact many lives *would* be saved, because people making left turns across oncoming traffic pose a significant road hazard. I daresay requiring left-turn signals would save many more lives than Megan's Law, Lizzie's Law, and all the other victim laws combined. Yet I have no emotional, tear-jerking story to tell, no martyrs to proffer; no politicians will trumpet left-turn signals to get votes.

My aim isn't in any way to denigrate the lives or memories of Megan Kanka, Kendra Webdale, or any of the other victims-turned-martyrs. I simply want to show how and why their deaths can be co-opted by political interests and their memories used for misguided and unnecessary laws. I would argue, in fact, that allowing special interests to use their images and deaths in such a way demeans them by casting them as mute, one-note exhibits trotted out for someone else's cause.

While the media closely followed the stories of missing kids like Elizabeth Smart and Danielle van Dam, missing young black children were virtually ignored. Alonzo Washington, a comic book artist from Kansas City, was "appalled at the lack of coverage some of these missing African-American children were getting compared to some of these missing white children." To address the issue, Washington began including missing kids information in his independent comic book *Omega Man* and on trading cards.[55]

Though stories of missing children grab the public's attention, there are other stories, just as tragic, that don't get widespread attention because the victims are over eighteen. Kym Pasqualini, director of the Center for Missing Adults, points out that "when you think of 'missing,' it's usually a child that jumps into your mind. But families of missing adults suffer no less than the families of missing children. And they rarely get the same kind of assistance."[56]

In stark contrast to the widespread legislation intended to protect children, some lawmakers have instead supported laws that make it easier to abandon children.

In 1996 Kelli Moye of Illinois left her newborn to freeze to death in a neighbor's snowy yard, having hidden her pregnancy from her parents.

Moye was convicted of involuntary manslaughter and served less than two years for killing her baby.[57] Two years later, a Buffalo, New York, teen also left her baby to die in subzero temperatures; she was sentenced to just a year in jail for killing her child and was spared a criminal record.[58] During a ten-month period in Houston, Texas, in 1999, thirteen babies were thrown away by their mothers. They were dumped in trash cans, suffocated in plastic bags, and drowned in toilets. What should society do when mothers decide they don't want their infants and kill them or leave them to die? Until recently, the obvious answer—prosecuting the mothers for the crime of child abandonment—was the law.

Then Texas lawmakers decided to rewrite the law to allow mothers to abandon their babies. The law was passed on September 1, 1999, allowing new mothers to anonymously give infants up to one month old to medical personnel at firehouses and hospitals. More than a dozen states, including New York, have legalized the practice, and many more have such bills under consideration.

Abandoning a newborn child and walking away thus dropped from a felony to a legally sanctioned act. Because the process is anonymous and entirely at the mother's discretion, the law denies fathers, grandparents, and other family members the opportunity to raise the child.

THE DRUG SCARE

America goes out of its way to protect its children in other ways as well. And once again, the popular solutions are ineffective because they don't address the real problems. As with sexual predators, the American public is ready to point blame for the drug problem anywhere—except the mirror. Many current drug prevention and education campaigns urge parents to talk to their kids about drugs, even calling parents the "anti-drug." While that tack may work for many families, it's way off the mark for others.

Who introduces American youth to drugs? The common perception is that of reckless drug gangs pushing their drugs on bored, rebellious, or otherwise alienated youth. Yet the truth is somewhat different. A survey of drug users in treatment programs found that one in five had been introduced to drugs by their parents, and drug users were nineteen times more likely to have been introduced to drugs by a family member than a professional drug dealer. And less than 1 percent were introduced to drugs by a professional dealer. Says David Rosenker, vice president of adolescent services at the Caron Foundation, a treatment program in Pennsylvania, "We already see it a lot: Baby boomer parents who are still using and still having a problem with their use. They're buying for their kids, smoking pot with their kids, using heroin with their kids."[59] Remember the short-lived antidrug public service announcement slogan of the 1990s, "Get involved with drugs before your kids do"? Well, that's exactly what's happening to a significant segment of drug users.

Ephrat Livni of ABC News reports that "Stephen Higgins, a professor of psychiatry and psychology at the University of Vermont in Burlington, says addiction professionals have known for some time that most people are introduced to drug use by friends and relatives and not by a professional pusher."[60]

According to a study sponsored by the Center on Addiction and Substance Abuse at Columbia University, two-thirds of baby boomer parents who experimented with illegal drugs expect their own children to do the same, and many don't consider that a crisis. Says the center's Joseph Califano, "What is infuriating . . . is the resignation of so many parents. That is not a climate that's sending a clear and loud message to a kid: 'Don't do drugs.'" Further highlighting the disconnect between parents and children, the study found that while 94 percent of parents claimed that they warned their teens about the dangers of drugs, 39 percent of teens don't remember hearing it.[61]

So we're left with many parents who are either indifferent to their children's drug use or actually encourage it. Though this may not represent the majority of parents, it is clearly a large percentage, and this should be cause for alarm. It should also help to illuminate some of the reasons why the war on drugs, as it is—and has been—fought, is largely a failure.

The results of the survey suggest that money and resources might be better spent focusing on stopping the cycle of drug use within families instead of on stopping the drug pusher on the street. Yet this approach is unlikely to take root; it's much easier to blame the "other," the demonized and maligned drug dealers. After all, news reports of big drug busts of organized drug rings are sexy; they make good news footage, as do busy and loud predawn raids on crack houses. Educational efforts to stop drug use in families is a much more subtle and private endeavor—with less dramatic results and less likelihood of funding. Again, our emotions lead us away from what's most effective. As Scott Basinger, chair of the Substance Abuse Assistance Council at Baylor College of Medicine, puts it, "This information suggests the problem is not 'out there' but 'in here.'" Dr. Mitchell Rosenthal, a child psychiatrist, concurs: "We have met the neighborhood pusher, and he is us."[62]

A similar misdirection of concern occurs in the case of children killed in car crashes. Though anti–drunk driving lobby groups (such as Mothers Against Drunk Driving) don't mention it much, the biggest threat to children in automobiles is not the drunken stranger on the road, it's their own driver—most likely one of their parents. According to an article in the May 2000 issue of the *Journal of the American Medical Association*, most children under fifteen who were killed in drunk-driving crashes were riding unrestrained in a car with someone old enough to be a parent or caregiver. Of 5,555 child vehicle deaths that involved drunken drivers, nearly two-thirds (64 percent) happened while the child's *own* driver was intoxicated. The authors further believe that the number of child deaths involving nonstranger drivers is, if anything, underreported in their findings. Dr. Kyran Quinlan, one of the study's authors, wrote, "This is different than what might be assumed from popular media reports of children who are killed when the vehicle in which they are riding is hit by a drinking driver." They also found that less than 20 percent of children were properly buckled in.[63] These statistics were not widely reported; child advocates don't like to hear them because it holds a mirror up to the real perpetrators of the crimes.

The Candy Scare

Each year many American parents, physicians, and police go through a ritual that has little if any actual value and instead "protects" children from a nonexistent threat. Every Halloween, police and medical centers across the country X-ray candy collected by trick-or-treaters to check for razors, needles, or pins that might have been placed there by evil strangers to hurt or kill innocent children. Yet this scary tale has no basis in truth; there has never been a case of this happening.[64]

X-raying candy lets parents feel like they are protecting their children, when in fact they are simply wasting time and resources and unnecessarily feeding children's fears. The fact that parents and police take the myth seriously tells children that the danger is real, and reinforces the untruth that strangers are trying to hurt or kill them. Surely there are better uses for the X-ray equipment than addressing phantom fears, such as offering free or low-cost X rays for poor families.

ANTITERRORISM LAWS

After members of Osama bin Laden's Al-Qaeda group attacked the United States on September 11, 2001, politicians and government officials scrambled for ways to prevent future attacks and make America safer. While some of the measures were well thought-out and rational (such as strengthening airline cockpit doors), others were clearly expensive, knee-jerk quick fixes with no hope of implementation or actual effect.

Many of the measures enacted by President George W. Bush were both ineffective and unworkable. As ABC News correspondent Josh Gerstein noted:

> According to pilots, security professionals, and longtime students of the issue, the current security crackdown suffers from three key misconceptions: 1) Security screening can keep small weapons from getting onto aircraft . . . 2) The next time terrorists strike they will attempt something similar to those who struck on September 11 . . . and 3) Intense screening and a uniformed military presence at airport security checkpoints will significantly diminish the threat of terrorism.[65]

Indeed, Gerstein writes,

> The president's Sept. 27 speech at O'Hare Airport rallied workers there, but left something to be desired in the candor department. In fact, many of the security measures he announced are largely cosmetic. He asked governors to send the National Guard into airports, but never really said what the troops are supposed to do.[66]

The National Guard did little but maintain a conspicuous presence (standing around in camouflage, carrying M-16 rifles that would be impractical for use inside a busy airport). The guard was finally dismissed from airports on May 31, 2002, not having caught any terrorists or prevented any known airliner attacks or hijackings.

Not only are most of these measures of dubious value, but they take resources and attention away from real problems. Lawmakers and the Bush administration imposed unrealistic deadlines for security measures such as the installation of bomb-detection devices to check luggage. Despite the Federal Aviation Administration's (FAA) clear and repeated congressional testimony that the announced goal of screening all checked luggage in two months was logistically and physically impossible, lawmakers were upset when told it could not be done. According to the FAA, the airports would need at least two thousand bag-screening machines in place within two months, yet the companies that make the machines could not produce that many in the next year.

When Transportation Secretary Norman Mineta announced that the checks could not be in place on time, it caused a stir. Despite that what Mineta said was obvious to anyone knowledgeable about airline security, lawmakers were outraged at the admission. Senate Commerce Chairman Ernest Hollings said that Mineta should "keep it quiet."[67] Thus the lawmakers prefer to ignore reality, fool the American people, and cover up the fact that they acted before thinking by ignorantly imposing unachievable goals.

Some of the airport security measures were clearly more cosmetic than real. Prohibiting knives and guns is obviously a good idea, as is reinforcing cockpit doors. But banning plastic food knives, nail clippers, small scissors, and other common, nonoffensive objects from airplanes is ineffective overkill. One airline even stopped serving powdered coffee creamer, as it could be mistaken for anthrax.

These measures ignore the fact that nearly anything can be used as a weapon in the right hands. If a terrorist is determined to kill passengers on a plane, nearly any object will do, from sharp plastic forks to canes, hands, or feet. The Colorado Supreme Court ruled that a foot can be a deadly weapon, pointing out that "body parts can be deadly weapons depending upon the manner in which they are used."[68] Obviously, by definition, deadly weapons will always be available on airplanes to those who wish to use them.

There are a few cases in which patently useless "security" precautions have been eliminated. In August 2002, for example, the Transportation Security Administration finally eliminated the routine questioning of airline passengers to ask if they had kept a close eye on their luggage. James Loy, head of the organization, said that the questioning was stopped because it created a hassle and had never prevented a hijacking or bombing in the sixteen years it was mandatory.[69]

The Emergency Broadcast System, the system supposed to send out important information to Americans in the case of an emergency, has also been useless. It was not activated during the September 11 attacks, nor during the anthrax scares. If the terrorist attacks don't qualify as a national emergency warranting activation, it's not clear what would.

HATE CRIME LAWS

After child molesters, the most despised group might be racists and bigots. Legislation to deal with them blossomed in the mid-1990s. Initially, hate crime laws were enacted to deal with assaults that were deemed to be racially motivated. After a gay Wyoming man, Matthew Shepard, was killed in October of 1998, public outrage led to violence against homosexuals being included in hate crime laws. Since then, the list of hate crime qualifying criteria has expanded to include religion, creed, and gender.

The fatal flaw in hate crime law is, of course, that hate is not illegal. American citizens have the inalienable right to hold whatever views and beliefs they wish; if a person acts on those beliefs and violates the law, his *actions* are punishable. But his beliefs are not. In the rush to demonstrate to ourselves and the world how socially enlightened and progressive America is, this self-evident fact seems to have eluded policy makers across the political spectrum. The limits of free speech laws don't come into play until they are tested with words that the majority consider wrong or inappropriate; politically correct speech will always be safe. To mean anything, free speech must protect *all* speech—hateful and otherwise. We don't have to like it, but we must tolerate it. Unless, apparently, that speech is said during the commission of a crime against a minority.

As *Washington Post* columnist Richard Cohen writes,

> [Hate crime laws] set a higher value on the lives or safety of certain people than on others. . . . Did [a defendant] beat someone up because he dated his girlfriend, took his parking space or because he was black? Are the welts on the victim's face any different in either case?[70]

What if you hate someone because he's materialistic or because you don't like his aftershave or because he laughs too loud at his own jokes? Is that hatred any more acceptable than hatred on any other basis?

Proponents of hate crime laws often fail to realize that such legislation makes it harder, not easier, to prosecute perpetrators because an additional burden of proof must be met. Prosecutors must not only prove that the defendant committed the crime, but also that hate was a motivating factor.

In his book *Damned Lies and Statistics,* Joel Best points out that the data used to evaluate and identify hate crimes is riddled with problems, and there is not even good agreement on the nature of the crime:

> There are real disagreements about how to define and measure hate crimes. Not surprisingly, some activists favor broad, inclusive standards that will avoid false negatives; some feminists, for example, argue that rapes automatically should be considered hate crimes (on the grounds that all rape is motivated by gender prejudice).[71]

Furthermore, according to Best, hate crime statistics (which, after all, are used by activists to identify and characterize the problem) are poorly measured and "may be a better measure of local officials' politics than of the incidence of hate crimes."[72]

THE BOUNTY HUNTER THREAT

On August 31, 1997, five masked men in body armor burst into a home in Phoenix, Arizona, held three children at gunpoint, and killed two people. Christopher Foote, age twenty-three, and his girlfriend, Spring Wright, age nineteen, were shot to death in bed. When two of the suspects,

Michael Sanders and David Brackney, were arrested, the pair explained that they were bounty hunters pursuing a bail jumper. Foote had reached for a gun, they said, and the couple had been killed in self-defense. It had all been a legitimate, legal process gone tragically wrong.

The media picked up on the story and it made international news. The idea that overzealous bounty hunters could kill innocent people in a no-knock predawn raid was unconscionable. Bounty hunters were depicted as reckless, violent renegades, answerable to no one while violating private citizens' rights with impunity. The furor was further fueled when it was publicized that bounty hunters had some legal powers that even police don't have. The news media dug up other people who had been victimized by the bounty-hunting industry, who told their tales of abuse and indifference to catching the wrong person. Professional bounty hunters lamented the slayings and admitted that they knew the day would come that one of their peers would step over the line. Foote's sister handed out flyers and protested, demanding accountability for bounty hunters. One state representative introduced legislation that would clean up the licensing and regulation of the sleazy, loose-cannon business. The killings prompted a new Arizona law requiring bounty hunters to be licensed and to get permission from a home's occupants before entering.

Amid all the public, activist, and legislative outrage, one little detail went virtually unnoticed: The men weren't bounty hunters. Phoenix police determined a few weeks later that the whole thing was a robbery, and that Sanders had lied about who they were. No one had jumped bail, no one was wanted by the police. Some news media grudgingly and cursorily updated the story, but by that time the tale had too much inertia for reality to slow the story's speed. The news media, antigun activists, and politicians had too much invested in the fable of the killer bounty hunters to conscientiously correct the facts.

Perhaps the bail-jumper retrieval business needed regulatory overhaul anyway. There may have been legitimate reasons to introduce legislation regarding bounty hunting, but the deaths of Christopher Foote and Spring Wright aren't two of them. Not every news story is a call to arms demanding action, and the public needs to be wary of jumping to conclusions and of vote-getting political quick fixes using taxpayer dollars.

PUSHING THE TEN COMMANDMENTS

After a seventh-grade student wounded four classmates at Fort Gibson Middle School in Fort Gibson, Oklahoma, parents and students attending a school meeting applauded loudly when a question was read: "Why not put the Ten Commandments and prayer back in school?" (They were apparently unaware that the shooter, Seth Trickey, was religious and attended church regularly.)[73] Similar sentiments were expressed following the Columbine shootings, and in 1999 Rep. Robert Alderholt of Alabama introduced legislation to do just that. As of February 2000, Ten Commandments legislation was proposed in ten states, including Colorado, Georgia, Florida, South Dakota, Oklahoma, and Kentucky. (Ironically, these attempts to introduce Christianity in schools to stop the killings came around the same time that Pope John Paul II acknowledged and apologized for mass murders and torture committed in the name of God by followers of the Roman Catholic Church.)

Aside from its obvious and grave conflict with the separation of church and state, the question fails on its own irrelevance and logic: There is no necessary link between the posting of biblical text and a lack of school shootings, or of religiosity and good behavior. In fact, statistics show quite the opposite. The United States, the most religious of industrialized nations, has the highest homicide rate in the world. In Japan, a country with very few Christians, violent crime is very rare.

The Bible Belt, ostensibly the most religious area of the United States, leads the nation in divorces (divorce rates in Tennessee, Alabama, Arkansas, and Oklahoma are roughly 50 percent higher than the national average) and hold among the highest domestic violence and murder rates in the country. Louisiana has the highest churchgoing rate in America—and also a murder rate twice the national average. God-fearing, Bible-toting Texas leads the nation in state executions, and ranks fourth in the nation for numbers of abortions.[74]

Natalie Angier, writing in the *New York Times Magazine*, notes:

> [T]he canard that godliness and goodliness are linked in any way but typographically must be taken on faith, for no evidence supports it. In one classic study, sociologists at the University of Washington compared students who were part of the "Jesus People" movement with a comparable group of professed atheists and found that atheists were no more likely to cheat on tests than were Christians and no less likely to volunteer at a hospital for the mentally disabled. Recent data compiled on the religious views among federal prisoners show that nonbelievers account for less than one percent of the total, significantly lower than for America as a whole. Admittedly, some of those true-believing inmates may have converted post-incarceration, but the data that exist in no way support the notion that atheism promotes criminal behavior.[75]

Putting a plaque of the Ten Commandments on school walls is just the sort of meaningless, knee-jerk, simplistic reaction that merely pretends to address problems. Incidentally, there are several different versions of the Ten Commandments, not just one. "For example, because

Catholics de-emphasize the prohibition on graven images, they number seven of the ten commandments differently from other faith communities," says Tom Flynn, editor of *Free Inquiry* magazine. "If you're accused of violating the sixth commandment, you have to know whether your accuser is Catholic to know if you're accused of adultery or murder."[76] The version in Representative Alderholt's bill was the Protestant version; the versions familiar to America's Roman Catholics, Lutherans, and Jews were ignored in favor of the one based on the King James Bible.

Barry Lynn, executive director of Americans United for Separation of Church and State, has noted that state legislators have used the spate of school shootings to push moments of silence, posting of the Ten Commandments, and other religious policies into public schools. "If these legislators can't find any better solution than moments of silence, they ought to find a new line of work," Lynn says. "This is not a very serious endeavor for solving real problems."[77]

Pat Robertson and other religious fundamentalists trying to get religion in school cite statistics, but their lack of logic is both blatant and troubling. For example, Nita Weis, in her book *Raising Achievers*, notes that since 1962, when the Supreme Court abolished school prayer, "violent crime has increased from 16.1 per 10,000 people to 75.8, and the illegitimacy rate has soared from 5.3 percent to 28 percent."[78] Aside from her suspect statistics, the obvious inference, that a lack of school prayer led to an increase in crime, is dead wrong and deeply flawed. Weis commits the logical fallacy of *post hoc ergo propter hoc* ("after this, therefore because of this"): Just because one thing (a rise in crime) happens after another (abolition of prayer) doesn't imply that one *caused* the other. "If you accept the fallacy once, you must accept it everywhere," notes Tom Flynn. "I can make a great argument that society has deteriorated sharply since the middle 1950s, when 'In God We Trust' was made the national motto and 'Under God' was added to the Pledge of Allegiance. What we need is some of that old-time secularism."[79]

WARTIME MYTHMAKING

Governments have their own reasons to engage in mythmaking and manipulation, usually as a campaign to rally public support for military or political action. This can be seen in the ways that governments demonize their political adversaries, often drawing upon the ultimate mythological personification of evil: Iran's Ayatollah Ruhollah Khomeini famously referred to the United States as the "Great Satan"; Ronald Reagan proclaimed the Soviet Union to be an "evil empire"; and George W. Bush began the year 2002 by naming Iraq, North Korea, and Iran as the "axis of evil." As Alice Chasan, editor of the *World Press Review*, noted, "An alarming amount of the domestic and international political debate shifted from substantive matters to quarreling over which regime if any deserves to be dubbed the principality of darkness."[80]

Usually these demonization campaigns highlight alleged mental deficiencies in foreign leaders. The favored angle to emphasize is that they are insane. North Korean leader Kim Jong Il had been vilified by the American government and press for decades, portrayed as an insane and dangerous leader who was rumored to bathe in the blood of virgins to stay young.[81] In an abrupt turnaround fueled by concerns over nuclear proliferation, North Korea was suddenly treated respectfully by the Clinton administration, which, for the first time in history, sent an American official, Secretary of State Madeleine Albright, to meet the leader in November 2000. A scant year later, the U.S. government again turned on the demonization machine, and George W. Bush declared North Korea an "evil" nation.

Ugandan dictator Idi Amin was said to be a cannibal. Iraq's Saddam Hussein was the target of many demonization attacks. Most of the time those in charge painted Hussein as a paranoid, insane psychopath. An op-ed piece in the September 3, 2000, *Albuquerque Journal* was titled, "Iraq's Saddam Still a Crazy Threat." Despite the title, the author, Jim Hoagland, seems to suggest quite the opposite, that Hussein is not crazy but rather quite crafty and clever.

Newsweek's Meg Greenfield pointed out that many of the derogatory terms used to define Hussein were not correct at all:

> Have you noticed how many of us have been saying how blood-chilling it is that all that unspeakable biological germ warfare material is in the hands of Saddam Hussein, who is "crazy" and/or a "nut"? He's not crazy. He's no nut. It's far more scary and dangerous than that. He is sane. He is evil. . . . We have a penchant in this country, when confronted by a genuine villain, especially one in a foreign government, to dehumanize him.[82]

The problem is not, of course, that such foreign leaders are necessarily innocent and wrongly accused. The problem is that this sort of demonization leads to simplistic us-versus-them, good-versus-bad thinking, and the world is much more complex than such an analogy allows. The notion that the United States is always right (and that anyone who disagrees with its foreign policy is ill-informed or insane) is a mentality more suited to a childhood playground than thoughtful world leaders.

This sort of stark polarity in rhetoric can also be seen in the language of contemporary neo-Nazis. Linguist Bernhard Poersken, who has studied neo-Nazi writings, has found that "[t]he neo-Nazi vocabulary is laden with simplistic concepts used to define 'the enemy'—a vocabulary that allows them to cast themselves as victims and legitimate their acts of violence as resistance."[83] His study showed how the neo-Nazi writings used metaphors that emphasized "the enemy's" aggressive character.

In *Time* magazine, Paul Gray commented that

> [t]he demonizing of Saddam has escalated along with the war and seems omnipresent in the West. . . . Long-distance psychoanalyzing of Saddam has been going on for some time, particularly in the U.S. and Israel, with not very helpful results. . . . The trouble with such statements, even if they could be proved accurate, is that they explain far too little. . . . The frequent allusions in the West to Saddam's "paranoia" thus make his behavior seem more complicated than it really is. He does not have to fantasize about enemies; he has inherited and made enough to last several lifetimes.[84]

Horrific stories circulated that when Hussein attacked Kuwait, Iraqi soldiers tore newborns from their incubators, leaving the helpless infants to die. This account was bolstered several months later by a teenage Kuwaiti girl, Nayirah, who tearfully recounted that and many other atrocities. She said that she had personally seen fifteen Kuwaiti babies dumped to their deaths.

In the wake of such emotional testimony, "Congressmen were moved to tears. Bush was moved to double the American troop presence in the Gulf. . . . Amnesty International picked up the story in its eighty-eight page report on human rights abuses in Kuwait, and the president cited the report repeatedly as rhetoric heated up and his deadlines came due." After the demonization of the Iraqis served its purpose, much of it was found to have been based on lies. The events never happened; no babies were cruelly torn from respirators. The teen Kuwaiti girl was not a refugee but the daughter of the ambassador to the United States who hadn't even been in Kuwait.[85]

Such emotional manipulation likely guided foreign policy. As John Stauber and Sheldon Rampton write in their 1995 book on public relations and the media, *Toxic Sludge Is Good for You*:

> If Nayirah's outrageous lie had been exposed at the time it was told, it might have at least caused some in Congress and the news media to soberly reevaluate the extent to which they were being skillfully manipulated to support military action. Public opinion was deeply divided on Bush's Gulf policy. As late as December 1990, a *New York Times*/CBS News poll indicated that 48 percent of the American people wanted Bush to wait before taking any action if Iraq failed to withdraw from Kuwait

> by Bush's January 15 deadline. On January 12, the US Senate voted by a narrow, five-vote margin to support the Bush administration in a declaration of war. Given the narrowness of the vote, the babies-thrown-from-incubators story may have turned the tide in Bush's favor.[86]

The myth of the incubator babies was not just a wartime rumor; it had been purposely spread by governments with the help of the lobbying and public relations company Rendon Group. Rendon had been paid to help circulate the rumor and mislead Americans. In 2002, when the Pentagon briefly discussed opening an Office of Strategic Information (to pursue more or less the same purpose following the September 11, 2001, attacks), the Rendon Group was once again hired to disseminate false information for the United States in propaganda campaigns.[87] Saddam Hussein is guilty of enough crimes that the American propaganda machine surely doesn't need to fabricate new ones.

Of course, at times the U.S. government's political opportunism comes back to haunt us. Corrupt foreign political leaders who serve American interests are embraced until the situation changes and they are turned from assets to liabilities. This was seen prominently in the case of Panamanian dictator Manuel Noriega, who was on the CIA's payroll for years despite clear and rampant involvement in drug trafficking and murder.

Another more recent example is the government of Peru, which plays an important role in the U.S. efforts to curb the drug trade. Writer Bruce Shapiro, in an article for Salon.com, notes:

> In 1998 [U.S. drug czar Barry] McCaffrey warmly praised Peru's shadowy secret police chief Vladimir Montesinos, only to back away from Montesinos after human rights advocates pointed out his role in the imprisonment of at least 1,500 innocent individuals under draconian anti-terrorism laws. But last year the McCaffrey-Montesinos relationship was rehabilitated, with the drug czar praising Montesinos during a visit to Lima.[88]

A year later, McCaffrey's friend Montesinos became Peru's most wanted fugitive, spawning an international manhunt that resulted in more than fifty charges including arms trading and human rights abuses—as well as drug trafficking.

These incidents should not surprise anyone; at times U.S. intelligence agencies must deal with unsavory characters, both foreign and domestic. But it does highlight the capriciousness of U.S. foreign policy and how quickly a leader can be transformed from a hero to a villain, depending on how useful he is to the U.S. government. The American public shouldn't be swayed much by our government's characterization of foreign leaders, realizing that the rhetoric can change instantly depending on what myths our government wants us to believe at the time. The effort to manipulate the public's perception of—and support for—foreign leaders is pervasive and constant.

A journalism think tank, the Project for Excellence in Journalism, studied news coverage following the September 11 attacks. It examined nearly twenty-five hundred television, newspaper, and magazine stories between mid-September and mid-December 2001. According to Associated Press writer Jennifer Loven:

> The study also concluded that coverage has heavily favored U.S. positions. About half of the relevant stories contained only viewpoints in line with American or Bush policy administration policy. Television news was measurably less likely than print stories to include criticism of the administration, the study found.[89]

Whose Anthrax?

The American public and government's reaction to the 2001–2002 anthrax scare is an instructive illustration of demonization and manipulation. On October 23, 2001, during a congressional briefing, Bush commented on the evil character of anyone who would develop or use anthrax: "It's hard for Americans to imagine how evil the people are who are doing this. We're having to adjust our thinking. We're a kind nation, we're a compassionate nation, we're a nation of strong values and we value life." In a radio address to the nation on November 3, 2001, Bush reiterated that "anyone who would try to infect other people with anthrax is guilty of an act of terror."

Just a month later the Bush administration was forced to admit that U.S. government scientists had been developing and weaponizing anthrax for years, despite signing an international treaty banning the development of biological weapons. Published reports in the *Washington Post*, the *New York Times*, and the *Baltimore Sun* confirmed that officials at Utah's Dugway Proving Ground had in recent years produced dry anthrax powder—the same strain, in fact, that was used to terrorize the United States. The Pentagon had secretly been devising ways of carrying out biological warfare and making even more damaging strains.[90] The Bush administration not only continued but expanded the germ warfare program. The *New York Times* reported that in early 2001, "the Pentagon drew up plans to engineer a potentially more potent variant of the bacterium that causes anthrax, a deadly disease ideal for germ warfare."[91]

So which is it? If Bush is correct that "anyone who would try to infect other people with anthrax is guilty of an act of terror," then that, by definition, makes the U.S. government guilty of engaging in terrorism.

Yet this news was released to a largely indifferent public. There was little public outcry, perhaps out of fear of seeming unpatriotic during the first few months after September 11. The Bush administration took the moral high ground regarding anthrax development until it had to admit doing the same thing. Suddenly the public moral outrage was stifled and the war on terrorism stepped up. The anthrax scare almost certainly prompted the government's admission. If massive investigations hadn't forced the disclosure, President Bush and the U.S. government would have kept up the hypocritical rhetoric vilifying and criticizing those who would develop anthrax, while funding the same activity.

In fact, not only had the American government been weaponizing anthrax, but it had been providing biological cultures to Iraq. As *Buffalo News* reporter Douglas Turner pointed out, "American research companies, with the approval of two previous presidential administrations, provided Iraq biological cultures that could be used for biological weapons, according to testimony to a U.S. Senate committee eight years ago."[92] Senate testimony showed that at least seventy-two shipments went from the United States to Iraq, many containing germs and "a nerve gas rated a million times more lethal than sarin." The shipments were made during the Reagan and Bush administrations. If Saddam Hussein did indeed have biological weapons at the time, as George W. Bush insisted, it is likely that they were developed from germ weapons the United States (and other countries) gave to the Iraqi government.

While Bush was accusing Saddam Hussein of helping to finance the Al-Qaeda terrorist network, the Bush administration had knowingly done the same thing—even after the September 11 attacks. In March 2002 the White House was involved in arranging a ransom payment to the radical Islamic group Abu Sayyaf in the Phillippines.[93]

ABC News reported that the U.S. government helped pay $300,000 in cash to the group, known to U.S. intelligence agencies as part of Osama bin Laden's Al-Qaeda network. The ransom was arranged to secure the release of two American missionaries taken hostage at a resort on May 27, 2001. The money was paid but the hostages were not released; one was later killed. Not only was the White House willing to fund bin Laden's group and negotiate with terrorists, the administration even changed its policy on ransom to accommodate the payments. In February 2002 the policy changed from stating that the U.S. government "will not pay ransom" to a more flexible policy allowing payments.[94]

NOTES

1. Adam J. Lieberman and Simona Kwon, *Facts Versus Fears: A Review of the Greatest Unfounded Health Scares of Recent Times* (New York: American Council on Science and Health, 1998), p. 43.

2. Ibid.

3. "Seton Hall Fined $12,600 For Fire," Associated Press [online], wire.ap.org [August 30, 2000]; Amy Westfeldt, "NJ Gov Considers Dorm Sprinkler Law," Associated Press [online], wire.ap.org [January 21, 2000].

4. David Shenk, *Data Smog* (New York: HarperCollins, 1997), p. 137.

5. "Senator Says Sex on Internet Is Reason for Bill to Protect Kids," Bloomberg News Service [online], quote.bloomberg.com/newsarchive [July 15, 1998]; John R. Quain, "The Fraud Squad," *Entertainment Weekly*, August 14, 1998.

6. "Calderon Legislation to Ban Crush Videos and Snuff Films Will Be Heard in Public Safety Committee on March 14," Assembly Member Thomas Calderon, press release, March 13, 2000.

7. "Australia to Crack Down on Internet Porn," Reuters [online], www.ee.survey.ac.uk/Contrib/Edupage/1999/03/21-03-1999.html#6 [March 23, 1999].

8. See, for example, Scott Stine, "The Snuff Film: The Making of an Urban Legend," *Skeptical Inquirer* (May/June 1999): 29–33; David Kerekes and David Slater, *Killing for Culture* (London: Creation Books, 1995); and Nadine Strossen, *Defending Pornography* (New York: Scribner, 1995). In 1999 two German men were convicted of murder during the course of what they claimed was the making of a snuff film. Yet no one was killed on-screen or at the time of filming, and it was never proven that a snuff film was intended or produced.

9. Kenneth Auchincloss, "The Year of the Tear," *Newsweek*, December 29, 1998/January 5, 1999, p. 40.

10. Dale Russakoff, "The Power of Grief," *Washington Post*, June 22, 1998.

11. Cynthia Crossen, *Tainted Truth: The Manipulation of Fact in America* (New York: Simon & Schuster, 1994), p. 135.

12. Gavin De Becker, *Protecting the Gift* (New York: Dial Press, 1999), p. 48.

13. Tadd Wilson, "Suffer the Missing Children?" *Reason* (November 1995): 47.

14. Barry Glassner, *The Culture of Fear* (New York: Basic Books, 1999), p. 61.

15. De Becker, *Protecting the Gift*, p. 47.

16. Barbara Whitaker, "Abducted California Boy Is Found Safe; Mother Is Being Held," *New York Times*, August 30, 2002.

17. "Texas Baby Reunited with Parents," CNN [online], www.cnn.com/2002/US/08/14/texas.infant.abduction [August 15, 2002].

18. Christina Almeida, "Rash of Kidnappings Is Making Parents Fearful," *Salt Lake Tribune* [online], www.sltrib.com/2002/aug/08102002/nation_W/760584.htm [August 10, 2002].

19. Antigone Barton, "Police: Victim Admits Kidnapping a Hoax," *Palm Beach Post*, September 11, 2002, p. 48. Readers may notice that in nearly all cases of hoax and false claims of child abductions given as examples in this book, the perpetrator is a woman. This is not selective reporting or gender bias on my part; the fact is that women are far more likely than men to perpetrate these acts.

20. Charlie Goodyear and Matthew B. Stannard, "Missing 6 Months, Girls Safe," *San Francisco Chronicle*, November 5, 2002, p. A-1.

21. Charnicia E. Huggins, "US Child Abuse Deaths Sharply Underestimated," Reuters [online], members.aol.com/smartnews/Sample-Issue-46.htm [August 5, 2002].

22. Brenda C. Coleman, "Child-Abuse Deaths Underreported," *Milwaukee Journal Sentinel* [online], www.jsonline.com/alive/news/aug99/childabuse deaths080399.asp [August 4, 1999].

23. "Study: Newscasts Create 'Climate of Fear' for Children But Don't Cover Issues Like Education," *Jefferson City (Mo.) News Tribune* [online], newstribune.com/stories/102301/ent_1023010923.asp [October 23, 2001].

24. Mark Memmott, "Sex Trade May Lure 325,000 U.S. Kids," *USA Today* [online], www.usatoday.com/news/nation/2001/09/10/sex-trade.htm [September 9, 2001].

25. "Shock Over US Child Sex Trade," BBC News [online], news.bbc.co.uk/1/hi/world/americas/1535199.stm [September 10, 2001].

26. David Finkelhor, personal communication with the author, February 7, 2002.

27. Ibid.

28. Eva Klain, personal communication with the author, February 26, 2002.

29. Interview transcript from *NewsHour with Jim Lehrer*, April 29, 1998.

30. Anita Wadwhani, "Police Probe Girl's Reappearance," Associated Press [online], wire.ap.org [August 16, 2000].

31. Alex Lyda, "Is Sex-Offender Registry Accurate?" Associated Press [online], wire.ap.org [November 4, 1999].

32. "Call for UK Newspaper to Be Prosecuted Over Paedophile Campaign," CNN [online], edition.cnn.com/2000/WORLD/europe/08/09/britain.protest/ [August 10, 2000].

33. Randolph E. Schmid, "Family Members Are Common Kidnappers," Associated Press [online], www.ipce.info/ipceweb/Library/ooang16c_other_statistics.htm [July 24, 2000].

34. John McAlpin, "N.J. to Consider New Pedophile Law," Associated Press [online], www.stopsexoffenders.com/registrynews/archives/2000/registrynews 1.shtml [September 24, 2000].

35. "Homeless Sex Offenders Returned to Prison," Associated Press [online], www.geocities.com/eadvocate/issues/issues-prison.html [October 10, 2000].

36. Ray Carbone, "Flaws Unfold in Megan's Law," *Foster's Sunday Citizen*, May 7, 2000.

37. Ibid.

38. Laura Ahearn, personal correspondence with author, May 27, 2003.

39. Amitai Etzioni, *The Limits of Privacy* (New York: Basic Books, 1999), p. 68.

40. "Samantha's Mom: 'Little Room for Anger,'" CNN [online], www.cnn.com/2002/US/07/26/lkl.erin.runnion/ [July 26, 2002].

41. Mike Allen, "Connecticut Killing Shows Limits of 'Megan's Law,'" *New York Times*, August 28, 1998.

42. McAlpin, "N.J. to Consider New Pedophile Law."

43. Matt Bai, "A Report from the Front in the War on Predators," *Newsweek*, May 19, 1997.

44. Steve Irsay, "Cold War Technology Helped Save Lives of Abducted Teens," CNN [online], edition.cnn.com/2002/LAW/08/05/ctv.alert/ [August 5, 2002].

45. Henry K. Lee, "Amber Alert Runs into Snags in Bay Area," *San Francisco Chronicle*, August 31, 2002, p. A-1.

46. Cynthia Gorney, "The Perils of a Posse on Wheels," *Buffalo News*, October 6, 2002.

47. Laura Barnhardt, "Woman Is Charged with Filing False Report about Abduction," *Baltimore Sun* [online], www.sunspot.net/news/local/crime/bal-md.abduct24apr24,0,2339917.story?coll=bal-local-headlines [April 24, 2003].

48. "House Moves to Protect Kids on Web," ABC News [online], abcnews.go.com/wire/SciTech/ap20020522_456.html [May 22, 2002.].

49. "Police: 2 Sides to Slain 6th Grader," ABC News [online], abcnews.go.com/wire/US/ap20020521_684.html [May 21, 2002].

50. Ibid.

51. "House OKs Bill Targeting Molesters," Associated Press [online], story.news.yahoo.com/news?tmpl=story&cid=536&ncid=703&e=5&u=/ap/20020521/ap_on_go_co/internet_children_2 [May 21, 2002].

52. "Aunt: Slain Teen Knew of Web Danger," Associated Press [online], www.haltabuse.org/about/news/020527.shtml [May 22, 2002].

53. David McGuire, "Economics of Kid-Friendly Domain Questioned," *Washington Post* [online], www.washingtonpost.com/wp-dyn/articles/A44122-2002Dec12.html [December 12, 2002].

54. Samuel Maull, "Man Convicted in Subway Assault," Associated Press [online], wire.ap.org [October 21, 2000].

55. Bryan Robinson, "Coming to a 'Forgotten' Child's Rescue," ABC News [online], abcnews.go.com/sections/us/DailyNews/comics_missingkids/020930.html [September 30, 2002].

56. Michael J. Weiss, "Without a Trace," *Ladies Home Journal*, October 2001, p. 188.

57. "Mom Guilty in Death of Her Infant," *Beloit (Wisc.) Daily News* [online], www.beloitdailynews.com/600/baby22.htm [June 22, 2000].

58. Matt Gryta, "Teen Gets 1-Year Term for Newborn's Freezing Death," *Buffalo News*, March 21, 2002.

59. Donna Leinwand, "When Kids Share Drugs with Their Parents," *USA Today*, August 23, 2000, p. A-01.

60. Ephrat Livni, "Survey Finds Some Parents Introduce Teenagers to Drugs," ABC News [online], abcnews.go.com/sections/living/DailyNews/drug_survey000823.html [August 24, 2000].

61. Lauran Neergaard, "Survey: Parents Okay with Teen Drug Use," Associated Press [online], www.positiveatheism.org/rw/teendrug.htm [September 9, 1996].

62. Adam Marcus, "Drug Use a Family Affair," HealthSCOUT [online], i-medreview.subportal.com/health/Drugs_Alcohol_Tobacco/Drugs_and_Kids/101667.html [August 24, 2000].

63. Michele Focht, "Precious Cargo: Child Endangerment," *Driven* [online], www.madd.org/news/0,1056,1249,00.html [fall 2000].

64. Despite e-mail warnings, urban legends, and Ann Landers columns to the contrary, there have been only two confirmed cases of children being killed by

poisoned Halloween candy, and in both cases the children were killed not in random acts by strangers but intentionally by one of their parents. The best-known case was that of Texan Ronald Clark O'Bryan, who killed his son by lacing his Pixie Stix with cyanide in 1974. See, for example, Joel Best's article "The Myth of the Halloween Sadist," *Psychology Today* (November 1985): 14–16.

65. Josh Gerstein, "Flaws in the Shield," ABC News [online], abcnews.go.com/sections/politics/WhitehouseWag/WTC_wag010927.html [September 27, 2001].

66. Josh Gerstein, "Rhetoric Check: Putting the Talk to the Test," ABC News [online], abcnews.go.com/sections/politics/WhitehouseWag/wag011011.html [October 11, 2001].

67. "Hollings: Keep Quiet on Bag Check Delays," CNN [online], www.cnn.com/2001/TRAVEL/NEWS/11/29/airlines.security/index.html [November 29, 2001].

68. Steven K. Paulson, "Foot Can Be Weapon, Court Says," *Newsday* [online], www.newsday.com/news/nationworld/wire/sns-ap-court-weapon0429apr29.story [April 29, 2002].

69. Leslie Miller, "Airlines Stop Baggage Questions," First Coast News [online], www.firstcoastnews.com/news/2002-08-29/usw_baggage.asp [August 29, 2002].

70. Richard Cohen, "The Trouble with Hate-Crime Laws," *Issues & Views*, (summer/fall 1999).

71. Joel Best, *Damned Lies and Statistics* (Berkeley: University of California Press, 2001), p. 68.

72. Ibid.

73. Renee Ruble, "School Shooting Baffles Okla. Town," Associated Press [online], www.greatdreams.com/gibson.htm [December 8, 1999].

74. On Bible Belt divorces, see David Crary, "Bible Belt Leads U.S. in Divorces," Associated Press [online], wire.ap.org [November 11, 1999]. On murder rates, see "Southern and Western States Log Highest Rates of Intimate Partner Homicide," Centers for Disease Control [online], www.cdc.gov/od/oc/media/pressrel/r011011.htm [October 11, 1002]; Steve Chapman, "Praise the Lord, Pass the Ammo," Slate [online], Slate.msn.com/id/31364 [July 1, 1999].

75. Natalie Angier, "Confessions of a Lonely Atheist," *New York Times Magazine*, January 14, 2001, p. 34.

76. Tom Flynn, personal correspondence with author, February 16, 2001.

77. Anjetta McQueen, "Students Encounter Prayer Policies," Associated Press [online], wire.ap.org [February 5, 2000].

78. Nita Weis, *Raising Achievers: A Parent's Plan for Motivating Children to Excel* (Nashville, Tenn.: Broadman & Holman, 1995).

79. Tom Flynn, personal correspondence with author, February 18, 2001.

80. Alice Chasan, "Deliver Us from Evil," *World Press Review* (April 2002): 3.

81. Massimo Calabresi, "Stranger in a Very Strange Land," *Time*, November 6, 2000, p. 6.

82. Meg Greenfield, "The Apple Looked Good," *Newsweek*, December 1, 1997, p. 98.

83. Matthias Arning, in *Frankfurter Rundschau*, quoted in *World Press Review* (November 2000): 47.

84. Paul Gray, "The Man Behind a Demonic Image," *Time*, February 11, 1991.

85. Bob Tamarkin, *Rumor Has It: A Curio of Lies, Hoaxes, and Hearsay* (New York: Prentice Hall, 1993), p. 144.

86. John Stauber and Sheldon Rampton, *Toxic Sludge Is Good for You* (Monroe, Maine: Common Courage Press, 1995), pp. 170–75.

87. James Dao and Eric Schmitt, "Pentagon Readies Efforts to Sway Sentiment Abroad," *New York Times* [online], www.nytimes.com/2002/02/19/international/19PENT.html [February 19, 2002].

88. Bruce Shapiro, "Guilty Until Proven Useful," Salon [online], archive.salon.com/news/feature/2000/09/15/berenson/ [September 15, 2000].

89. Jennifer Loven, "Study: Fewer Facts in Media Coverage," Associated Press [online], home.earthlink.net/~mjohnsen/Post_911/few_facts_study.html [January 28, 2002].

90. "Report: U.S. Army Weaponized Ames Anthrax; FBI to Mail Bids for Help," ABC News [online], abcnews.go.com [December 13, 2001].

91. Judith Miller, Stephen Engelberg, and William J. Broad, "U.S. Germ Warfare Research Pushes Treaty Limits," *New York Times*, September 4, 2001.

92. Douglas Turner, "U.S. Sent Iraq Germs in Mid-80s," *Buffalo News* [online], www.buffalonews.com/editorial/200209023/1048504.asp [September 23, 2002].

93. John McWethy, "Ransom Arranged to Rebel Group," ABC News [online], abcnews.go.com/sections/wnt/DailyNews/Philippines_ransomD20411.html [April 11, 2002].

94. Marc Lerner, "Rebels Funnel Ransom Money to Al Qaeda," *Washington Times*, April 4, 2002.

Part 4

THE WAGES OF FEAR

the consequences of a public blinded by myths

10

LOSING TRUST AND RESOURCES

If the consequences of misplaced trust weren't so dire, the constant barrage of manipulation wouldn't be so damaging. When we are misled about where problems and solutions lie, enormous amounts of time, energy, and money can be misdirected or wasted. For example, in the 1990s, many feminists and the media claimed that women's health was being shortchanged in preference for men's health issues. Groups such as the National Women's Health Network claimed that medical research had mainly been done on men and for the benefit of men.

To be sure, there were areas in which the medical community was failing women (and men, for that matter). But the cause went beyond an awareness campaign for women's health care. Congress, under pressure from women's groups, passed legislation requiring all federally funded clinical studies to include enough women and minorities to analyze the results by sex and race.

Yet the claims of gender bias in medical research have been largely discredited. There is no systematic bias against women's health concerns; men's and women's health issues get about equal research and funding. In fact, as *Reason* reporter Cathy Young found, breast cancer (which strikes many times more women than men) got much more funding than many health problems that strike men only:

> From 1966 to 1986, there were over 400 clinical trials on breast cancer and 121 on prostate cancer; and in 1990, the National Cancer Institute spent $81 million on breast cancer research and $13.2 million on prostate cancer, which causes nearly as many deaths.[1]

Whether through innocent misunderstanding or intentional deception, a problem was greatly exaggerated, and consequently time was lost, laws were passed, and resources were misdirected in trying to fix a problem that never really was.

On one level, society recognizes the dangers inherent in emotion and the value in deliberative thought. That's one reason vigilantism is anathema to our justice system, and why juries are encouraged to take as much time as they need to rationally review the evidence and render an impartial verdict. Evidence for mistakes made in the emotional rush to judge are too numerous to recount; here I will highlight a few cases.

THE BEARDSTOWN LADIES

In 1995 a group of elderly women from Beardstown, a small town in west-central Illinois, became famous. The kindly group of grandmothers made news not for prize-winning pie recipes or knitting sweaters but for playing—and beating— the stock market. Using "commonsense" advice, the geriatric group garnered a very impressive return of 23.4 percent over ten years. Their first book, *The Beardstown Ladies' Common-Sense Investment Guide: How We Beat the Stock Market—and How You Can, Too,*[2] sold more than eight hundred thousand copies. Based largely upon their dramatic rate of return, they wrote several more books, advising down-home investors on where to put their money. Several of the books touted the Ladies' impressive investment record on their covers.

America loved the story: sweet, silver-haired grandmothers showing up hard-nosed, uptight Wall Street investors with homespun wisdom on investing. The story sounded too good to be true, and in 1998 Shane Tritsch, managing editor of *Chicago* magazine, decided to do a little checking. Following an article by Tritsch, an audit by Price Waterhouse LLP found that, contrary to the Ladies' claims of a 23.4 percent annual return on the club's investment portfolio from 1984 through 1993, their actual return was 9.1 percent. That rate of return was, in fact, almost 40 percent behind the Standard & Poor's 500 index. In addition, the Ladies had outperformed the index in only three of the fourteen years audited. When confronted with the numbers, Betty Sinnock, the longtime treasurer, claimed that the problem was a computer input error. The rate apparently only applied to a two-year period for 1991 to 1992, not the ten-year period between 1984 and 1993.

Tritsch got hate mail and accusations of "granny bashing" for his efforts to uncover the truth. Had it been a large investment house that reported a return almost 15 percent higher than it actually had, a flurry of lawsuits would likely have immediately followed. When it's grannies giving the same advice, the public is much more forgiving.

It's not been reported how many people lost money following the

Beardstown Ladies' advice, but since more than a million of their books were sold, it's likely that considerable savings were lost. If even one person in a hundred who bought their book invested just $1,000, that's $10 million allocated according to their skewed advice, and millions lost. And while it's true that they may have encouraged investors to join the market at a good time, that same money could have been much, much more wisely invested. In a lawsuit against Hyperion Press, the book's publisher, some readers claimed that they were misled by a blurb on the book jacket, touting the 23.4 percent figure. Hyperion apparently made no attempt to correct the mistake after it had been revealed, and left the incorrect figure on the book's cover to sell more copies. This, according to the plaintiffs, amounted to false advertising and cost them dearly.[3]

The mere fact that the Ladies made a mistake is beside the point; innocent calculation errors occur all the time. The real question is why it took three years for the error to be caught. The most likely explanation is emotion. People wanted to believe that the grannies had outsmarted Wall Street, and that desire to believe, probably coupled with the ultimately thankless job of debunking a cherished myth, averted questions and skepticism.

No one claims that the Ladies were out to cheat anyone. But the fact remains that the very basis of their fame was derived from a claim that no one apparently checked out until three years later. The down-home wisdom the Ladies were famous for didn't extend to having someone double-check their claim of beating the market by a two-to-one margin. The writer who first brought the Ladies' claim to the public eye didn't question the numbers: "I'm not a business reporter," she said. "It was pitched as a human-interest story. It was the small-town, older-lady thing. So it never occurred to me to question the financial returns. It's so out of my league."[4]

RACIST CHURCH FIRES

In May 1996 a rash of twelve church fires was reported nationwide, five of which served mostly black congregations. The arsons were seen by many as being racially motivated, fueled in part by stories like the one that appeared in the September 2, 1996, issue of *Newsweek*: Below the headline, "We Live in Daily Fear" is the slug, "Greenville, Texas, thought it had outgrown its racist past. That was 41 fires ago." The article went on to describe two recent church arsons in the town of Greenville.

Curiously, the article notes that, in the case of both Greenville churches highlighted therein, "[P]olice recently charged a retarded 18-year-old black man with both church blazes."[5] If that's true (and the man did in fact do it), why did the reporters frame the story as racially motivated? This seemingly thesis-nullifying statement was brushed aside for a discussion on Greenville's racist past. The jump was already made, the news bias was already set: The fires were motivated by racism. Any facts suggesting otherwise were ignored or downplayed.

The following month President Clinton highlighted the problem in an address to the nation and announced that a national task force would be organized to investigate and combat the crimes. A year later the task force concluded that many of the 429 fires they examined were not racist but copycat crimes. They found no evidence of a racist conspiracy or even a clear pattern to the crimes. Many were committed by individuals acting alone, and, of those arrested, 42 percent were juveniles. Though some of the fires were traced to racist motives, other arsons were committed for profit, vandalism, or revenge. Of the 199 people arrested in incidents dating back to 1995, 160 were white, 34 were black, and 5 were Latino.

The Insurance Information Institute, a trade group that collects data regarding insurance companies, examined the rash of fires and concluded that: (1) most of the fires were set by serial arsonists; (2) the number of fires in white churches also increased in 1995; (3) in Florida, Georgia, Tennessee, Oklahoma, and Virginia, fires destroyed more white churches than black ones; and (4) in nine of fifteen black church fires, black suspects were named.[6]

Eric Daniel Harris, former pastor of a rural Baptist church, confessed that he set his own Kentucky church on fire. Harris, who had implied that he thought the fire was either a hate crime or an act of vandalism, said he burned his church to unite his flock. In Wichita Falls, Texas, a minister and three others were accused of burning down their own church to collect $270,000 in insurance in November of 1996.[7]

Perversely, Clinton's announcement actually led to more, not fewer, church arsons: Following the president's speech, the number of incidents nearly quadrupled. Forty-seven churches were targets of fires or bombs, nineteen of which were black churches. This increase was mainly attributed to copycat crimes: Treasury Secretary James E. Johnson reported that some of those arrested said "they saw it on the news, and this became the thing to do."[8]

An editorial in the June 11, 1997, *Albuquerque Journal* reflected on the rush to judge:

> It was far easier last year to jump to conclusions from the meager information and wealth of speculation. It was widely asserted that the fires were sparked by racism in America. . . . Victims of the May 1996 fires, however, were not exclusively black or even mostly black. Of the 12 churches torched in May 1996, five served predominantly black congregations. The destruction of houses of worship turns out to have been an equal opportunity crime cutting across racial, ethnic, and ecumenical lines.[9]

In many of these cases the problem was compounded by the news bias: The reporters went into the story with preset assumptions regarding what the story was about.

This bias isn't restricted to journalists, of course: We all do it. When we see a person simply arrested for a crime, our first instinct is usually to assume that the person is probably guilty of something, the presumption of innocence notwithstanding. We know that the person may, in fact, eventually be shown innocent, but more likely we assume that there's some valid evidence pointing to the person's guilt. There must be some reason, we say, that a police officer or judge believed that the person should be picked up and questioned. But because journalists have more power than the layman, it is more important that they be vigilant to their news bias.

The media have done a good job raising awareness of the dangers and injustice of prejudice. Most of us know that discrimination against people because of their gender, race, religion, and the like is wrong. We're warned of the dangers and immorality of rushing to judge others negatively based on emotion or prejudice. While the media does this, it does not at the same time encourage skepticism: The rush to judge cuts both ways, and there is also a danger of being too quick to judge something good or worthy of support, money, or legislation.

SPORTS ROLE MODELS

Aside from jingoism there is probably no other feeling that brings people together like sports fervor. It feeds on collective, raw emotions. At times that feeling carries over outside the baseball diamond, football gridiron, or basketball court. The adoration and emulation of sports heroes can encourage youth to strive for athletic greatness and pursue their dreams. But it can also lead to a reverence of people who may, by example, teach our kids things we may not want them to learn.

The Slugger's Steroids

Cardinals slugger Mark McGwire was featured in full-page ads for CaP CURE, an association that promotes research into a cure for prostate cancer. He is pictured hitting a baseball, under the words, "Help me set the most important home run record of all . . . the one that beats prostate cancer." McGwire's endorsement is apropos, since the baseball hero publicly announced that he had taken the steroid androstenedione. According to a study published in the *Journal of the American Medical Association*, the use of androstenedione has been associated with many health risks, including prostate dysfunction, stunted growth, and testicular dysfunction. The drug is banned in the Olympics and in professional football, tennis, and basketball. Sales of the drug soared after his announcement, and McGwire's use undoubtedly encouraged many youngsters to take steroids. After all, a kid may wonder, if the record-breaking baseball hero takes them, how bad can they be? Following the news that McGwire used another muscle-building drug, creatine, a survey of more than one thousand students found kids were using the substance as early as sixth grade.[10]

Hopefully some of the money McGwire helped raise will go to treat the youngsters who will eventually have health problems due to the steroid abuse his use of androstenedione encouraged. Amid the hero-worship and nightly news updates on McGwire's latest home run and how much his home-run balls were selling for, little criticism was heard about his de facto endorsement of the drugs. In 1998 shot-putter Randy Barnes was disgraced when he made headlines for a positive steroid test; the following year McGwire—also discovered to be using steroids—was touted as a hero. Just over a decade ago, Lyle Alzado, a former football player for the Oakland Raiders, traveled the country warning kids of the dangers of taking steroids. He died in 1989 at the age of thirty-eight from a heart attack allegedly brought about from steroid abuse.

Women's World Cup Soccer

McGwire's accomplishments were soon overshadowed by perhaps the biggest sports story of 1999: The United States's victory over China at the third Women's World Cup soccer game. After 120 scoreless minutes of regulation and overtime, the win came down to penalty kicks. China converted four of its five penalty kicks, and the United States scored on all five of their attempts.

When the U.S. team defeated China, the country erupted with resounding congratulations. The victory made international news, and Brandi Chastain, Michele Akers, Mia Hamm, and the rest of the team were touted as heroes and made the media rounds. Women's sports had its highest-profile success ever, and the media was abuzz for weeks discussing how far women's sports had come. In the months following, the soccer team became a merchandising franchise, spawning books, posters, calendars, and even their own breakfast cereal, Golden Goals.

Yet not everyone was applauding the victory: The Chinese team accused the United States of cheating. The reason the Chinese could not convert the one missed goal, the Chinese team claimed, is because U.S. goalkeeper Briana Scurry violated the rule against moving forward before the Chinese team kicked the ball. Instant replay bore out the truth of the complaints. At the time, the accusation was largely treated as sour grapes in most quarters. But a frame-by-frame replay clearly showed

Sports Illustrated named the U.S. Women's Soccer team its "Sportswomen of the Year."

Scurry illegally taking several steps forward before Liu Ying hit her penalty kick. In the end it was quietly and grudgingly acknowledged that, yes, the U.S. team had violated the rules.

Sports Illustrated justified Scurry's move thusly:

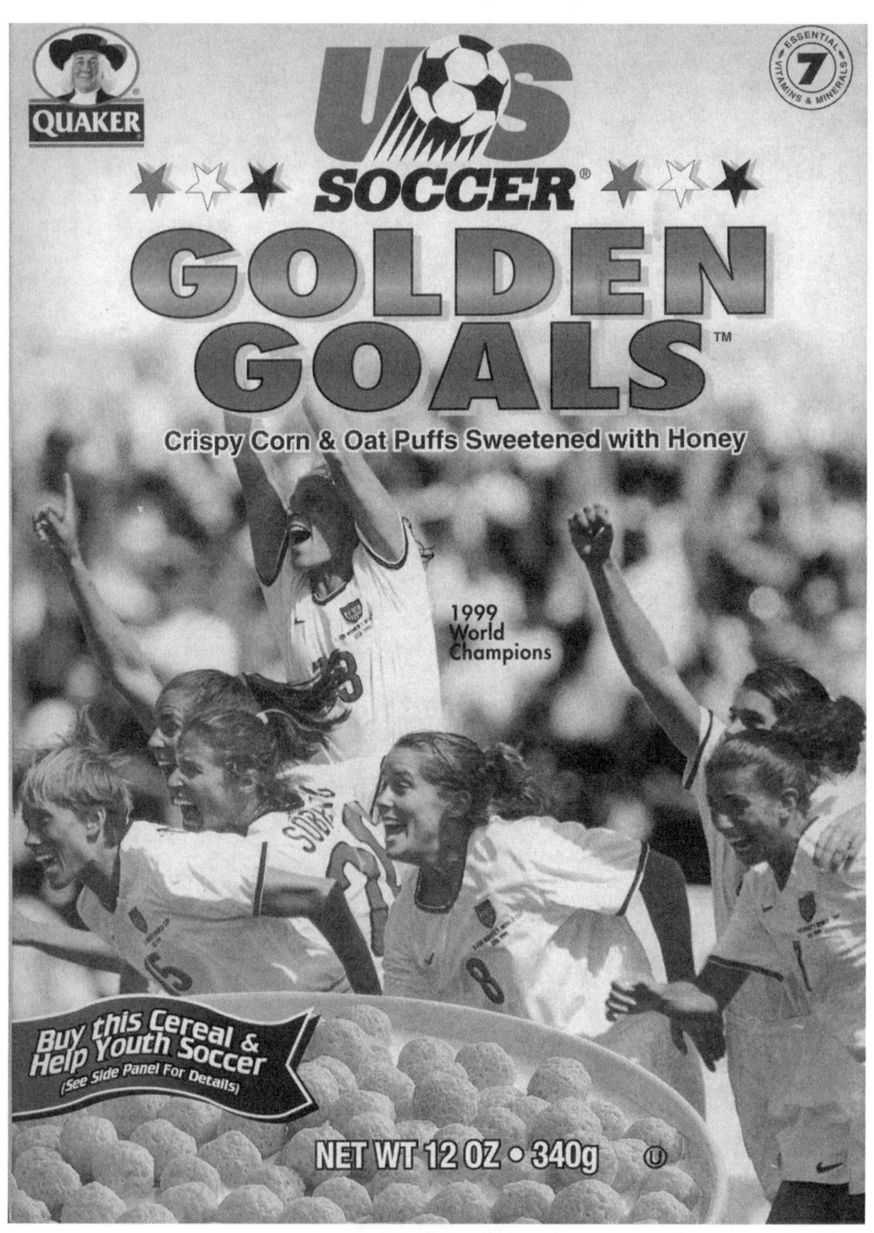

Golden Goals, the U.S. Women's Soccer team's breakfast cereal.

> Briana Scurry, the U.S. goalkeeper, stopped the third of China's bullets from 12 yards out by doing what every NBA forward does under the boards, stretching the rules as much as possible without getting caught.[11]

The magazine, instead of taking a stand on the slippery slope of validating sly cheaters, did just the opposite. *Sports Illustrated* devoted just two paragraphs of an eleven-page article to the question of whether or not the team deserved the victory. *Time* magazine, which featured the team on its July 19, 1999, cover, devoted seven pages to "The New Dream Team"—without a word about the disputed goal. And the magazine wasn't the only one ignoring the scandal: Not one of the readers' follow-up letters to *Time*, published August 9, mentioned it.

For their part, the team, Scurry, and the coach were unapologetic. When asked if what she did was illegal, Scurry replied with a mischievous grin, "a little bit." She even admitted that she had done it earlier in the game, on the shootout's first kick. Yet her story changed as the days wore on, and in later interviews she claimed she didn't remember if she moved forward or not. U.S. coach Tony DiCicco defended the cheating by saying, "You've got to get any edge you can."[12]

As *Sports Illustrated* continued:

> People want to know if Scurry cheated by taking a step or two forward before each of the Chinese penalty kicks. Clearly Scurry had violated the letter of the rule, which prohibits forward movements before the ball is kicked. In Akers's opinion, though, that does not constitute an ethical lapse. . . . "The keeper has to do everything she can to stop the ball. It's the referee's job to make sure she's doing it right. And if the shoe were on the other foot, if the Chinese had stopped one of our penalty kicks by moving forward, I guarantee you we would have said, 'Hey, she cheated.' Every last one of us."[13]

And perhaps that's the whole point: The Chinese goalie *didn't* cheat, *didn't* move forward. She played ethically and by the rules, and lost because of it. Deliberately breaking rules is wrong, because it gives the cheater an unfair advantage over her rule-following opponents. The team's message seemed to be: It's okay if you have to cheat to win the game, just don't get caught; if the referee doesn't see it, it didn't happen. Honorable behavior is thus not an issue for an internal moral compass but should be left to referees to decide. The mercenary "everybody does it" excuse is particularly unseemly given the role model status the team embraced. An action is either ethical or it isn't, regardless of whether the cheater gets caught.

Presumably the U.S. soccer team's ethical standards could be used to justify doping and steroid use in the Olympics. Using their logic, it would be acceptable for athletes to try to gain unfair advantage over their opponents by using banned muscle-building or endurance-enhancing substances. It would only be wrong if drug testing caught the athlete; otherwise it's perfectly acceptable to cheat if it helps to win a medal.

Despite the admission of cheating, the team was honored as the 1999 *Sports Illustrated*'s Sportswomen of the Year. It's one thing to celebrate the team's accomplishments, but quite another to single them out as examples of sportsmanship. The *American Heritage Dictionary* defines sportsmanship as "conduct and attitude considered as befitting participants in sports, especially fair play, courtesy, striving spirit, and grace in losing." Apparently the first attribute, fair play, isn't requisite for the honor of Sportswomen of the Year.

The reason the cheating charge was largely ignored is easy to see: America was drunk on the elation and emotions of victory, and no one wanted to delve too deeply into the controversy. No one wanted to rain on the parade of beautiful, talented, strong sportswomen in their finest moment.

The women's soccer team played hard and deserves credit for its efforts. But it is a fair question to ask whether it deserved to win. It must be remembered that the players sullied their own victory (with a little help from careless officials); they—and we—will never know what would have happened had they played fairly. I hope and expect that the result would have been the same, but either way, we could be sure that the victory was pure. It's sad that the victory, for all its hype, came at the price of Brianna Scurry's integrity. It's even sadder that most Americans (and female athletes) probably don't care about what we had to do to win the game.

That question aside, most soccer fans and players will be the first to admit that penalty kicks probably should not be permitted to decide a soccer match. It gives no real indication of who the better team is. To have won the match on a penalty kick is already something of a hollow victory; to win it by cheating on a penalty kick is even less of an accomplishment.

Italian soccer referee Pierluigi Collina, who officiated in the opening game of the Euro2000 games, said that players should be ashamed of trying to cheat each other. "It is a way of trying to gain advantage without using ability," he said. "The players are doing the same job, they should show more respect for their opponent."[14]

The U.S. soccer team's lax ethics may be symptomatic of a larger problem. A 1998 survey of high-level youth soccer players found that 84 percent would intentionally foul an opponent in some game situations. Purdue researchers Joan Duda and Marta Guivernau studied responses of 135 boys and 159 girls at a summer soccer camp. They were asked their reactions to certain game situations and how they would handle them. Journalist Ira Dreyfuss reported,

> In one instance, the players were asked if they would tackle the opposing team's best player from behind while the player was dribbling toward the goal and there was no other way to prevent the score. In the questionnaire, the players were told that this foul is wrong, and would probably hurt the opposing player. Eighty-four percent said they would do it anyway.[15]

The study also found that the coach's willingness to break rules had a very powerful influence on whether or not the players found such conduct acceptable. In Brianna Scurry's case, coach Tony DiCicco defended his player's cheating. In a climate of such widespread willingness to injure other players and cheat, the need for positive role models in ethics and sportsmanship is perhaps stronger than ever.

By way of comparison, see the example set by Jeffrey Glick, a student at Clarence High School near Buffalo, New York. The score was tied 15–15 in their final volleyball game against Williamsville North High School. The referee awarded a point to Glick's team, ruling that the opposing team had committed a foul. But Glick knew that the ball had in fact touched *his* wrist during play, and therefore his team didn't deserve the point. He told the referee, and the team lost the game on the replay. Glick, in effect, likely cost his team the match—and perhaps a spot in the postseason tournament. Glick's coach, Kevin Starr, tells all his players to make such "honor calls," informing referees when they mistakenly make rulings in the team's favor. Said Glick, "If I didn't say anything and we won, I would have known it happened on a bad call. Not saying anything just wouldn't have been the right thing to do."[16]

McGwire and the U.S. Women's Soccer team are fine athletes deserving of recognition. But they are not necessarily the role models they are held up to be.

MILKING THE PUBLIC'S MONEY AND TRUST

A few days before Christmas 1995, a young boy's tragic tale touched hearts across the country. In Salt Lake City, a twelve-year-old was found abandoned at a bus stop. He had few clothes but carried a letter from his stepmother saying that she could no longer care for the boy because his father had died of AIDS and his birth mother was dead. He told officials that he had never been to school and that his family had led a nomadic life, finding shelter where they could. The local media picked up the story, and it ran nationwide. As Christmas approached, donations poured in, with people offering money, gifts, and even their homes. Trust funds for the young boy were set up by the state and a local newspaper. But a few days later, the story began to unravel.

The "boy" turned out to be a twenty-five-year-old woman, Birdie Jo Hoaks, who lived as a boy and had pulled similar scams in a dozen other states. In April, while in South Dakota, Hoaks had claimed to be thirteen-year-old Nathan Devine, who had been abandoned by his mother. She received more than $700 in cash and benefits before anyone became suspicious. Previously she had received free medical care, money, and gifts from kindly citizens. In 1993 police spent two days trying to locate "his" parents before Hoaks's true identity was discovered. Hoaks eventually confessed and claimed that she was simply looking for a place to stay, though her record showed a long history of scams, fraud, and jail terms.[17]

In June 1999 a thirteen-year-old Honduran boy, Edwin Sabillon, "had New Yorkers reaching for their handkerchiefs with a heartbreaking tale of how Hurricane Mitch had killed his family and how he had trekked 3,200 miles to New York to be with a father he'd never met. He arrived alone Sunday at LaGuardia Airport, and a concerned taxi driver took him to police. After the story broke, hundreds of people offered gifts and clothes; some said they'd adopt Edwin if his father didn't appear."[18] Police spent two days looking for Edwin's father, while Mayor Rudolph Giuliani publicly urged him to come forward.

Yet once again emotions were used to abuse the public's trust. Two days later the boy admitted that his story was a hoax; he was in fact a runaway who had been living with an aunt in Florida. His father had in fact died, but not in Hurricane Mitch, and his mother was alive and well.

Margo Blunk, the wife of a former Tulsa, Oklahoma, police officer, made impassioned cries for help when her young daughter needed a bone marrow transplant because of leukemia. Nearly $50,000 was raised and collected by the Blunks before it was discovered that their daughter did not in fact have leukemia or need a marrow transplant. Margo Blunk pleaded guilty to a charge of fraudulently obtaining money, and promised to make restitution. She said some of the proceeds went to pay for the couple's surrogacy expenses, groceries, and utilities.[19]

A Philadelphia woman, Sonya Furlow, was key in what was perhaps the worst case of emotional manipulation in recent memory. Furlow ran a company called Tender Hearts Adoption Facilitation Services, promising to help match pregnant women with parents desperate for children. When one couple contracted with her, Furlow related dramatic stories about the different birth mothers the couple could choose from, including "Andrea," a high-school cheerleader, and "Roxanne," a young woman with a boyfriend. The couple chose Roxanne, and Furlow sent frequent e-mail updates with soap-opera details of Roxanne's life. When the baby was born, Furlow sent for the couple, who flew to Philadelphia to pick up their baby.

When the couple arrived, however, Furlow said that Roxanne was having second thoughts. The couple waited in their hotel room for days, agonizing over whether they would return home with a child. But as it turned out, there was no baby for them to adopt: Roxanne, the baby, and everything had been a cruel scam. The couple was one of forty-four scammed out of a total of $215,000. Said one woman, who lost $15,500 to Furlow, "It's easy money. You're not dealing with selling a car. You're dealing with people's emotions." Furlow was indicted on twenty counts of mail fraud, and in July 2000 pleaded guilty to three.[20]

What is the lesson from these cases? That our society should become coldhearted? That we should dam the famous American generosity because people take advantage of us? Of course not. But these examples (and many others like them) serve to show just how vulnerable we are when emotions are involved, and we buy into myths before examining them. And these are only a small sample of the cases that have been uncovered; who knows how many others go unreported out of sympathy or embarrassment? These fictions become woven into the collective understanding of reality, and the problem comes in when decisions are based upon such myths.

NOTES

1. Cathy Young, "False Diagnosis," *Reason* (May 2001): 23.

2. The Beardstown Ladies Investment Club, *The Beardstown Ladies' Common-Sense Investment Guide: How We Beat the Market—and How You Can, Too* (New York: Hyperion, 1996).

3. Steven Brill, "Selling Snake Oil," *Brill's Content* (February 2000): 66.

4. Elizabeth Lesly Stevens, "He Cracked the Numbers Racket" *Brill's Content* (July/August 1998): 58; Martha Irvine, "Beardstown Ladies Admit Club's Bullishness Was Bull, *Corpus Christi (Tex.) Caller-Times* [online], www.caller2.com/busarch/bus3691.html [March 18, 1998].

5. Mark Miller and Marc Peyser, "We Live in Daily Fear," *Newsweek*, September 2, 1996, p. 52.

6. "Conspiracy of Racism Nonexistent in Church Fires," *Skeptic* 4, no. 3 (1996): 12.

7. "Pastor Accused in Texas Church Fire," Associated Press [online], wire.ap.org [November 8, 1999]; "Pastor Pleads Guilty to Church Arson," Associated Press [online], wire.ap.org [November 9, 1999].

8. David G. Savage, "No Conspiracy Found in Church Arsons," *Albuquerque Journal*, June 9, 1997, p. A-1.

9. "Church Arson Report Found No Conspiracy," *Albuquerque Journal*, June 11, 1997, p. A-14.

10. Scott Dickensheets, "Roid Rage," *Playboy* (July 2001): 129.

11. Michael Bamberger, "Dream Come True," *Sports Illustrated*, December 20, 1999, p. 48.

12. Mike Penner, "Bare Facts Make These Two Heroes," *Los Angeles Times*, July 11, 1999.

13. Michael Bamberger, "Dream Come True," *Sports Illustrated*, December 20, 1999, pp. 55–56.

14. Simon Evans, "Soccer-Euro2000-Referees Vow to Clamp Down on 'Divers,'" Reuters [online], www.reuters.com [June 8, 2000].

15. Ira Dreyfuss, "Cheating May Now Be Moral Norm," Associated Press [online], wire.ap.org [June 21, 1998].

16. Peter Simon, "Student Puts Honesty Over Winning," *Buffalo News*, October 21, 2000, p. A-1.

17. Kimberley Murphy, "Abandoned 'Boy' Exposed as Woman, 25," *Albuquerque Journal*, December 28, 1995, p. A-1; Matthew Brown, "Waif Impostor Is Charged with Forgery," *Albuquerque Journal*, December 30, 1995.

18. Quotes from Donna De La Cruz, "Honduran Boy Admits Tale Was a Lie," Associated Press [online], wire.ap.org [June 30, 1999].

19. Bill Braun, "Woman Says She Regrets Fund Fraud," *Tulsa (Okla.) World*, May 5, 1998.

20. Amanda Ripley, "The Empty Crib," *Time*, July 17, 2000, p. 46.

11

THREATS TO LIFE AND HEALTH

The threats from the media's mythmakers aren't only to our money and trust, but in some cases to our very health and lives. When our attentions and resources are misdirected, the consequences can be deadly. For example, an estimated 5 to 10 percent of sudden infant death syndrome (SIDS) deaths each year are, in fact, infanticides. The mysterious nature of SIDS allowed many mothers and fathers to kill their infants without arousing suspicion. A 1997 book on the topic, *The Death of Innocents*, uncovered several cases where this clearly occurred, and pointed to many more.[1] Why did this problem take so long to be discovered? Part of the answer can be found when the situation is viewed as a battle for public awareness: There are several organizations raising awareness about SIDS, but few, if any, raising awareness about parents who kill their newborns.[2]

In this chapter, we'll examine a few examples of the medical consequences of emotional manipulation and hysteria.

BREAST IMPLANTS

The saga of silicone breast implants is a curious one, filled with moving personal accounts and litigation-happy lawyers. It is most notable, however, for its complete lack of scientific evidence to back up the emotional claims of harm. Unlike other health scares that were backed up by evidence (such as the furor over the diet drug combination Fen-Phen), emotion and fear successfully obscured the fact that evidence against implants was lacking. Pseudoscience and faulty logic flooded courtrooms, which were usually so successful at keeping out junk science.

Most of the complaints involved women who claimed to suffer from autoimmune and connective tissue disorders caused by leaking gel from the implants. In December 1991 a California court ruled that Dow Corning Corporation, one of the largest makers of silicone breast implants, had to pay a $7.3-million judgment. In January of the following year, an FDA moratorium on the implants effectively eliminated their use. The implant lawsuits drove the company to seek Chapter 11 bankruptcy protection in 1995. The bankruptcy would have set aside $2.4 billion to settle the claims, but lawyers for the plaintiffs wanted more money. That same year French health officials *lifted* a three-year moratorium on implants, following the careful analysis of a body of exhaustive international research demonstrating the implants' safety. Following protracted negotiations, Dow Corning offered $3 billion to settle the claims.

The talk show industry sought out and booked breast implant horror stories; perhaps the most dramatic was the case of Laura Thorpe, a woman from the small town of Bloomfield, in northern New Mexico. In 1992 Thorpe, after hearing numerous media reports of the dangers of breast implants, became so emotional and alarmed that she cut out her own implants with a razor. Thorpe was later assessed as suffering severe depression or a psychotic break, according to Jeanne Heaton and Nona Wilson, two psychologists who researched the case. Talk show host Maury Povich featured Thorpe on a program titled "Breast Implant Horror." Barry Glassner describes the episode: "It took all of Povich's interviewing skills, Heaton and Wilson show, to keep Thorpe from sounding deranged during the broadcast. In answer to questions about the implants, she rambled on about having grown up in orphanages and foster homes, her unemployed husband, and feeling sorry for men because they have to shave."[3] No evidence was produced that her implants caused or contributed to her real or imagined ails. The fact that the star of Povich's show was likely unreliable and had no proof for her health damage claims was apparently not of concern. The goal was entertainment, not truth; heat, not light.

The implant controversy also had high-profile activists, including talk show host Jenny Jones, who told her story during sweeps month on February 24, 1992. On *Donahue*, her own program, and in a *People* magazine cover story, Jones discussed the six implant operations since 1981 that left her chest scarred and numb.

Repeated studies at top research institutions across the globe have consistently failed to substantiate a link between connective tissue disorders and silicone breast implants. Yes, some women with breast implants were getting ill—at the same rate as the general population. At the request of Congress, the Institute of Medicine (the medical branch of the National Academy of Sciences) convened an independent panel of thirteen scientists to study the implant controversy. The panel concluded that silicone breast implants do not cause any major diseases. In the March 2000 issue of the *New England Journal of Medicine*, an analysis of twenty previous studies showed once again that breast implants are safe.

The case has also come to symbolize "junk science," in which emotional testimony and anecdote replace good science. As *Newsweek* writer Sharon Begley wrote, "Because courts allowed 'junk science' into evidence, argues Dr. Marcia Angell in her recent book 'Science on Trial,' one woman won millions of dollars from Dow Corning even though her own rheumatologist testified that her symptoms of connective-tissue disease began before she received the implants (other doctors disagreed)."[4]

Lawyers pounced on the implant claims, and solicited clients through television and in newspaper ads. Many lawyers took as much as 40 percent of the awards, collecting tens of millions of dollars. Though fueled by greedy lawyers, the controversy was also driven in large part by alarmist media reports and emotional, anecdotal testimony. With a few exceptions, reporters didn't wait for evidence before reporting on the sad cases. Juries and courts valued the emotional testimony while ignoring overwhelming evidence that implants were in fact safe.

THE NORPLANT SCARE

Another, closely related example of a baseless scare in women's health is the contraceptive Norplant. Norplant consists of six small capsules containing a synthetic hormone inserted under the skin. The hormone, progestin, is the same as one of the hormones used in birth control pills; only the method of delivery is different, with the added benefit that the capsules are effective for five years but can be removed at any time.

When Norplant was first introduced in Britain in 1993, its effects had been studied since the 1960s. In the United States it was approved in 1990 and introduced in 1991. In the wake of the breast implant rulings, however, claims that Norplant was dangerous began to surface. Some women complained of pain and difficulty in removing the implants, excessive weight gain, headaches, and various other problems.

A few complaints about Norplant reached American lawyers who had received lucrative settlements from breast implant litigation. Soon the lawyers were actively soliciting Norplant users, hoping to find victims willing to join a class-action lawsuit against Wyeth-Ayerst, Norplant's manufacturer.

The lawsuits weren't the only things scaring women away from Norplant. As with breast implants a few years earlier, hundreds of horrific, emotional stories flooded the media; feature stories on women with health problems they attributed to Norplant appeared in magazines and in national and local newspapers. A segment on the television newsmagazine *Eye to Eye* with Connie Chung that aired May 12, 1994, featured several Norplant users who complained of pain and scarring when having the devices removed.

Throughout the furor and hysteria, the simple fact that Norplant had been unfairly maligned went virtually unheard. The public listens to a woman on a television newsmagazine weeping about her painful experience while they ignore doctors, studies, and statistics showing how rare such complications actually are and explaining that the woman's health problems may be unrelated to Norplant.

Certainly, some women experienced side effects when using Norplant. All drugs, from aspirin to Zantac, have side effects. Norplant's promotional literature and informational videos were clear about the drug's side effects, and doctors were urged to convey those precautions to patients. And it's true that not all doctors were competent at explaining risks or at inserting and removing the capsules. But in those cases blame lies with the doctor, not the manufacturer. To blame Norplant is like suing the paint manufacturer because a painter did a bad job on your house.

Glamour magazine, in a 1999 article examining the Norplant controversy, found plaintiffs in lawsuits against Norplant who

> kept their Norplant inserted in their arms for years after signing up for the suit, because they didn't want to relinquish what they considered an effective contraceptive; never mentioned to their doctors anything about problems they charged Norplant caused; claimed to have experienced Norplant-related symptoms that cross-examination by a Wyeth-Ayerst attorney revealed had existed prior to their getting the device, or stemmed from other causes; and admitted under oath that they weren't sure they'd experienced the side effects they'd originally complained of at all.[5]

In 1995 the Food and Drug Administration reviewed several years of Norplant data and found "no basis for questioning the safety and effectiveness" of the contraceptive. In 1998 the World Health Organization, the American College of Obstetrics and Gynecologists, and Britain's Family Planning Association issued a statement reassuring the public that Norplant was "safe and effective."

Many women's rights and family planning organizations were and are supporters of Norplant. In 1999, Marie Stopes International (MSI), a family planning organization, released a statement that said, "(MSI) welcomes the collapse of the litigation case against the manufacturers of Norplant, Hoechst Marion Roussel. . . . Dr. Judy Murty, one of MSI's family planning doctors, commented, 'MSI is very pleased the the action against HMR has been dropped. There has been a lot of very negative and misleading publicity surrounding Norplant. The fact is, it is safe, effective, and offers women more choice.'"

It's important to recognize that the litigation craze affects more than just Norplant and its manufacturers. When a drug company spends millions of dollars to develop, test, and market a product, has it approved as safe and effective by the FDA, and *still* ends up having to pay millions or billions of dollars in lawyer fees and settlements based upon anecdotal, emotional, and unscientific claims, it does little to encourage new research. Even though some Norplant suits have been dismissed, and perhaps eventually all will be, much of the damage has already been done: In April 1998, the United Kingdom distributor announced that Norplant would be taken off the market there, as it was no longer commercially viable due to lawsuits and negative publicity. And in America, the latest sales figures show less than $5 million per year in sales, a dramatic drop from $141 million in 1992, the first full year on the market.

Frank Furedi, a sociologist at the University of Kent at Canterbury, lamented Norplant's demise as a dangerous sign. "The victim-is-always-right mentality of the media is unlikely to change. But maybe it will come to recognize that trashing a technology can also create victims."[6]

AUTISM: FOSTERING FALSE HOPES

In other cases, rushing forward blindly and emotionally can foster false hopes and encourage quack medicine. Several such cases involving autistic children have surfaced over the past decade. Autism is a severe developmental disability affecting about four to five out of every ten thousand children, and is characterized by delayed and often abnormal communication and behavior. The disease is heartbreaking, in part perhaps because many autistic children look otherwise normal, which can inspire hope that they may just snap out of it one day and start talking and laughing like a "normal" child.

One woman's emotional story led thousands of parents to invest money and hope in a cure for autism that so far has been shown to be worthless. In 1997 Victoria Beck, the New Hampshire mother of an autistic child, claimed that one dose of the digestive enzyme secretin given during a diagnostic test had brought her son out of autistic isolation. Since then, thousands of parents have sought doctors willing to give their autistic children intravenous doses of the $180-per-vial enzyme. Though the anecdotal evidence was moving, the effects vanished when subjected to rigorous scientific studies.

A series of studies were designed and conducted to test secretin against a placebo. The first two studies completed showed no benefit from secretin. Dr. Duane Alexander, director of the National Institute of Child Health and Human Development, said that the findings "strongly suggest that secretin should not be recommended to treat autism until the results of our other ongoing studies are known."[7] Nonetheless, many parents desperate for a cure will likely continue to hold out hopes and money.

In the 1980s and 1990s, many parents of autistic children turned to a technique called facilitated communication (FC), which had been claimed to help autistic children (and others who have limited communication abilities) to communicate better. The idea behind FC is based on the premise that the lack of communication is not due to an underlying cognitive disorder, but instead to motor disorders such as coordinating speech. What is needed, FC advocates claim, is a trained facilitator to help the autistic children by holding their hands, fingers, or elbows while the child types on a keyboard or points to lists of letters, words, or symbols to communicate. In this way, the child can break through the tragic block of her disorder and speak, perhaps for the first time, to her parents and loved ones.

This technique was developed in the 1970s by Rosemary Crossley and others at the Dignity Through Education and Language Communications Centre in Melbourne, Australia. It was introduced in the United States by Douglas Biklen, a special education director at Syracuse University.

Anecdotal stories of children who had been silent all their lives but could now form sentences, express their dreams and fears, and even write poetry encouraged many parents to sign up for classes and hire facilitators. They saw the results as a miraculous breakthrough and signed up for FC workshops and sessions costing hundreds of dollars; specialized equipment cost around $800 more.

Yet the celebration was premature. As the technique and phenomenon were studied further, glaring problems became apparent. The premise that communication problems in autistic patients came from speech motor dysfunction was unsupported by medical science. The messages that the autistic children were sending much more closely matched those of the facilitator than the child. The words, diction, nuances, and grammatical structures used in the messages frequently far exceeded what an autistic child could have learned. (This, however, rarely deterred FC proponents, who stubbornly took this troublesome evidence instead as proof that doctors were underestimating the autistic childrens' abilities.)

Frequently the child wasn't even looking at the keyboard or letters, yet continued to type out her messages. Furthermore, when the child was asked questions only the child knew (but the facilitator didn't), the child was unresponsive or gave incorrect answers; similarly, when the facilitator and child were shown two pictures independently, the child responded correctly only when the same pictures were also seen by the facilitator. In short, it was clear that the facilitators were fooling themselves and simply typing out what they *thought* the child would say.

Numerous studies over two decades have failed to validate the claims of Crossley, Biklen, and others. The American Psychological Association has found no scientific evidence that FC works, and Gina Green, director of research at the New England Center of Autism, likened the technique to "dowsing sticks and the ouija board." No one claims that FC proponents or facilitators maliciously deceived parents of autistic children. Yet money was lost and hopes were raised—then shattered—when hope and emotion jumped ahead of science and reason.[8]

AIDS AND SEX: THE PRICE OF KEEPING CHILDREN IGNORANT

Another way in which emotion and hysteria have hurt American health is in sexual health education. Surgeon General Joycelyn Elders, who spoke out at the United Nations AIDS Day 1994, was asked to resign in late December of that year by the Clinton administration. Her offense? Rationally and candidly discussing masturbation, specifically as a preventive tool against sexually transmitted diseases, including AIDS, and teen sex. Elders had recently called on schools to consider teaching students about masturbation.

Given the outcry over AIDS, the long history of misinformation about masturbation (and sex and AIDS, for that matter), and the high rates of AIDS, other sexually transmitted diseases, and teen pregnancy, one might think that Elders's suggestion was a good one. Long before Elders was nominated for her post, as head of the Arkansas health department, she was one of the nation's most outspoken advocates of wide-ranging sex education and known for her direct, no-nonsense approach.

The furor was swift and loud: Conservatives (and some liberals) were mortified that the surgeon general would publicly say the word "masturbation," much less advocate teaching kids about it. Yet Elders simply suggested *that it be considered* to be taught along with the rest of the sex education curriculum. In education circles, Elders wasn't saying anything particularly novel or lascivious: The guidelines for the Sexuality Information and Education Council (the main source for sex education materials adopted by the U.S. Department of Education) support dissemination of accurate information about masturbation. Nearly all states require or encourage sex education, though many forbid teaching about masturbation.

But President Clinton, shaken by disastrous midterm elections, acutely felt the political heat and turned against Elders. He fired the surgeon general—for taking a stand and doing her job—after just over fifteen months.

Elders later reflected on the hysteria and furor over her comments:

> Informed decisions require knowledge. To ensure the health and well-being of a patient, age-appropriate information must be made available. Some call it candor— I call it common sense and good medicine. On the other hand, coquetries can be more than deceptive: both the refrain from self-gratification and the concealment of it can result in sexual dysfunction. Yet to study masturbation would be to admit its role in our lives—one that many of us are not comfortable with. Instead, we discourage the practice in our children, dispensing cautionary tales that read like Stephen King novellas. These myths were more understandable before Pasteur enlightened the world to the presence of germs in the 1870s; prior to his discovery, no one really knew where diseases came from. Masturbation was blamed for dreaded conditions like syphilis and gonorrhea, as well as for their ramifications: dementia, blindness and infertility, to name a few. . . . Parents need to let go of the idea that ignorance maintains innocence and begin teaching age-appropriate facts to children.[9]

Secretary of State Colin Powell also drew sharp criticism for encouraging the use of condoms to prevent AIDS and other sexually transmitted diseases. During an interview on MTV in February 2002, Powell was asked about his position on condom use. He replied that "[i]t is important that the whole international community come together, speak candidly about it, forget about taboos, forget about conservative ideas with respect to what you should tell young people about it. It's the lives of young people that are put at risk by unsafe sex, and therefore protect yourself."[10]

Though the Bush White House had little comment on Powell's remarks, James Dobson, president of the conservative group Focus on the Family, shot back that Powell was secretary of state, not secretary of health, and "talking about a subject he doesn't understand." Christian activist Gary Bauer also criticized Powell.[11]

The dangers of denying accurate sex information was highlighted by *60 Minutes II* correspondent Ed Bradley in an hourlong special on AIDS in Africa, which aired on June 27, 2000. Though AIDS is at epidemic levels throughout much of Africa, one success story stands out: Uganda. While the governmental programs of South Africa, Zimbabwe, Kenya, and others have little effect on AIDS rates, Uganda has achieved significant success because officials talk about AIDS candidly and often. President Yoweri Kaguta Museveni discusses contraception proudly and publicly, recognizing that accurate sex education information may be a difficult subject to broach, but that doesn't mean the facts shouldn't be discussed.

And lest one be tempted to say that such AIDS myths are only prevalent in Africa, recall that not long ago many people in the United States believed that AIDS could be contracted from donating blood. As a result, blood donations dropped markedly. The problem got to be so bad that the Red Cross and blood banks launched information campaigns to counter this dangerous myth. And a poll taken in 2000 of teens and young adults showed many people still deeply misinformed about AIDS. Thirty percent said that they thought that only people who share needles can get HIV, and 25 percent believed that only promiscuous people were in danger of infection. Sixteen percent said that only homosexuals get AIDS, and 12 percent thought AIDS could be transmitted through kissing.[12]

Sex advice writers and columnists are nearly universally discouraged by the level of sexual ignorance today. Writes Michael Castleman:

> Answering sex questions is a job fraught with mixed emotions—chief among them, feelings of being overwhelmed and profound sadness at the sexual ignorance apparent in so many letters. . . . [T]he questions they ask, often tinged with desperation, suggest that 30 years after the so-called sexual revolution . . . Americans are no better informed about sex and no happier in bed than their parents or grandparents were.[13]

Says Thrive Online/Oxygen sex advice columnist Sandor Gardos, "I'm often shocked at the level of cluelessness out there."[14]

The public's puritanical efforts to keep their children sexually ignorant has a long tradition. When Ida Craddock wrote several pamphlets about sex (with such titles as *The Wedding Night* and *Right Marital Living*) in the early 1900s, she was persecuted for it. She dared to give women accurate (and, for the time, explicit) information about sex. Anthony Comstock, a special agent to the U.S. Post Office and secretary of the New York Society for the Suppression of Vice (and rabid sexual puritan) had Craddock arrested. The charge was violating obscenity laws, and Comstock's harassment of Craddock soon drove her to suicide. Before she died, Craddock decried a "social superstition that young people should be kept as ignorant as possible of all that pertains to the marriage relation. It is thought by many people that it would somehow render young people impure if they were told previous to marriage anything of details. . . . It does not matter how delicately and chastely the teacher may instruct that young girl or boy; that she should instruct them at all is expatiated on as an effort to corrupt the morals of innocent youth."[15]

In 1901 Dr. Prince Morrow began studying prostitutes and sexually transmitted diseases. He found that the problem was worse than anyone had expected, costing many lives. Yet when he tried to warn people of the severity of the problem, he found society unwilling to address the epidemic. In 1908 he wrote that the cause of the great tragedy was "the parental policy of mock modesty and silence with their sons and daughters about their physical selves. . . . If parents would only believe this one vital truth—that it is ignorance that ruins little girls, not innocence that protects them."[16] A century later, that lesson is still lost.

NOTES

1. Richard Firstman and Jamie Talan, *The Death of Innocents* (New York: Bantam Books, 1997).
2. Sharon Begley, "The Nursery's Littlest Victims," *Newsweek*, September 22, 1997, p. 72.
3. Barry Glassner, *The Culture of Fear* (New York: Basic Books, 1999), p. 168.
4. Sharon Begley, "The Trials of Silicone," *Newsweek*, December 16, 1996, p. 56.
5. Leslie Laurence, "Your Perfect Birth Control . . . Blocked?" *Glamour* (September 1999): 307.
6. Frank Furedi, "Mud Sticks," *New Scientist*, July 3, 1999, p. 51.
7. Janet McConnaughey, "Autism Studies Show No Enzyme Benefit," South Coast Today [online], www.s-t./daily/12-99/12-14-99/C06he099.htm [December 8, 1999].
8. James A. Mulick, John W. Jacobson, and Frank H. Kobe, "Anguished Silence and Helping Hands: Autism and Facilitated Communication," *Skeptical Inquirer* 17, no. 3 (spring 1993): 273; Kathleen M. Dillon, "Facilitated Communication, Autism, and Ouija,"*Skeptical Inquirer* 17, no. 3 (spring 1993): 284; R. A. Cummins and M. P. Prior, "Autism and Facilitated Communication: A Reply to Biklen," *Harvard Educational Review* 62 (1992): 228; James D. Herbert, Ian A. Sharp, and Brandon Gaudiano, "Separating Fact from Fiction in the Etiology and Treatment of Autism," *Scientific Review of Mental Health Practice* 1, no. 1 (2000): 23–43.
9. Joycelyn Elders and Rev. Dr. Barbara Kilgore, "The Dreaded 'M' Word," Nerve [online], www.nervemag.com/Dispatches/Elders/mword [June 26, 1997].
10. "Powell Gets Quizzed on MTV," Fox News [online], www.headliner.nl/headliner.php?c=us&abbr=foxnews&id=3323 [February 14, 2002].
11. "Colin Powell's Stance on Condoms Draws Fire," Reuters [online], www/drbobmartin/2002_02_15news13.html [February 15, 2002].
12. "HIV/AIDS Infections Rise to 36 Million in 2000," Reuters [online], etherlabs.net/m.werneburg/words/reality/aids_world_dc_1.html [November 28, 2000].
13. Michael Castleman, "Can Dry Humping Get Me Pregnant?" Salon [online], archive.www.salon.com/sex/feature/2001/03/14/columnists_1/ [March 14, 2001].
14. Ibid.
15. James R. Petersen, *The Century of Sex: Playboy's History of the Sexual Revolution, 1900–1999* (New York: Grove Press, 1999), p. 17.
16. Ibid., p. 88.

12

THREATS TO FREEDOM AND JUSTICE

Threats to our liberty come not only from intentional infringement of our rights, but also from overreaction to the media's scares. When emotions run out of control, particularly among those of influence and power, even the most well-intentioned measures can turn against the common good.

POST-COLUMBINE HYSTERIA

In the wake of the spate of school shootings in 1999 and 2000, many civil rights groups complained of crackdowns on students' civil rights. Reports emerged almost monthly of cases in which students were singled out for suspension or segregation out of fear of crime.

About a month before the Columbine shooting, eighteen-year-old student Antonius Brown wrote a story in his English class journal about a deranged student who massacred people at his Atlanta school. *Time* reporter John Cloud described the result:

> Eventually officials heard about it and suspended him for 20 days. But Brown happened to return from that suspension on April 20, the day of the Columbine massacre. He was expelled two days later in the fearful atmosphere of the moment. Police charged him with making terrorist threats. Brown spent three days in jail, and then a municipal judge ordered him to leave town for two months.[1]

Charles Carithers, a junior at Boston's Latin Academy, was assigned to write a descriptive horror story for an English class in May 2000. He fulfilled his assignment with a story about a student who attacked his high school English teacher with a chainsaw. In a surprise ending, however, it was the character's aunt who died. Carithers's teacher reported the story as a possible threat of bodily harm and Carithers was given a three-day suspension. The suspension was later overturned by a school hearing officer, who said that officials should have considered other factors, including the boy's academic record.[2]

In another case, a fourteen-year-old Pennsylvania girl told a teacher during a discussion on the Columbine shootings that she could understand how someone who is constantly teased and persecuted could snap; she was suspended for expressing that opinion. In Columbia, South Carolina, police arrested three high school students after they were sent to the principal's office simply for wearing all-black clothes. And an eight-year-old Arkansas boy was suspended from school for three days for pointing a piece of breaded chicken at a teacher and saying, "Pow, pow, pow." These, and many other cases like them, had civil rights groups concerned about protecting students' rights.[3]

Following a chorus of stinging criticisms that police and school officials ignored clear warning signs that the Columbine killers planned their rampage and bragged about it (on Web sites and in personal communication), an emphasis has also been placed on identifying potential killers before they act. The FBI has been enlisted to help schools in "student profiling." Law enforcement agencies have developed a list of traits to help teachers, parents, and others identify angry or maladjusted students who might be at risk for violence. All this despite the fact that most students, at one time or another, probably would answer questions in a way that would raise flags. Students who fit broad profiles can be required to undergo counseling, be suspended, or be transferred to alternative education programs. And what of students who are targeted for being maladjusted? What happens to them?

Increased criteria for excluding students leads to increases in student suspensions, which in turn leads to an increase in dropouts. A report by the Justice Policy Institute/Children's Law Center stated:

> Consistently, research has pointed to a strong correlation between school suspensions and dropping out of school. One study published in the Teachers College Record found that sophomores who are suspended drop out at three times the rate of their peers. . . . [A 1994] CDC study found that youth who were not in school were more likely to have been involved in a physical fight and more likely to carry a weapon [as well as] to smoke and use alcohol, marijuana and cocaine.[4]

The report further cited reassuring facts. The Centers for Disease Control found that there is a less than one in a million chance of a school-aged youth dying or committing suicide on school grounds or on the way to school: "Studies by the Bureau of Justice Statistics, the National Center of Education Statistics and various other sources found violent crime was relatively rare in schools and not on the increase."[5]

While many politicians, school officials, and parents demand metal detectors and security guards in schools, this knee-jerk reaction may instead exacerbate the problem. Matthew J. Mayer and Peter E. Leone, researchers at the Department of Special Education at the University of Maryland, analyzed data compiled for the 1995 National Crime Victimization Survey and sorted the responses of nine thousand youth in school. Of those, the responses were divided between those students who attended schools with "secure buildings" (with metal detectors, locked doors, and personal searches) and those who attended schools with rule enforcement policies (schools where the rules were emphasized and the consequences of breaking the rules were known).

They found that the greater the effort to enforce a "secure building" through metal detectors and guards, the more victimization, fights, and theft were reported, and the less safe kids reported feeling. Mayer and Leone write, "Creating an unwelcoming, almost jail-like, heavily scrutinized environment may foster the violence and disorder administrators hope to avoid."[6]

Parents are much more concerned about their childrens' safety than their children are. Some have apparently taken the media's fear-mongering to heart. In Norwalk, Connecticut, a twenty-seven-year-old mother of two elementary school boys was charged with arming her children with a hammer and screwdriver to fend off attacks.[7]

The overreaction wasn't limited to schools. In September 1999 Sears halted sales of a twelve-inch action figure called "The Villain" because three people complained that the armed dolls came with trench coats. The toys, manufactured by 21st Century Toys, were designed more than a year earlier but had the misfortune of coming out around the time of the Columbine massacre. Other figures in the series included soldiers from Vietnam and World War II. A Sears spokeswoman said of those who complained, "Their concerns were very sincere and heartfelt." A Colorado mother, Kim Carpenter, complained after her two boys, aged eight and ten, saw the doll in a catalog and told her that they thought it looked like the "Trench Coat Mafia."[8]

When the dust and hysteria settled, the final report on the Columbine massacre revealed that the two killers were not in fact part of any so-called Trench Coat Mafia. But as long as, in the opinion of eight- and ten-year-olds, a doll *seems* to look like a real killer (based, ultimately, upon incorrect information), consumers across the country were kept from choosing a product they could otherwise purchase. For Sears, wanting to preserve its family-friendly image, the bad publicity that might follow was not worth standing up to one mother. Such is the power of emotion and hysteria.

The removal of a doll might seem insignificant, but take a second to understand what happened: A pair of children and their mother forced a national chain to remove one of its products—not for safety reasons, but because it came with clothes similar to the Columbine killers'. Sears could have politely but firmly explained to the mother and children that just because *they* imagined some link between the doll and the crimes doesn't mean there *was* one, and that they don't get to decide what other people should be able to buy. If the mother found the doll objectionable, she could simply not order it from the catalog.

THE RAILROADING OF WEN HO LEE

Wen Ho Lee, a computer scientist at Los Alamos National Labs in New Mexico, was arrested in March 1999, accused of downloading top-secret documents. He was initially charged with giving classified information about a W-88 nuclear warhead to China. Those charges were dropped by December of that year, and reduced to mishandling government documents. Lee was released after pleading guilty to improperly downloading classified material onto an unsecured computer. The other fifty-eight counts were dropped, and he was sentenced to time already served. During Lee's nine-month incarceration, he was held in solitary confinement, routinely shackled, and allowed to see his family for only one hour per week.

The accusations against Lee did not appear in a vacuum. By the time Lee was fired in March 1999, the United States had endured months of heated accusations, vehement denials, and contradictory information about China spying on U.S. nuclear secrets.

The government prosecutors had done their best to demonize Lee and inflate the charges against him. Los Alamos scientist Richard Krajcik said that the documents Lee allegedly downloaded represented "the crown jewels of nuclear design assessment capability of the United States."[9] In fact, the material was not even classified as secret, much less top secret, when Lee supposedly took the data. A defense witness testified that "99 percent" of the material was already available to the public.

Much of the scientific community rallied around Lee, including Bruce Alberts, president of the National Academy of Sciences; William Wulf, president of the National Academy of Engineering; and Kenneth I. Shine, president of the Institute of Medicine. In a joint, open letter to Attorney General Janet Reno, they protested Lee's treatment. Many supporters, and Lee himself, accused the government investigators and prosecutors of singling him out because of his Chinese ancestry.

In the government's fervor to keep Lee in jail, FBI agent Robert Messemer and U.S. Attorney for New Mexico John Kelly misled U.S. District Judge James Parker about Lee's actions and the consequences of releasing Lee on bail. In a statement to Lee, Judge Parker said, "I tell you with great sadness that I feel I was led astray last December by the executive branch of our government through the Department of Justice, by its Federal Bureau of Investigation and by the United States Attorney for the District of New Mexico [John Kelly], who held office at that time."[10]

Messemer testified under oath that Lee lied to a colleague to gain access to a computer and that Lee had sent letters to foreign scientific organizations, ostensibly seeking an overseas job. Those statements, in part, led Judge Parker to deny Lee bail in December 1999; he called them "deeply troubling" deceptions. Messemer later admitted that his "testimony was incorrect," but said that he didn't think his (apparent) lying under oath, which led to Lee's denial of bail, was a serious error.[11]

Upon freeing Lee on September 13, 2000, Judge Parker apologized to the scientist: "I sincerely apologize to you, Mr. Lee, for the unfair manner in which you were held in custody by the executive branch." The Departments of Justice and Energy, Parker said, "have embarrassed our entire nation and each of us who is a citizen of it."[12]

Judge Parker's integrity and apology are very rarely seen; all too often, those unfairly hounded by the press or judicial system may gain monetary damages, but a simple apology is rare indeed. In the end, several senators and law professors called for an investigation into the government's conduct.

A Justice Department report on the matter by former federal prosecutor Randy Bellows concluded that the FBI wasted four years investigating Lee because it failed to correct misleading information provided by the Department of Energy (DOE). The DOE's 1996 inquiry into Lee was, according to Bellows, "a deeply flawed product whose shortcomings went unrecognized and unaddressed due to the FBI's own inadequate investigation. . . . Had either the FBI or DOE done what it should have, the FBI could have been investigating in the year 1996 what it is now investigating in the year 2000." Bellows notes that the DOE also misled the FBI by inaccurately reporting the findings of a panel of scientists assembled to assess whether China had breached U.S. security. The Department of Energy's deception "resulted in the FBI spending years investigating the wrong crime."[13]

And what of the media's role in this sorry affair? While many newspapers were careful in their reporting of the case, the *New York Times,* one of the country's most respected newspapers, was not so on the ball. The case against Wen Ho Lee unfolded in the *Times* in a series of front-page reports by Jeff Gerth and James Risen. In his article in *Brill's Content* on the matter, Robert Schmidt wrote that the tone of Gerth and Risen's articles seemed to suggest that the case against Lee was solid, and that "[their] word choices seemed freighted with guilty connotations. . . . Whenever possible, it seemed, Gerth and Risen emphasized the information that seemed consistent with Lee's guilt."[14]

In September 1999 the *Times* ran a piece by William Broad, a science reporter with a background in nuclear weaponry. Broad's article made several points that showed the flaws in the case against Lee, and strongly suggested that the investigation focused on Lee too quickly. As Schmidt notes, "Broad's story was meticulously reported. But it left out one salient fact: The *New York Times* itself had been largely responsible for fueling the scandal and portraying Wen Ho Lee as a traitor."[15]

That task finally fell to the *Times* itself, in its September 26, 2000, edition. In an unprecedented, 1,680-word note from the editors, the *New York Times* admitted that its coverage of the Wen Ho Lee case was flawed. It said that on the whole the paper's staff remained proud of their work,

> But looking back, we also found some things we wish we had done differently in the course of the coverage to give Dr. Lee the benefit of the doubt. In those months, we could have pushed harder to uncover weaknesses in the F.B.I. case against Dr. Lee. . . . In place of a tone of journalistic detachment from our sources, we occasionally used language that adopted [a] sense of alarm.[16]

The *Times* deserves credit for making the announcement—more journalists should run such corrections when they make mistakes—though one wonders why it was so long in coming. Serious doubts about the coverage had been raised long before: The *Times*'s own Broad article was published in September 1999, and the *Brill's Content* article appeared two months later in November. Nearly a year passed before Lee was freed and the *Times* ran its note admitting its errors.

The fallout from the Wen Ho Lee case goes far beyond the damage to Lee's (and the FBI's) reputation; it extends to issues of national security. As often happens, those in power reacted to myths instead of realities.

Alan Zelicoff, a senior scientist in the Center for National Security and Arms Control at Sandia National Labs, explains what happened:

> In the wake of the Wen Ho Lee debacle in 1999, bureaucratic Washington, in search of a "quick fix" [to the exaggerated spying crisis] made the classic bureaucratic mistake: doing something first, and thinking later. . . . Instead of doing the difficult but correct thing—reinstating guards at entry points into the Labs . . . [the Energy Secretary] elected to

> recommend a widespread, screening polygraph program throughout the Department of Energy. Congress went along, and real security was sacrificed at the altar of politics.[17]

Many known spies, such as Aldrich Ames, routinely passed polygraph tests during their employment in intelligence agencies. A study commissioned by the Department of Energy and conducted by the National Academy of Sciences found that "the polygraph's accuracy is not good enough for security screening," and that polygraph testing "now rests on weak scientific underpinnings despite nearly a century of study."[18]

The polygraphs, Zelicoff says, undermine national security by creating a false sense of security, draining resources from effective and proven security measures, and demoralizing staff by subjecting innocent employees to useless and invasive questioning. In 2003, despite ample evidence of inefficacy, the Department of Energy sought to continue the polygraph program at national laboratories.

THE SATANIC ABUSE SCARE

Throughout the 1980s and early 1990s, a rash of child abuse cases horrified America. Children accused adults of ritual rape, torture, and abuse, and the news media gleefully reported the lurid stories. Though some media reports were carefully researched and stuck to the facts, most were heavily sensationalized. The pinnacle was perhaps Geraldo Rivera's infamous NBC special *Devil-Worship: Exposing Satan's Underground,* which aired on October 28, 1988.

On the special (as well as on his syndicated talk show), Rivera mixed together a stew of self-proclaimed "Satanism experts," misleading and inaccurate statistics, crimes with only tenuous links to "Satanism," and sensationalized media reports. What came out was a rancid yet irresistible two hours that garnered the largest viewership for a documentary in television history—though "documentary" is perhaps giving it too much credit. Rivera did his best to whip up emotions, paranoia, and fear, claiming that an organized Satanic conspiracy was at work killing babies, murdering innocents, conducting ghastly rituals, and having orgies, all to appease evil incarnate, Satan. The notable lack of evidence for the Satanic crimes was seen not as a reason to question the claims, but simply as proof of how well organized and shrewd the Satanic conspiracy really had become.

Satan's Underground was also the title of a 1991 book in which author Lauren Stratford relates her experiences inside a Satanic cult.[19] Stratford tells a horrific first-person story of Satanism, pornography, infanticide, torture, and rape. She claims to have been continually physically and sexually abused by her parents and forced into child prostitution and pornography. She was forced, she says, to attend Satanic rituals, including sacrificing a baby. At one point she was locked in a metal drum with the bodies of four babies who had been sacrificed. Her terrifying account became a best-seller. It has since been used to support claims promoting and validating Satanic ritual abuse and "repressed memories."[20]

Several journalists with *Cornerstone*, a Christian magazine, looked into the story behind the book. As Bob and Gretchen Passantino and Jon Trott discovered:

> As it turned out, none of it was true. There was no documentation, corroboration, or evidence. Careful research . . . revealed that author Lauren Stratford was actually Laurel Rose Willson, a troubled woman from Washington State who spent most of her teen and adult life fabricating horrendous stories of victimization by a variety of people in a variety of settings. . . . In the mid-1980s, when the scare about ritual child abuse in day cares gained momentum, she produced a new story incorporating Satanic Ritual Abuse's most sensational features. That story metamorphosed over three years to become the story of *Satan's Underground*.[21]

According to the authors, Stratford has since changed her name to Laura Grabowski and was recently claiming to be a Jewish Holocaust survivor.

In the wake of the emotional manipulation and media hype, terrible injustices were committed. Hundreds of people were accused of horrible crimes; ostracized by their friends, families, and communities; and even sentenced to prison. Though many of the convictions have been overturned and falsely accused people set free, others remain in prison. A few of the most notorious cases:

Manhattan Beach, California (1983)

In the longest and costliest trial in U.S. history (seven years and $14 million), preschool teacher Ray Buckey; his mother, Peggy McMartin Buckey; his sister, Peggy Ann; his grandmother Virginia McMartin; and three other teachers at the McMartin Preschool were accused of sexual abuse. Of 400 children questioned by a child welfare agency, 369 were determined to have been molested. The first charges were brought by Judy Johnson, who claimed that Ray Buckey, along with her estranged husband, had abused her two-and-a-half-year-old son. She also complained to prosecutors that someone sodomized her dog; in 1985 she was found to be an acute paranoid schizophrenic. The childrens' stories included tales of being abused in a secret tunnel underneath the school, being taken to a church where strangers killed a rabbit and forced them to drink its blood, jumping out of airplanes, digging up dead bodies at a cemetery, and even more fantastic stories. When asked to identify molesters, children fingered community leaders, store clerks, and even a picture of actor Chuck Norris. Nonetheless, fueled by zeal (and, undoubtedly, pressure from a scared public convinced of the reality of the Satanic cults), prosecutors believed these outlandish tales. Eventually charges were dropped against Peggy Ann, Virginia, and the three other teachers; Ray spent five years in prison during the trial; his mother, two years.[22]

Malden, Massachusetts (1984)

Gerald Amirault; his mother, Violet Amirault; and his sister, Cheryl LaFave, were accused of torturing children at the Fells Acres Day Care Center. One child said that he had seen a four-year-old sodomized with a foot-long butcher knife that got stuck; another said that he had been tortured by a "bad clown" in a "secret room"; yet another claimed that if the children tried to refuse sex, a robot would bite their arms. Gerald Amirault was sentenced to thirty to forty years in prison; his mother and sister each served eight years, having been denied parole because they maintained their innocence. As of this writing, Gerald remains in prison, having exhausted his appeals.[23]

Edenton, North Carolina (1989)

Robert Kelly Jr. was convicted in 1992 on ninety-nine counts of sexually abusing a dozen children at his Little Rascals Day Care Center. One boy claimed that Kelly prayed to the devil; another claimed that Kelly took the children on a boat trip and pushed a boy overboard to circling sharks; and one girl said that he raped and drugged her, then photographed her performing sex acts with another child. Little or no evidence was found that supported any of the accusations. Kelly was sentenced to twelve consecutive life sentences, one for each child. In May 1997, after he had served more than six years in prison, all ninety-nine charges against Kelly were dropped.[24]

Wenatchee, Washington (1994)

When sex crimes investigator Robert Perez's nine-year-old foster daughter told him of a church-based pedophile group, he drove her around town and asked her to point out who had abused children. She accused dozens of townspeople, and the search was on to find more victims. Finally other children joined in; one told of mass child rapes by men in black and women holding colored pencils; another spoke of wild orgies involving dozens of people held at the local Pentecostal church. When the investigations were completed, some twenty-nine thousand charges were brought against twenty-eight people. Eventually, nineteen people were convicted or pleaded guilty. Most of the defendants had developmental disabilities, low IQs, or limited English skills. Lawyers from the volunteer group Innocence Project Northwest have helped overturn convictions.

The initial accuser recanted her accusation in 1996, then later withdrew it. One girl claimed that she and her sister had been forced by Perez to make false accusations; a former social worker said that, when interviewing a third-grade girl, Perez placed his gun on the table in front of her and repeatedly told her that she wouldn't be allowed to go back to school until she told him about abuse. Meanwhile, Perez remains adamant he did nothing wrong: "I'll never apologize for the work I did."[25]

Similar cases occurred in Maplewood, New Jersey, in 1985; Olympia, Washington, in 1988; and Martensville, Saskatchewan, in 1991. In nearly all the cases, social workers, police, and detectives asked leading questions of children in their efforts to uncover the "truth." At times the interviewers badgered the children until they said what the interviewer wanted to hear. And throughout, there was a stunning lack of physical evidence to back up the wild (and, at times, physically impossible) accusations. The emotional will to "believe the children" (a popular slogan adopted by many child advocates) overrode common sense and defendants' rights. Superior Court Judge Isaac Borenstein's 1998 comment on the Cheryl LeFave prosecution is typical of the abuse cases: "There are so many examples in the evidence of this case of improper procedures that it would take days to go through them. This case should leave no one confident except for one thing—justice was not done."[26]

In another case, two young children were taken from their parents' home in Escondido, California, in the middle of the night in 1991. This was done—without a judge's order—to take the children into protective custody. The upcoming third birthday of one child coincided with the autumnal equinox, and police believed that the parents were planning to kill him in a sacrifice to Satan. The children were kept in various foster homes for nearly three months, despite investigations that found no evidence at all of either Satanism or abuse of any sort. In 2000, after years of legal battles, the parents were awarded $750,000 in compensation for the police department's violation of their rights.[27]

Incidentally, Geraldo Rivera eventually retracted his belief in the Satanism scare. On a CNBC special that aired December 12, 1995, Rivera announced that he had been "terribly wrong" and acknowledged that many innocent people had been falsely accused in the hysteria he had helped foment.

THE MEDIA AND COPYCAT CRIMES

Another detrimental aspect of the barrage of emotional media content is the potential it has to encourage copycat crimes. The media have influence (advertisers wouldn't spend billions of dollars if they didn't), but at times the influence goes beyond informing and entertaining the public and telling them which pain reliever to buy—it can also lead to crimes and deaths.

Following the coverage of the school shootings, and the Columbine event in particular, schools across the country were plagued by copycat rumors. In the months that followed the Columbine shooting, investigators were concerned that, due in part to the extensive media coverage, others would try to emulate or duplicate the killers' crimes. One newspaper article said that "[investigator and bomb technician Rick] Young and other officials are so worried the killers' plans and arsenal could be used as a blueprint to launch other attacks, they would not tell the [Columbine Review] commission why the bombs failed."[28]

In the weeks following the April 20 massacre and bombing (and the resulting media coverage), the National Safety Center estimated that at least three thousand copycat bomb threats were made, and there have been reports of mimicking behavior at schools in nearly every state.[29]

And though many of the copycat incidents were relatively minor (such as bomb scares), others were much more serious:

- Days after the Columbine massacre, a fifteen-year-old boy went on a rampage at his Alberta high school, shooting two people and killing one. The boy's mother described her son as being depressed and obsessed with the Columbine shootings.
- On the one-month anniversary of the Columbine shootings, a teenage boy shot and wounded six students at Heritage High School in suburban Atlanta. Attorney General Janet Reno referred to the incident as a "copycat" shooting.
- On December 6, 1999, Seth Trickey, a thirteen-year-old Oklahoma boy, shot at his Fort Gibson Middle School classmates, wounding five of them. According to his case file and Dr. Shreekumar Vinekar, the psychiatrist who testified at his court hearing, Trickey was strongly influenced by media accounts of the Columbine shootings eight months earlier: "He started wondering what he

would do if he were placed in the role of the perpetrators that were previously depicted on the TV and in the media."[30]

- Al DeGuzman, a nineteen-year-old student at De Anza College in Cupertino, California, apparently planned to carry out a bombing at his school. DeGuzman was arrested after photographing himself with guns and sixty explosives. The sophomore reportedly idolized Columbine killers Klebold and Harris, calling them "the only thing that's real."[31]

The media's barrage of tragedy coverage tells viewers that the crimes they hype are significant. This emphasis encourages copycats, because they want to do something that will get attention, and a copycat isn't going to copy a crime not worth reporting. Thus the news media's hype helps perpetuate copycat crimes.

A judge in Salamanca, New York, refused to release a hearing transcript from a racially charged murder case on the basis that the news coverage could incite copycat crimes. In his ruling, Judge William Mountain III criticized the news media's coverage of crime:

> The norm in this day and age seems to be the news media circling like vultures, each hoping to be the first to feast on the gory details of a story such as this. Perhaps if the media were to refrain from dwelling on this carrion, we would have fewer "copycat killers." Perhaps, we would also be spared the attempts of disturbed children to attain their 15 minutes of fame by murdering their peers . . . if the public were not endlessly bombarded by pictures and grisly details of prior senseless tragedies of the same ilk by the news media.[32]

When police were searching for suspect Buford Furrow following a shooting at a Los Angeles Jewish center, cable news networks covered the story live. Sid Bedingfield, executive vice president of CNN USA, said that during the coverage his network was aware of and concerned about the risk of encouraging copycats, "[b]ut on the other hand, you can't not cover the story. You can try to cover it responsibly and with perspective. But I don't think it helps to ignore the story."[33]

A few newspapers were so concerned about their coverage that they actually changed the way they handle news stories. The most prominent example was when Nigel Wade, editor of the *Chicago Sun-Times*, decided not to cover the Littleton shootings on the front page. "Littleton was the biggest story of that day and we carried every detail of it," Wade said in an interview on ABC's *Nightline*. "We carried six pages of it, in fact, but we just didn't start it on page one, page one being so often all that a young person might see of the newspaper." The paper made a similar editorial decision when Kip Kinkel opened fire on his schoolmates in

Springfield, Oregon, in May 1999. Instead of front-page emphasis, the story ran on pages 2 and 3.[34]

MYTHMAKING FOLLOWING TERRORISM

Several myths have emerged in the aftermath of the September 11, 2001, attacks. One common myth was that people who have attacked and terrified Americans are mostly foreigners. The most devastating (and most recent) attacks were clearly committed by foreigners, but a survey of bombings, attacks, and terrorism scares reveals that the threats to our country often come from within:

- April 19, 1995: Americans Timothy McVeigh and Terry Nichols bombed a federal building in Oklahoma City, Oklahoma, killing 168 people.
- July 27, 1996: American Eric Rudolph (captured in May 2003 after five years at large) is suspected of several bombings, including the 1996 Olympic Park bombing, which killed two people and injured more than a hundred others.
- Late 2001: Anthrax-laced letters were sent to journalists and politicians. Five people died, more than two dozen contracted anthrax, and innumerable people panicked. The case remains unsolved, but there is no indication the terrorist was a foreigner, and in fact the investigation has so far suggested it may be an American scientist.
- October 2002: Two snipers terrorized America, killing thirteen and wounding six. Two suspected were captured; one is an American, the other is a Jamaican.
- May 2002: A series of seemingly random bombings occurred throughout the Midwest, injuring seven people. American Luke Helder was arrested for the crime.

There are, of course, many other notorious American terrorists, including Theodore Kaczynski (the Unabomber). Foreign terrorists are a real threat, but the reality is that American terrorists have shown just as little regard as foreign terrorists for American lives.

Instead of being "united against terrorism," many Americans have been participating in the terrorism. In the weeks and months after the September 11 attacks and anthrax scares, thousands of Americans called in fake bomb threats and anthrax hoaxes. From mid-October to early November 2001 alone, the Postal Inspection System received more than eighty-six hundred anthrax-related hoax threats.[35] The FBI also saw thousands of practical jokes, false alarms, and hoaxes.

And it's not just pranking teenagers scaring Americans with false anthrax warnings. Many hoaxers are adults in the professions we have come to see as heroes:

- Pennsylvania firefighter Steve Welch was charged with making false reports and tampering with or fabricating evidence.
- Chicago county prosecutor James Vasselli resigned after admitting he put an envelope of sugar in a coworker's desk.
- A Kentucky sheriff planted unmarked envelopes of crushed aspirin on desks.[36]
- A Chicago postal worker wrote "antrax inclosed" on a package as a prank.[37]
- A Washington, D.C., police officer was suspended for leaving a note and powdery substance in an office building.[38]
- Two Philadelphia police officers were charged with sending an anthrax hoax from their patrol car computer.[39]
- A Virginia postal worker opened mail and sprinkled baby powder inside. She was upset because she didn't feel that the anthrax threat was being taken seriously enough by her supervisors.[40]

Those who we would think are the most afraid of anthrax threats are, in some cases, the very ones who are causing the fear: children. In a study of anthrax hoaxing by the Center for Nonproliferation Studies, 172 false threats were made between January 1998 and April 2001. Of 40 anthrax hoaxes in which the perpetrators were caught, over a quarter of them were made by children between twelve and eighteen.[41]

These hoaxes are very costly in terms of both time and money. Each hoax can cost tens of thousands of dollars in materials used, lost productivity from shutting down offices and buildings, overtime pay for police, and so on. Laboratories are swamped with requests to test specimens for anthrax, delaying treatment and evaluation for others in need of medical diagnosis.

Said New Jersey State Police Col. Carson J. Dunbar Jr., "I want people to be cautious, but the media in this country has done a really good job of just scaring the daylights out of people."[42]

Of course, the ultimate responsibility for any copycat crime lies not with the media but the individual who commits the crime. The news media's role in encouraging the crimes, however, cannot be ignored. Certainly, some of the shooters inspired by the Columbine massacre might have committed their crimes anyway, but there can be little doubt that the emotion-laden saturation coverage of the shootings contributed to these tragedies. Had the stories been reported in an objective tone, keeping perspective in mind, with equal emphasis on the week's other news stories, it's likely many fewer copycat incidents would have occurred.

The Reason for September 11

In the wake of the September 11 attacks, Americans naturally asked why it happened. In part because of our inadequate and xenophobic news media, many Americans were jarred by the realization that our country had made important enemies in the world. Why did Osama bin Laden attack the United States? What was the motivation for such a destructive act?

There were several answers to the question, though the Bush administration's official line was quickly and carefully set: The United States was attacked because Osama bin Laden hates our American freedoms. President Bush said the terrorists are a "barbaric enemy that hates what we stand for, hates our freedoms, hates our openness."[43] Using the wonderfully abstract and patriotic word *freedom,* Bush recast the war in his own simplified and politically convenient terms: "We will defend freedom; we will defend the values we hold dear." How bin Laden (or Saddam Hussein, for that matter) threatens American freedoms or values is not explained.

The president's explanations aside, there can be little doubt as to why bin Laden attacked the United States. He explained his motivations clearly and repeatedly in his writings and speeches: His chief complaint is the presence of infidels (i.e., Christian American troops) in the holy land (i.e., Saudi Arabia, homeland to Mecca and Medina, Islam's shrines). He may be a terrorist, but he's a *religious* terrorist, and from those motivations come his actions.

In a December 22, 1998, interview with ABC News, Osama bin Laden began by stating that "we, in the World Islamic Front for *jihad* [holy war] against Jews and Crusaders, have . . . issued a crystal clear *fatwa* [religious ruling] calling on the Nation to carry on *jihad* aimed at liberating Islamic holy sites . . . and all Islamic lands."[44] Bin Laden repeated the purpose of the war on the United States several times, including making statements such as, "We will continue this course because it is part of our religion, and because God . . . ordered us to carry out *jihad*" and because of the "unjust American occupation of the land of the two mosques."

How this was interpreted to mean that bin Laden hates American freedom and openness is unclear. It is not American freedom he objects to, it is American religion and foreign policy. Sean O'Neill, of London's *Daily Telegraph,* noted that "[m]ore than any other cause it was the presence of 'crusader' forces in the land of Islam's holiest sites . . . that turned bin Laden from Afghan *jihadi* to an international terrorist."[45] Yet instead of trying to address the root of the problem, the Bush administration ignored the real causes and pursued its own agenda. Bush avoided mentioning the real reasons for the attacks in an effort to downplay religious tensions and not alienate the nation's (few) Muslim allies. But bombing straw men (and their arguments) is a dangerous approach to international politics.

President Bush, a born-again Christian, has made no secret of his faith. Both Bush and Osama bin Laden are deeply religious men, and each has claimed that his own nation has been chosen by God. Bin Laden has called for a *jihad* against Christian America; Bush has called for a "crusade" against Muslim terrorists. There is plenty of ammunition in both the Bible and Koran for those looking to justify their wars. Unfortunately, those who do not share either leader's extremist views (i.e., much of the world) are caught in the middle.

In the wake of a series of highly public political embarrassments (the Immigration and Naturalization Service issuing visas for known terrorists, the inability to locate Osama bin Laden, seizing—then releasing—a North Korean ship containing secret missiles to our allies, and so on), the Bush administration's focus turned from its repeated failures to an old enemy: Iraq's Saddam Hussein.

To legitimize an attack on Iraq, Bush had to somehow link Iraq and Saddam to Bin Laden. It is well documented that Saddam Hussein does not share bin Laden's fundamentalist fanaticism. This is an important point, because the very reason the United States was attacked is wholly missing from the Iraqi situation: a fanatical religious leader. Saddam and bin Laden are not ideological brethren. Bin Laden, in fact, offered to fight against Saddam when Iraq invaded Kuwait. Bush, apparently unaware of how he undermines his own arguments, at times went out of his way to tar Saddam Hussein as nonreligious.[46]

Another justification for attacking Iraq was that the country was harboring many dangerous weapons of mass destruction. Government officials repeatedly asserted that not only was Saddam intent on a massive attack on the United States, he also had the capacity to execute such an attack. Yet when American troops invaded Iraq in March 2003, the supposed biological and chemical weapons were not used. While the military desperately searched for the banned weapons, the Bush administration assured Americans and the international community that they would soon be found.

Captured Iraqi scientists (who presumably had nothing left to fear from the deposed—and possibly killed—Saddam Hussein) continued to claim that Iraq had none of the weapons the U.S. government had claimed. As this book goes to press, despite searching the country for more than three months, the Bush administration has yet to find any hard evidence of the weapons it claimed justified the attack. Unless the alleged huge stockpiles are eventually discovered, the United States's credibility in the international community will be sorely diminished. Whether the mythmaking was intentional or the result of honest mistakes based on faulty intelligence, it appears that the campaign to attack Iraq was based largely upon myths.

There may have been legitimate reasons to invade the country and force Saddam Hussein from power, but two of the most widely cited reasons do not withstand scrutiny. Rumors and myths cannot be used to justify preemptive military attacks on sovereign countries, no matter how despicable their leaders.

NOTES

1. John Cloud, "The Columbine Effect," *Time*, December 6, 1999, p. 51.
2. "Boston Schools Drop Suspension of Chain-Saw Storyteller," Associated Press [online], www.freedomforum.org/templates/document.asp?documentID=12497 [May 18, 2000].
3. Amy Beth Graves, "ACLU Swamped with Complaints after Colorado Shootings," Associated Press [online], www.copaa.net/newstand/acluboston.html [May 10, 1999].
4. Kim Brooks, Vincent Schiraldi, and Jason Ziedenberg, "School House Hype: Two Years Later," Justice Policy Institute/Children's Law Center [online], www.cjcj.org/pubs/schoolhousehype/shh2.html [April 2000].
5. Ibid.
6. Ibid.
7. "Mother Charged with Arming Children," Associated Press [online], fact-on.ca/news/news0003/ap000309.htm [March 9, 2000].
8. "Sears Cancels Sales of Doll," *Beloit Daily News* [online], www.beloitdailynews.com/999/lill21.htm [September 21, 1999].
9. Sue Major Holmes, "FBI Testimony 'Incorrect,'" Associated Press [online], abcnews.go.com/sections/us/DailyNews/wenholee000818.html [August 18, 2000].
10. James Sterngold, "A Judge's Indignation," *New York Times* [online], www.nytimes.com/2000/09/15/national/15JUDG.html?ex=1054094400&en=801089582340763eb&ei=5070 [September 15, 2000].
11. Holmes, "FBI Testimony 'Incorrect.'"
12. Richard Benke, "Intelligence Chiefs Defend Lee," *Washington Post* [online], www.washingtonpost.com/wp-srv/aponline/20000901/aponline102020_000.htm [September 1, 2000].
13. Beverly Lumpkin, "Thank You, Randy!" ABC News [online], abcnews.go.com/sections/us/HallsOfJustice/hallsofjustice91.html [August 17, 2001].
14. Robert Schmidt, "Crash Landing," *Brill's Content* (November 1999): 68.
15. Ibid.
16. "The *Times* and Wen Ho Lee," *New York Times* [online], tms.physics.lsa.umich.edu/214/other/news/092600edno.html.
17. Alan P. Zelicoff, "Polygraphs and the National Labs: Dangerous Ruse Undermines National Security," *Skeptical Inquirer* (July/August 2001): 22.

18. Committee to Review the Scientific Evidence on the Polygraph, *The Polygraph and Lie Detection* (Washington, D.C.: National Academy of Sciences, 2003).

19. Lauren Stratford, *Satan's Underground* (Gretna, La.: Pelican Publishing, 1991).

20. Bob Passantino, Gretchen Passantino, and Jon Trott, "Lauren Stratford: From Satanic Ritual Abuse to Jewish Holocaust Survivor," *Cornerstone* 28, no. 117 [online], www.cornerstonemag.com/features/iss117/lauren.htm.

21. Bob Passantino, Gretchen Passantino, and Jon Trott, "Satan's Sideshow: The True Lauren Stratford Story," *Cornerstone* 18, no. 90 (1990): 24.

22. Richard Lacayo, "The Longest Mistrial," *Time*, August 6, 1990, p. 28.

23. Margaret Carlson, "Six Years of Trial by Torture," *Time*, January 29, 1990, p. 26.

24. Marc Barnes, "Edenton Over—Last Kelly Abuse Charges Dropped," *Fayetteville (N.C.) Observer-Times*, September 23, 1999.

25. Peggy Andersen, "4 Exonerated in Sex Case Now Suing," Associated Press [online], www.skeptictank.org/hs/fmemcase.htm [June 4, 1998].

26. *Commonwealth of Massachusetts* v. *Cheryl Amirault LeFave* (1998), comment of Isaac Borenstein, users.rcn.com/kyp/borenstn.html.

27. Mark Sauer, "Escondido to Pay $750,000 to Parents of 2 Seized Kids," *San Diego Union-Tribune*, November 2, 2000.

28. "Columbine Attackers Had Big Arsenal," *USA Today* [online], www.usatoday.com/news/index/colo/colo185.htm [February 14, 2000].

29. Karen Testa, "Courts and Jails Now Teeming with 'Columbine Copycats,'" Online Athens [online], www.onlineathens.com/stories/100399/new_1003990010.shtml [October 3, 1999]; Kenneth J. Cooper, "This Time, Copycat Wave Is Broader," *Washington Post*, May 1, 1999, p. A6.

30. "Columbine May Have Influenced Boy," Associated Press [online], wire.ap.org [June 11, 2000].

31. Rachele Kanigel and Jeffrey Ressner, "The Copycat?" *Time*, February 12, 2001.

32. "Judge Attacks Media in Murder Case," Associated Press [online], wire.ap.org [July 16, 1999].

33. David Bauder, "Tragedy Gets Blanket TV Coverage," Associated Press [online], wire.ap.org [August 12, 1999].

34. For more on Nigel Wade and the *Sun-Times* decision, see pp. 308–309.

35. Darlene Superville, "System Has Little Patience for Anthrax Hoaxers," Associated Press [online], www.buffzone.com/news/terror/nov01/041hoax2.html [November 3, 2001].

36. "Anthrax: Pranksters Getting Little Sympathy from Authorities," *Topeka Capital-Journal* [online], cjonline.com/stories/110401/ter_pranksters.shtml [November 4, 2001].

37. "Postal Worker Indicted in Anthrax Hoax," Associated Press [online], wire.ap.org [November 9, 2001].

38. Laurie Kellman, "Capitol Police Suspend Officer on Suspicion of Anthrax Hoax," Associated Press [online], multimedia.belointeractive.com/attack/bioterror/1113police.html [November 13, 2001].

39. Joann Loviglio, "Philly Cops Charged in Anthrax Hoax," Associated Press [online], wire.ap.org [November 20, 2001].

40. "Virginia Postal Worker Charged with Anthrax Hoax," Court TV [online], www.courttv.com/assault_on_america/1102_anthraxhoax_ap.html [November 2, 2001]; Brooke Masters, "Va. Postal Worker Charged in Hoax," *Washington Post*, November 2, 2001, p. B1.

41. Erica Goode, "Anthrax Hoaxes Hinder Effort to Cope with Real Threats," *New York Times*, October 15, 2001.

42. Ceci Connolly and Avram Goldstein, "Deluge of Hoaxes Spurs Authorities to Launch Crackdown," *Washington Post*, October 17, 2001, p. A-1.

43. Bush made this statement at a March 5, 2002, Minnesota Republican dinner; available online at www.whitehouse.gov/news/releases/2002/03/20020304-14.html.

44. "Terror Suspect," ABC News [online], http://abcnews.go.com/sections/world/DailyNews/transcript_binladen1_981228.html [September 11, 2001]. This statement was also repeated in an interview published in the January 11, 1999, issue of *Time* magazine.

45. Sean O'Neill, "Bin Laden's Main Demand Is Met," *Daily Telegraph* [online], www.telegraph.co.uk/news/main.jhtml?xml=/news/2003/04/30/wsaud230.xml/ [April 30, 2003]. The fact that fifteen of the nineteen September 11 hijackers were Saudi citizens further illustrates the religious and political message. Ironically, in April 2003 the Bush Administration met bin Laden's demand and announced it would withdraw all combat forces from Saudi Arabia by the end of the summer. It is possible that if America had done in 2000 what it did three years later, we might have been spared the devastation of the September 11 attacks.

46. See, for example, the White House's statement that "experts know that Saddam Hussein is a non-religious man from a secular—even atheistic—party." *Apparatus of Lies: Saddam's Disinformation and Propaganda, 1990–2003* [online], www.whitehouse.gov/ogc/apparatus-of-lies.pdf.

Conclusion

TOWARD SOLUTIONS

This book has explored some of the ways in which we are manipulated and misled by journalists, activists, and politicians. Though the problem is both pervasive and insidious, there are ways we can protect ourselves. Some in the media, as well, have come to recognize the dangers inherent in emotion-driven, context-barren news content.

Just because Americans tune in to emotional media circuses in droves doesn't necessarily mean they approve of what they see. In a 1999 poll conducted by the Gallup Organization and the Pew Research Center for People and the Press, nearly 60 percent of those polled thought the media coverage of John F. Kennedy Jr.'s death was excessive. Two years earlier, polls showed that about half of the public felt that coverage of Princess Diana's death was excessive. Bob Giles, executive director of the Freedom Forum's Media Studies Center, notes, "The public tunes in because they want news. But part of the reaction is because the 24-hour news channels and the main networks . . . kept that story on even when there was nothing new to report."[1]

In a 1999 poll by Penn, Schoen, and Berland Associates, Inc. and commissioned by *Brill's Content*, participants were asked if they agreed with the following proposed policy: "The news organization would agree not to show a current photograph or image of family members who have lost a loved one within the prior week, and will not post reporters outside the family's home or any other place to wait to interview or photograph the family members without their consent." Eighty-six percent of the respondents thought that news organizations should adopt this policy; 9 percent said they should not.

Similarly, when asked if they supported this policy: "The news organization would agree not to photograph grieving family members at funerals if asked by family members," 80 percent thought news organizations should adopt it, while 15 percent said they should not.[2]

CHANGING THE NEWS MEDIA

In April 2000 the Justice Policy Institute issued a report titled "School House Hype: Two Years Later," dealing with the debate about school violence. The report concluded with several recommendations on dealing with the tragedies, including adding more context to media coverage. According to the authors:

> The crime and public opinion data in this report indicate that Americans are not just misinformed, but are in many cases exponentially misinformed, by the hyperbole that too often follows school shootings. Americans don't know what they know about youth violence from personal experience, they know what they know about youth violence from the media. . . . We need our media professionals to remind viewers and readers that the school shootings they are covering are exceedingly rare, that they are not on the increase, and that the current crime data shows violence by youths in and out of schools to be on the decline. Phrases like "another in a series of school shootings" and "an all-too-common phenomenon" should be dropped from the lexicon of evening news casts. . . . Finally, efforts should be made to give less prominence to idiosyncratic crimes, even when they are clearly newsworthy. While no one is suggesting that such shootings should be ignored, it is not mandatory that they make front page or top of the evening news.

As the report goes on to note, several media outlets have decided to accept some responsibility for how they treat such news. Among the most prominent is the *Chicago Sun-Times*, which decreed that it would no longer cover out-of-state shootings on its front page. The move came after a shooting in Springfield, Oregon, when the news media were criticized for giving such incidents too much emphasis and blowing them out of proportion.

The decision was made by Nigel Wade, editor-in-chief of the *Sun-Times*. The story of Kip Kinkel shooting his classmates still ran in the newspaper, and in full; it just wasn't on the front page. It ran on pages 2 and 3. Wade felt that since the story wasn't local, and because saturated media coverage might spur copycats, front-page treatment of the gory details and photos was both unnecessary and irresponsible: "It was a question of editorial judgment, of balancing news reporting responsibilities against responsibilities to society as a whole."

Orville Schell, dean of the Graduate School of Journalism at the University of California at Berkeley, was among the many who applauded Wade's decision:

> Having more bodies piled up on the front page may sell papers, but there is a great distinction between selling papers and news of significance. I mean, if you can't cover a massacre in Rwanda where a half-million people have died on the front page, then in the grand scale of things a wacko teenager hosing down his classmates with an automatic weapon is not of more consequence.[3]

By November 2000 it seemed apparent that some in the news media had finally learned their lesson. In a suburb of Dallas, a high school student with a loaded 9mm handgun took eighteen classmates and their pregnant teacher hostage. No one was killed, and police eventually overpowered the youth and arrested him. The national news media, however, barely mentioned the story. This time, there was little of the alarmist rhetoric about school violence that had come to characterize coverage just two years before.[4]

ABC television affiliate KVUE-TV in Austin, Texas, decided in 1996 to change the way it reported on crime stories. The station decided that crime stories would not be covered unless they met at least one of five criteria: (1) Does action need to be taken?; (2) Is there an immediate threat to safety?; (3) Is there a threat to children?; (4) Does the crime have significant community impact?; and (5) Does the story lend itself to a crime prevention effort?

The initiative was taken by news director Carole Kneeland and executive producer Cathy McFeaters, who both felt that television provided excessive and sensationalized coverage of crime. The pair encouraged their news staff to examine why and how their station covered crime stories. Clearly, crime is important and newsworthy; the question was how to cover it. "What we're trying to get away from is an automatic response to the way we cover crime," McFeaters said. "We're not trying to deny the ugliness in the world; that's not what this is all about. However, we have a responsibility not to give the ugliness more play than it deserves."

Austin Police Chief Elizabeth Watson applauded the station's approach: "I think that it is commendable for a major TV news station to really take a look at responsible reporting, commendable from a community service standpoint. Sensationalized reporting fuels fear. It makes people feel powerless."[5]

Following the school shootings in Conyers, Georgia, ABC's *Nightline* aired a segment about the news media's role in (and responsibility for) reporting violence.[6] Among the guests were Andy Hill, president of programming for Channel One, a news service that airs in schools nationwide; Deborah Potter, a former CBS and CNN correspondent; and Earl Casey, managing editor of domestic news gathering for CNN. The guests all said they believed that improvements had been made in the journalism industry, particularly following criticism of the media's coverage of school violence. They emphasized that progress wouldn't come overnight, but the fact that such topics were being discussed was a good sign. Said Earl Casey, "We learned from Littleton."

MEDIA LITERACY

Another way to help people understand the media is through media literacy classes in high school and college. George Ventura, a teacher of media studies at Ontario's West Toronto Collegiate Institute, notes, "We teach kids how to read books, we teach kids how to analyze poetry, but we don't teach them how to read a TV program or how a news program is constructed or what's beside the article in the newspaper or who's the advertiser in the magazine. Those are all things that they need to be told." David Reed, another Toronto media literacy teacher, suggests that a critical eye for the media helps people recognize when they are being manipulated. When students see that they don't have to conform to fads or what's 'in,' he says, "the pressure to conform isn't so great."[7]

This opinion was also borne out in a study undertaken by The New Mexico Media Literacy Project (NMMLP), a nonprofit educational organization. The group implemented a program titled *Media 2000* at six New Mexico schools. According to Bob McCannon, executive director of NMMLP, "Statistical analysis of survey results showed that media literacy presentations helped students question the reality of what they saw in the media. Students were less likely to believe the hyperbole presented in alcohol and tobacco advertising, and they were less likely to identify favorably with the people they saw on TV."[8]

Michael Gartner, the ombudsman for *Brill's Content* magazine, suggested ten insightful yet simple questions to ask as you read, watch, or surf the news:

1. Is the expert you're listening to getting paid? Does he have a vested interest in what he tells you?
2. Who posted it? Web and Internet information is as good or bad as the author.
3. Who said it? Not only is the expert credible (and within his or her field of expertise), but is the source even cited?
4. What was the question? If a story features the results of a poll,

does it list the sample size, whether the sample is random, or the wording of a sample question?
5. What is the answer? If an allegation is made about a topic, is an answer provided?
6. Why should the audience believe the journalist? Does she provide facts to support assertions and opinions?
7. Does the reporter inject opinion into his straight journalism?
8. Do Americans really believe what is claimed? is a "man on the street" interview really representative of the population claimed?
9. Are the words loaded, or the language neutral?
10. Do you really care? Don't assume that whatever news directors and reporters think is important really is. Decide for yourself what is worth paying attention to.[9]

A CALL FOR CONTEXT

Nearly ten years ago, Richard Harwood, a former ombudsman of the *Washington Post*, wrote a piece decrying the media's lack of depth and context in its crime coverage:

> A great nerve has been touched in the country. Crime has become politicized. There are demands for more jails, more police on the streets, longer sentences, fewer paroles and gun control. We faithfully report these developments along with the latest casualties on the streets and in the alleys. But the media do not explain very well the nature and incidence of the plague.... [There] are questions the media need to deal with as crime enters the political arena and inspires legislative remedies that may prove to be as useless as much of the legislation of the past quarter-century. There is, for example, a chorus of demands for "more cops on the beat." What is the correlation between "more cops" and homicide rates? Washington, with the highest homicide rate among American cities, also has more police per square foot than any city in the Western world....[10]

To this list, one could also add many of the issues dealt with in other sections of this book.

Some network news departments have been better than others at unbiased reporting with context and depth. On May 24, 2000, for example, the *ABC Evening News* ran a substantive story about how television networks (including ABC) have a vested interest in keeping political finance reform from reducing campaign ad spending. The report was very up-front about the networks' role in lobbying against curbing political candidates' use of television advertising because of the big money to be made. Two years later, however, when the bill finally came to a vote, the networks—including ABC—were conspicuously silent about their lobbying efforts.

Two months later, on July 11, ABC News correspondent James Walker did a report on Toysmart.com, an Internet business that went bankrupt while holding its customer database list among its assets. The problem was that Toysmart shoppers were promised that their consumer information would never be sold, though it now seemed likely that just that would happen. The piece was somewhat critical of Disney, and privacy concerns were aired, as was the disclosure that Disney owned both Toysmart and ABC News. Such disclosure is a good model for other news departments to follow.

ABC was, however, the network that ran a one-on-one interview on the environment with President Clinton on Earth Day 2000. And which knowledgeable and experienced journalist was chosen for the task? Ted Koppel? Barbara Walters? No, *Titanic* star and then-hot actor Leonardo DiCaprio. ABC also was ready to axe the award-winning news show *Nightline* and replace it with David Letterman's talk show in 2002. ABC's credibility seems to take one step back for every two steps forward.

In some cases, the public's response to potentially inflammatory topics has been admirably measured. Take, for example, the publication in 2000 of the book *Taboo: Why Black Athletes Dominate Sports and Why We're Afraid to Talk about It*, by Jon Etine. The book examines why it is that black athletes seem to dominate many sports (such as basketball, football, baseball, boxing, and sprinting). Though the book is by most accounts well researched, evenhanded, and not racist, it is easy to see why such a topic might ignite racial tensions. Suggestions of racial differences, especially those quantified by scientific research, tread on sensitive ground.

Etine is an investigative journalist and Emmy Award–winning producer for ABC and NBC News. To help guide him through the minefield of research, he assembled advisors from many disciplines—including biologists, anthropologists, and sociologists. Yet despite his solid pedigree (and endorsement of his findings from the prestigious scholars, both black and white), Etine reports that his book was rejected by publisher after publisher. *Skeptic* magazine did a special section on the book and its controversy. There, Etine notes that, when trying to get his book into print, he got a consistently negative response from publishers,

> [M]any of whom refused to even read it—"on principle." Again and again, I heard: "This is a racist subject. By even suggesting that blacks may have a genetic edge in sports, you are opening up the Pandora's box of intellectual inferiority." . . . In early January, just before the book was released, the *New York Times Magazine* informed me that it was

killing plans to publish an adaptation, calling the book's thesis potentially "dangerous."

Yet the publishers underestimated the critics' and public's reactions. The responses to the book have so far been very positive, surprising even Etine. Scholars and reviewers, both black and white, generally praised Etine and his book as responsible and thorough.[11]

TAMING EMOTIONS

Much of the manipulation discussed in this book is based upon emotional appeals such as sympathy, patriotism, fear, and outrage. This manipulation is especially effective because emotions fail us badly when used to make important choices in our lives. Decisions made based on emotion are very likely to be poor ones for several reasons.

- Emotions can be fleeting and capricious. While a given emotion may pass in days, hours, or even minutes, the consequences of decisions you make while under the influence of those emotions may last a lifetime. A woman who meets a stranger in a bar and lets her passions cloud her judgment about safe sex may end up with AIDS or a child; a person who attacks another in a fit of anger may kill or injure that person permanently and end up in prison or dead. While these examples may seem extreme, they happen all the time.
- People are vulnerable to emotional appeals, which require no basis in reality. There's a reason that advertisers use emotion to sell products and activists use it to scare people: Emotion moves people. If a person can't convince you of the worth of his cause through logic or rationality, emotion is always the easy route. Cults use emotion to cloud the judgment of their followers; Adolf Hitler and Joseph Goebbels were masters at using emotion and propaganda to manipulate crowds and further the Third Reich. It is easy to get swept up in the heat of the moment when emotions are running high and fears are manipulated.
- Emotions ignore complexity. Emotions are frequently extreme and can blind people to important shades of gray in situations and problem-solving discussions. As simplistic as bumper sticker slogans, emotions are frequently reduced to likes or dislikes, and are rarely open to other information. But the world isn't black and white; it is a complex web of choices, decisions, and causes that emotions are simply poorly equipped to deal with.

- Feelings and emotions can inhibit rational problem solving. Because emotions are usually considered subjective, sacred, and inviolable (and therefore outside the realm of debate), nothing puts a stop to a discussion faster than saying, "Well, that's just the way I feel." Feelings have no truth-value, no inherent validity. Feelings, unlike factual statements, are neither true nor false, valid nor invalid: they simply *are*. Feelings can and should be taken into account in discussions and analyses, but it's important to recognize their limits. Each person is entitled to her own feelings and opinions, but hopefully most people can offer at least *some* reason or evidence to support them other than "That's just how I feel."
- Emotions have a way of blowing events way out of proportion; tiny fears and grievances can seem enormously important and urgent. There are many examples of this problem. In February 2000 in San Jose, California, a man grabbed a dog and hurled it into traffic following a minor fender-bender. The media picked up the story, showing video of Leo, the photogenic white bichon frise, and his weeping owner. Animal lovers (and nearly everyone else) were outraged at the cruelty of the crime. Leo became a cause célebre, and by March nearly $110,000 had been donated as a reward for anyone who could provide information leading to the arrest and conviction of the perpetrator.

  Certainly what the man did was wrong and he should be punished. But $110,000 is more money than is frequently offered for information leading to people who kill *human beings*. If the animal lovers were really concerned with preventing canine deaths, $110,000 would go a long way toward spaying and neutering San Jose's living animals, whose stray babies will likely be roaming the city's streets in years to come, only to be rounded up and killed later on.
- Feelings and emotion seem inherently natural and "right." Emotions are rarely questioned or consciously supported; they simply exist. We may be able to retrospectively explain why we felt a certain way, but even then we apply convenient labels after the fact. Yet emotional certainty doesn't imply truth. An anorexic girl may truly feel that she's too fat; a child abuser might honestly believe his rage is justified; an alcoholic may genuinely feel she doesn't have a problem. In each case, the person has used the malleability of emotion to insulate him- or herself from reality and truth. But respect for the "truth" of their feelings must end in order for them to get help. Not challenging their beliefs out of respect for their emotions is inviting tragedy.

Following the September 11 terrorist attacks, many people took the opportunity to reevaluate their personal lives. Some said the tragedy made them think about what was important to them and focus on that. Some people decided to go ahead with life decisions they had put off: getting married, having children, going to school. Interestingly, others reevaluated their lives in a different light and decided to do the opposite. One person wrote that she became less forgiving, not more, in the wake of the tragedy: "I broke up with someone I've lived with for many years. Although there were times when I was forgiving, this time I just thought about how precious life is . . . and that I wanted to live that life with joy, with laughter."

Yet psychologists worry that those who make snap decisions in a crisis can make poor choices based on panic and insecurity. Some people, for example, have left cities altogether, believing they will be at less risk elsewhere. Says psychologist Joseph Weintraub, "Don't rush into decisions without thinking about how others might be affected by your decisions. Pulling your kids out of school and moving to the woods is not likely to give your family the sense of security that you hoped to accomplish."[11]

The challenge is to be able to set aside (or overcome) emotions when necessary and recognize when others try to manipulate us using our fears and feelings. Some people go through life as marionettes, buying the products and supporting the causes that tug hardest on their heartstrings while forgetting to engage their critical thinking. A clear hand, unclouded by emotion, is the best defense we have against those who would exploit and manipulate us.

* * *

The issues raised in this book are complex, and no one solution will fix everything. Just as I have railed against simplistic explanations and facile solutions to all the mythmaking, I can offer no magic bullets. The roots of the problem lie in the way the media operates, the way we view and understand the nature of news, and the way we react to it. But the deeper and more resilient issue is within ourselves. It's the question of how we train ourselves to not respond on cue, reaching for our wallets whenever someone offers us simple solutions and tragic stories. It's a skill, like any other, and it requires practice. If the simple solution or tragic story still seems good after rational reflection, then by all means we should give the money or support the cause.

The manipulation we are routinely exposed to is, in a real way, a threat to democracy. The idea of democracy assumes an informed populace exchanging ideas in good faith and acting upon them; instead we have a nation that relies on the news media to tell us what we need to know about the world, including what the important issues are. Yet the media frequently fail at their job, preferring to air emotion over substance, heat over light.

In this book I have identified many of the factors and forces that manipulate us and lead us astray. Reporters, politicians, and activists are all part of the problem, but they are only one side of the equation. Much of the blame lies with ourselves as news consumers and as citizens. It has been said that each country gets the government it deserves. I believe that is partially true of its news media as well. We deserve better news media than we get; we deserve better coverage, more understanding, more answers. But until we refuse to accept nonanswers to questions and nonsolutions to problems, we will get what we deserve.

NOTES

1. Will Lestern, "Most Followed Story of Kennedy's Death; Thought Coverage Was Excessive," *Boston Globe* [online], www.boston.com/news/packages/jfkjr/0727_polls.htm [July 27, 1999].

2. Steven Brill, "Curiosity vs. Privacy," *Brill's Content* (October 1999): 102.

3. Lori Leibovich, "When a School Massacre Isn't Page 1 News," Salon [online], archive.salon.com/media/1998/os/22medialab.html [May 22, 1999].

4. "Armed Student Takes Class Hostage," Associated Press [online], www.ogo.org/newsclips.htm#armed%20studetn [November 2, 2000].

5. Quotes from Joe Holley, "Should The Coverage Fit the Crime? A Texas TV Station Tries to Resist the Allure of Mayhem," In *The Media and Morality,* ed. Robert M. Baird, William E. Loges, and Stuart Rosenbaum (Amherst, N.Y.: Prometheus Books, 1999).

6. "The Dilemma," *Nightline,* May 20, 1999.

7. Rachel Taylor, "Media 101," *Brill's Content* (July/August 1998): 78.

8. Bob McCannon, "Four Studies: Media Literacy Works!" *State of Media Education* (fall/winter/spring 2000) [online], www.nmmlp.org/spring00.pdf.

9. Michael Gartner, "Report from the Ombudsman," *Brill's Content* (November 2000): 31.

10. Richard Harwood, "Media Goes Around Crime Beat Missing Central Questions," *Albuquerque Journal,* December 26, 1993.

11. Jon Etine, "Breaking the Taboo," *Skeptic* 8, no. 1 (2000).

12. Geraldine Sealey, "How We've Changed," ABC News [online], abcnews.go.com/sections/us/DailyNews/STRIKE_lifechange011017.html [October 17, 2001].

INDEX